The NEW ENCYCLOPEDIA *of* SOUTHERN CULTURE

VOLUME 17 : EDUCATION

Volumes to appear in

The New Encyclopedia of Southern Culture

are:

The NEW

ENCYCLOPEDIA *of* SOUTHERN CULTURE

CHARLES REAGAN WILSON General Editor

JAMES G. THOMAS JR. Managing Editor

ANN J. ABADIE Associate Editor

VOLUME 17

Education

CLARENCE L. MOHR Volume Editor

Sponsored by

THE CENTER FOR THE STUDY OF SOUTHERN CULTURE

at the University of Mississippi

THE UNIVERSITY OF NORTH CAROLINA PRESS

Chapel Hill

This book was published with the
assistance of the Anniversary Endowment Fund
of the University of North Carolina Press.

Designed by Richard Hendel
Set in Minion types by Tseng Information Systems, Inc.
Manufactured in the United States of America
The paper in this book meets the guidelines for permanence and durability of the Committee on Production Guidelines for Book Longevity of the Council on Library Resources.
The University of North Carolina Press has been a member of the Green Press Initiative since 2003.
Library of Congress Cataloging-in-Publication Data
Education / Clarence L. Mohr, volume editor.
p. 24 cm. — (The new encyclopedia of Southern culture ; v. 17)
"Sponsored by The Center for the Study of Southern Culture at the University of Mississippi."
Includes bibliographical references and index.
ISBN 978-0-8078-3491-6 (alk. paper) —
ISBN 978-0-8078-7201-7 (pbk. : alk. paper)
1. American Education—Southern States—Encyclopedias.
2. Universities and colleges—Southern States—Encyclopedias.
3. Popular culture—Southern States—Encyclopedias. 4. Southern States—Social conditions—Encyclopedias. 5. Southern States—Social life and customs—Encyclopedias. I. Mohr, Clarence L.
II. University of Mississippi. Center for the Study of Southern Culture. III. Series.
F209 .N47 2006 vol. 17
[LA230.5.S6]
975.003 S—dc22
2011655000
The *Encyclopedia of Southern Culture*, sponsored by the Center for the Study of Southern Culture at the University of Mississippi, was published by the University of North Carolina Press in 1989.
cloth 15 14 13 12 11 5 4 3 2 1
paper 15 14 13 12 11 5 4 3 2 1

Tell about the South. What's it like there.

What do they do there. Why do they live there.

Why do they live at all.

WILLIAM FAULKNER

Absalom, Absalom!

To the Memory of

CHRISTINE EVELYN SHAW,

Marine City High School, Class of 1932,

Holder of Certificate of Merit for Straight-A Academic Record,

Inducted into National Honor Society

CONTENTS

GENERAL INTRODUCTION

In 1989 years of planning and hard work came to fruition when the University of North Carolina Press joined the Center for the Study of Southern Culture at the University of Mississippi to publish the *Encyclopedia of Southern Culture*. While all those involved in writing, reviewing, editing, and producing the volume believed it would be received as a vital contribution to our understanding of the American South, no one could have anticipated fully the widespread acclaim it would receive from reviewers and other commentators. But the *Encyclopedia* was indeed celebrated, not only by scholars but also by popular audiences with a deep, abiding interest in the region. At a time when some people talked of the "vanishing South," the book helped remind a national audience that the region was alive and well, and it has continued to shape national perceptions of the South through the work of its many users—journalists, scholars, teachers, students, and general readers.

As the introduction to the *Encyclopedia* noted, its conceptualization and organization reflected a cultural approach to the South. It highlighted such issues as the core zones and margins of southern culture, the boundaries where "the South" overlapped with other cultures, the role of history in contemporary culture, and the centrality of regional consciousness, symbolism, and mythology. By 1989 scholars had moved beyond the idea of cultures as real, tangible entities, viewing them instead as abstractions. The *Encyclopedia*'s editors and contributors thus included a full range of social indicators, trait groupings, literary concepts, and historical evidence typically used in regional studies, carefully working to address the distinctive and characteristic traits that made the American South a particular place. The introduction to the *Encyclopedia* concluded that the fundamental uniqueness of southern culture was reflected in the volume's composite portrait of the South. We asked contributors to consider aspects that were unique to the region but also those that suggested its internal diversity. The volume was not a reference book of southern history, which explained something of the design of entries. There were fewer essays on colonial and antebellum history than on the postbellum and modern periods, befitting our conception of the volume as one trying not only to chart the cultural landscape of the South but also to illuminate the contemporary era.

When C. Vann Woodward reviewed the *Encyclopedia* in the *New York Review of Books*, he concluded his review by noting "the continued liveliness of interest in the South and its seeming inexhaustibility as a field of study." Research on the South, he wrote, furnishes "proof of the value of the *Encyclopedia* as a scholarly undertaking as well as suggesting future needs for revision or supplement to keep up with ongoing scholarship." The two decades since the publication of the *Encyclopedia of Southern Culture* have certainly suggested that Woodward was correct. The American South has undergone significant changes that make for a different context for the study of the region. The South has undergone social, economic, political, intellectual, and literary transformations, creating the need for a new edition of the *Encyclopedia* that will remain relevant to a changing region. Globalization has become a major issue, seen in the South through the appearance of Japanese automobile factories, Hispanic workers who have immigrated from Latin America or Cuba, and a new prominence for Asian and Middle Eastern religions that were hardly present in the 1980s South. The African American return migration to the South, which started in the 1970s, dramatically increased in the 1990s, as countless books simultaneously appeared asserting powerfully the claims of African Americans as formative influences on southern culture. Politically, southerners from both parties have played crucial leadership roles in national politics, and the Republican Party has dominated a near-solid South in national elections. Meanwhile, new forms of music, like hip-hop, have emerged with distinct southern expressions, and the term "dirty South" has taken on new musical meanings not thought of in 1989. New genres of writing by creative southerners, such as gay and lesbian literature and "white trash" writing, extend the southern literary tradition.

Meanwhile, as Woodward foresaw, scholars have continued their engagement with the history and culture of the South since the publication of the *Encyclopedia*, raising new scholarly issues and opening new areas of study. Historians have moved beyond their earlier preoccupation with social history to write new cultural history as well. They have used the categories of race, social class, and gender to illuminate the diversity of the South, rather than a unified "mind of the South." Previously underexplored areas within the field of southern historical studies, such as the colonial era, are now seen as formative periods of the region's character, with the South's positioning within a larger Atlantic world a productive new area of study. Cultural memory has become a major topic in the exploration of how the social construction of "the South" benefited some social groups and exploited others. Scholars in many disciplines have made the southern identity a major topic, and they have used a variety of methodologies to suggest what that identity has meant to different social groups. Literary critics have adapted cultural theories to the South and have raised the issue of postsouthern literature to a major category of concern as well as exploring the links between the literature of the American South and that of the Caribbean. Anthropologists have used different theoretical formulations from literary critics, providing models for their fieldwork in southern communities. In the past 30 years anthropologists have set increasing numbers of their ethnographic studies in the South, with many of them now exploring topics specifically linked to southern cultural issues. Scholars now place the Native American story, from prehistory to the contemporary era, as a central part of southern history. Comparative and interdisciplinary approaches to the South have encouraged scholars to look at such issues as the borders and boundaries of the South, specific places and spaces with distinct identities within the American South, and the global and transnational Souths, linking the American South with many formerly colonial societies around the world.

The first edition of the *Encyclopedia of Southern Culture* anticipated many of these approaches and indeed stimulated the growth of Southern Studies as a distinct interdisciplinary field. The Center for the Study of Southern Culture has worked for more than three decades to encourage research and teaching about the American South. Its academic programs have produced graduates who have gone on to write interdisciplinary studies of the South, while others have staffed the cultural institutions of the region and in turn encouraged those institutions to document and present the South's culture to broad public audiences. The center's conferences and publications have continued its long tradition of promoting understanding of the history, literature, and music of the South, with new initiatives focused on southern foodways, the future of the South, and the global Souths, expressing the center's mission to bring the best current scholarship to broad public audiences. Its documentary studies projects build oral and visual archives, and the New Directions in Southern Studies book series, published by the University of North Carolina Press, offers an important venue for innovative scholarship.

Since the *Encyclopedia of Southern Culture* appeared, the field of Southern Studies has dramatically developed, with an extensive network now of academic and research institutions whose projects focus specifically on the interdisciplinary study of the South. The Center for the Study of the American South at the University of North Carolina at Chapel Hill, led by Director Harry Watson and Associate Director and *Encyclopedia* coeditor William Ferris, publishes the lively journal *Southern Cultures* and is now at the organizational center of many other Southern Studies projects. The Institute for Southern Studies at the University of South Carolina, the Southern Intellectual History Circle, the Society for the Study of Southern Literature, the Southern Studies Forum of the European American Studies Association, Emory University's SouthernSpaces.org, and the South Atlantic Humanities Center (at the Virginia Foundation for the Humanities, the University of Virginia, and Virginia Polytechnic Institute and State University) express the recent expansion of interest in regional study.

Observers of the American South have had much to absorb, given the rapid pace of recent change. The institutional framework for studying the South is broader and deeper than ever, yet the relationship between the older verities of regional study and new realities remains unclear. Given the extent of changes in the American South and in Southern Studies since the publication of the *Encyclopedia of Southern Culture*, the need for a new edition of that work is clear. Therefore, the Center for the Study of Southern Culture has once again joined the University of North Carolina Press to produce *The New Encyclopedia of Southern Culture*. As readers of the original edition will quickly see, *The New Encyclopedia* follows many of the scholarly principles and editorial conventions established in the original, but with one key difference; rather than being published in a single hardback volume, *The New Encyclopedia* is presented in a series of shorter individual volumes that build on the 24 original subject categories used in the *Encyclopedia* and adapt them to new scholarly developments. Some earlier *Encyclopedia* categories have been reconceptualized in light of new academic interests. For example, the subject section originally titled "Women's Life" is reconceived as a new volume, *Gender*, and the original "Black Life" section is more broadly interpreted as a volume on race. These changes reflect new analytical concerns that place the study of women and blacks in broader cultural systems, reflecting the emergence of, among other topics, the study of male culture and of whiteness. Both volumes draw as well from the rich recent scholarship on women's life and black life. In addition, topics with some thematic coherence are combined in a volume, such as *Law and Politics* and *Agriculture and Industry*. One new topic, *Foodways*, is the basis of a separate volume, reflecting its new prominence in the interdisciplinary study of southern culture.

Numerous individual topical volumes together make up *The New Encyclopedia of Southern Culture* and extend the reach of the reference work to wider audiences. This approach should enhance the use of the *Encyclopedia* in academic courses and is intended to be convenient for readers with more focused interests within the larger context of southern culture. Readers will have handy access to one-volume, authoritative, and comprehensive scholarly treatments of the major areas of southern culture.

We have been fortunate that, in nearly all cases, subject consultants who offered crucial direction in shaping the topical sections for the original edition have agreed to join us in this new endeavor as volume editors. When new volume editors have been added, we have again looked for respected figures who can provide not only their own expertise but also strong networks of scholars to help develop relevant lists of topics and to serve as contributors in their areas. The reputations of all our volume editors as leading scholars in their areas encouraged the contributions of other scholars and added to *The New Encyclopedia*'s authority as a reference work.

The New Encyclopedia of Southern Culture builds on the strengths of articles in the original edition in several ways. For many existing articles, original authors agreed to update their contributions with new interpretations and theoretical perspectives, current statistics, new bibliographies, or simple factual developments that needed to be included. If the original contributor was unable to update an article, the editorial staff added new material or sent it to another scholar for assessment. In some cases, the general editor and volume editors selected a new contributor if an article seemed particularly dated and new work indicated the need for a fresh perspective. And importantly, where new developments have warranted treatment of topics not addressed in the original edition, volume editors have commissioned entirely new essays and articles that are published here for the first time.

The American South embodies a powerful historical and mythical presence, both a complex environmental and geographic landscape and a place of the imagination. Changes in the region's contemporary socioeconomic realities and new developments in scholarship have been incorporated in the conceptualization and approach of *The New Encyclopedia of Southern Culture*. Anthropologist Clifford Geertz has spoken of culture as context, and this encyclopedia looks at the American South as a complex place that has served as the context for cultural expression. This volume provides information and perspective on the diversity of cultures in a geographic and imaginative place with a long history and distinctive character.

The *Encyclopedia of Southern Culture* was produced through major grants from the Program for Research Tools and Reference Works of the National Endowment for the Humanities, the Ford Foundation, the Atlantic-Richfield Foundation, and the Mary Doyle Trust. We are grateful as well to the College of Liberal Arts at the University of Mississippi for support and to the individual donors to the Center for the Study of Southern Culture who have directly or indirectly supported work on *The New Encyclopedia of Southern Culture*. We thank the volume editors for their ideas in reimagining their subjects and the contributors of articles for their work in extending the usefulness of the book in new ways. We acknowledge the support and contributions of the faculty and staff at the Center for the Study of Southern Culture. Finally, we want especially to honor the work of William Ferris and Mary Hart on the *Encyclopedia of Southern Culture*. Bill, the founding director of the Center for the Study of Southern Culture, was coeditor, and his good work recruiting authors, editing text, selecting images, and publicizing the volume among a wide network of people was, of course, invaluable. Despite the many changes in the new encyclopedia, Bill's influence remains. Mary "Sue" Hart was also an invaluable member of the original encyclopedia team, bringing the careful and precise eye of the librarian, and an iconoclastic spirit, to our work.

INTRODUCTION

Schools are central to cultural life—the repositories of knowledge and sources of innovation. The institutions of learning in the South have played a key role in reflecting and shaping southern cultural ways, from racial segregation to religious values to social class differences. The region struggled through the 19th century, though, to establish a system of public education, but the Progressive Era in the early 20th century saw improved formal education as a main reform goal. Persisting individualism and localism, however, strengthened the resistance of many southerners to entrusting educational policy to a distant state-level educational bureaucracy, and many people trusted instead in the informal folk knowledge embodied for so long in a predominantly agrarian society. The South's poverty limited its resources for educational development, and its public commitment to racial segregation made the school an institution for social orthodoxy, constraining the pursuit of new ideas so often associated with educational inquiry. Still, schools were seats of progress in the South, providing poor children needed skills and black children the ability to rise to success within the limits of Jim Crow. Institutions of higher learning have, at their best, nurtured ideals of academic freedom and the humanities and are now positioned to provide key resources for regional economic development.

The *Education* volume of *The New Encyclopedia of Southern Culture* places education in the broader context of southern society and regional cultural identity. Race has permeated discussion of formal education in the South, as well as other aspects of regional life, and this volume analyzes the educational parameters for education under Jim Crow. Articles assess the region's transition from segregation to desegregation and give special attention to the long-held faith in education among African Americans. Philanthropic foundations have played a crucial role in fostering education for African American children and poorer southerners in general from the General Education Board in the late 19th century to the Southern Education Foundation in the 20th century. An important component of higher education is generation of scholarship, and this volume explores the contributions of scholars of the South from classicist Basil Gildersleeve to renowned sociologist Howard Odum to literary critic Allen Tate to historians C. Vann Woodward and John Hope Franklin.

Editors have provided a generous helping of entries on individual institutions, selecting these entries on the basis of their reputations for quality, historic roles, or embodiment of a diverse set of missions. The volume's topical entries emphasize the region's wealth of religious schools and military schools, reflecting regional cultural values. The region's commitment to liberal arts education is highlighted here as well, through entries on such specific institutions as Hampden-Sydney College, the University of the South, and Millsaps College. The region's leading public universities and agricultural colleges are well represented. The commitment of African American southerners to education, often under trying circumstances, is seen in the many separate entries on historically black colleges and universities. Teachers are central figures in this volume, reflecting their key contributions.

The contemporary southern context is rapidly changing, with globalization creating new challenges and opportunities for the region's people, and this volume takes a reading on the South's educational history and contemporary developments at a time of transition.

The NEW ENCYCLOPEDIA *of* SOUTHERN CULTURE

VOLUME 17 : EDUCATION

EDUCATION IN THE SOUTH

Once you have counted James Branch Cabell . . . you will not find a single southern prose writer who can actually write. . . . [B]ut when you come to critics, musical composers, painters, sculptors, architects and the like, you will have to give it up, for there is not even a bad one between the Potomac mudflats and the Gulf. Nor an historian. Nor a sociologist. Nor a philosopher. Nor a theologian. Nor a scientist. In all these fields the South is an awe-inspiring blank.
—H. L. MENCKEN, "The Sahara of the Bozart," in *Prejudices: Second Series* (1920)

Decayed and hopeless men writing editorials at midnight for leading papers in Mississippi, Arkansas, and Alabama. . . . Presidents of one-building universities in the rural fastness of Kentucky and Tennessee.
—H. L. MENCKEN, "Virtue," in *Prejudices: Third Series* (1922)

For those who recall the unflattering depictions of southern intellectual life advanced during the 1920s by Baltimore journalist H. L. Mencken, the idea of exploring regional culture through the study of education may seem like a dubious exercise, if not actually a fool's errand. A moment's reflection reminds one, however, that Mencken himself took education quite seriously and wrote in the hope of elevating the South's intellectual standards. In this respect at least Mencken's strictures speak to one of the central themes in southern educational history—the Janus-faced quest to elevate the South and strengthen regional consciousness by embracing institutional models and intellectual standards imported from other parts of the nation. That this effort, prompted in part by Yankee influences clothed in the garb of regional uplift, often went against the grain of conservative southern values simply underscores education's key role in mediating between the parochial and the cosmopolitan elements—the inwardly and outwardly directed components—of regional identity.

The southern educational landscape has, of course, changed profoundly over the span of four centuries, as formal learning moved gradually from the margin to the center of daily life. Aware that education at once reflected and shaped the region's evolving social fabric, scholars of the past few decades have taken important steps toward incorporating educational developments into the larger narrative of the South's past. And while no writer has yet produced a comprehensive account of the dynamic tension between formal learning and the nonformal education embedded in patterns of regional folk culture, a sizeable body of recent scholarship has explored the role of schooling in shaping the South's troubled passage into the mainstream of American life. Whether the issue is the suppression of free thought in the Old South, disputes over the amount and type of schooling provided to ex-slaves and their descendants, the struggle for control and authority over tax-supported rural schools in the Progressive Era, the rise and fall of racial segregation, the place of religion in the public sphere, or the century-long concern over southern educational backwardness, few episodes in the history of regional modernization can be adequately discussed apart from their educational dimension. Work on these and many related problems is ongoing. Without presuming to offer a systematic reinterpretation of southern educational history, the present volume, in addition to providing a convenient source of factual reference, seeks to call attention to some of the more significant ways in which the study of education has come to illuminate the subject of regional identity in the states of the former Confederacy.

Early Educational Patterns. During the colonial era most southerners accepted the English notion of education as a private responsibility. As a result, a stigma surrounded publicly supported education, resulting in the frequent disparagement of those individuals who were unable to pay for instruction. The conservative outlook of the South's governing elite was captured in a 1671 pronouncement by Virginia's outspoken Gov. William Berkeley. When asked what course was taken for the religious instruction of the colony's population, Berkeley replied, "The same that is taken in England out of towns, every man according to his ability instructing his children. I thank God there are no free schools nor printing presses, and I hope we shall not have them these hundred years; for learning has brought disobedience, and heresy, and sects into the world, and printing has divulged them and libels against the best of governments: God keep us from both!" Strictly speaking, free education was not unknown in the colonial South. Many apprentice contracts contained educational provisions, and one or two privately endowed schools were providing free education to some Virginia children even during Berkeley's tenure as governor. Nonetheless, as historian Rhys Isaac has pointed out, literacy was more important as a line of social demarcation than as a path to upward mobility in colonial society. Many factors including sparseness of settlement, fear of slave literacy, and a lack of effective governmental apparatus inhibited the growth of schools in the South. Thus, the socializing effects of education were usually confined to areas where sufficient collective wealth existed to pay tutors for the education of children or where the means of an individual planter or merchant permitted the underwriting of his children's education. Although accurate statistics are unavailable, it seems probable that as late as the middle of the 18th century at least half of the South's white women and one third of its white men were illiterate. Literacy among the black population was extremely rare.

Higher education received scant attention in the pre-Revolutionary South. Some southerners sent their sons to one of the eight colonial colleges located in New England and the Middle Colonies, while others arranged to educate their male offspring abroad. The College of William and Mary, chartered in 1693 and achieving true collegiate status by the third decade of the 18th century, was the first college located in the South. Nearly a century would pass before additional colleges appeared. Initial steps toward establishing the College of Charleston in 1770 were met with objections that "learning would become cheap and too common." (The school was eventually chartered in 1785.) A few other unsuccessful attempts at college founding took place, most notably perhaps the effort mounted by the trustees of Georgia to transfer a college planned for Bermuda to Georgia and a later plan designed by the evangelist George Whitefield, which envisioned the establishment of what would have been a denominational college in Savannah. William and Mary, however, remained the South's only college at the time of the American Revolution.

The growth of republican ideology that accompanied American independence contributed to a new interest in tax-supported schooling. In Virginia and several other southern states, plans evolved for unitary systems of education with state universities at the top, supported by a system of academies and common schools. Most of these plans failed, although Georgia, Tennessee, South Carolina, and North Carolina all chartered state-supported colleges prior to 1800. A few colleges with no direct ties to the states also appeared in the immediate post-Revolutionary years. During the later antebellum era, as the older state universities achieved a degree of stability, the South would experience the same proliferation of small, financially weak, denominational and private colleges that typified other parts of the nation.

In many respects, the South's educational system in the generation before the Civil War reflected the region's descent into a conservative bunker mentality. William R. Taylor has argued that the 1830s witnessed a reactionary shift in southern educational thought, as sectional tensions led slave-state residents to repudiate much of the liberal Revolutionary heritage. Not only did schooling come, once again, to be seen as a private or, at best, a local matter, but the object of education ceased to be preparing a citizenry to guard its liberties and place a check on government. Instead, Taylor argues, education became a means of inculcating orthodoxies and fending off outside criticism—a means of social control in which the young were prepared to "do battle for the very orthodoxies that it had become heretic to question or examine." The popularity of military schools, with their stress on discipline and applied subjects, might be seen as one symptom of this reactionary drift. Wealthy southerners hired private tutors for their children's instruction, while middling folk and the moderately well-to-do created private contract schools and academies. Higher education catered to the children of the elite, and the collegiate curricula reflected the fondness of the privileged for classicism and the values of an earlier age. In church colleges piety took precedence over critical thought. The region also rejected formal schooling for its black population. All southern states prohibited teaching slaves to read and the efforts of white religious reformers to legalize slave literacy came to nothing. Some African Americans surmounted these educational obstacles. Perhaps 3 to 5 percent of slaves and a somewhat larger portion of free blacks were literate by the 1850s.

For much of the antebellum period public education, in the modern sense of the term, remained a foreign concept below the Potomac. But if most of the region's schools remained privately financed, a genuine system of public schools began to take shape in the South's major port cities. The South's oldest public school system was that of Baltimore, Md. Founded in 1829 with minimal funding from a municipal tax, the Baltimore schools operated for a decade on the monitorial system devised by the British educational reformer Joseph Lancaster. The system was never popular with parents, and during its final year of operation in 1838 only eight teachers were employed to teach the 675 students in Baltimore's public system. With the shift to a new pedagogy of group-based "simultaneous recitation" enrollment grew rapidly—to 1,126 students and 16 teachers in 1839 and more than 7,000 students and 119 teachers by 1850. A decade later enrollment was approaching 13,000 students served by a teaching staff of over 300. Well before that time the system had been reorganized to include separately designated grammar and primary schools as well as male and female high schools. Throughout the decades in question Baltimore's large free black population (numbering over 25,000 in 1850) was taxed to support the public schools that their children were forbidden to attend. Between 1839 and 1850 three separate requests to either provide schools for free black children or exempt their parents from school taxation fell upon deaf ears.

Elsewhere, the pace of school creation began to accelerate during the 1840s and 1850s as the accomplishments of Horace Mann and other northeastern school reformers inspired supporters of public education in New Orleans, Mobile, and Charleston. Efforts to create a school system in New Orleans were complicated by the bitter rivalry between American residents and French-speaking Creoles, a conflict that led in 1836 to the division of the city into three, self-governing "municipalities." In 1841 merchant-activists in the American-dominated Second Municipality, many of whom were transplanted northeasterners, secured passage of state legislation that authorized the formation of a school system governed by a 16-man board of commissioners. Under the leadership of John Angier Shaw, a native New Englander and ally of Horace Mann, the Second Municipality's first public schools opened in 1842. Within a year more than 1,000 students had enrolled, and by the late 1850s average daily attendance surpassed 3,600. On the eve of the Civil War the system included modern high schools for girls and boys modeled after the famous Boston Latin School, free textbooks, and a free library for teachers and students, as well as evening schools for working youth and adults. Progress in the other municipalities was less impressive, slowed by factional rivalries and disputes over finances and bilingual instruction. Nevertheless, the city's Creoles eventually embraced much of the example set by the American sector and became strong supporters of public instruction. It was, in fact, Alexander Fabre, the superintendent of the French Quarter schools, who delivered what has been rightly characterized as the most eloquent defense of public education in antebellum New Orleans. Speaking in 1852, Fabre extolled the city's schools for being "essentially public, not intended for any particular *class, but for the whole rising generation. . . .* In the empire of the *mind*, at least, let there be no *Monopoly*, no *caste*, no privilege," he declared.

No other southern city equaled New Orleans's record of educational accomplishment, but the decade of the 1850s witnessed the development of public schools in several other port cities. After several false starts in the 1840s, Mobile, Ala., launched a public school system in 1852, following the election of a board of 12 school commissioners, five of whom had moved to Mobile from the North. Mayor Kiah B. Sewell urged the city to follow the example of New York, Boston, Portland, and New Orleans in creating a three-tiered system of primary, grammar, and high school instruction, financed at taxpayer expense. The new system grew rapidly. In 1851 some 42 percent of Mobile's 3,524 school-age white children attended no institution of formal education. The rest were divided between private and parochial schools and various charity schools scattered across the city. By the end of the decade the public system included more than one fourth of all school-age white children from six school districts in the city and 17 districts in the county outside the city limits. Annual educational expenditures averaged four dollars per school-age child. Uniquely among southern cities, Mobile operated a publicly funded school for the children of the city's black Creole population, whose citizenship rights were guaranteed under the Louisiana Purchase Treaty of 1803 and the Adams-Onis Treaty of 1819. Attendance was limited to children who could prove descent from "free

Colored Creoles" residing in west Florida at the time of Spain's transfer of the territory to the United States.

Charleston, S.C., long a citadel of social elitism, launched its public school system in 1856, nearly two decades after the city assumed financial responsibility for the College of Charleston. The leading proponent of the new system was Christopher G. Memminger, one of the state's leading politicians and a crusader for many civic causes. The orphaned child of German immigrants, Memminger was adopted by a prominent Charleston family at age 11 and reared in an environment of wealth and privilege. An ardent defender of southern interests, including slavery, he nonetheless traveled widely outside the region and kept abreast of developments in other cities. During 1855–56 Memminger spent several weeks studying the public schools of Boston, New York, and Philadelphia, purchasing books and equipment, and hiring experienced teachers, nine of whom came south to teach Charleston's newly consolidated primary and high schools. Memminger's educational ideas were also shaped by correspondence and personal acquaintance with Connecticut school reformer Henry Barnard, who would later found the *American Journal of Education* and serve as the first United States commissioner of education. Barnard himself visited Charleston in 1855 to help launch the school system that was modeled on that of New York and presided over by his protégé, the former Brooklyn school superintendent Frederick A. Sawyer. Prior to 1850 less than 500 "poor scholars" had attended the city's unkempt, underfinanced, and poorly staffed charity schools. The graded schools of the new public system attracted a steadily rising enrollment that grew from 1,698 in 1857 to over 4,000 in 1861. Other towns including Savannah, Ga., took tentative steps toward public schooling in the late 1850s, but in most places the South's only tax-supported schools were the "poor" schools, set aside for those youths who would take a demeaning pauper's oath.

Although the circumstances giving rise to urban public school campaigns differed according to the political makeup of each city, several common threads run through the larger story. First, and most obviously, public schools were located in the South's major seaports, where commerce brought civic leaders into frequent contact with people and ideas from other places. In each of the cities just named, transplanted northerners joined native-born educational reformers to press for tax-supported schools. The resulting coalitions looked to northern models in their quest for educational arrangements that would promote Protestant morality, social stability, and economic growth. In Baltimore the statistically "typical" advocate of public education in the 1820s was a 41-year-old lawyer, merchant, manufacturer, or newspaper editor who had been born outside the city and affiliated with the Presbyterian, Episcopal, or Unitarian faith. Opponents of public schooling in Baltimore were almost exclusively native-born conservatives whose ranks included many leading members of the city's landed-merchant elite. Their preference for private schools was shaped by a static commitment to the status-based, paternalistic order of the 18th century, in which the poor were assumed to be a permanent social group. School supporters, by contrast, had a more fluid conception of society. Employing the language of post-Revolutionary republicanism, school advocates stressed the need to bridge the distance between social classes and demonstrate that individual achievement, and upward mobility, would result from moral, industrious behavior.

To one degree or another, similar motives for public schooling existed in New Orleans, Mobile, and Charleston, although by the 1840s and 1850s mass immigration from Ireland, Germany, and other places had created concern over social stability and the place of a foreign-born urban proletariat in a slave society. Fearing that white workers could be "marshaled against the Planters upon the idea that they were fighting against the Aristocracy," Charleston's Christopher Memminger argued that bringing the children of the rich and the poor together in public schools would "benefit both by removing from one any disposition to arrogance and self-will, and from the other the spirit of envy and jealousy."

In contrast to the incipient "melting pot" rationale advanced for urban public schools, higher education in the Old South catered to the children of the wealthy. By design most southern colleges were located in small, interior towns where students could supposedly be shielded from the moral temptations and intellectual heresies of city life. But if the collegiate curricula reflected the fondness of the privileged for classicism and the values of an earlier age, southern colleges were not impervious to the educational ideas of the mid-19th century. Indeed, as Caroline Winterer has recently noted, throughout America from the 1820s onward, an increasingly historical approach to classical study was embraced as an antidote to rampant materialism, political "mobocracy," and uncouth rhetoric. These goals struck a responsive chord in the antebellum South, where the ancient world was often appropriated as a cultural antecedent for contemporary slave society. In addition to broadening the scope of classical instruction beyond simple grammar, southern schools also experimented with the introduction of collateral courses of study in the natural sciences and foreign languages. Colleges began to admit older students of lower social station who either worked their way through school or received financial aid. Graduates of southern colleges, regardless of their social origins, played influential roles in the region's affairs both before and after the Civil War. In a few places southerners also succeeded in establishing higher education for women on approximately the same level as that of the region's colleges for men. In Macon, Ga., for example, the Georgia Female College (later Wesleyan) offered a level of education that was genuinely collegiate. For most women, however, opportunities for schooling beyond the academy level were all but nonexistent. Between the 1780s and the 1850s the South made impressive strides in the field of higher learning, only to see many of the gains squandered as southern colleges increasingly became tools for the confirmation of regional values.

Civil War and Beyond. The Civil War disrupted education in the South, just as thoroughly as it disrupted the activities of other peacetime institutions. After the war, education resumed rather quickly at both lower and higher levels. Colleges that had been forced to close during the war now reopened, as did academies and other lower schools. During Reconstruction most state governments made appropriations for common-school education. Perhaps the most significant question addressed during Reconstruction, however, related to the availability of education for newly freed slaves. Agents of the Freedmen's Bureau and representatives of northern missionary societies began educational efforts in parts of the South even before the close of hostilities. With the coming of peace, large numbers of northern teachers came south to educate the freedmen. Blacks greeted the prospect of education with great enthusiasm, viewing education as a "badge of freedom" and ticket to greater equality in the white man's society. During Radical Reconstruction, educational provisions found their way into the new state constitutions, where for the first time in southern history universal education was recognized as a right of all citizens. In addition to the constitutional provisions, state legislators passed laws that established in every southern state a state superintendent of public instruction, made provisions for the training of teachers, and authorized taxes in support of education. The region's poverty, persistent white resistance to educating blacks, and corruption in the management of state government limited the achievements of the educational reforms introduced during Reconstruction. Nevertheless, Reconstruction introduced the region to the concept of universal education as a public responsibility.

Throughout the 1880s and 1890s southern cities developed systems of racially segregated graded schooling. The emphasis was on elementary instruction lasting five to seven years for most students. Publicly funded high school instruction, rarely available to black students, was limited largely to white children from affluent families. Once Supreme Court decisions in the 1880s ended all hope of federal support for school integration, urban blacks campaigned successfully for the employment of African American teachers and administrators in the schools their children attended. In the rural South ungraded one-room schools controlled by families in local neighborhoods became the educational norm. The quality of instruction, vividly recounted in books such as William Owens's classic memoir *This Stubborn Soil*, varied widely and was largely a reflection of the wealth and educational level of the residents in local districts. Although the racial division of meager state educational appropriations was more equitable in the late 19th century than would be true after 1900, black communities had little choice but to fall back on their own resources to pay teachers and provide school facilities. As Ned Cobb, a black Alabama sharecropper, recalled, "Sometimes school wouldn't run over a month and a half or two months and they'd send out word. . . . 'Close the schools down, close the schools down. Money's out.'"

By the turn of the century, southern schools had fallen further and further behind the rest of the nation. In 1900, when the average amount expended per child for education in the United States was slightly less than three dollars, Alabama and North Carolina (at the lower end of the southern scale) provided only 50 cents per child, while Florida and Texas (at the upper end) provided slightly less than a dollar and a half per child. School terms in the South were less than 100 days in length as opposed to 145 days on average for other regions of the United States. Teachers, an increasing number of whom were female, remained very poorly trained and were pitifully paid, averaging only about one-half the amount paid teachers elsewhere in the nation. Only one southern state required school attendance, and as a result, only about 40 percent of the region's children went to school on a regular basis. Of those who did, only one in 10 completed the fourth grade. Schoolhouses were unbelievably primitive in the rural areas and in black neighborhoods within the cities. Private academies offered college preparation for those who could pay, but outside of major cities, public secondary education throughout the region was virtually nonexistent. Illiteracy rates for the southern states greatly exceeded those in any other part of the nation. Census statistics indicated that at least half of the region's blacks could not read. Undoubtedly, even larger numbers could have been classified as functionally illiterate.

Southern colleges and universities made some progress from the close of Reconstruction until the turn of the century, but by and large they suffered from problems generated by the region's poverty. The Morrill Act of 1862 provided federal funds to designated institutions in the southern states, but state appropriations to public institutions remained quite low and, in some cases, nonexistent, as conservative southern legislators clung to a laissez-faire philosophy toward higher education. Private institutions struggled to survive on gifts from sponsoring denominations and tuition from students.

Writing in 1884–85 Charles Forster Smith, a professor of English at Vanderbilt University, painted an unflattering picture of higher learning in the New South. After corresponding extensively with college faculty members and headmasters of private preparatory schools across the region, Smith reported wide agreement that higher learning had been profoundly affected by the pressures of post-Reconstruction life. For young men of the 1880s the importance of classical instruction was no longer self-evident and the prerequisites for advanced study were neither uniform nor easily satisfied. Few private or public high schools provided genuine college preparation to southern youth, who were increasingly subject to the pull of an all-powerful commercial spirit. Business had displaced *otium cum dignitate* ("dignified leisure") as a cultural dictum, resulting in a pervasive "eagerness, impatience, haste to get into employment." Leading educators complained that "young men will not take the time to prepare for college nor stay in college when they get there." Colleges themselves had encouraged superficiality by lowering admission standards in a desperate competition for tuition revenue. Throughout the former Confederacy the postwar decades witnessed the wholesale resort to elective courses and improvised degrees, conferred in many cases by small, impoverished, academically suspect "universities" that sprang up like toadstools in what had once been a well-manicured collegiate landscape. Smith acknowledged that these developments had "opened higher education to those who have no classical training [and] who were formerly excluded by the curriculum." But increased access had come at a price. With many schools offering "a course beginning at 'a b c' and ending with A.B.," the very meaning of higher education seemed in doubt. There was, Smith insisted, an inverse relationship between the quantity and quality of southern collegiate institutions.

Separate black colleges that opened soon after the close of the Civil War with assistance from various northern agencies had difficulty surviving in an atmosphere of white hostility. The American Missionary Association, a Congregational body, chartered six black colleges in rapid succession: Berea in Kentucky, Hampton in Virginia, Talladega in Alabama, Tougaloo in Mississippi, Straight (later Dillard) in New Orleans, and Fisk in Nashville. Northern Methodists and Baptists were equally active, sponsoring more than twenty colleges, founded mainly during the 1870s and 1880s when most southern states also created at least one publicly supported black institution, typically for teacher training and industrial education. When Congress passed the Second Morrill

Act in 1890, providing annual appropriations to be shared between white and black land-grant schools, Alabama, Arkansas, Florida, Texas, Kentucky, Virginia, Mississippi, and Missouri chose existing black institutions to receive the federal funds. In other southern states new black Agricultural and Mechanical colleges were created in response to the law.

From the 1860s and 1870s through the decade of World War I most black colleges and universities resembled grammar and normal schools that offered advanced work to a small number of students. During the mid-1890s just over 11 percent, or 1,020 of the 9,066 students enrolled in colleges supported by northern mission groups, were classified as college or professional students. The picture had changed very little by 1914–15 when 9,144 out of 12,894 students (some 71 percent) were enrolled in elementary, grammar, and secondary courses at the same institutions. Notwithstanding their frequent "Industrial" or "A&M" designations, the real mission of black colleges, apart from providing elementary and secondary classes, was training teachers, and to a lesser extent ministers, who would return to educate the children of black communities across the South. This was true even of schools such as Tuskegee Institute where the blending of academic and industrial courses was emphasized. In 1889 more than two thirds of Tuskegee's 321 graduates were employed as schoolteachers. Of 1,883 graduates of some 30 black colleges in 1900, over one third were employed as teachers while only 1.4 percent engaged in farming.

The rudimentary nature of much of the academic work at black colleges should not be allowed to obscure the significance of African American higher learning for the reshaping of regional values. Black schooling of any type involved a tacit acknowledgement on the part of southern whites that the aspirations of freedpeople and their children must be taken into account when charting a course to the future. In the deteriorating racial climate of the late 19th century this was no small thing. Just as important, blacks themselves drew a sharp distinction between the enforced humiliations of the Jim Crow system and the racial separateness of the Negro campus. From Reconstruction onward, black colleges sought to inspire their students with a sense of higher learning's relevance to the task of collective racial uplift. In time the colleges, like the African American churches, would become, in Adam Fairclough's phrase, "part of the sinew, brains, and soul of the black community."

Although the South's late 19th-century educational universe was in a state of flux, most black and white colleges continued to offer a liberal arts curriculum. Calls for engineering schools and modern technological training generated much rhetoric and occasional action, resulting most notably in the founding of the Georgia School of Technology. A few state universities and some of the black institutions sought to incorporate agricultural and industrial training into their programs of study. Widespread education of teachers in a collegiate setting would await the second decade of the 20th century.

Reform Efforts. A major campaign to provide public schooling to the southern white masses took place from the 1890s through World War I. Leaders such as southern expatriate Walter Hines Page, Charles B. Aycock and Edwin A. Alderman of North Carolina, Thomas U. Dudley of Kentucky, Charles W. Dabney of Tennessee, James H. Dillard of Louisiana, William N. Sheats of Florida, Oscar Cooper of Texas, J. J. Doyne of Arkansas, Braxton B. Comer of Alabama, Walter B. Hill of Georgia, and William H. Hand of South Carolina approached the task of school reform with a crusading zeal. Their efforts were part of a larger program of regional economic modernization, which coincided with the disfranchisement of black voters and a major shift in the focus of southern white reform ideology. Convinced that progress would occur when each race fostered its unique spirit or folk genius, moderate white reformers after 1900 subscribed to a philosophy of racial essentialism that diverted attention away from black schooling, and the "Negro problem" in general, and focused instead upon the seemingly more urgent work of nurturing, through education, the cultural development of common whites. This outlook, which Joel Williamson has termed "Volksgeistian Conservatism," infused white school campaigns with a new moral energy even as it provided a convenient excuse for turning a blind eye to the gross inequalities of state-mandated segregation.

Funds provided by George Peabody, a Massachusetts banker, for the improvement of education at the elementary and secondary levels promoted the establishment of model schools and the improvement of individual schools. J. L. M. Curry, administrator of the Peabody Fund, proselytized throughout the region on behalf of education. Another eastern philanthropist, Robert C. Ogden, with the aid of people like Curry, established a series of educational conferences that were held across the South. What began as the "Ogden movement" evolved quickly into a multiyear campaign to build political support for public school expansion. Financed by Rockefeller funds channeled through the Southern Education Board, the school campaigns enlisted the active support of urban, middle-class women who formed organizations such as the Richmond Education Association and the Women's Association for the Betterment of Public School Houses in North Carolina, to say nothing of the dozens of local school improvement leagues that sprang up across the rural and small-town South. The pre–World War I school campaigns comprised one element in the larger modernizing agenda of southern Progressivism. Progressive southern governors sponsored legislation and constitutional revisions that led to dramatic increases in school revenues, a lengthening of the school terms, increases in the salaries of teachers, and decreases in the illiteracy rate. Consolidation of rural schools followed, and by 1920 important strides had been taken toward establishing widespread public secondary education. During the first three decades of the 20th century, appropriations for education in all the southern states rose dramatically but stayed well below the national average.

Like other Progressive measures such as child labor restrictions and public health programs, school reform encountered substantial opposition from rural neighborhoods that were reluctant to cede decision-making power to middle-class bureaucrats in distant locales. Such opposition, which has been carefully examined in the work of William A. Link, points toward the larger social and psychological meaning of school modernization. In his insightful book *Schooling the New South*, historian James L. Leloudis traces the movement of white children in North Carolina from the loose informality of family-, church-, and community-centered neighborhood schools to the more externally oriented and competitive environment of larger graded schools. In this new setting children were exposed to object teaching, silent reading (rather than recitation), standardized numeric evaluation of performance, and disciplinary methods that substituted ambition, guilt, and conscience in place of corporal punishment. Viewed in this light, southern school reform not only mirrored the requirements of the commercial market, but, perhaps more important, contributed to an increased emphasis upon the "primacy of the self" in turn-of-the-century southern life. Just as important, as Ann C. Rose has argued, northern philanthropic support of southern school reform brought with it a new perspective on childhood that stressed the developmental aspects of personality and emphasized environmental influence over natural endowments. Ultimately this logic would prove inimical to the southern defense of racial segregation.

Considering the attitudes of white reformers, and the political consequences of disfranchisement, it is hardly surprising that blacks derived few advantages from the educational programs of the pre–New Deal South. The 1899 U.S. Supreme Court ruling in *Cumming v. Board of Education of Richmond County, Georgia* made a mockery of the "separate-but-equal" doctrine enunciated in the 1896 *Plessy v. Ferguson* decision and opened the door for blatant racial discrimination in the allocation of state school funds by local authorities. In areas of high black population, white children were the chief beneficiaries of educational appropriations made on a per capita basis. It is important to note, however, that not all southern whites turned a blind eye to racial injustice in education and other aspects of daily life. Tulane's James H. Dillard, a vocal opponent of lynching during the 1890s, went on to head the Anna T. Jeanes Negro Rural School Fund in 1907 and the John F. Slater Fund in 1910. Among other activities, these agencies sponsored industrial "county training schools" that provided the only publicly funded secondary education available to most blacks. Eventually, many of these schools would become standard high schools. Aware that white voters had little enthusiasm for educating blacks, Dillard required Jeanes and Slater applicants to provide matching funds, thus reducing, if only slightly, the cost to stingy local school officials. In addition, philanthropies like the Rosenwald Foundation contributed millions of dollars toward the construction of black schools. For the most part, however, black communities fell back on their own resources to augment meager state support for local schools.

Despite the improvements in both black and white education during the Progressive Era, the region's schools remained woefully inadequate. A few centers of achievement did appear, most notably in higher education, and the South committed an increasingly large percentage of its resources to the support of education. Southern schools, however, made relatively little progress in the game of catch-up, which they would play for decades to come. The agricultural depression of the 1920s and the Great Depression of the 1930s compounded an already difficult fiscal situation. Also, the region's largely rural culture placed a low premium on education for both whites and blacks. Whites refused to acknowledge that blacks should receive equal education, or for that matter be educated beyond even the barest rudiments. State legislators throughout the region saw that black schools received only a fraction of the meager support that flowed to all of education. And local school boards typically made sure that white schools received the lion's share of state funds appropriated on the basis of total school-age population.

On the positive side of the ledger, one is struck by the determination of leaders in higher education to overcome fiscal and cultural obstacles to institutional development. In time—how much varied from school to school and from state to state—southern institutions modernized their curricula, enlarged their faculties, adopted the departmental system of organization, and began to exhibit a spirit of disciplinary loyalty and professionalism. Regional accrediting bodies gained support, and loosely standardized admission requirements helped clarify the educational mission of schools at all levels. Church colleges moved to town, grew worldly, and sought Yankee patronage, even as newer urban universities and technological schools arose. Outside the athletic realm, where football flourished, southern schools led in little and lagged in much. But during each major phase in the structural evolution of higher education be-

Mother teaching children in a sharecropper home, Transylvania, La., 1939 (Russell Lee, photographer, Library of Congress [LC-USF34-T01-031938-D], Washington, D.C.)

tween the 1890s and World War II southern schools moved haltingly down the path toward eventual convergence with external norms. This was true despite the Vanderbilt and Louisiana State University agrarians' antimodernist celebration of sectional peculiarity and notwithstanding the seeming anomaly presented by racial segregation and the exclusion of blacks from white colleges—a phenomenon scarcely confined to the South in practice.

One of the clearest indications of the power of outside models to shape and inspire academics below the Potomac was the growing importance attached to research and graduate training. The generation of college administrators who assumed the reins of power in the South after World War I perceived the widening gulf between their own institutions and the emerging research universities of the Northeast. Seeing the gap, they resolved to narrow it. The formation in 1927 of the Conference of Deans of Southern Graduate Schools, even more than the founding of the Southern Association of Colleges and Secondary Schools three decades earlier, signaled the determination of southern educators to embrace qualitative standards that would be consistent with the requirements of serious scholarship and academic science. Impatient with long decades of apology for regional backwardness, spokesmen for leading southern universities sought progress through a frank assessment of existing conditions and the conscious emulation of more prestigious institutions in the East and Midwest—where many southern scholars, deans, and college presidents had received their own advanced training.

Wilson Gee's 1932 study *Research Barriers in the South*, although cast in the form of a tabular jeremiad, can more accurately be seen as an expression of the commitment leading southern universities had already made to follow the path marked out by the elite schools of the Northeast and Midwest, where private philanthropy had brought about a functioning system of research institutions. A few numbers may clarify the point. In her careful investigation of graduate work in the South, begun as a North Carolina doctoral dissertation in 1942 and published five years later with support from the Conference of Deans of Southern Graduate Schools, Mary Bynum Pierson provides the best available overview of when and where in the South the training of new Ph.D. students took root. Prior to 1920 such activity was of negligible significance at all schools, and the situation would change very little for many of the region's state universities over the next two decades. In the strongest institutions, however, primarily those that had gained early membership in the Association of American Universities, a different picture emerged. During the decade of the 1920s doctoral training took on a new importance for schools such as Duke, Vanderbilt, and the Universities of Virginia, North Carolina, and Texas. Between 1920 and 1930 Texas, Chapel Hill (N.C.), and Virginia produced respectively 31, 70, and 89 Ph.D.s, with science doctorates being most numerous, followed by degrees in English, history, and education. The next decade (1931–41) witnessed a major upsurge in doctoral work at these and other schools. The University of Texas alone granted 332 Ph.D.s, followed by Duke with 276, Chapel Hill with 264, and Virginia with 255. Vanderbilt also entered the ranks of doctoral institutions, awarding 106 Ph.D. degrees, including 38 in the field of English literature—an indication of the regional impact of the self-styled Agrarian movement and the New Criticism. All told, the above mentioned schools accounted for 1,233 new doctoral recipients during an era of extreme financial stringency for southern higher learning. As in the 1920s, much doctoral work was concentrated in scientific fields, especially the medical sciences and public health, followed by history, literature, and the social sciences such as economics, sociology, and psychology.

No doubt many factors, including the creation of the $40 million Duke Endowment in 1924 and the all-important stimulus of funding from major philanthropies, helped account for the expansion of graduate work during the interwar decades. And yet much of the impetus for expanding research and graduate study came from within the South and was closely tied to a sense of regional identity that linked intellectual accomplishment with the struggle for sectional uplift and Yankee recognition. Indeed, even W. J. Cash's classic 1941 endorsement of Henry Adams's belief that southerners typically "had no mind" can be seen as an implicit acknowledgement of their need to acquire one. In speaking of the period from 1920 to 1927 Cash noted, with obvious approval, the influx from the North of brilliant and distinguished academics, both Yankees and native southerners educated above the Mason-Dixon line. By 1940 Cash believed the South enjoyed the best intellectual leadership in its history, "the first which really deserved the adjective."

Expansion of Education after World War II. As the Depression closed and World War II began, the southern economy entered a period of growth and increasing prosperity. A high birthrate after the war and rapid urbanization helped create a stronger demand for quality education. The growing prosperity of the region promoted increases in funding for education. Consolidation of schools became a hallmark in rural education, while in cities and suburbs massive construction programs were made possible by steadily increasing appropriations from state legislators. After 1950, school systems near major military bases and defense installations also benefited from government aid to schools in "federally impacted" areas. The congressional formula granting such aid to districts with higher-than-average taxes and lower-than-average spending per pupil corresponded closely with the conditions prevailing in many southern communities of the postwar era. In addition to physical growth the region also turned its attention to salaries of teachers and requirements for teacher certification. In the 1952–53 school year some 78.8 percent of white teachers and 73.3 percent of black teachers possessed college degrees. By the end of the decade a bachelor's degree was required for teacher certification in all southern states, and in 1966 more than 97 percent of the South's high school teachers were college graduates, with some 25 percent holding a master's degree. Libraries and curricula grew, and secondary schools increasingly provided not only college preparatory education but also vocational-technical education. In many school systems programs of "distributive education" or other cooperative arrangements allowed high school students to gain work experience prior to graduation.

Increased support for elementary and secondary education went hand in hand with more generous appropriations for the region's public colleges and universities. Long hampered by pitiful support from the states and by inferior facilities and faculties, these institutions now benefited from a growing awareness of the importance of higher education to the modernization of southern society. The appearance of large numbers of veterans on southern campuses following World War II added a much-welcomed source of revenue. The veterans' presence on campus helped to change the orientation of the institutions away from a strict *in loco parentis* posture. Enrollments in many southern colleges more than doubled during the late 1940s as a result of the presence of the veterans. The southern record in higher education, however, remained well below that of the nation. Institutions such as the University of North Carolina or the University of Texas occasionally achieved national recognition for individual programs, but the achievements of most public and private universities in the region were not compatible with national norms. Indeed, many southern *universities* remained little more than large liberal arts *colleges* with a modicum of professional education. Fledgling graduate programs, struggling to recover from wartime neglect, were still in their infancy. During the six-year period from 1948 to 1953 no less than 13 southern institutions, mainly state universities and engineering schools, granted their first earned doctorates, while at least three additional campuses revived Ph.D. programs after decades of quiescence. From the early 1950s through the early 1960s the South's annual production of Ph.D.s in the liberal arts and sciences (excluding education degrees) averaged 23 doctorates per institution. The University of Texas led the way with an average of 125 new Ph.D.s per year followed by the University of North Carolina with 82, Duke University with 69, and the University of Florida with 65.

In the early 1950s academicians and politicians developed an enlarged awareness of the importance of research in a university environment and a nascent recognition of the availability of federal and foundation funds for the support of research. Accordingly, in the 1950s many state and private institutions hired faculty who had both instructional and research skills. Their research led to a growth in outside funding for the university programs during the late 1950s. With passage of the National Defense Education Act (NDEA), in the wake of the Russian launching of Sputnik, federal support increased exponentially. Enacted in 1958 at the behest of Congressman Carl Elliott of Alabama and his Senate colleague Lister Hill, over strong opposition from Republicans and conservative southern Democrats, the NDEA was dramatically expanded in 1964. Among the bill's more important provisions were fellowships for graduate study as well as low-interest undergraduate loans. Like federal science traineeships, NDEA awards were granted to institutions rather than to individual students. This resulted in a more even geographical distribution of graduate aid. During the first seven years of the program (1958–64) the majority of NDEA fellowships went to schools "in regions most deficient in graduate facilities."

The South, which produced 9 percent of all U.S. doctorates during these years, received 22 percent of all NDEA fellowship awards.

The new dollars strengthened research and instruction at the South's major institutions. For the next 30 years southern universities steadily built their research components and worked to achieve the depth and rigor that characterized advanced study at the nation's leading schools. Measured in terms of spending on research and development, the South could claim 32 of the nation's top 100 universities in the year 2000. Using the same standard, some 23 of the South's top universities ranked higher in 2000 than they had in 1985. Moreover, the share of research funding in the South derived from federal sources (54 percent) was only slightly lower than the national average. At the beginning of the 21st century the South still had no "flagship" public universities fully equal to the University of California at Berkeley or the University of Wisconsin, although the principal state universities of Virginia, Texas, North Carolina, Florida, and Georgia enjoyed a substantial degree of national visibility. Among private schools Duke, Rice, Vanderbilt, and Emory now appeared with increasing frequency in various national rankings of research universities. The same could be said of the region's best liberal arts colleges, schools such as Birmingham Southern, Davidson, Millsaps, Furman, Washington and Lee, Rhodes, Sewanee, Centre, and the other eight members of the Associated Colleges of the South, as well as women's colleges such as Mary Baldwin, Sweet Briar, and Mississippi University for Women, which are widely acclaimed for maintaining high intellectual standards and fostering humane learning in an age of rampant vocationalism.

Outside the realm of status competition among elite universities and colleges, the most significant development in southern higher education has been the quiet revolution in college attendance that has gone on unabated for the past two generations. Access to higher education expanded dramatically after World War II, beginning with the G.I. Bill and the Higher Education Act of 1965 and its subsequent amendments. In 1956 approximately 5 percent of adult southerners had a bachelor's degree. By 2007 the figure was 23 percent. Although these numbers represent no gain in degree attainment relative to the rest of America (southern figures have been in the low 90 percent range of the national average since the 1960s), the absolute increase is still highly significant. Some of the growth in bachelor's degrees has occurred as a result of higher enrollment at flagship schools or former teachers colleges legislatively elevated to university status. But the post-1945 decades also witnessed an upsurge of educational demand in many southern cities where new schools were established or where branch campuses of state universities gained independent status. As Tennant S. McWilliams has noted, the rise of urban public universities was part of a larger shift in the rural versus urban balance of political power in the postwar South. Serving many students unable to "go away" to college, the new urban commuter schools typically admitted all comers, providing high-quality intellectual training to serious students and granting employment credentials to many others. Over time, graduate programs were added to the curriculum of most publicly financed urban schools.

By the start of the 21st century such institutions, sometimes designated "metropolitan universities," faced a deepening identity crisis. Were young metropolitan schools in some sense an urban equivalent of older land grant universities? If so, was their primary mission to serve local communities through open-admissions undergraduate classes and professional training in the applied fields, thereby renouncing aspirations to the research university status that older, land-grant schools had long since achieved? The question pointed to potential conflicts between research, liberal learning, and vocational training—a confusion of purpose symbolized by the difference between teaching "best practices" in a professional setting or pursuing basic research that would enlarge the scope of fundamental knowledge in the sciences and humanities. Finite resources precluded giving equal weight to the demands of all claimants, leaving college administrators to devise mission statements that were at best loosely connected to budgetary reality. Similar tensions existed in a more muted form at wealthier flagship schools, where differing conceptions of higher learning operated in a fuzzy state of neutral coexistence.

Properly understood, the tensions within southern universities were simply reflections of the larger triumph of an instrumentalist view of higher education that had long been gathering momentum. At bottom this outlook rested upon an implicit rejection of the value of creative and intellectual activity as an end in itself. Increasingly pressed to adopt a business-oriented calculus of marginal utility, those guiding the destiny of southern (and American) universities often discovered that the life of the mind (as traditionally understood) was a luxury their schools could ill afford. Against this background, part-time faculty, like online courses and Division-I football, took on a strong appeal. All were efficient means of attracting more students and producing more graduates, the meaning of whose degrees seemed increasingly suspect amid the ruins of a national economic meltdown accompanied by accreditors' insistent demands for the quantitative measurement of student learning. In the post-1960s South many thoughtful members of the academy had grown increasingly fearful of the consequences that would inevitably follow higher learning's embrace of narrowly utilitarian aims and entrepreneurial values. Would a generation of students who had been encouraged to see themselves as customers purchasing a fungible commodity called education be prepared to cope with the ugly reality of a global economic meltdown? Would the seemingly endless post-1945 expansion of higher education come to be regarded as little more than a generational Ponzi Scheme? In the second decade of the 21st century, as southern colleges absorbed the fiscal consequences of America's post-1980 infatuation with free market ideology, the question remained altogether too delicate for robust public discussion.

As the preceding paragraphs have indicated, the spurt in growth of southern education after World War II stopped well short of bringing the region to a position of parity with other parts of the United States. Without a concomitant move toward establishing equal educational opportunities for blacks and whites, southern education was doomed to remain grossly inferior. This was true not only because of the expense involved in maintaining dual educational systems and the historic neglect of black schools, but also because of the constraints on intellectual freedom imposed by segregationist orthodoxy. During the 1950s most southern states sought to paper over segregation's contradictions by adopting "minimum foundation" schemes for school funding and asking blacks to "voluntarily" accept segregation, even as state legislatures conducted witch hunts against integrationists, "Communists," and homosexuals in the teaching ranks. Amid a wave of equalization lawsuits filed by attorneys from the NAACP Legal Defense Fund, improvements and increased funding flowed to black schools as white southerners attempted to avert integration through achieving a closer approximation of the separate-but-equal formula prescribed in the 1896 Supreme Court decision *Plessy v. Ferguson*. Although a certain amount of regional modernization was achieved during the last years of segregation, whites' hopes that integration could be avoided were derailed with the *Brown v. Board of Education* decision in 1954.

Race Relations and Educational Quality. From the mid-1950s through the early 1960s the South's public schools and colleges became a primary focus of civil rights activity. As blacks pressed for desegregation, ambitious white politicians endorsed a program of "massive resistance," replete with demagogic attempts to negate federal court rulings through the "interposition" of state authority. In Little Rock and New Orleans, as well as at Ole Miss and the University of Alabama, states' rights oratory and mob violence became the hallmark of opposition to racial change. Pressure for desegregation came from local black communities together with federal officials, the national press, and major philanthropic foundations outside the region. White resistance dragged on until the early 1970s, when the combined effect of legal decisions and federal legislation brought integration to most of the region's public schools and colleges. For a time the South led the nation in the percentage of students attending racially mixed classes, but a slow retreat from integration and "forced busing" resulted in substantial resegregation during the closing decades of the 20th century. Antibusing court decisions together with white flight to the suburbs accounted for much of the racial homogeneity in individual schools. But black disillusionment with integration also played a role. Having watched while black schools were closed and black teachers and administrators fired or demoted during the initial stages of desegregation, many African Americans began to lament the fracturing of community and loss of control that came with integration. In time, ambivalence over integration would give rise to something like nostalgia and an ill-defined sense of loss among black youth who had never experienced life under the Old Regime. Carried to an extreme, emphasis on the psychologically nurturing environment of pre-1960 black schools could make segregation seem like a warm security blanket instead of a barbed wire cage. By the 1990s some black writers were openly calling for a voluntary return to neighborhood schools in which residential patterns would result in schools attended overwhelmingly by a single race. Considerable school resegregation did, in fact, take place in the late 20th and early 21st centuries, resulting in an enrollment shift that placed more than 70 percent of the South's black and Latino students in predominantly minority schools. The change was significant, but its consequences paled against the larger reality of continued racial mixing and social contact among black and white children. Students arriving on southern college campuses in the years preceding the election of President Barack Obama no longer carried the burden of guilt, anger, resentment, and humiliation that their predecessors had known. Race had not disappeared as a factor in southern educational life, but it had ceased to be a consuming obsession.

With the defeat of legally sanctioned Jim Crow policies in the mid-1960s, political leaders were free to address the long-standing educational gap between the South and other regions. The 1970s saw the emergence of a group of "New South" governors such as Georgia's Jimmy Carter, Alabama's Albert Brewer, South Carolina's John West, and Florida's Ruben Askew, racial moderates who looked to education and economic development as an alternative to the bankrupt politics of white supremacy. The taproot of their reformist outlook, as Gordon Harvey correctly notes, ran to the cautious business Progressivism of the 1920s rather than to a more radical Great Society heritage. The latter fact together with the political makeup of individual states determined the practical limits of educational reform. Florida's diverse electorate and relatively tranquil racial climate allowed Ruben Askew to speak out forcefully against antibusing efforts and to secure passage in 1973 of a $1.1 billion educational finance bill that added $200 million to the previous year's appropriation and funded schools at a base rate of $587 per pupil. In Alabama, where Albert Brewer became governor upon Lurleen Wallace's death in 1968, spending for public schools would not reach the 1973 Florida level until 1987. The $100 million increase in educational spending that Brewer secured in 1969 was impressive by state standards but paltry in comparison to the task at hand. Although the South still lagged behind other regions in 1980, the end of massive resistance had unquestionably opened the door to educational progress. Virtually all areas of educational activity reflected the great increases in funds, and southern spokesmen prophesied that the region would one day become an example to the rest of the nation in the pursuit of academic excellence and equality.

By the early 1980s racial issues had largely taken second place to issues of quality at all levels of southern education. Beginning in 1983 most southern legislatures inaugurated far-reaching educational reforms aimed at upgrading elementary and secondary education, with special attention given to such quality indicators as teacher salaries and qualifications. During the next quarter century efforts at educational reform and improvement continued, reflecting a growing awareness of the link between education and economic development in what came to be called the "information age." The pace of change was uneven, reflecting wealth disparities between locales, to say nothing of peaks and valleys in the economy of individual states. Kindergarten, preschool, and adult education programs became more common, but by no means universal. Beginning in 2001 the federal "No Child Left Behind" act required states to report annual progress toward meeting state proficiency standards in math and science for elementary and high school students. Since each state established (and frequently changed) its standards, generalizations about educational quality based on state scores are problematic at best. Between 2003 and 2007 nearly all southern states reported gains in the percentage of fourth graders meeting state goals. For the South as a whole the median average of those passing state tests rose from 62 to 85 percent. The performance of southern students, as measured by the National Assessment of Educational Progress, looked somewhat less impressive. In 2007 the percentage of southern fourth graders scoring at or above the basic level of "partial mastery" in reading and math was nearly the same as that for students throughout America (65 percent in reading and 81 percent in math). At the next level only 29 percent and 35 percent of southern students were deemed "proficient" by demonstrating "competence over challenging subject matter" in reading and math. These scores fell 4 to 5 percent below national norms.

Still, outside observers found many reasons for optimism. In 2007 the South's poorest areas including the Alabama Black Belt and the Mississippi Delta remained educational backwaters but, as the *Christian Science Monitor* noted, the top five places in *Newsweek*'s ranking of U.S. public high schools went to schools below the Mason-Dixon line. These and other top performing schools had "risen against the odds," teaching racially diverse and often poor students with initially weak academic preparation. Critics charged that some districts manipulated test data, and that high-stakes testing and accountability were a double-edged sword that led to high failure rates in the ninth grade, followed by declining rates of high school completion. But if a declaration of educational "mission accomplished" seems premature, there can be little question that real progress has been achieved in the decades since Jim Crow's demise. Gene Bottoms of the Southern Regional Education Board put the matter succinctly when he observed that "if you looked at where the South was 20 years ago [i.e. in 1987], there's very little comparison to what exists today."

The passage of another generation will permit a more confident verdict on the state of southern education in the first decade of the 21st century. At present a few points seem clear. Southern schools, like those in other regions, have unquestionably been affected by the educational mandates of President George Bush and his secretary of education, Margaret Spellings. On the positive side, future teachers are required to take more college classes in the academic subjects they will later teach. But gains in subject knowledge have at times been offset by a new accountability mania that places a premium on classroom activities resulting in higher standardized test scores. "Teaching the tests" with an emphasis on factual recall and mechanical methods of problem solving seemed an imperfect substitute for deeper forms of intellectual engagement. It is, after all, quite possible to solve a problem in chemistry or mathematics without understanding what has been done or why an answer is correct. In 2009, for example, a sixth-grade math teacher in Mobile, Ala., was teaching students to reduce the fraction 310 over 1,000 by dividing the numerator and the denominator by a common number. Her efforts were short-circuited when a well-meaning "literacy coach" intervened to tell the students that they should "write 310 over 1,000 and cross out a zero from each number."

In many southern communities the late 20th century also witnessed a slow erosion of confidence in public education among some segments of the population. One symptom of this was the gradual growth in "homeschooling." After a slow beginning the trend gained momentum in the late 20th century. Between 1999 and 2003 the number of homeschooled students in the South rose from 355,000 (some 2 percent of the student population) to 445,000 (2.6 percent). Although the numbers are small, they reflect larger currents of cultural and pedagogical dissent that are more commonly associated with the growth of private education. Beginning with the "segregation academies" of the 1960s, many Protestant groups founded private elementary and high schools that, like the older Catholic parochial schools in some southern cities, siphoned off students and parental support from the public system. From the 1970s onward, private schools were no longer committed to racial segregation in an explicit way. Their appeal was part of a larger cultural backlash against the perceived excesses of the 1960s, including concern over violence, drug usage, and weak instruction in the public sector. The situation was further complicated by the emergence of culturally polarizing special interest groups demanding ideologically based curricular models ranging from Afrocentrism on the one hand to Creationism on the other. These challenges to the civic consensus necessary to sustain public schools coincided with the rise of the "religious right" in national politics and the accompanying critique of what was depicted as rampant secularism in American life. The South's Christian academies attracted parents angered by the constitutional ban on public school prayer and opposed to the teaching of evolution. As William Martin has observed, Christian academies provided "a well ordered atmosphere in which religious beliefs, patriotic sentiments, and conservative behavioral norms were reinforced rather than challenged." In each of these respects one might argue that the Christian schools of the 21st century resembled nothing so much as the typical southern public school of the early 1950s.

Conclusion. For most of the past century formal education has provided an important mechanism for blending tradition with modernity in the minds of southern youth. The shift to graded, consolidated, and bureaucratically administered schools in the decades surrounding World War I drew subsequent generations of rural students off the farm and into the cultural orbit of the urban middle class. As important as this change was, it did little to weaken the pull of conservative cultural norms until well after the civil rights battles of the 1960s. Before that time the walling off of blacks and whites in segregated schools provided constant and highly visible institutional underpinning to dogmas of white supremacy that lay at the core of regional identity. Historian Francis Butler Simkins once noted that "among Southerners there is the education which does not educate." The home rather than the school, Simkins believed, determined the cultural outlook of southern students who were predisposed to accept some ideas while rejecting others. Certainly this was and continues to be true of many private schools established in the wake of desegregation where, as one study found, both students and teachers sought to escape social realities deemed unacceptable. With respect to religion, patriotism, athletics, and authoritarian discipline, the new private schools of the mid-1970s represented "a logical and coherent extension" of the home environment. At the beginning of the 21st century, moreover, many homeschoolers and private evangelical academies espoused an "America as a Christian nation" history curriculum that venerated Stonewall Jackson and spoke with a decidedly southern and pro-Confederate accent.

Whether southern schools, either public or private, will continue to reinforce conservative local values in the era of the Internet, global trade, and unprecedented levels of foreign immigration seems very much open to question. The evangelical retreat into educational privatism appears almost inconsequential when weighed against the demands for mass education in an increasingly globalized world. In the second decade of the 21st century bilingual instruction is no longer a novelty in southern school districts that were once overwhelmingly WASP in makeup and parochial in outlook. One might reasonably envision a time in the not very distant future when southern schools will perform the "melting pot" function associated with northeastern education in the late 19th and early 20th centuries. Some version of regional identity will undoubtedly emerge from the new multiracial and multinational educational environment that is now taking shape. Its outlines are as yet indistinct, but one feels safe in predicting that the next "New South," deprived of an obvious "other" against which to define itself, will bear little resemblance to the proto-Dorian monolith evoked by Wilbur J. Cash in 1941. The "typical southerner" who graduates from high school in 2041 will be in some sense a descendant of Cash's South, but the family resemblance may be that of a third cousin twice removed.

CLARENCE L. MOHR
University of South Alabama

Clinton B. Allison, *Teachers for the South: Pedagogy and Educationists in the University of Tennessee, 1844–1995* (1998), in *Essays in Twentieth-Century Southern Education: Exceptionalism and Its Limits*, ed. Wayne J. Urban (1999); Eric Anderson and Alfred A. Moss Jr., *Dangerous Donations: Northern Philanthropy and Southern Black Education, 1902–1930* (1999); James D. Anderson, *The Education of Blacks in the South, 1860–1935* (1988); Rod Andrew, *Journal of Southern History* (November 1998); Susan Youngblood Ashmore, in *The New Deal and Beyond: Social Welfare in the South since 1930*, ed. Elna C.

Green (2003); Liva Baker, *The Second Battle of New Orleans: The Hundred Year Struggle to Integrate the Schools* (1996); William Billingsley, *Communists on Campus: Race, Politics, and the Public University in Sixties North Carolina* (1999); Amy J. Binder, *Contentious Curricula: Afrocentrism and Creationism in American Public Schools* (2004); Jason C. Bivins, *The Fracture of Good Order: Christian Antiliberalism and the Challenge to American Politics* (2003); John Charles Boger and Gary Orfield, eds., *School Resegregation: Must the South Turn Back?* (2005); John B. Boles, *University Builder: Edgar Odell Lovett and the Founding of Rice Institute* (2007); Charles C. Bolton, *The Hardest Deal of All: The Battle over School Integration in Mississippi, 1870–1980* (2005); Horace Mann Bond, *Negro Education in Alabama: A Study in Cotton and Steel* (1939); Steven Brint and Jerome Karabel, *The Diverted Dream: Community Colleges and the Promise of Educational Opportunity in America, 1900–1985* (1989); Laura Fairchild Brodie, *Breaking Out: VMI and the Coming of Women* (2000); Philip A. Bruce, *Social Life in Old Virginia* (1965); Henry Allen Bullock, *A History of Negro Education in the South from 1619 to the Present* (1967); Helen Jones Campbell, *William and Mary Quarterly* (January 1940); Allan M. Cartter, *Southern Economic Journal* (July 1965); David S. Cecelski, *Along Freedom Road: Hyde County, North Carolina, and the Fate of Black Schools in the South* (1994); Ann Short Chirhart, *Torches of Light: Georgia Teachers and the Coming of the Modern South* (2005); E. Culpepper Clark, *The Schoolhouse Door: Segregation's Last Stand at the University of Alabama* (1993); Robert Cohen, *Georgia Historical Quarterly* (Fall 1996), *When the Old Left Was Young: Student Radicals and America's First Mass Student Movement, 1929–1941* (1993); Crystal Collins and Marilyn Thomas, *Set for Success: Improving Reading and Mathematics Achievement in the Early Grades* (2008); Paul K. Conkin, *Peabody College: From a Frontier Academy to the Frontiers of Teaching and Learning* (2002); E. Merton Coulter, *College Life in the Old South* (1983); Lawrence A. Cremin, *American Education: The Colonial Experience, 1607–1783* (1970), *American Education: The National Experience, 1783–1876* (1980), *American Education: The Metropolitan Experience, 1876–1980* (1988), *The Transformation of the School: Progressivism in American Education, 1876–1957* (1961); Merrimon Cuninggim, *Perkins Led the Way: The Story of Desegregation at Southern Methodist University* (1994); Merle Curti, *The Social Ideals of American Educators, with a New Chapter on the Last Twenty-five Years* (1959); Charles W. Dabney, *Universal Education in the South*, 2 vols. (1936); Michael Dennis, *Lessons in Progress: State Universities and Progressivism in the New South, 1880–1920* (2001), *Journal of the Historical Society* (June 2008); Donald E. Devore and Joseph Logsdon, *Crescent City Schools: Public Education in New Orleans, 1841–1991* (1991); Davison M. Douglas, *Reading, Writing, and Race: The Desegregation of Charlotte Schools* (1995); Thomas G. Dyer, in *The American South in the Twentieth Century*, ed. Craig S. Pascoe, Karen Traham Leathem, and Andy Ambrose (2005), *The University of Georgia: A Bicentennial History* (1985), in *The Web of Southern Social Relations*, ed. Walter J. Fraser and Jon Wakelyn (1986); Clement Eaton, *The Freedom-of-Thought Struggle in the Old South* (1964); Bruce W. Eelman, *History of Education Quarterly* (Summer 2004); Adam Fairclough, *A Class of Their Own: Black Teachers in the Segregated South* (2007), *Teaching Equality: Black Schools in the Age of Jim Crow* (2001); Christie Ann Farnham, *The Education of the Southern Belle: Higher Education and Student Socialization in the Antebellum South* (1994); Michael Fultz, *History of Education Quarterly* (Winter 1995); Michael W. Fuquay, *History of Education Quarterly* (Summer 2002); Frye Gaillard, *The Dream Long Deferred: The Landmark Struggle for Desegregation in Charlotte, North Carolina* (2006); Willard B. Gatewood, *Preachers, Pedagogues, and Politicians: The Evolution Controversy in North Carolina, 1920–1927* (1966); Roger L. Geiger, *Research and Relevant Knowledge: American Research Universities since World War II* (1993), ed., "Southern Higher Education in the 20th Century," special edition, *Perspectives on the History of Higher Education Annual* (1999); Irving Gershenberg, *Journal of Negro Education* (Winter 1970); Ronald K. Goodenow and Arthur O. White, eds., *Education and the Rise of the New South* (1981); Patricia Albjerg Graham, in *Community and Class in American Education, 1865–1918* (1974); Jennifer R. Green, *Military Education and the Emerging Middle Class in the Old South* (2008); Louis R. Harlan, *American Historical Review* (April 1962), *Separate and Unequal: Public School Campaigns and Racism in the Southern Seaboard States, 1901–1915* (1958); Carl V. Harris, *Journal of Southern History* (August 1985); Gordon Harvey, *A Question of Justice: New South Governors and Education, 1968–1976* (2002); A. Scott Henderson, *South Carolina Historical Magazine* (January 2005); Richard Hofstadter and C. DeWitt Hardy, *The Development and Scope of Higher Education in the United States* (1952); Helen Lefkowitz Horowitz, *Campus Life: Undergraduate Subcultures from the End of the Eighteenth Century to the Present* (1987); Rhys Isaac, *The Transformation of Virginia, 1740–1790* (1982); Charles A. Israel, *Before Scopes: Evangelical Education and Evolution in Tennessee, 1870–1925* (2004); Daniel M. Johnson and David A. Bell, eds., *Metropolitan Universities: An Emerging Model in Higher Education* (1995); William R. Johnson, *History of Education Quarterly* (Spring 1994); Jacqueline Jones, *Solders of Light and Love: Northern Teachers and Georgia Blacks, 1865–1873* (1980); Patrik Jonsson, *Christian Science Monitor* (11 September 2007); Laylon Wayne Jordan, *South Carolina Historical Magazine* (April 1982); Carl F. Kaestle, *Pillars of the Republic: Common Schools and American Society, 1780–1860* (1983); Melissa Kean, *Desegregating Private Higher Education in the South: Duke, Emory, Rice, Tulane, and Vanderbilt* (2009); Edgar W. Knight, *Public Education in the South* (1922), ed., *A Documentary History of Education in the South before 1860*, 5 vols. (1949–53); Alexander S. Leidholdt, *Stand before the Shouting Mob: Lenoir Chambers and Virginia's Massive Resistance to Public-School Integration* (1997); James L. Leloudis, *Schooling the New South: Pedagogy, Self, and Society in North Carolina, 1880–1920* (1996); William A. Link, in *Essays in Twentieth-Century Southern Education: Exceptionalism and Its Limits*, ed. Wayne J. Urban (1999), *A Hard Country and a Lonely Place:*

Schooling, Society, and Reform in Rural Virginia, 1870–1920 (1986), *William Friday: Power and Purpose in American Higher Education* (1995); Alex Macaulay, *Southern Cultures* (Fall 2005); Joan Malczewski, *Journal of Southern History* (November 2009); Catherine S. Manegold, *In Glory's Shadow: Shannon Faulkner, the Citadel, and a Changing America* (1999); Joseph L. Marks, *Fact Book on Higher Education, 2007* (2007); William Martin, *With God on Our Side: The Rise of the Religious Right in America* (1996); Amy T. McCandless, *The Past in the Present: Women's Higher Education in the Twentieth-Century American South* (1999); Robert L. McCaul, *Georgia Historical Quarterly* (September 1956); Tennant S. McWilliams, *New Lights in the Valley: The Emergence of UAB* (2007); Gregg Michel, *South Carolina Historical Magazine* (January 2008), *Struggle for a Better South: The Southern Student Organizing Committee, 1964–1969* (2004); Theodore R. Mitchell, *Educational Theory* (Fall 1989); Clarence L. Mohr, in *Remaking Dixie: The Impact of World War II on the American South* (1997); Clarence L. Mohr and Joseph E. Gordon, *Tulane: The Emergence of a Modern University, 1945–1980* (2001); Edmund S. Morgan, *Virginians at Home: Family Life in the Eighteenth Century* (1952); Robert C. Morris, *Reading, 'Riting, and Reconstruction: The Education of Freedmen in the South* (1981); Mary Lee Muller, *Louisiana History* (Winter 1976); David Nevin and Robert E. Bills, *The Schools that Fear Built: Segregationist Academies in the South* (1976); Joseph W. Newman, in *Southern Cities, Southern Schools: Public Education in the Urban South*, ed. David N. Plank and Rick Ginsberg (1990); William A. Owens, *This Stubborn Soil: A Frontier Boyhood* (1966); Robert F. Pace, *Halls of Honor: College Men in the Old South* (2004); Charles S. Padgett, *History of Education Quarterly* (Summer 2001), *Alabama Review* (October 2003); Stephen Eugene Parr, "The Forgotten Radicals: The New Left in the Deep South, Florida State University, 1960–1972," Ph.D. dissertation, Florida State University, 2000; Daniel Perlstein, *History of Education Quarterly* (Autumn 1990); David R. Poole Jr., *Methodist History* (1977); Robert A. Pratt, *The Color of Their Skin: Education and Race in Richmond, Virginia, 1954–1989* (1991), *We Shall Not Be Moved: The Desegregation of the University of Georgia* (2002); Richard A. Pride, *The Burden of Busing: The Politics of Desegregation in Nashville, Tennessee* (1985), *The Political Use of Racial Narratives: School Desegregation in Mobile, Alabama, 1954–1997* (2002); Sonya Ramsey, *Reading, Writing, and Segregation: A Century of Black Women Teachers in Nashville* (2008); Diane Ravitch, *The Troubled Crusade: American Education, 1945–1980* (1983); Ralph Eugene Reed Jr., "Fortress of Faith: Design and Experience at Southern Evangelical Colleges, 1830–1900," Ph.D. dissertation, Emory University, 1991; Joe M. Richardson, *Christian Reconstruction: The American Missionary Association and Southern Blacks, 1861–1890* (1986); Joe M. Richardson and Maxine D. Jones, *Education for Liberation: The American Missionary Association and African Americans, 1890 to the Civil Rights Movement* (2009); Anne C. Rose, *History of Psychology*, vol. 10, no. 3 (2007); Theodore Rosengarten, ed., *All God's Dangers: The Life of Nate Shaw* (1974); Douglas C. Rossinow, *The*

Politics of Authenticity: Liberalism, Christianity, and the New Left in America (1998); David G. Sansing, *Making Haste Slowly: The Troubled History of Higher Education in Mississippi* (1990); Amilcar Shabazz, *Advancing Democracy: African Americans and the Struggle for Access and Equality in Higher Education in Texas* (2004); Jeff Sharlet, *Harper's Magazine* (December 2006); Tina H. Sheller, *History of Education Quarterly* (Spring 1982); Wilson Smith and Thomas Bender, eds., *American Higher Education Transformed, 1940–2005: Documenting the National Discourse* (2008); Barbara Miller Solomon, *In the Company of Educated Women: A History of Women and Higher Education in America* (1985); Southern Regional Education Board, *Fact Book Bulletin* (May 2002); Julia Cherry Spruill, *Women's Life and Work in the Southern Colonies* (1938, 1972); Lester D. Stephens, *Joseph LeConte: Gentle Prophet of Evolution* (1982); Mitchell L. Stevens, *Kingdom of Children: Culture and Controversy in the Homeschooling Movement* (2003); Jesse Stuart, *The Thread That Runs So True* (2006); William R. Taylor, *Harvard Educational Review* (1966); John R. Thelin, *A History of American Higher Education* (2004); J. Mills Thornton III, in *Region, Race, and Reconstruction: Essays in Honor of C. Vann Woodward*, ed. J. Morgan Kousser and James M. McPherson (1982); Courtney L. Tollison, in *History of Higher Education Annual* (2003–4), "Moral Imperative and Financial Practicality: Desegregation of South Carolina's Denominationally Affiliated Colleges and Universities" (Ph.D. dissertation, University of South Carolina, 2003); Allen W. Trelease, *Making North Carolina Literate: The University of North Carolina at Greensboro from Normal School to Metropolitan University* (2004); Jeffrey A. Turner, *Gulf South Historical Review* (Fall 2000), in *History of Higher Education Annual* (2001); Mark V. Tushnet, *The NAACP's Legal Strategy against Segregated Education, 1925–1950* (1987); David Tyack, Robert Lowe, and Elizabeth Hansot, *Public Schools in Hard Times: The Great Depression and Recent Years* (1984); U.S. Department of Education, Institute of Education Sciences, National Center for Education Statistics, *Homeschooling in the United States: 2003 Statistical Analysis and Report* (2006); William P. Vaughan, *Schools for All: The Blacks and Public Education in the South, 1865–1877* (1974); Laurence R. Veysey, *The Emergence of the American University* (1965); Richard C. Wade, *Slavery in the Cities* (1964); Pamela Barnhouse Walters and David R. James, *American Sociological Review* (October 1992); Thomas L. Webber, *Deep Like the Rivers: Education in the Slave Quarter Community, 1831–1865* (1978); Stephen H. Wheeler, in *The Vietnam War on Campus: Other Voices, More Distant Drums*, ed. Marc Jason Gilbert (2001); Zachery R. Williams, *In Search of the Talented Tenth: Howard University Public Intellectuals and the Dilemmas of Race, 1926–1970* (2010); Joy Ann Williamson, *Radicalizing the Ebony Tower: Black Colleges and the Black Freedom Struggle in Mississippi* (2008); Raymond Wolters, *The New Negro on Campus: Black College Rebellions of the 1920s* (1975); Bertram Wyatt-Brown, in *The Web of Southern Social Relations: Women, Family, and Education*, ed. Walter J. Fraser, R. Frank Saunders, and Jon L. Wakelyn (1983).

Academic Freedom

Southern culture has presented distinctive problems for academic freedom. Sectional characteristics of religion, race relations, political conservatism, and history have sometimes brought conflicts so violent that bodily harm was threatened along with freedom of thought.

More than in any other section of the country, the people of the Bible Belt have had a personal and emotional contact with their religion rather than a mere institutional membership. Believers were expected to defend their faith and did so with passions frequently dividing towns, families, and educational institutions into hostile camps. As the mission of the church was to proselytize and to educate its members in its doctrine, so the free exercise of religion demanded the ability to create educational institutions to train preachers and lay readers. The absence of tax-supported public schools in the region motivated the growth of institutes, academies, and colleges with denominational affiliation. As naturally as the churches chose only members of their own religion to be their ministers, they chose only like-minded teachers for their institutions. The proprietary nature of such schools so conflicted with the theory of academic freedom that their character as institutions of higher education has been called into doubt, although many carried on the development of intellects with distinction. The conflicting claim of academics to the right of intellectual freedom and of the churches to the right to establish and maintain colleges is one of the abiding paradoxes of southern culture.

Instances of direct conflict of intellectual freedom with institutional purpose arose when professors changed their beliefs or when they found themselves caught in one of the frequent doctrinal splits in the denominations. The situation could be alleviated if the sect had a powerful central body that could exercise rigid control over the institutions. The upper offices tended to be held by the more liberal elements, which protected the institutions from the radical conservatism sometimes found in the pew. Where government remained on the congregational level, as it did among the Baptists, the Pentecostals, and the Churches of Christ, it was harder for the ecclesiastical hierarchy of the churches to closely supervise the institutions, which sometimes fell under the control of special interests, especially those led by a powerful preacher or those people or factions that could offer large financial incentives. Although many southern colleges and universities continue to have denominational ties, the tendency has been to weaken the sectarian contribution and control so that it is rare to find religious requirements for faculty membership, except in departments such as religion or Bible study.

With the rise of the scientific method and the influence of Darwinism, an attempt to accommodate theology to new discoveries became common on religious campuses. In some cases the new theories were so contrary to the older doctrines that charges of heresy could be brought, as in the case of the general assembly's 1888 judgment against James Woodrow in the South Carolina Presbyterian synod. At the same time, and from the opposite direction, a new spirit of hostility toward theological concepts was manifesting itself, tending to claim an exclusive right to the title "intellectualism," and in a few cases going so far as to create a new outlook actively hostile to orthodox Christianity. In a number of cases the men who espoused the new ideas gained control of institutions created under the denominations and separated them from the churches, as at Vanderbilt.

The rise of the public schools in the early 20th century provided a new competition for the church schools, which they were not completely willing or able to face. Tax-supported education would, it was assumed, be religiously neutral because of the separation of church and state mandated by the U.S. Constitution. The new Darwinian theories presented a problem for that neutrality insofar as they dealt directly with the religiously pivotal issues of the nature and origin of man. Moderates in most denominations had already accommodated evolution to the Scriptures by using figurative interpretations of the Old Testament and including a reservation that the human soul, at least, was a special creation of God. They were willing for the tax-supported schools to teach the theories of evolution so long as they handled the matter of human development (and especially the nature of the human soul) with discretion and made no reference to the Bible.

By the 1920s, however, there were reports that a few teachers were using the classrooms to attack the Bible and to inculcate new religious doctrines based upon Darwinism. Such violations of the religious neutrality of the public school motivated appeals to the antiestablishment clause of the First Amendment. Fundamentalists wanted to prohibit all teaching of the evolution of man, while moderates proposed only a clarification of the constitutional infringement involved in a tax-supported assault on some religious beliefs. Proposals in several states were defeated by the divisions between these factions. When a law was proposed in Tennessee, its heading was worded so as to satisfy the fundamentalists while its body prohibited only the teaching that used the theory of the evolution of man in express contradiction to the Bible. Even the opponents were mollified, because the wording was so vague that they did not believe it enforceable. The Scopes Trial in June 1925 was supposed to decide the constitutionality of the law, but the tactics of the defense turned it into a contest between the Bible and evolution. The result was that many southerners who had previously accepted both were now convinced the two were mutually exclusive and rejected Darwin to keep God. The South-baiting of the 1920s, so prevalent in the prosecution case and in the reporting of the trial, made many loyal southerners espouse anti-intellectualism and made it harder for the moderates to continue to control denominations and institutions; academic freedom thereby suffered. The present attempts in some states to force "creationism" into the classroom or the textbooks have the same roots.

U.S. Supreme Court rulings since the 1950s on Bible reading, prayer, and integration in the public schools have provided new incentives for the formation of church-related primary and high schools, which tend to be under the control of the most conservative local churches and to have associations with the fundamentalist, or "religious right," wing of the denominations. The lack of academic freedom in these Christian academies has not received the attention it would in higher education. The main controversies instead are over teacher qualifications, certification, and tuition tax credits.

Political and economic conservatism has created serious problems for academic freedom, especially in the periods of the reinstitution of Democratic control after the Civil War (during the years of Ku Klux Klan domination), the Red Scare, and the McCarthy era. Other sections suffered from the same turmoil, though perhaps not to the same extent.

The most emotional issue for southerners has been that of race relations. Even before the Civil War the controversy had become a struggle for freedom of thought and expression. Almost from the beginning, relations with the slaves and the ex-slaves took on the volatile mixture of racism, political interests, religious concerns, and sectional pride, and the bloody tragedy engulfed the section for years. After Reconstruction and the reestablishment of white political supremacy, black students and faculty were routinely denied academic freedom as well as civil rights, and the occasional white who defended them was in peril of ostracism, loss of position, and even violence. As the civil rights campaign of the 1950s and 1960s grew, it frequently found its leadership on the campuses. Especially during the integration conflicts, southern campuses witnessed the presence of marshals, militiamen, tear gas, and even death. Although not all questions are settled, the basic issues have moved toward resolution so that freedom of thought and expression is no more an issue for the South than for other regions.

CHARLES F. OGILVIE
University of Tennessee at Martin

Clement Eaton, *The Freedom-of-Thought Struggle in the Old South* (1964); Richard Hofstadter and Walter P. Metzger, *Development of Academic Freedom* (1955); James W. Silver, *Mississippi: The Closed Society* (1964).

Agricultural Education

Generations of farmers learned traditional techniques associated with southern crops and stock at the sides of their elders. Yet, as science and technology fundamentally changed agricultural practices, and as farming transitioned from a lifestyle that most southerners engaged in to a business that fewer and fewer invested in, different interest groups took different approaches to championing agricultural education. The debate about whom agricultural education benefited and who should support it created deep divisions among southerners, pitted races and classes against each other, and galvanized philanthropists as well as local, state, and national politicians to either advocate or criticize public funding for agricultural education. The debate transcended sectional borders. Agricultural education even became part of informal foreign relations as well as foreign policy, with both black and white southerners playing critical roles.

During the 18th and early 19th centuries, planters and progressive farmers educated themselves, gaining information about the merits of new implements, seeds, and cultivation techniques from British publications. For example, by 1760 Virginia planter George Washington had implemented revolutionary new methods in crop cultivation, devised and widely publicized by Jethro Tull via his *Horse-Hoeing Husbandry*. Other planters and farmers accessed weather forecasts and other relevant information from almanacs, annual publications that came to be known as "farmers' almanacs." Two early examples were African American Benjamin Banneker's almanac that served Pennsylvania, Delaware, Maryland, and Virginia (1792–97) and immigrant John Gruber's *Neuer Hagerstauner Calender Stadt und Land* (*Hagers-Town Town and Country Almanack*) (1797–present) that focused on Maryland.

Printers believed that agriculturalists could benefit from periodicals that included articles and advertisements as well as running commentary between southern agriculturalists. John D. Legare began one of the earliest in the South, the *Southern Agriculturalist, Horticulturist, and Register of Rural Affairs*, in 1828. Other southern agricultural periodicals that appeared in print prior to the Civil War included *DeBow's Review*, launched in 1846 by James D. B. DeBow of New Orleans to educate readers about scientific agriculture. Readers furthered the goal, and through letters to the editor they debated slave management, sugar refining, and cotton cultivation, among other topics. Farmers and planters often did not agree, so the copy reflected the dynamic nature of antebellum southern agriculture and the need for practical if informal education in farming methods, markets, and business practices.

Slavery made agriculture an intensely political issue in the South, and publishers regularly used their serials as outlets for their political views. Sometimes the views of the editor did not reflect those of the intended readership. DeBow used his *Review* to argue for more commercial and industrial development to create a more independent South, which likely reduced elite planters' support for his periodical. But it reflected an important aspect of Civil War–era southern nationalism and the role that practitioners played prior to the development of formalized agricultural education.

Some southern farm periodicals remained in production after the war, but new journals appeared as well. One of the most successful, Leonidas L. Polk's *Progressive Farmer*, began in North Carolina in 1886 with the goal of furthering "the industrial and educational interests of our people paramount to all other considerations of state." Polk and other members of the Grange believed that farmers had to educate themselves to make farming a profitable undertaking. Many Grangers sought reform of public education to make the curriculum more meaningful to farmers. Grangers educated themselves through Grange meetings and local, state, and national newspapers published by and for Grange members. Yet, efforts to provide stable sources of information proved challenging as Grangers bickered among themselves about which newspapers to endorse.

Grangers also urged their legislators to take advantage of the Morrill Act of 1862, supporting formal, practical education in agriculture and the mechanical arts, which the national government had committed itself to on 2 July 1862, when President Abraham Lincoln signed the act into law. The act outlined the policy of land-grant funding to "promote the liberal and practical education of the industrial classes in the several pursuits and professions in life." State legislators bore the responsibility of prescribing a system to educate its citizens in agriculture and mechanical arts "without excluding other scientific and classical studies, and including military tactics." The act made agricultural education a part of national war policy insofar as states in rebellion were prohibited from realizing any benefits from the legislation. After readmission into the Union, many southern states accepted the land-grant funds but did not immediately invest in higher agricultural education. For example, Texas legislators accepted Morrill land-grant funds in 1871, but did not open the Agricultural and Mechanical College of Texas (now Texas A&M University) until 1876. North Carolinians began collecting Morrill funds in 1875 but did not charter North Carolina State University until 12 years later. The last of the ex-Confederate states to comply, South Carolina, did not officially establish its land-grant college, Clemson, until 1889.

During the decade of the 1880s, reformers' advocacy for improved agricultural education did not wane even as economic conditions across the South worsened and support for the Grange declined. Polk continued to champion the merits of formal education to improve rural life through the *Progressive Farmer*. At the same time, farmers became more politically self-conscious as Farmers' Alliance membership grew across the South. By 1890 Polk was elected president of the Southern Alliance, and the People's Party had emerged as an influential third party. Such politically motivated farmers helped ensure passage of important legislation related to agricultural research and education either directly through populist influence or indirectly through Democrat and Republican efforts to disarm the populist threat. The Hatch Act of 1887, sponsored by southerners William Hatch of Missouri and James Z. George of Mississippi, set aside national funding to help states establish agricultural experiment stations administered through the land-grant colleges and charged them with "acquiring and diffusing among the people of the United States useful and practical information on subjects connected with agriculture." In 1889 Alabamans used Hatch funding to establish secondary agricultural schools along with branch agricultural experiment stations in each congressional district in the state. By doing so they improved rural secondary education and began a trend across the South.

In 1890 the U.S. Congress passed, and President Benjamin Harrison signed, the Second Morrill Act into law. The act stipulated that states should use proceeds from land grants to more completely endow and support colleges devoted to agricultural and mechanical arts. It also indicated that states could use a portion of the money to prepare instructors to teach these subjects. The Second Morrill Act, however, also recognized southern segregation and did not penalize the land-grant colleges for segregating white and black students.

African Americans, increasingly isolated from influence in white politics as a result of white supremacy, found ways to secure authority over their own agricultural education. In 1876, the same year that Texas A&M University opened, Texas legislators voted to establish an agricultural and mechanical college for the benefit of colored youth. White Democrats in Texas, however, did not provide adequate funding to the college, nor invest proportionately in its development as a land-grant college. The Second Morrill Act provided additional funding but reinforced the model of racial segregation that the 1896 U.S. Supreme Court decision *Plessy v. Ferguson* made legal. The defeat of the Populist challenge in 1896 further reduced African American authority in the countryside as white southern Democrats returned to power in southern politics. African Americans, however, remained committed to rural and agricultural education, and they remained visible members of southern communities and taxpayers to county government through the peak in African American landownership during the 1920s. These black farmers influenced local governments to allot meager funds to black educational goals, both formal and informal. They also secured private funding, either from among their race or from white, often northern, philanthropists. Not until the 1950s did a backlash against rural racism cause rural black parents to encourage their children to do anything other than pursue an agricultural education. Those who persisted often earned their education in northern and midwestern land-grant institutions, thus exacerbating the brain drain on southern agricultural education.

While African Americans and poor white farmers found their political voices muted during the 1890s, others realized their goals of furthering agricultural education. In 1893 Alfred C. True became director of the United States Department of Agriculture's Office of Experiment Stations, and he commissioned a study of how nature and agriculture were taught in country schools. In 1895 the American Association of Agricultural Colleges and Experiment Stations, an organization composed of presidents of land-grant colleges and professors of agriculture, created a standing committee to document existing methods of teaching agriculture. By 1902 the committee reported that "agriculture has . . . been almost entirely neglected in the high school programmes, and it is high time that the friends of agricultural education should make a systematic effort to have the claims of this fundamental industry acknowledged and satisfied in the curricula of the public schools." The obvious interest in forging a relationship between experiment stations and rural education and the success in Alabama caused southern states to invest in secondary schools in rural areas. Georgia did so in 1907, Virginia and Mississippi in 1908, and Arkansas in 1909. Farmers' Union members continued the calls for improved rural education into the 1910s, often helping forge connections between rural libraries, rural schools, and Boys' Corn Clubs and Girls' Domestic Science Clubs that demonstration agents had begun.

Not all southerners, however, advocated increased national influence over state agricultural education. Many southern states established departments of agriculture and farmers' institutes and even state and regional fairs during the late 19th and early 20th centuries in an effort to retain local and state control of agricultural education. National legislation in the form of the Hatch Act and the Second Morrill Act, however, provided funding that helped land-grant colleges become dominant providers of agricultural education.

Two additional pieces of national legislation, both written by southerners, helped consolidate public land-grant colleges' domination of agricultural education in the South. The Smith-Lever Act of 1914, championed by Senator Hoke Smith (Ga.) and Representative Asbury Lever (S.C.), helped diffuse "useful and practical information on subjects relating to agriculture and home economics, and to encourage application of the same." The legislation complied with the system of racial segregation enforced across the South, providing extension education through segregated schools and segregated programs with lower levels of funding and staffing for African Americans. Finally, the National Vocational Education Act, also known as the Smith-Hughes Act of 1917, promoted education in agriculture and the trades and industries by providing funds to improve salaries and teacher preparation in agriculture and vocational subjects such as home economics, trades, and industry. Georgians Hoke Smith in the Senate and Dudley Hughes in the House proposed this legislation.

After passage of the 1917 act, state and federal agencies cooperated to ensure that teachers of agriculture, home economics, and other vocational subjects at the secondary level met regularly with experts to discuss the latest subject matter and pedagogy. State extension services and the faculty at land-grant institutions provided leadership to achieve Smith-Hughes Act goals.

Organizations to support teachers as well as students were established. The Future Farmers of Virginia provided a model for a national organization, Future Farmers of America (FFA), which emerged out of the third annual meeting of the National Congress of Vocational Agricultural Students, in 1927. But because this special interest group was segregated, African American students and teachers organized their own clubs, and state organizations began to appear across the South, such as the New Farmers of Virginia. The first sectional meeting of such clubs occurred at Virginia State University in 1927. By 1931 Dr. H. O. Sargent, the federal agent in charge of agricultural education for African Americans, employed by the U.S. Office of Education, helped formalize a national organization, New Farmers of America. It held its first meeting at Tuskegee Institute in 1935. In 1965 the New Farmers of America merged with the Future Farmers of America, and in 1988 the organization changed its name to National Future Farmers of America Organization (NFFAO).

During the era of the Cold War, agricultural education took on new meaning beyond the South. The Point Four program emerged as an international relief effort undertaken by the U.S. Department of State. Harry S. Truman introduced the idea as the fourth point in his inauguration address on 20 January 1949. He indicated that the United States must boldly provide technical assistance to poor people in "underdeveloped areas" who suffer because of "primitive and stagnant" economies. By doing so, experts in agricultural methods gained new educational outlets, and southern universities became involved in national defense efforts. Specifically, if Americans could improve the living standards of foreigners, those same foreigners might look more favorably on democracy rather than communism as a political philosophy. White as well as African American extension agents and vocational agriculture teachers served two-year stints as technical experts. African Americans often found themselves in places such as Liberia where they tried to raise the nation's standard of living and develop its economic resources. White participants were often stationed in the Middle East or India.

The U.S. Department of Agriculture's Office of Foreign Agricultural Relations (OFAR), reconstituted from its foreign relations branch during the late 1930s, extended scientific agricultural and technical assistance to "friends from (and within) foreign lands." In 1949 OFAR launched an effort to adapt the extension model of education to countries around the world. In the process, southern land-grant universities became involved in foreign agricultural education. Competition broke out between different white and black land-grant institutions over which schools would be assigned to which places and projects. Prairie View A&M University, Texas's historically black land-grant institution, worked through this program to rehabilitate the Booker T. Washington Industrial Institute in Kakata, Liberia, founded by James L. Sibley, a reformer who had also introduced the Jeanes system of teacher enrichment to Liberia. In addition to modernizing the Washington Institute's physical plant, technical assistance helped train Liberians to assume faculty positions there. The undertaking generated increased support for agricultural education at Prairie View A&M, afforded an international work experience for selected staff, and provided an opportunity for African American extension agents and technical experts to apply their goals of racial uplift to the African continent.

In the early 21st century, as the number of farmers declines steadily, the interest in agricultural education remains steady, largely because of the expansion of urban as well as rural employment in agribusiness. The NFFAO remains active in junior high and high schools, with students drawn from both genders and reflecting the ethnic and racial makeup of the schools. Land-grant institutions remain the primary purveyors of both higher agricultural education and agricultural extension education. Topics covered in university curricula and through county and state extension offices appeal to a wide audience ranging from future agriculture teachers to organic farmers, market gardeners, stock and crop farmers, and agribusiness interests, demonstrating the diversity of agriculture in a region known historically for cash-crop production and today for modern agribusiness and megafarming.

DEBRA A. REID
Eastern Illinois University

Debra A. Reid, *Reaping a Greater Harvest: African Americans, the Extension Service, and Rural Reform in Jim Crow Texas* (2007); Theodore Saloutos, *Farmer Movements in the South, 1865–1933* (1960); Elizabeth Sanders, *Roots of Reform: Farmers, Workers, and the American State, 1877–1917* (1999).

Athletics and Education

Modern American athletics emerged in the years between 1880 and 1920. Beginning with a concern for nurturing "the strenuous life" in an urban, industrial society, Americans created a highly organized spectator and participant system of athletic activities for their young. These developments began in the Northeast, spread then to the Middle West, and came late to the South, where athletics became an important part of southern education and helped to define a distinctive southern culture.

Americans at the turn of the 20th century articulated a sports ideology that spoke of "muscular Christianity," which stressed the religious significance of manliness and the importance of play for proper physical, spiritual, and mental development. The Young Men's Christian Association, city playground associations, church leagues, business-sponsored community leagues, and the public school athletic leagues all reflected an urban-centered ideology that had come to the South by the 1920s. However, the South's relative lack of urban areas in the early 20th century limited the importance of the interest in organized athletics until after 1920. The South's predominantly rural schools, oriented to a seasonal farm cycle, had little interest in, or ability to nurture, extracurricular activities such as athletics. Sports had long been important to rural southerners, but primarily in the form of outdoor activities like hunting and fishing. Eventually, though, southerners became convinced of the need for adult management of youthful activities as a way to nurture cultural values. The emergence of "comprehensive" high schools encouraged adult management of youth sports. Athletics were said to help channel adolescent sexual energy into constructive social and moral habits and to help redirect potentially rebellious students into more socially acceptable activities.

Since the 1920s, when interscholastic leagues were created to allow relatively equal competition between schools of similar enrollment, high school athletics

Georgetown vs. Washington and Lee football game, November 1928 (Photographer unknown, Library of Congress [LC-DIG-npcc-00838], Washington, D.C.)

has become an integral part of southern education in urban and rural schools alike. High school sports in the South have helped to give an identity and sense of common purpose to neighborhoods, towns, and cities. Historian Thomas D. Clark has noted that the enthusiasm for school athletics has placed schools "in a curious kind of public domain." As Clark notes, "Even hardened old rednecks who have wandered in from the cotton fields have caught the fever. Fifty years ago they would have regarded these sports as either effeminate or juvenile. Not so the modern southerner." The emphasis on athletics has brought the general population into close association "with the forms if not the substance of education."

Each fall, football becomes the prime focus for school athletics. It is a major southern ritual occasion and a complex cultural event involving more than players on the field. Cheerleaders, baton twirlers, trainers, and marching bands are actively involved, while the stands are filled with students, former players who have graduated and returned to cheer for their team, parents, and friends. As historian Lawrence Goodwyn has written of Texas, schoolboy football "was an instrument of psychic survival and, as such, a centerpiece of the regional culture." When the local high school team was having a bad season, an "uneasiness" settled over the entire community. Journalist James J. Kilpatrick has noted that while high school athletics are also taken seriously in the Midwest, in the South, "they're a religion." Local people read in their Saturday papers or their weeklies of the feats of Panthers, Rebels, Bisons, Rockets, Trojans, Bulldogs, Wildcats, Warriors, Whippets, Raiders, Tigers, and Golden Eagles.

Basketball was a rallying point for communities whose schools were too poor or too small to field football teams. In Kentucky, where basketball so dominates the culture that local storytellers joke that "a Kentucky homosexual is a boy who likes girls more than basketball," many small towns have enjoyed lasting distinction on the basis of their high school team's accomplishments in the state tournament. Girls' basketball was also deeply rooted in southern schools long before the recent growth in women's sports.

The appearance of comprehensive high schools in the early 20th century necessitated the development of large-scale extracurricular athletic activities. However, initially many small towns in the South were reluctant to accept large, consolidated county high schools because the local community's identity was tied to a small school, and the boys and girls who comprised the varsity basketball teams were genuine community heroes and heroines. In this setting, the basketball games became the major social activity throughout most of the school year for both the adults and children of the community. These get-togethers provided inexpensive, family-oriented socialization for the rural populace and were carefully scheduled so as not conflict with church activities—the other, major focal point of small-town community life.

By the 1960s most rural southern counties contained a "big school"—a county-seat high school with 500 to 2,000 students. However, the county was also still dotted with "country schools," which contained 300 to 600 students in grades 1 through 12. By the late 1960s and early 1970s consolidation and "progress" closed most of these small, country high schools. The "farmers" rode the big yellow school buses, often for several hours each day, to attend bigger and, ostensibly, better schools. Some of these rural youngsters who had been "top dog" at their small school were too intimidated to participate in extracurricular activities and sports at their new school. Others would have been involved in after-school sports but had to ride the bus home in order to assist with daily chores. In exchange for a broader curriculum and other big-school amenities, many rural youngsters lost an opportunity to build confidence and leadership abilities through participation in sports, clubs, and other extracurricular activities. On the positive side, big-school education unquestionably led more rural youngsters to attend college.

By the 1980s some of the little high schools that once pumped lifeblood into local communities had become grade schools. Many others stood as empty and crumbling monuments to a part of southern life that had been lost forever. The dissolution of the small country high school led to a concomitant disappearance of community spirit and identity and left a part of the rural populace frustrated, disoriented, and nostalgic for the good old days when a last-minute victory over an archrival lit fires of community pride that were rekindled by generations of storytellers. As University of Alabama football coach Paul "Bear" Bryant once observed, "It's hard to rally 'round a math class." For rural southerners, it was hard to rally around an empty building.

The stress on athletics glorified success on the playing field at the expense of other forms of educational achievement in the South, as across the nation. In the high school social structure, the athlete ranks near the top. In the 1980s, Texas led a movement to reduce the role of athletics in high schools, when the state board of education passed a rule, which was authorized by the state legislature, barring students from extracurricular activities if they did not pass every subject they took in the previous six-week examining period. The "no pass, no play" provision was promoted by businessman H. Ross Perot, who headed an advisory committee on educational excellence. The *New York Times* (28 April 1985) said the rule had "stirred about as much emotion in Texas as anything since Santa Anna overran the Alamo." The state's business and political leaders pledged a strong commitment to it, but coaches and parents expressed concern over its fundamental challenge to athletic values in Texas schools. Other southern states followed suit and enacted programs to promote educational improvement, but, none adopted the Texas model at the state level.

Athletics played an important role in the desegregation of southern schools. Skilled black athletes, such as Marcus Dupree from Philadelphia, Miss., Herschel Walker from Wrightsville, Ga., and Perry Wallace from Nashville, Tenn., became community heroes. The stress on school athletics, however, channeled black achievement disproportionately into sports at the expense of other activities, according to critics. Moreover, the achievements of black athletes did not always translate into later success for athletes when their collegiate playing days ended.

Women's sports were slow to develop because of 19th and early 20th century notions of the lady as a passive and fragile southern belle. By the 1920s, women's sports programs in swimming, track and field, basketball, and gymnastics had expanded because of the Amateur Athletic Union. Schools began to develop better programs in tennis, golf, and swimming, but were slower to start up more vigorous sports such as basketball and softball. By the middle of the 20th century, the South rose above the national average in financial support of men's sports programs but well below the national average in financial support of women's sports. Women found athletic opportunities in bowling leagues and through industrial league softball and basketball teams. The late 1960s and 1970s witnessed a revolution in women's sports. Title IX of the Education Amendments of 1972 outlawed sexual discrimination in public schools and institutions of higher learning. The hope was to expand programs through increased funding while avoiding the high-pressure, competitive problems of men's sports. Between 1972 and the present, women's sports at all educational levels increased dramatically. However, this growth, particularly at the collegiate level, paralleled men's sports and stressed recruiting, giving scholarships, and winning in order to develop a broad base of spectator support. During this period of growth, many good high school players continued basketball careers in college and a few went on to play professionally in the Women's Basketball Association. Icons emerged, most notably Pat Summit, the women's basketball coach at the University of Tennessee, who has amassed the most wins of any coach in the history of college basketball.

College and university athletics have reflected many of the same growth patterns found in public high schools. College football, for example, began in the Northeast in the late 19th century, and southern teams earned little national acclaim until the 1920s. The hot climate, regional provincialism, and wide distribution of good players in many small colleges supposedly prevented the emergence of powerful teams. The 1920–45 period witnessed a dramatic change. On 1 January 1926, Coach Wallace Wade's University of Alabama team defeated Washington State in the Rose Bowl, a landmark intersectional game. The University of Georgia defeated Yale three times in a four-year period, and, by the post–World War II years, southern teams were frequently winning national championships. Southerners responded to these triumphs with an outburst of regional enthusiasm. "Indeed, pride in the strength of sectional football teams took its place along with pride in the valor of the Confederate army as a major source of Southern chauvinism," wrote historians Francis Butler Simkins and Charles Roland in *A History of the South* (1972). The athlete became a glamorous new southern hero and his coach was much better known than the university president. Athletics soon emerged as a sometimes consuming affair for students and alumni. Bonfires, cheerleaders, pep bands, and other ingredients of a new ritualism led one writer in 1930 to remark that football was "medieval pageantry long forgotten outside the South."

In the last decades of the 20th century, school and collegiate athletics grew in direct proportion to the athletes. From the 1940s to the mid-1960s, few male basketball teams had a player who could dunk. Forty years later, at least half of the players on a high school team could dunk, and a six-foot three-inch player was more likely to be a guard than a center. The growth in the size of schoolboy football players was equally dramatic. From the 1940s to the 1960s, a six-foot, 185-pound athlete would probably be the anchor of the line, in an era when good players usually played on both offense and defense. By the turn of the 21st century, high school players often averaged 250 pounds across the offensive line.

At the same time, college players and programs grew enormously. Big-time college basketball teams played in modern arenas before 10,000 to 20,000 fans, but less than half of the attendees would be students. College basketball became big business, and the best players rarely graduated; rather they played a year or two of college ball to improve their crossover dribble or to add 20 pounds of muscle before turning pro. College football players were equally large and gifted—measured by the demands of their sport—but they tended to stay in school longer. The rosters of the great American professional spectator sports of baseball, basketball, and football include numerous athletes from both high school and colleges in the South. In fact, some of these gifted athletes—like Deion Sanders, Bo Jackson, and Steve Hamilton—distinguished themselves in two professional sports.

In the mid-20th century, colleges had freshman teams and varsity teams, so that first-year players could adjust to the physical demands of collegiate sports. By the end of the century, high school players were so physically ready that many of them skipped college and turned pro. At the turn of the new century, the tail wagged the dog: sports were no longer a part of education, as much as educational institutions coexisted with their athletic teams. Yet much good had come from this enormous growth, including the desegregation of athletics, the growth of women's sports, and increased opportunities for participation in a wider spectrum of both public school and collegiate sports.

JAMES M. GIFFORD
Jesse Stuart Foundation

Thomas Rosandich, *Education* (Spring 2002).

Black Education

As aspects of the Old South crumbled because of the success of Union armies and the difficulty of conducting what many white southerners considered a total war, many black southerners attempted to reshape their lives to meet their notions of the meaning of freedom. And for a small number of them the Civil

War represented an expansion of freedom rather than a new birth of freedom. Still, the newly freed and those free before the war were united around several shared goals, including access to education. They started the education quest much less disadvantaged than their previous slave status might suggest. Southern states had embraced the idea of universal education only reluctantly and failed to fund public education even to that tepid level of support. As a result, few southern children, black or white, enjoyed the benefits of education, especially schools funded by public dollars.

The Civil War and the period of Reconstruction dramatically improved the opportunities to obtain education for blacks throughout the South. The four-year-long Civil War was marked by intense fighting and high casualty rates. But the experiences of soldiers included much more than preparation for battles and fighting them. For some Union soldiers at least, their experiences also included giving literacy instruction to the many slaves who made their way to Union camps. And as Union soldiers captured and secured additional Confederate territory, the number of black southerners freed from slavery increased, thus straining the capacity of Union soldiers to provide literacy instruction and demonstrating the need to better organize the nascent education effort.

The initial education program reflected local and regional concerns and power relations. Still, some developmental patterns were common throughout the South. Army commanders, for example, established agencies to supervise and coordinate black education programs in several states prior to the end of the war. In addition, northern missionary organizations sent teachers and established schools in rural areas, small towns, and cities. Indeed, as early as September 1861 the American Missionary Association (AMA) operated a school in Hampton, Va. The AMA continued to build on that effort, establishing schools and championing black education in plantation settings like Port Royal, S.C., and urban environments like New Orleans, La.

In 1865 Congress created the Bureau of Refugees, Freedmen, and Abandoned Lands. Among its many responsibilities, the Freedmen's Bureau became a chief provider of black education and coordinated that work through its Bureau of Education. The bureau supported an expansive idea of the potential and importance of education and helped establish elementary and secondary schools. Many black southerners experienced their first educational opportunities through the bureau's work. This success resulted from the often diligent and sincere effort of bureau agents and educators. They were aided, however, by black southerners who embraced and fought for expanded public education.

The change in the education landscape that the Civil War and Reconstruction produced faced serious challenges in the 1880s and 1890s but could not be totally reversed. As a result, and despite the loss of political influence and suffrage and an upsurge in political and economic violence, the idea that African Americans would be a part of the South's education program was established. What type of education they should receive, however, remained contested decades into the 20th century. Many white southern leaders wanted black public education in particular limited to the grammar grades, with some even advocating its restriction to the lower and middle grades. Typical were the situations in Augusta, Ga., and New Orleans, La.

In the mid-1890s Richmond County, Ga., still supported a high school for African Americans, Ware High School. In July 1897, however, Richmond County school officials closed it, asserting that the board's limited funds were needed to support primary and grammar schools for African Americans. School leaders indicated that they would reopen Ware when funds permitted. Given the poor state of southern race relations in counties like Richmond and cities like Augusta, where the school was located, African American leaders placed little faith in the board's pledge. Local black leaders J. W. Cumming, James Harper, and John Ladeveze sued the school board and the county tax collector. The joy from a favorable decision from the Superior Court was brief, for school officials won a reversal on appeal to the Georgia Supreme Court. The United States Supreme Court later sustained it in *Cumming v. School Board of Richmond County*.

The 1899 *Cumming* decision influenced education policy throughout the South. For example, school officials in New Orleans, having already discontinued funding for black secondary education, decided in 1900 to support black education only through the fifth grade. Black leaders in New Orleans waged a slow but sustained and ultimately successful effort to restore the upper grammar grades and the opening of a high school. The campaigns for improved education helped to maintain a degree of political awareness and civic engagement in communities and cities throughout the South. Because of educational battles like those in Richmond County and New Orleans, African American education advanced during the era of legal segregation, though it continued to lag behind the educational opportunities provided to white students.

Advancing black education in the South, an effort described by W. E. B. Du Bois as "weary work," was carried out by determined efforts of African American community leaders and parents. The South's long ordeal of racial segregation gave black leaders sufficient opportunities to continue to act on the communal ethos that had sustained them through slavery. One illustration of this pattern was the school construction program supported by Julius Rosenwald and the Rosenwald Fund. The first school completed under the construction program was located in Lee County, Ala., and it marked the beginning of a significant rural school building program. During the program's existence, the fund helped build nearly 5,000 rural black schools with the capacity to house 660,000 students. All southern states benefited to some degree from the program. Construction was greatest in North Carolina, with 787 schools and Mississippi with 557. On average, though, Rosenwald funds accounted for approximately 15 percent of the building cost. On the other hand, African Americans contributed slightly more, nearly 17 percent. The remaining funding came from white southerners (4.27 percent) and public taxes (63.73 percent). In addition to the Rosenwald Fund, several other funds contributed to black education between 1900 and 1940: George Peabody Fund, John F. Slater Fund, General Education Board, Anna T. Jeanes Fund, and Caroline Phelps-Stokes Fund. And organizations affiliated with religious groups or closely associated with them continued to assist black education.

Expanding the educational infrastructure through school construction was only part of the challenge of ensuring that education served as a means of racial uplift and individual advancement. Another challenge, and usually fought with few white allies, involved struggles over the type of education African Americans should receive and for what purpose. Education scholars have rightly pointed out that a main goal of white northern philanthropists and white southern leaders for black education was to produce a disciplined and docile work force. Scholars have also noted the differing views of black education leaders such as Booker T. Washington and W. E. B. Du Bois, especially regarding the primacy of vocational and industrial education. Those often competing views of black southern education, however, were not alone in shaping its development. African American teachers, community leaders, parents, and students themselves helped to formulate black education policy in the South. Their goals, aspirations, and persistent work produced many of the gains achieved during the Jim Crow period, including increases in the percentage of school-age children attending school, in the number of school days, in per capita annual funding, in teachers' salaries, and in teacher quality. And by the 1940s, students were staying in school longer, as evidenced by a sharp increase in the number of black public high schools.

Once America entered World War II, the next few years witnessed a lull in the struggle for improved schools and education. No such lull persisted, however, with the war's end. The education work resumed at a pace that pleased its many proponents to the same degree that it dismayed its many opponents. What resulted, the noted historian John Hope Franklin observed, was a substantial increase in public funding for black education that produced new and renovated schools, expanded curricula, and increased teacher-to-student ratios. Indeed, in terms of closing the educational opportunity gap between white and black students, the period 1945–60 could be considered, after the Reconstruction period, as close to a golden age of southern support for black education as any.

The cooperation and enthusiasm that greeted white southern leaders and school officials in 1945 as they embarked on their much-delayed program to provide black southerners with an education program comparable to white southerners had waned considerably by 1960. The resistance that they encountered was not connected to their work to improve black education but to their still fervently held view that the improvement should remain within the segregated system. The United States Supreme Court decision in *Brown v. Board of Education* dealt a legal blow to racial segregation. Education again became, as it had been at the turn of the 20th century, the contested southern institution that would determine race relations. African American leaders and parents resumed their familiar role of battling school officials. They battled in the 1960s and 1970s to dismantle one of the main pillars of racial differences in the South: segregated school systems.

Supreme Court decisions are not self-implementing, and implementation of the *Brown* decision became the most contentious in the nation's history. The South's strategy to prevent or delay implementation through legislation, litigation, and administrative procedures proved successful during the first decade following the decision. To label the pace of school desegregation between 1955 and 1965 slow would be a gross understatement. As late as the 1965–66 school year, seven southern states had less than 3 percent of their African American students enrolled in formerly all-white schools. And three of them—Alabama, Louisiana, and Mississippi—had less than 1 percent. Indeed, of the 11 former Confederate states, only Texas, with 20 percent, and Virginia, with 14, appeared to be making a good-faith effort to end their dual systems of education. Eventually the Supreme Court justices, perhaps believing that public education was now freed from bearing the main burden of improving southern race relations because of the successes of the civil rights movement, the 1964 Civil Rights Act, and the 1965 Voting Rights Act, ordered the immediate end to school segregation.

To the surprise of only a few, school desegregation did not solve all the problems that had historically affected African American education. And some have argued that school desegregation caused additional challenges. Still, in the early years of the 21st century black education is fundamentally improved from what existed in the opening decades of the 20th century.

DONALD E. DEVORE
University of South Alabama

James D. Anderson, *The Education of Blacks in the South, 1860–1935* (1988); Horace Mann Bond, *The Education of the Negro in the American Social Order* (1934); Lawrence A. Cremin, *American Education: The Metropolitan Experience, 1876–1980* (1988); Donald E. DeVore and Joseph Logsdon, *Crescent City Schools: Public Education in New Orleans, 1841–1991* (1991); Adam Fairclough, *A Class of Their Own: Black Teachers in the Segregated South* (2007); Mary S. Hoffschwelle, *The Rosenwald Schools of the American South* (2006); Charles S. Johnson, *The Negro Public Schools: A Social and Educational Survey* (1942); Leon Litwack, *Trouble in Mind: Black Southerners in the Age of Jim Crow* (1998).

Black Public Colleges

The history of black public colleges and universities has been in many ways a microcosm of the African American struggle for education advancement in America, especially in the South. The majority of the black public colleges were founded during the waning days of Reconstruction and the post-Reconstruction period. As state-organized and state-supported institutions, they were segregated from the start. Reflecting the tenor of late-19th-century race relations, white southerners intended that black public colleges would support and sustain rather than challenge the emerging racial order of white superiority and black inferiority.

All of the 15 states that maintained legal slavery in 1861 established at least one historically black public college. Three other states and the District of Columbia also established black public colleges, and one of them, Pennsylvania, established two colleges for African Americans prior to the Civil War—Cheyney University of Pennsylvania and Lincoln University. Several of the black public colleges started after the Civil War shared similar origins and developments (including modifications to their original names). One feature of their early development was, in fact, their lack of development as four-year postsecondary schools. Their real value to African American education advancement until after World War I, then, consisted of contributions to elementary and secondary education.

Several factors contributed to their slow development as schools of higher education. First, the lack of a sufficient number of black elementary schools, and later high schools, in the South influenced or forced the black public colleges to offer instruction at both the elementary and secondary levels as separate program units within the schools. Indeed, as late as 1915 the black public colleges still offered little college instruction. Second, state control did not mean adequate state financial support for any of the various types of education programs at the schools. To supplement state funding the schools increasingly relied on tuition and donations to meet expenses. For example, revenues from tuition and fees increased as a percentage of their budgets between 1915 and 1930, making attendance that much more expensive for most African Americans. Third, to a degree greater than that experienced by most private black colleges, the public colleges were trapped in the early-20th-century debate on the proper education for African Americans, such as whether the emphasis should be on vocational training or on academics, which slowed their emergence as four-year colleges. A 1927 government study noted: "In general, the private colleges emphasized an academic curriculum, while the public colleges emphasized more vocational training." That was especially the case at the black land-grant colleges.

The 16 black land-grant colleges were founded or repurposed under provisions of the First and Second Morrill Acts. In 1909 Tennessee established the last of the black public colleges to receive land-grant status, and in June 1912 Tennessee State University held its first classes. The legislation creating the land-grant colleges had a clear purpose: instruction and research in "agriculture, home economics, mechanical arts, and other useful professions." And in the 1920s the black land-grant colleges and the other black public colleges expanded their academic programs. The belief that improved and expanded post-secondary education was essential for both personal advancement and group advancement encouraged African American leaders to persist in their efforts to strengthen black public colleges.

Between 1920 and 1960 black public colleges became the institutions that the many founders had envisioned. This resulted, in part, from expansion and improvements in black elementary and secondary education because of African American advocacy and increased local and state support. Black public colleges closed their remaining secondary departments and focused exclusively on building their higher education programs. One response to the changed focus was the expansion of normal school programs early in the period to meet the demand for more teachers. Later, as states raised teacher certification requirements to include a degree from a four-year college, the colleges expanded to meet this demand as well. During the period of legal segregation the black public colleges contributed to the overall growth of black professionals. And racial segregation's decline caused an unanticipated but welcomed strengthening of black public colleges. Successful higher education equalization suits brought by the National Association for the Advancement of Colored People influenced all the southern states to increase funding and support for their black public colleges. The growth in funding produced improved and new undergraduate and graduate programs.

But the new era of school desegregation produced both opportunities and challenges. Black public colleges had to compete with traditionally white colleges for African American students beginning in the 1950s and in later years for African American faculty as well. One response to that challenge was the successful effort by most black public colleges to improve their programs, facilities, and relationships with students. They also embraced increased student diversity while attempting to maintain aspects of their traditional identities as historically black institutions. The majority of the African American students who attend those universities want and expect that special tradition to continue.

DONALD E. DEVORE
University of South Alabama

James D. Anderson, *The Education of Blacks in the South, 1860–1935* (1988); Ralph D. Christy and Lionel Williamson, eds., *A Century of Service: Land-Grant Colleges and Universities, 1890–1990* (1992); John A. Hardin, *Fifty Years of Segregation: Black Higher Education in Kentucky, 1904–1954* (1997); Robert G. Sherer, *Subordination or Liberation?: The Development and Conflicting Theories of Black Education in Nineteenth-Century Alabama* (1977); William H. Watkins, *The White Architects of Black Education: Ideology and Power in America, 1865–1954* (2001); Karl E. Westhauser, Elaine M. Smith, and Jennifer A. Fremlin, eds., *Creating Community: Life and Learning at Montgomery's Black University* (2005).

Busing

During the 1970s busing achieved more urban desegregation in the South, especially in Florida, Kentucky, North Carolina, and Tennessee, than it did in the North and the West. Legally, southern cities were more vulnerable to court-ordered remedies because of their past records of school segregation. Administratively, it was easier to implement metropolitan busing in southern communities, where the county was the "basic educational unit" (Florida and Kentucky), the number of school districts was relatively small, and "white flight" to suburbia had not undermined the possibility of creating reasonable black-white pupil ratios in city schools.

In the first major and decisive southern busing case, *Swann v. Charlotte-*

Mecklenburg Board of Education (1971), the U.S. Supreme Court upheld an extensive busing order—of more than 43,000 children—for the largest school system in the Carolinas and the 43rd largest in the nation. Under a proportional plan, black pupils would be transported from central-city to suburban schools, so that each school in the consolidated system would have a balanced black-white ratio. Busing between noncontiguous zones, the Supreme Court ruled, was a permissible remedy, if the school closest to home was racially segregated.

Although metropolitan solutions were implemented in Florida (statewide) and in Charlotte-Mecklenburg, Nashville-Davidson, and Louisville-Jefferson, busing was legally stopped at the city line in Richmond (by a divided Supreme Court) and exchanged in Atlanta for the appointment of more—over half—black school administrators (compromise of 1973). The Supreme Court extended to northern and western communities (*Keyes v. School District No. 1, Denver, Colorado*, 1973) Swann's school-desegregation requirement, but Detroit and similar cities thwarted metropolitan busing plans. In the absence of proof of prior official discrimination and its "interdistrict effect" on suburban areas, "an interdistrict remedy" was not legally justified (*Milliken v. Bradley*, 1974).

Opposition to busing became a heated political issue in the 1972 presidential campaign, when antibusing candidate Gov. George C. Wallace of Alabama won the Florida and Michigan Democratic primaries. The Nixon administration championed the neighborhood school concept and opposed busing. During the 1980s, the Reagan administration argued vigorously that busing neither improved the educational achievements of minority pupils nor increased racial tolerance. In the changing political climate that resulted, some southern cities reformulated busing plans that they instituted in the 1970s. For example, in Memphis in 1982 the city and the NAACP Legal Defense and Education Fund reached an agreement that allowed the city to limit busing and restore neighborhood status to a number of schools. The revamped busing plans coupled with aggressive school-improvement efforts enabled the Memphis public schools between 1981 and 1985 to lure back some 3,500 students who had fled the city system in the wake of earlier desegregation plans. Supported by the Reagan administration, many southern communities—including the bellwether city of Charlotte—began emphasizing alternatives to busing such as magnet schools, which were intended to offer enriched public school opportunities and encourage voluntary integration. During the 1980s such approaches became more popular as court requirements for busing were eased or reversed. In 1986, for example, the Fourth Circuit Court of Appeals ruled that Norfolk, Va., could curtail the court-ordered busing that had been instituted in 1971.

Since the Norfolk ruling, at least three other Supreme Court rulings have accelerated the trend away from busing and even from the maintenance of desegregation. In the 1991 case of *Oklahoma v. Dowell*, the court ruled that once a school district had been declared unitary, or fully desegregated, it was no longer required to preserve integration. In the Georgia case of *Freeman v. Pitts* the court concluded that school districts were not required to make "heroic" efforts to maintain desegregation and could be released from that obligation even if schools were not fully integrated. And finally, in 2002, the Supreme Court upheld a lower court ruling in a reopening of the Charlotte-Mecklenburg case, prohibiting the use of race in school assignments even when the goal was desegregation.

In their book *Dismantling Desegregation*, Harvard education professor Gary Orfield and coauthor Susan Eaton concluded in 1996 that the South as a whole still had the nation's most integrated schools, after more than 100 districts in the region aggressively desegregated in the 1970s and 1980s. But by the mid-1990s, noted Orfield, the southern states of Alabama, Tennessee, and North Carolina had joined New York, New Jersey, Illinois, and Michigan on the list of those with the most segregated schools.

MARCIA G. SYNNOTT
University of South Carolina at Columbia

FRYE GAILLARD
University of South Alabama

Thomas J. Cottle, *Busing* (1976); Jonathan Kozol, *The Shame of the Nation: The Restoration of Apartheid Schooling in America* (2005); Ellie McGrath, *Time* (6 February 1984); Nicolaus Mills, *The Great School Bus Controversy* (1973), ed., *Busing U.S.A.* (1979); *Newsweek* (17 December 1984); Gary Orfield, *Must We Bus?: Segregated Schools and National Policy* (1978); Gary Orfield and Susan Eaton, *Dismantling Desegregation: The Quiet Reversal of* Brown v. Board of Education (1996); Andy Paztor, *Wall Street Journal* (10 February 1986); William E. Schmidt, *New York Times* (25 May 1985).

Desegregation

With the collapse of two brief, but notable, biracial experiments in the New Orleans public schools (1870–77) and at the University of South Carolina (1873–77), racially dual school systems would be required by law in 17 "southern" states—the 11 former Confederate states, plus Delaware, Kentucky, Maryland, Missouri, Oklahoma, and West Virginia—and the District of Columbia (where Congress had provided separate black schools). Separate-but-equal public schools and accommodations received U.S. Supreme Court sanction in *Plessy v.*

Ferguson (1896) and expanded in the North with the Great Migration of blacks (1890–1930) to Chicago, Indianapolis, and Philadelphia.

The desegregation of southern education occurred in several phases over 80 years: (1) 1930–45, inauguration of the National Association for the Advancement of Colored People's (NAACP) desegregation campaign, which ended the era of virtually unchallenged Jim Crowism; (2) 1945–54, overturning the separate-but-equal doctrine, first in graduate and professional education and then in elementary and secondary schools; (3) 1955–64, massive southern white resistance countered by escalating federal intervention to enforce court-ordered desegregation and by passage of the 1964 Civil Rights Act; (4) 1965–92, extensive desegregation of southern school districts and dismantling of racially dual systems of higher education by court decisions, civil rights enforcement, and threats of withholding federal education funds; and (5) since the 1990s legal and legislative challenges to public school desegregation plans and college and university affirmative action programs.

Initially, Charles Hamilton Houston and Thurgood Marshall, NAACP Legal Defense and Education Fund attorneys, attacked segregation indirectly through lawsuits aimed at equalizing black and white schools in terms of curricula, teachers' salaries, and physical equipment. At the graduate and professional levels, states were forced either to establish new schools for blacks or to admit them to existing all-white universities. In 1936 the Maryland Court of Appeals ordered Donald G. Murray admitted to the state university's law school, because none existed for blacks. Two years later, the U.S. Supreme Court ruled that Missouri could not meet the Fourteenth Amendment's equal-protection requirement by giving plaintiff Lloyd Gaines a tuition grant to study law in a nonsegregated state; after Gaines's unaccounted disappearance, Missouri established a Jim Crow law school. Other reverses followed in Kentucky and Tennessee, although West Virginia in 1938 voluntarily admitted black graduate and professional students.

In 1945, Marshall shifted to a direct attack on separate-but-equal education, which opened the doors of graduate and/or law schools at the universities of Oklahoma, Kentucky, Texas, Virginia, Missouri, and Louisiana State University, while Delaware and Arkansas voluntarily admitted blacks. In the pivotal 1950 *Sweatt v. Painter* and *McLaurin v. Oklahoma State Regents for Higher Education*, the U.S. Supreme Court unanimously ruled, first, that the University of Texas Law School had to admit Heman Sweatt because the new black law school was academically inferior, and then ordered the University of Oklahoma to accord George McLaurin equal, nonsegregated treatment in the classrooms, cafeteria, and library.

James Meredith, escorted by U.S. marshals, on the University of Mississippi campus in Oxford, 1962 (Marion S. Trikosko, photographer, Library of Congress [LC-U9-8556-24], Washington, D.C.)

Buoyed by victories and supported by reports of President Harry Truman's Committee on Civil Rights and Commission on Higher Education, the NAACP directly attacked segregated public elementary and secondary schools. On 17 May 1954 the U.S. Supreme Court unanimously ruled in the five cases comprising *Brown v. Board of Education* that "separate educational facilities are inherently unequal" and deprived plaintiffs of equal protection of the laws. In 1955 it remanded these cases to federal district courts for the ordering of desegregation "with all deliberate speed."

Swept up by massive white resistance, southern states enacted new laws to prohibit or indefinitely postpone integration: pupil-placement laws, freedom-of-choice amendments, tuition grants, repeal of compulsory attendance laws, modification of teacher tenure, public school closings (Norfolk and Prince Edward County, Va.), state interposition and nullification of the *Brown* decision, and mob violence (University of Alabama, 1956; Little Rock Central High School, 1957; University of Georgia, 1961; and University of Mississippi, 1962). Federal judicial and military supremacy ultimately triumphed—paratroopers returned nine black students to Little Rock Central High School, while the army secured James Meredith's enrollment at Ole Miss. In 1963, despite Governor George C. Wallace's televised "schoolhouse door" stand, responsible University of Alabama leadership registered two black students, and Clemson and the University of South Carolina integrated with dignity. By the early 1960s, Duke, Emory, Rice, Tulane, and Vanderbilt also desegregated, yielding to pressures from philanthropic foundations, accrediting and scholarly associations, federal granting agencies, and some progressive administrators, alumni, faculty, students, and trustees.

Significant public school desegregation occurred only after the 1964 Civil Rights Act empowered the U.S. attorney general to bring lawsuits on behalf of black plaintiffs and prohibited, under Title VI, spending funds of the Elementary and Secondary Education and Higher Education acts in segregated schools and colleges. To counteract white flight to the suburbs or to private, "segregation," academies, courts ordered students bused citywide and from urban centers to surrounding counties. Angry whites supported conservative, antibusing political candidates, who endorsed freedom-of-choice plans that racially segregated public schools. The Supreme Court's 1968 ruling in *Green v. County School Board of New Kent County, Virginia* established the new requirement that desegregation plans must "ensure racial balance" by maintaining reasonable black-white ratios among students and faculty and by equalizing facilities, transportation, and extracurricular activities. Then, in *Alexander v. Holmes County (Mississippi) Board of Education* (1969) the Supreme Court unanimously ordered all school segregation ended immediately through the creation of unitary schools. By 1971, the year the Supreme Court upheld central-city to suburban busing in *Swann v. Charlotte-Mecklenburg (North Carolina) Board of Education*, busing had more than doubled to 79 percent those southern black students attending integrated schools. A divided Supreme Court halted busing at the Richmond, Va., city line and in Detroit, Mich.

Meanwhile, the U.S. Office for Civil Rights required Predominantly White Institutions (PWIs) in 10 southern and border states, including Oklahoma and Pennsylvania, to submit comprehensive desegregation plans for increasing the number of black students and faculty, expanding financial-aid and remedial programs, and electing black trustees (*Adams v. Richardson*, 1973). The NAACP returned to court to obtain more specific criteria (*Adams v. Califano*, 1977) that would enhance the quality of Historically Black Colleges and Universities (HBCUs). Mississippi blacks filed lawsuits under the name of sharecropper Jake Ayers (*Ayers v. Allain*, 1987 and 1990). In *United States v. Fordice* (1992), the Supreme Court ruled that Mississippi's "race-neutral" admission policies had not eradicated its dual system of higher education. A settlement was finally reached after nine years of further litigation (*Ayers v. Musgrove*, 2001). More than $503 million was awarded to the three public HBCUs to strengthen their academic and summer developmental education programs and to fund endowments and capital improvements. Despite a strict desegregation mandate that offered applicants admission through several flexible pathways to any four-year public institution, Mississippi's enrollment patterns showed residual segregation. Between 1984 and 2004, white enrollment at its three HBCUs increased only from 1.7 percent to 2.9 percent, while black enrollment at its five PWIs rose from 13 percent to 22 percent. Segregated college enrollment patterns also occurred in North Carolina under a consent decree that gave students freedom of choice. Between 1984 and 2004, the percentage of white students at the five HBCUs dropped from 14.5 percent to 10.3 percent, while the percentage of blacks at the 10 PWIs and one historically American Indian institution rose from 8.2 percent to 11.3 percent. To increase black enrollment, the University of North Carolina at Chapel Hill's Carolina Covenant Program provided tuition grants to pay all expenses for students from families at or below 150 percent of the federal poverty level.

Drawing upon the state's 30 percent black population, the University of South Carolina in Columbia led all other flagship state universities in black enrollment in 2000: 17.6 percent of freshmen and 18.7 percent of undergraduates. By 2007, while total freshman enrollment had increased by two-thirds, black freshmen dropped to 8 percent and total black enrollment fell to 12.5 percent. USC required higher SAT scores and more than $8,800 in tuition and fees for in-state undergraduates, making it one of the most expensive public universities in the South. In response, its Gamecock Guarantee offered grants and scholarships to academically qualified first-time South Carolina freshmen from low-income families.

Court decrees and voter-approved bans have limited affirmative action programs. In *Regents of the University of California v. Bakke* (1978), the Supreme Court upheld the use of race in admissions, while rejecting an explicit quota for minority students at the University of California at Davis Medical School. Discretionary admissions policies at public universities led to further judicial and political challenges. The Fifth Circuit Court of Appeals ruled, in *Hopwood v. State of Texas* (1996), that the Fourteenth Amendment did not permit the University of Texas Law School to discriminate against whites and "nonpreferred minorities" to increase the admission of blacks and Mexican Americans. Percentages of black freshmen at California's public universities dropped sharply after voters approved Proposition 209 (1996), a constitutional amendment outlawing racial, ethnic, and gender preferences "in public employment, public education or public contracting." In 1998, Washington imposed a voter-approved ban on racial and gender preferences in public colleges and government agencies. In *Johnson v. Board of Regents of University of Georgia* (2001), the Eleventh Circuit Court ruled that race-based scholarships and fixed numerical points awarded to nonwhite freshman applicants violated the Fourteenth Amendment. Defending their HBCUs, Georgia blacks complained that legislative cost-cutting proposals to merge two of them with PWIs threatened their cultural heritage.

The University of Michigan became an affirmative action battleground after white plaintiffs appealed two cases from the Sixth Circuit Court to the U.S. Supreme Court. Briefs by private and public universities, Fortune 500 companies, and retired military officers persuaded the Supreme Court, in *Grutter v. Bollinger* (2003), to decisively uphold the use of race, if holistically applied, in admitting diverse and talented individuals to the law school. The companion *Gratz v. Bollinger* struck down as mechanistic the point system benefiting minority undergraduate applicants to its College of Literature, Science, and the Arts.

Florida and Texas developed alternative plans to increase black enrollments. In 1999, Governor Jeb Bush announced his "One Florida" plan that guaranteed students ranking in the top 20 percent of their high school class admission to one of the state's public universities. In Texas, Governor George W. Bush obtained legislative support for the "Texas 10 Percent Plan" guaranteeing the top tenth of high school graduates admission to their preferred state university. By 2007, black enrollment at the University of Texas at Austin, which had dropped after *Hopwood*, climbed to about 5 percent. A 2008 study suggested that minority students in the top 10 percent of their high school classes were more likely to graduate within six years if they attended the competitive UT-Austin or Texas A&M at College Station, calling into question the so-called "minority mismatch theory" that assumed black graduation rates were higher at less competitive institutions. In the 16 member states surveyed by the Southern Regional Education Board, black college enrollment had grown by 52 percent, to 1.1 million by 2005; only 19 percent of blacks attended HBCUs. Of the 136,122 bachelor's degrees awarded to blacks, more than twice as many as in 1990, two thirds were earned by black women.

Despite impressive increases in college and school integration, new patterns of segregation developed. Middle-class parents in both southern and nonsouthern states politically campaigned for a voucher system based on their right to choose the best available schools for their children. A proposed voucher system in South Carolina would assist parents with income of $75,000 or less in paying for private or parochial school tuition, homeschooling, or transferring their child to another public school. According to a 1999 ruling of the South Carolina Supreme Court (*Abbeville v. The State of South Carolina et al.*, 2005), public schools are constitutionally required to provide only a "minimally adequate education."

Districts faced legal challenges when they sought to diversify schools segregated by housing patterns. In 2007 the Supreme Court ruled that assignment programs in Louisville, Ky., and Seattle, Wash., violated the rights of individual students. In *Meredith v. Jefferson County (Kentucky) Board of Education et al.*, the Court reviewed the "managed choice" program implemented in 2000 after dissolution of the county's 25-year-old court-ordered desegregation plan. By assigning students to schools after considering parental/student preferences, student needs, school programs, building size, pupil capacity, and the district's educational mission, "managed choice" aimed to maintain black enrollment at no lower than 15 percent, but not over 50 percent at any school. In *Parents Involved in Community Schools Inc. v. Seattle School District No. 1 et al.*, plaintiffs sought an injunction barring use of race in school placement, applied as "a tiebreaker" when the number of applicants exceeded the available seats and its nonwhite enrollment was either more than 15 percent higher or lower than the district's nonwhite population. Since Louisville had fulfilled its court-ordered desegregation, while Seattle schools had never been legally segregated, neither had a "compelling interest" to remedy previous intentional discrimination. Though Chief Justice John G. Roberts argued, "The way to stop discrimination on the basis of race is to stop discriminating on the basis of race," *full integration* remains an elusive goal.

MARCIA G. SYNNOTT
University of South Carolina at Columbia

Robert Barnes, *Washington Post* (29 June 2007); Nadine Cohodas, *The Band Played Dixie: Race and the Liberal Conscience at Ole Miss* (1997); Davison M. Douglas, *Reading, Writing, and Race: The Desegregation of the Charlotte Schools* (1995); *Journal of Blacks in Higher Education* (Autumn 2003, Autumn 2007, Spring 2008); Melissa Kean, *Desegregating Private Higher Education in the South: Duke, Emory, Rice, Tulane, and Vanderbilt* (2008); Richard Kluger, *Simple Justice: The History of* Brown v. Board of Education *and Black America's Struggle for Equality* (2004); Thurgood Marshall, *Journal of Negro Education* (Summer 1952); James T. Minor, *American Educational Research Journal* (December 2008); Gary Orfield, *Must We Bus?: Segregated Schools and National Policy* (1978), *The Reconstruction of Southern Education: The Schools and the 1964 Civil Rights Act* (1969); Jean L. Preer, *Lawyers v. Educators: Black Colleges and Desegregation in Public Higher Education* (1982); President's Commission on Higher

Education, *Higher Education for American Democracy: A Report* (1947); President's Committee on Civil Rights, *To Secure These Rights: The Report of the President's Committee on Civil Rights* (1947); Jeffrey A. Raffel, *Historical Dictionary of School Segregation and Desegregation: The American Experience* (1998); Jacqueline A. Stefkovich and Terrence Leas, *Journal of Negro Education* (Summer 1994); Marcia G. Synnott, *Cornell Law Review* (January 2005); Calvin Trillin, *An Education in Georgia: The Integration of Charlayne Hunter and Hamilton Holmes* (1964); Peter Wallenstein, ed., *Higher Education and the Civil Rights Movement: White Supremacy, Black Southerners, and College Campuses* (2008); Stephen L. Wasby, Anthony A. D'Amato, and Rosemary Metrailer, *Desegregation from Brown to Alexander: An Exploration of Supreme Court Strategies* (1977).

Desegregation of College Sports

College sports have enjoyed widespread popularity and inspired great passion among southerners of all backgrounds since the dawn of the 20th century. Until the mid-1960s, however, southern white opinion demanded that athletic competition at all levels within the region be segregated by race, as part of its ubiquitous Jim Crow system. Since higher education itself was rigidly segregated, athletic teams from white and black colleges consequently existed in separate and unequal sporting worlds. White colleges extended this color line even further by refusing to compete against integrated northern or western teams until well after World War II. Starting in the mid-1960s, though, after federal action had forced white universities to admit African Americans, coaches at these schools cautiously began the process of recruiting African American athletes for their teams. By 1973 this trend had transformed southern college sports, as every major university then fielded integrated football and basketball teams. During the rest of the decade, increasing numbers of black stars came to share the spotlight with their white counterparts. Despite complaints from a few whites, these integrated teams retained their previous popularity and provided white and black fans with unifying symbols that both could support, thereby furthering the process of racial reconciliation within the region.

The young sport of football invaded the South from northeastern colleges in the late 19th century. Despite opposition from ministers, faculty, and administrators, male students eagerly embraced football and the rough physical contact that the sport required. The first game between two southern white colleges took place in the fall of 1888, when the University of North Carolina defeated Wake Forest by a score of 6–4. In the first recognized game between black colleges, host Johnson C. Smith College (then Biddle University) of North Carolina defeated Livingstone College 4–0 in 1892. Baseball also enjoyed considerable popularity on campus in the late 19th century, but the newer game of basketball did not spread across the South until the first decade of the following century.

During the early 1900s, the more ambitious southern teams began to schedule an occasional intersectional game against a northern opponent in pursuit of gate receipts and glory. These contests usually involved southern football teams heading north in the fall or northern baseball squads coming south in the early spring to take advantage of warmer weather. Most of these games proved uneventful, but the rare presence of an African American athlete on a northern team generated intense conflict. In June 1907, for example, the University of Alabama baseball team forfeited a game at the University of Vermont when the host squad refused to bench its two black players.

In order to avoid such last-minute confrontations, southern educators eventually convinced northern officials that it was unreasonable for them to expect southern white athletes to compete against black players. Southerners argued that to compete against even one African American in an athletic event would violate the basic tenets of white supremacy, dishonor the participants, and promote social equality across the South. By the time of World War I, northern schools had acquiesced in this unofficial but widely understood policy of racial exclusion, which came to be known as the Gentleman's Agreement. According to this code, northern institutions would automatically act as gracious hosts or polite visitors by benching any black players on their roster when challenging a southern white team, regardless of the game's location. This informal agreement governed intersectional competition for the next two decades.

Many northern universities willingly colluded with southern schools to maintain this color line. In fact, some of them practiced racial exclusion within their own region. In the early years of the 20th century a few northern teams had refused to compete against black athletes on rival teams. In the Big Ten Conference, all but two member schools excluded African Americans from their basketball teams until the 1950s. Thus, prior to World War II racial discrimination in college sports was not exclusively a southern custom but rather a widespread American practice. In the latter half of the 1930s, however, a few southern universities opportunistically abandoned the Gentlemen's Agreement for several high-profile games held outside the South. In the South Atlantic region, the University of North Carolina, Duke University, and the University of Maryland all played against at least one integrated team in the North in the late 1930s, as the cost of seeking greater national recognition. In the Southwest, a group of Texas colleges led by Southern Methodist University likewise rejected racial exclusion for an occasional game held on the West Coast, in hopes of improving their chances to be invited to the prestigious Rose Bowl classic on New Year's Day.

The democratic ideology and patriotic inclusiveness that World War II rhetoric emphasized helped undermine the color line's grip on intersectional competition. In the late 1940s and early 1950s, southern colleges increasingly scheduled games in the North and West against integrated teams. However, the extreme reaction by southern politicians to the Supreme Court's famous school desegregation ruling of *Brown v. Board of Education* temporarily slowed down the trend towards expanded interracial competition. In the most dramatic action, the Louisiana legislature in 1956 adopted a law that prohibited integrated social and athletic events within the state, part of which survived legal challenge until 1963. In the state of Mississippi, massive resistance to desegregation forced Mississippi State University officials to refuse to allow the school's championship basketball teams to participate in the NCAA tournament in 1959, 1961, and 1962, because the squad would have played against integrated teams. In the spring of 1963 the Bulldog team, once again the Southeastern Conference champion, literally sneaked out of the state in order to evade a temporary legal injunction prohibiting the school from participating in the national tournament. Nonetheless, by the mid-1960s integrated competition had become acceptable even to white colleges in Mississippi, leaving coaches with the dilemma of whether or not to recruit black athletes for their own teams.

There were several noticeable patterns in the transition from all-white to integrated teams at southern colleges. The first white colleges to desegregate their varsity football and basketball teams were located near the geographical borders of the South, while schools in the Deep South were the last to accept African American players. Teams in the Southeastern Conference were somewhat slower to integrate their rosters than were members of the Atlantic Coast Conference and the old Southwest Conference. Colleges lacking a conference affiliation (Independents), schools that played mostly against nonsouthern teams (such as the University of Louisville), and church-related institutions were usually more willing to seek out black prospects than were most state-supported colleges. Basketball coaches were initially more successful in recruiting African Americans than football coaches, despite having fewer scholarships to give out. Not surprisingly, coaches at losing programs were also more aggressive in seeking out minority athletes than their more successful and better-known counterparts. Moreover, integration also turned out to be mostly a one-way street. In the 1970s, as black high school stars increasingly enrolled at white colleges, only a tiny number of white athletes replaced them at black colleges.

Texas Western College (now the University of Texas at El Paso), the University of North Texas, the University of Louisville, the University of Houston, and the University of Maryland were the first major southern colleges to integrate their athletic teams. In the fall of 1956 transfers Charles and Cecil Brown joined the Texas Western basketball squad, becoming the first black players at a major white college in an ex-Confederate state. The University of North Texas fielded the next integrated varsity basketball team in the 1961–62 season, while Louisville, which played mostly midwestern opponents, did so during the 1964–65 season. The earliest southern colleges to integrate their varsity football teams were Louisville in 1954, North Texas in 1957, and Texas Western in 1959.

In the Atlantic Coast Conference, Maryland took the lead in both football and basketball integration. In 1963 Naval Academy transfer Darryl Hill joined the Terrapin varsity football team, while two years later Billy Jones made his appearance on the Maryland basketball team. Out in the Southwest Conference, Jerry Levias of SMU and John Westbrook of Baylor became the league's first black varsity football players in September 1966. A few months later, James Cash of Texas Christian University broke the conference's color line on the basketball court. In the Southeastern Conference (SEC), the college sports world's "final citadel of segregation," Nat Northington at Kentucky in 1967 and Lester McClain at Tennessee in 1968 became the first African Americans to see varsity football action. Vanderbilt's Perry Wallace stood out as the only black player in the SEC during the 1967–68 basketball season, and he was not joined by another African American until Henry Harris took the court for Auburn two years later. One of the first white players to compete for a southern black school was Joseph Malbouef of Detroit, Mich., who played for the Tuskegee University football team from 1968 through 1971.

Several famous southern coaches including Alabama's Paul "Bear" Bryant and Kentucky's Adolph Rupp did not play a prominent role in sports integration. The later success of Bryant's teams, aided by his eventual recruitment of black players, obliterated awareness of his earlier hesitancy over desegregation and even led to inflated claims that he had been a leader in dismantling the SEC's color line. On the other hand, Adolph Rupp's uneasiness over recruiting African Americans was neither forgotten nor forgiven. Many sports writers and especially black fans continued to criticize Rupp after his retirement, and his racial legacy remains a bitterly contested issue for some die-hard Wildcat fans still today.

The desegregation of southern football and basketball teams eventually produced new stars and unifying symbols for black and white southerners. Outstanding black football players like Herschel Walker at Georgia, "Bo" Jackson at Auburn, and Earl Campbell at Texas helped win championships and make integration acceptable to white fans. Basketball stars like David Thompson at North Carolina State and Charles Scott at the University of North Carolina likewise inspired white and black fans alike. The example of integrated teams on which black and white players worked together in pursuit of mutual success offered a valuable model of interracial cooperation in the 1970s and 1980s, as white and black southerners adjusted to profound changes in their society. Athletic desegregation thus represented a positive but sometimes overlooked achievement of the civil rights era.

CHARLES H. MARTIN
University of Texas at El Paso

Allen Barra, *The Last Coach: A Life of Paul "Bear" Bryant* (2005); Charles H. Martin, *Benching Jim Crow: The Rise and Fall of the Color Line in Southern College Sports, 1890–1980* (2010).

Desegregation of Private Universities and Colleges

The desegregation of the public universities in the South is one of the most familiar and dramatic stories of the civil rights movement. Images of George Wallace's "stand in the schoolhouse door" at the University of Alabama, of federal marshals at the University of Mississippi, and student riots at the University of Georgia following the enrollment of Hamilton Holmes and Charlayne Hunter are now indelibly part of the popular understanding of the region's turbulent racial transformation in the 1960s. In stark contrast, most people know little, if anything, about how southern private colleges and universities came to admit black students. That change took place almost entirely outside the glare of national publicity, with little open acrimony or fanfare. What drama there was took place quietly, usually behind closed doors.

In the struggle to desegregate, the critical difference between public colleges and private ones was the source of their funds. Reliance on public tax monies left the state schools open to legal compulsion to desegregate through the Equal Protection Clause of the Fourteenth Amendment. NAACP lawyers could thus use the federal courts to force their desegregation, beginning with the University of Maryland in 1938 and gradually picking up steam through the 1940s and 1950s, culminating in the dramatic events of the 1960s. The private universities and colleges, on the other hand, were considered at the time to be beyond the reach of the Fourteenth Amendment: most of their revenue came from private donors, religious organizations, and tuition. This financial reality, coupled with a long and fiercely guarded tradition of independence, discouraged frontal assaults on the racial policies of private schools.

The same pressures, though, that lay behind the desegregation of the South's public universities also gave rise to internal conflict over racial policies at the private schools. In the aftermath of the Second World War, the South began a period of dramatic demographic, economic, and social transformation. Cities grew rapidly as industry expanded and relocated in the South, providing better-paying alternatives to agricultural work. The region's population, including its black population, became more mobile, more prosperous, and better educated. The rise of the grassroots civil rights movement began to directly challenge institutional white supremacy. Pressure to change southern race relations also came from outside the region. The Truman administration, for example, undertook a series of minor but real steps to loosen racial restrictions within the federal government. The President's Commission on Higher Education began the era with a ringing condemnation of segregation and a call for broader democracy in American schooling. Other changes were far more immediate. National academic professional organizations and accrediting bodies, both critically important in the drive to improve instruction and build reputation, grew reluctant to tolerate racial discrimination in their membership. Faculty members and students alike became increasingly vocal about the immorality of banning blacks from their schools for no reason other than their color.

Southern higher education itself was undergoing a profound transformation during the postwar years. For most of their existence, private colleges in the South lagged far behind their counterparts in the rest of the nation. Most were (or began as) religious schools founded by Protestant denominations, with a handful of Catholic colleges, mainly in urban areas. They were often sleepy, isolated institutions, thoroughly local and focused on teaching a classical curriculum and Christian theology to undergraduates of good families. Nearly all of them were chronically hard-pressed for money, as local and regional church bodies, not wealthy themselves, struggled to support them. With only a couple of exceptions, notably Berea College, these schools were also rigidly segregated. Those that had been founded after the Civil War (the Rice Institute is a prominent example) typically had charter provisions banning black students. Those founded earlier tended not to have such prohibitions in their founding documents—it would hardly have been necessary—but various post-Reconstruction state laws made it illegal for white and black students to be taught together.

Amid the growing prosperity of the post–World War II era the leadership at many of the private universities saw an opportunity to leap forward to national respectability and even prominence by tapping into the river of money that began to flow from the federal government during the war and continued after it, as well as by cultivating the aid of several national foundations that made the improvement of southern higher education a prominent goal. These efforts were in many cases astonishingly successful and led to dramatic changes on many campuses. The larger and most ambitious schools began to develop more and significantly better graduate and professional programs. They successfully recruited important scholars and researchers and stronger student bodies, now drawing more applications from outside the South. Smaller private schools also participated in these changes, expanding their curricula, focusing on improving the quality of instruction, and opening up to new kinds of students and faculty. Unsurprisingly, in the middle of such deep transformation, many people (mainly alumni, trustees, and a handful of senior faculty members) associated with the southern colleges began to grow unsettled. To them, segregation came to represent their institution's last meaningful connection to cherished local and regional traditions, to real "southernness," and they were willing to fight to keep it. In order to continue moving towards the mainstream of American higher education, the South's private colleges and universities would thus have to confront not outsiders, but their own traditions.

In some cases, the change was relatively easy. During the late 1940s, a few private schools began to desegregate willingly, even eagerly. Most of these schools were grounded less in southern than in religious tradition and were driven by a calling to serve all. They simply began to do so, quietly, as soon as they were legally able. Some were undergraduate colleges, others seminaries. All were located in border states or the District of Columbia. As the NAACP's legal campaign to open admissions to public universities first gained ground in these states, these schools took advantage of the court decisions. When the United States Supreme Court ordered the integration of the graduate school at University of Kentucky in 1949, for example, the state legislature was forced to repeal its ban on integrated education. Four private schools in Louisville—Nazareth College, Louisville Theological Seminary, Ursuline College, and the Southern Baptist Theological Seminary—almost immediately opened admissions to blacks. Others no doubt simply saw the handwriting on the wall and chose not to resist. By 1951, at least 20 private colleges or universities had integrated, including institutions as different as Berea College and Washington University in St. Louis.

During the early 1950s, a few private schools in the Deep South also desegregated. In early 1954 Loyola of New Orleans and Spring Hill in Alabama, both Jesuit institutions, ended segregation on their campuses. These decisions, unsurprisingly, were more difficult and in both cases came only after several years of internal debate that pitted the claims of religious mission against the fear of alienating local and regional supporters. Many other private schools came to terms with desegregation in the aftermath of the May 1954 U.S. Supreme Court decision in *Brown v. Board of Education*, which banned segregation in public schools. Although this decision did not affect private colleges directly, events now pointed clearly in one direction and leaders at these schools chose to confront the problem before they were forced to do so. Each school had its own debate, differing in details and intensity, but revolving around the now clear conflict between upholding southern tradition and entering the main currents of American higher education. Within four years of *Brown*, more than half of the South's 233 church-related colleges and universities and about a quarter of the private schools without religious affiliation had voluntarily desegregated. Somewhat surprisingly, given the growing racial turmoil in the region, in most cases there was little or no adverse public reaction.

The laggards in the process of desegregation turned out to be some of the South's most successful and respected private universities. Ironically, these were the very institutions that had the most to gain by desegregating. Successful fundraising, sustained focus on academic improvement, and intense recruitment of faculty and graduate students had already transformed the major private schools, including Duke, Emory, Rice, Tulane, and Vanderbilt, so that by the late 1950s they had emerged as legitimate national research universities. Perhaps because schools like these had undergone such wholesale, rapid change, they also experienced more—and more intense—internal conflict over segregation. Many of their trustees in particular came to insist that they could maintain both progress and tradition indefinitely, that they could join the American mainstream and compete at the highest levels of academia while remaining unbending on segregation. They were wrong. For these schools to continue on their upward path, they depended entirely on their ability to continue raising money from the federal government and from large private philanthropies. By the early 1960s, the federal government adopted nondiscrimination policies that made segregated universities ineligible for grants and contracts, and the major private donors also made it clear that they would send no more money to segregated institutions. Only when thus confronted squarely with the choice between desegregation and probably irreversible academic decline did these elite schools open their doors to blacks.

Thus, by the middle of the 1960s most southern private universities and colleges had peacefully, if not thoroughly, desegregated. Black students were accepted in the classroom (although acceptance in extracurricular and other social activities often came more slowly) and settled into the business of education with a minimum of disruption. The institutions themselves, having shed the last truly meaningful vestige of regional identity, were now fully part of the national academic mainstream, competing with schools throughout the country for students, faculty, funding, and prestige.

MELISSA KEAN
Rice University

Melissa Kean, *Desegregating Private Higher Education in the South: Duke, Emory, Rice, Tulane, and Vanderbilt* (2008); Clarence L. Mohr, in *Remaking Dixie: The Impact of World War II on the American South*, ed. Neil R. McMillen (1997); Peter Wallenstein, ed., *Higher Education and the Civil Rights Movement: White Supremacy, Black Southerners, and College Campuses* (2008).

Fraternities and Sororities

The first Greek-letter society, Phi Beta Kappa, was founded in Virginia at the College of William and Mary on 5 December 1776 as a secret social organization; only later did it become the nation's leading scholastic honor society. It succeeded the earlier Flat Hat Club at William and Mary, to which Thomas Jefferson had belonged. Phi Beta Kappa members went on to found the original Kappa Alpha at the University of North Carolina in 1812. Before it became defunct in 1855, this fraternity had 12 "circles," all in the South.

Despite these beginnings, the progenitors of today's college fraternities are considered to be the three fraternities of the "Union Triad," founded at Union College, Schenectady, N.Y., between 1825 and 1827. By 1850 there were 16 men's fraternities in the country, all founded in the North, but 12 of which had chapters established on southern campuses before secession. First to come South was the Mystical Seven, founded at Wesleyan University in 1837, which established a chapter at the University of Georgia in 1839 and later merged with Beta Theta Pi. The first college fraternity founded in the South was the Rainbow Fraternity, or "WWW," established at the University of Mississippi in 1849. In 1886 it merged with Delta Tau Delta, itself established in 1858 at Bethany College, Va. (now W.Va.). Neither Epsilon Alpha at the University of Virginia nor Alpha Kappa Phi at Kentucky's Centre College survived the Civil War.

The first Greek-letter society founded in Dixie to take permanent root was Sigma Alpha Epsilon, begun in 1856 at the University of Alabama. Sigma Alpha, or the Black Badge Society, founded at Roanoke College in Salem, Va., in 1859, and eventually having eight southern chapters, was disbanded in 1882. The fraternity system flourished in the South before the Civil War, so that at the University of Mississippi, for example, 11 fraternities could be found among a small male student body at the time of secession. When the Civil War began, fraternities folded up on nearly every southern college campus as the male students left for battle. However, war did not kill southern Greek-letter societies. During the Atlanta Campaign, five Sigma Chi's from various colleges formed the Constantine Chapter of Sigma Chi in Gen. Joseph E. Johnston's Army of Tennessee and initiated two Confederate soldiers on the night of 17 September 1864 near Jonesboro, Ga., where a monument commemorates the event.

After the Civil War, southern students, mainly Confederate veterans or military college cadets, organized several new fraternities in the South: Alpha Tau Omega in 1865, Kappa Sigma Kappa in 1867 (which merged with Theta Chi in 1962), and Sigma Nu in 1869 at the Virginia Military Institute (VMI); Kappa Alpha Order, at what is now Washington and Lee, in 1865; and Pi Kappa Alpha in 1868 and Kappa Sigma in 1869 at the University of Virginia. Other southern fraternities that appeared later were Sigma Phi Epsilon, founded at the University of Richmond in 1901, and Phi Kappa Phi at the College of Charleston in 1904.

The first Greek-letter women's social organization in the United States was Alpha Delta Pi, begun at Wesleyan College in Macon, Ga., in 1851, closely followed there the next year by Phi Mu. Chi Omega started at the University of Arkansas in 1895. Virginia State Normal School (now Longwood College) in Farmville gave birth to four sororities: Kappa Delta in 1897, Sigma Sigma Sigma and Zeta Tau Alpha in 1898, and Alpha Sigma Alpha in 1901.

Early in the 20th century, black college fraternities and sororities also appeared. The first black men's Greek-letter society was Alpha Phi Alpha at Cornell in 1906, followed by Kappa Alpha Psi at Indiana in 1911. As might be expected, Howard University in Washington, D.C., was the incubator for two black fraternities and three black sororities. For men there were Omega Psi Phi in 1911 and Phi Beta Sigma in 1914, and for women there were Alpha Kappa Alpha in 1908, Delta Sigma Theta in 1913, and Zeta Phi Beta in 1920. Sigma Gamma Rho became a black collegiate sorority at Butler University in Indianapolis in 1929. All these groups are found on southern campuses.

Southern social fraternities and sororities have had their ups and downs, as have others across the nation, in peace as well as in war. Secret societies were eventually suppressed at military colleges, such as VMI and the Citadel. Yet at some southern land-grant colleges once run on military lines there were social organizations, such as Lee Guard and George Rifles at Mississippi A&M (now Mississippi State University), that later became chapters of national men's social fraternities. Early in the last century, southern governors and legislatures in predominantly rural and agrarian states succeeded in banning Greek-letter societies on public campuses, such as in South Carolina from 1897 to 1929 and in Mississippi from 1912 to 1926. However, they continued to exist sub rosa in some cases and eventually returned stronger than ever.

Certain southern campuses have long been noted for their hospitality to "the Greeks," most notably the University of Alabama, which in 1963 on the eve of the Vietnam War was the home of 26 men's and 16 women's Greek-letter social organizations. The wave of social protest that swept over American campuses during the 1960s and 1970s was heralded in some quarters as dooming fraternities and sororities. Although the Greek system suffered elsewhere in the country, especially in the Northeast and Far West, it was not damaged noticeably in the South.

The national leadership of Greek organizations has reacted to increasing pressure by parents and college officials concerned about the brutality of certain hazing and initiation rituals. The resistance by Greek organizations to the alteration of these practices stems from the emphasis members place on the secrecy of rituals and on loyalty, both to each other and to the traditions of their groups. As a result of the recent deaths of some fraternity pledges during hazing rituals and the publicity the deaths received, the campaign against hazing has progressed in the South as elsewhere. The national fraternities, as well as the National Interfraternity Conference, have rules prohibiting hazing, and 18 states have laws against hazing practices. Many campuses, such as the University of Texas at Austin, have taken strong stands against the rituals, expelling students and even fraternities on occasion for their participation.

Fraternity and sorority participation at southern schools appears to be increasing, consistent with the national trend. College students join Greek organizations looking for camaraderie, social status, and the feeling of group unity. The gregariousness, conviviality, and love of ritualistic pomp and hierarchical status usually associated with southerners may account for the seemingly enduring popularity of Greek organizations in the region. Some college students are influenced by members of their families to join a particular Greek society.

Since the 1970s membership in both fraternities and sororities has risen steadily nationwide. In the past 20 years, national membership has increased from about 400,000 to around 600,000 in 2008. The percentage of students in Greek organizations varies widely on southern college campuses, though the percentage of involvement is not necessarily indicative of the strength of the Greek system on any given campus. Fraternity participation in the South ranges from 70 percent of male students at Louisiana State University in Baton Rouge and at Centre College in Kentucky, to 5 percent of male students at East Carolina University and Tuskegee Institute. Sorority participation on southern campuses ranges from 65 percent of the female students at Shorter College in Georgia, to 4 percent of females at Tuskegee Institute and at North Carolina State University.

Although a strong Greek system has sometimes been associated with a "party campus" and considered antithetical to a serious academic emphasis, several southern institutions with excellent academic reputations have flourishing Greek organizations, among them Birmingham-Southern College in Alabama, Duke University in North Carolina, Emory University in Georgia, Millsaps College in Mississippi, and Vanderbilt University in Tennessee. Some southern schools have no fraternities and sororities at all. These include Berea College in Kentucky, the University of Dallas, Eckerd College in Florida, and Texas A&M University.

JOHN HAWKINS NAPIER III
Montgomery, Alabama

Allen Cabaniss, *A History of the University of Mississippi* (1949); Clyde S. Johnson, *Fraternities in Our Colleges* (1972); Thomas J. Meyer, *Chronicle of Higher Education* (12 March 1986); John Hawkins Napier III, *The Mississippian* (20 February 1948); John Robson, ed., *Baird's Manual of American College Fraternities* (19th ed., 1977), *The College Fraternity and Its Modern Role* (1966).

Illiteracy and Least Literate

Inability to read and write in any language has been the conventional definition of illiteracy and the basis of most illiteracy statistics. The concept of "functional" illiteracy was advanced during World War II as a result of the U.S. Army's experience with soldiers who "could not understand written instructions about basic military tasks." The South has exceeded the rest of the nation in illiteracy, whether defined in functional terms or as the inability to read and write in any language.

A 1992 National Adult Literacy Survey (NALS) was followed by a National Assessment of Adult Literacy in 2003 to establish the national trends in "literacy." Analysis of a representative sample of 189,500 adults 16 years of age and older produced estimates of three types of literacy, classified as "prose," "document," and "mathematical." An Adult Literacy Supplemental Assessment

(ALSA) found that the highest concentration of "least literate in reading skills" was in the Southeast.

Information from the U.S. Census of 1870 illustrates the South's heritage of illiteracy. No area of the region had less than 12 percent illiteracy. The cotton-culture subregions, particularly the river valleys and deltas and the Piedmont and coastal plain, were 40 percent or more illiterate. The South was predominantly agricultural, and agriculture depended less upon science than upon traditional practices—learning by doing rather than by reading. The 1870 census estimated there were 4.53 million persons 10 years of age and older unable to read in the nation; 73.7 percent of them resided in the South. Four-fifths of blacks were then illiterate.

The agricultural economy rested upon a sparsely distributed population, the use of child labor that discouraged school attendance, and a prejudiced and often fatalistic people who lacked the means for upward mobility in the expanding industrial system of the nation. The church was more important as a social institution than the school; word of mouth, song, and story were prominent means of cultural transmission. Under these conditions illiteracy served to conserve tradition and retard cultural change, whereas a more general literacy would have accelerated adaptation and change. Said a Jasper County, Miss., man: "My grandfather—he raised me—figured going to school wouldn't help me pick cotton any better."

Illiteracy has declined both in the South and in the nation as a whole. As educational benefits were extended to blacks through both public and private schools (including schools sponsored by religious groups, such as the Congregational Church, and by private foundations, such as the Rosenwald Fund), illiteracy rates dropped.

When the education of a generation of children is neglected, the deficiency persists throughout a lifetime. As important as it is to teach adults to read, in terms of eliminating illiteracy, mortality and out-migration from the South have been more effective. The neglect of a generation of school children during the Civil War (those five to 14 years of age in 1860) resulted in higher illiteracy rates for the native white population in 1900 (who then were 45 to 54 years of age) than for either the preceding or succeeding generation. The illiteracy rates by age of the black population of Louisiana, from 1890 to 1930, shown in Table 1, illustrate the dogged tenacity of illiteracy, despite mortality and out-migration. The population represented below the dashed line lived under pre–Civil War conditions. The older the population in 1890, the lower the rate of change in illiteracy to the terminal age group. As time progressed, reductions in illiteracy among the 10 to 14 age group accelerated.

Data from Georgia from 1960 and 1970 illustrate the source of gains and losses in the number of illiterates in a state. The number of Georgia illiterates in 1960 was reduced by 45 percent in 1970. Some 22,530 were estimated to have died during the decade, and 23,840 were lost through out-migration. The Adult Basic Education Program of the state taught 14,380 to read during the period. However, 6,290 new illiterates, aged 14 to 24 years in 1970, entered the illiterate category. This new group testifies to the failure of the family and the school to inculcate literacy skills.

The most extensive recent testing of reading and writing has been conducted by the National Assessment of Educational Progress. In tests of 17-year-olds, the Southeast (which differs from the Census's definition of the South by excluding Texas, Oklahoma, Maryland, Delaware, and the District of Columbia) scored lower than any other region; the results illustrate functional, rather than conventional, illiteracy. This is especially revealing because the 17-year-old is the product of the present school system.

Although some industrial plants will not hire illiterates, the prevalence of illiteracy in the South apparently has not affected plant location. Following World War II, as more oil, chemical, atomic energy, and other technological industries located in the South, educational requirements for employment rose, and, except for common labor, the illiterate worker was less likely to find employment. Not surprisingly, the unemployment rate of illiterates is higher than that of literates. Southern migrants to the North who found jobs in the automobile industry were able to perform the work but often encountered off-the-job difficulties: they overextended themselves in credit installment purchases, failed to adjust to city life, or returned home without receiving permission from supervisors. Their absentee rates were higher than those of other workers. Similar employment difficulties evidently plague Latinos in the Southwest. Indeed, policymakers also find low literacy associated with poverty, incarceration, and poor health.

In general, illiterates are more likely to have diminished learning capacity, to be welfare recipients, and to be rejected for military service. If female, they have higher fertility rates and their children have a higher incidence of infant mortality. And the rate of illiteracy is higher in rural than in urban areas.

The 1980 Census and the November 1979 Current Population Survey found approximately 398,000 illiterates in the South. The distribution by color was white, 44.9 percent; black, 51.4 percent; other nonwhite, 3.7 percent. By age, they were 14–24 years, 9.2 percent; 25–44 years, 17.0 percent; 45–64 years, 32.2 percent; and 65 years and over, 41.6 percent. These are individuals unable to

TABLE 1. *Illiteracy Rates among Blacks in Louisiana, by Age, 1890–1930*

Age	1890	1900	1910	1920	1930
10–14	60.3	49.7	40.0	25.4	7.7
15–24	66.3	54.3	41.5	31.5	14.7
25–34	70.7	58.7	43.9	34.6	21.3
35–44	78.7	65.7	51.0	41.7	26.7
45–54	86.0	76.7	60.5	51.2	34.7
55–64	89.5	84.8	72.4	63.5	45.6
65 and up	92.6	89.9	81.4	77.5	64.4

Source: U.S. Department of Education, Institute of Education Sciences, Center for Education Statistics, 1992 National Adult Literacy Survey and 2003 National Assessment of Adult Literacy.

read and write, according to census definitions; functional illiterates are more numerous. A more precise definition of least-literate adults, however, gives us a more accurate definition of the problem.

The more positive concept, literacy, was adopted as the statistic beginning 1992. The National Adult Literacy Survey has replaced illiteracy with a comparable measure, the *least literate*. The least literate were those adults who were unable to complete the standard Adult Literacy survey and who, when administered a special instrument, could not read the standard questions. They were shown 3-D objects such as food boxes and drug labels, since the least literate rely upon context for comprehension. Some 79 questions assessed the least-literate adults' background, knowledge, basic reading skills, and inferential literacy skills.

In 1992, the "least literate" were 18 percent of the population of the 12 southeastern states (omitting Texas, Oklahoma, and the District of Columbia but including West Virginia). This represented approximately 8,501,400 adults. Mississippi, with 25 percent, had the highest rate, followed by Louisiana and Alabama, each with 21 percent. Eleven years later, however, the literacy problem had improved. The 2003 survey found 11.3 percent of the population illiterate in the Southeast, representing 5,962,000 adults. Mississippi, Louisiana, and Alabama no longer led the list; instead Florida, with 20 percent least literate, led the states, it being the only state not improving. The percentages are presented in Table 2.

TABLE 2. *Indirect Estimates of the Percentage of the Population Lacking Basic Prose Literacy Skills, Southeastern States, 1992 and 2003*

State	1992 (%)	2003 (%)
Alabama	21	15
Arkansas	19	14
Florida	15	20
Georgia	18	17
Kentucky	19	8
Louisiana	21	16
Mississippi	25	16
North Carolina	18	14
South Carolina	20	15
Tennessee	19	13
Virginia	15	12
West Virginia	17	13
Southeast	18.0	11.3

Source: U.S. Department of Education, Institute of Education Sciences, Center for Education Statistics, 1992 National Adult Literacy Survey and 2003 National Assessment of Adult Literacy.

As in other sections of the country, southeastern states have programs to teach prose literacy. For example, South Carolina during 2002–3 had 80,000 adult learners in its Adult Education and Literacy program. The state realizes that the economy depends upon an adequate pool of educated, well-trained workers.

ABBOTT L. FERRISS
Emory University

Sterling G. Brinkley, *Journal of Experimental Education* (September 1957); John K. Folger and Charles B. Nam, *Education of the American Population* (1967); Eli Ginzberg and Douglas W. Bray, *The Uneducated* (1953); *Historical Statistics of the United States to 1970* (1975); Carman St. John Hunter with David Harman, *Adult Illiteracy in the United States: A Report to the Ford Foundation* (1979); *National Assessment of Educational Progress*, Report No. 11-R-02 (1982), Report No. 10-W-01 (1980); *U.S. Bureau of the Census, Current Population Reports*, Series P-23, No. 6 (November 1959), No. 8 (February 1963), No. 116 (March 1982); Series P-20, No. 99 (March 1959), No. 217 (March 1971); Sanford Winston, *Illiteracy in the United States* (1930).

Medical Education

Southern medical education has always been shaped by the South's distinctive climate and disease environment, its medical profession and health care institutions, and its educational system. All of these in turn have been strongly influenced by the South's racial and economic history of cash-crop agriculture dependent on slave labor, which set it apart from the urban Northeast, the power center of American academic medicine. Well into the 19th century, most aspiring southern physicians either apprenticed themselves to an experienced practitioner or attended the small, independent proprietary schools that proliferated beginning in the 1820s. Many chose to attend the better-established northern schools, and a handful studied in Europe. On the eve of the Civil War, most southern medical students at northern schools, including 300 in Philadelphia alone, withdrew to enroll in southern schools. By 1860 the South had established 23 medical schools, 15 of which were concentrated in Maryland, Virginia, the District of Columbia, Tennessee, and Kentucky. During the antebellum period, sectionalist physicians such as Samuel Cartwright embraced "states' rights medicine," which held that the southern environment had modified common diseases or created entirely new ones that could only be understood and treated effectively by physicians trained in southern schools. Southern medical professors and textbook authors were also among the chief proponents of biological black inferiority based on racist concepts of comparative anatomy and physiology, which would subsequently become widely accepted outside the South as well. Charity Hospital in New Orleans, the teaching hospital for the medical schools of Tulane University and later Louisiana State University, became a center of research on race-based differences in disease.

After the Civil War, both black and white physicians founded numerous proprietary medical schools. At this time, even Harvard Medical School had no admissions requirements, grades, or laboratory work, except for anatomy. The founding of the Johns Hopkins Medical School in 1893 as the first modern medical school, the formation of the American Medical Association Council on Medical Education in 1900, and Abraham Flexner's 1910 report to the Carnegie Foundation on medical education in the United States and Canada together ushered in sweeping reforms that made medicine the most expensive form of higher education and decimated the southern schools, particularly those for blacks. Between 1900 and 1923 the number of black schools shrank from 10 to 2, Howard University in Washington, D.C., and Meharry Medical College in Nashville, Tenn., which henceforth educated the vast majority of black physicians. Abraham Flexner concluded in his report on the South that medical education there was "trembling on the verge of extinction," but he still urged the General Education Board to fund specific measures to improve the schools, ranging from construction of laboratory facilities to establishing residency programs to creating a $500,000 endowment for teaching and equipment at Howard, which Flexner insisted "must not be permitted to disappear." Despite Flexner's low opinion of most southern schools, he and Carnegie Foundation president Henry S. Pritchett recognized the limitations posed by southern conditions and advocated tolerance of "greater unevenness." All the South's medical schools were handicapped by the serious underdevelopment of its public and higher education systems as well as its health care institutions. Southern university endowments were uniformly low; the only three (Duke, Texas, and Vanderbilt) with more than $25 million before World War II also boasted the best medical schools. In 1914, Flexner, Pritchett, and the Southern Medical College Association threatened to remove southern schools from the American Medical Association Council on Medical Education's authority unless they were given time to adjust to the new admissions standards. Although Flexner, a native of Louisville, Ky., considered black physicians better suited to be hygienists than surgeons, he also made sustained efforts to secure major grants to improve southern medical schools for blacks as well as whites. By 1930 nearly all the southern schools required a liberal arts degree for admission and offered three to four years of graded instruction in medicine and surgery.

By World War II, of 76 medical schools in the United States, one third were in the South, but most were at private universities, which severely limited access to medical education in the nation's poorest region. The dire shortage of health personnel, particularly those with even minimal public health training, was a major obstacle to delivering health services to the South's poor, widely scattered population. Physician-to-population ratios indicate the magnitude of disparity: in 1940, one physician practiced for every 592 persons in the Northeast and 755 persons in the nation, versus 1,064 persons in the South. For African Americans, the ratio was one black physician per 3,681 black population nationally, per 6,204 in the South, per 12,561 in South Carolina, and per 18,132 in Mississippi. Moreover, physicians were heavily concentrated in cities in a region that remained largely rural. Black physicians who were willing to give up their civil rights to practice in the segregated South were even less likely than white practitioners to locate in rural areas.

The Great Depression and World War II were catalysts for federal and state programs to address the major deficiencies in the South's health and educational systems. The South's high rates of maternal and infant mortality, low percentage of doctor-attended hospital births, and disproportionate number of World War II draft rejections all prompted southern medical societies and state legislatures to make increasing the supply of doctors and hospital beds a top priority. In Alabama and North Carolina, wartime health reform centered on campaigns to build a new four-year state medical school, as did postwar health reform in Florida and Kentucky. Progressive southern governors such as Earl Long of Louisiana and Sid McMath of Arkansas raised taxes to fund new public schools and enhancements to the state university system and also oversaw the refurbishing of state hospitals and mental institutions, all of which contributed to an improved environment for medical education.

As southern state governments grew more willing to spend tax dollars on health care and education, they also exhibited a hardening resolve to defend segregation. *Gaines v. Missouri* (1938) and subsequent Supreme Court decisions required public graduate and professional schools to admit qualified black applicants if no "separate but equal" school for blacks existed. Led by Florida governor Millard F. Caldwell, the Southern Governors Conference created the Southern Regional Education Board (SREB) in 1948 to promote interstate cooperation and sharing of resources to improve and expand expensive graduate and professional programs for both black and white students. The primary focus of the SREB in its early years was medicine, dentistry, nursing, and pharmacy. To avoid building expensive new schools, southern states agreed to subsidize tuition for their residents at existing schools in other member states, including Emory, Tulane, and the University of Alabama. The largest recipient of SREB funding was Meharry Medical College, which received $2.5 million from 1949 to 1961 to aid approximately 500 black medical students and an additional $1 million for black dental students. Although the agreement with Meharry originated as a way for southern state governments to avoid desegregating medical schools, it made increasing the supply of black physicians a goal of southern public policy long before the advent of affirmative action or diversity programs, even after the 1954 *Brown* decision and white backlash. The SREB soon evolved to become a force for both racial equality and federal funding for medical education. In the late 1940s, the National Medical Association and the NAACP mounted a joint campaign to end segregation in medical education, and Thurgood Marshall urged black students to apply to white medical schools. Between 1948 and 1951, the state universities of Arkansas, Texas, and North Carolina, the University of Louisville, and the Medical College of Virginia admitted their first black medical students, and by the late 1960s, even schools in the Deep South were actively recruiting minority applicants with support from foundations such as the Commonwealth Fund and the Josiah H. Macy Foundation.

Major federal funding helped to more than triple the number of southern state medical schools from seven in 1940 to 23 by 1985, and existing schools also increased their class sizes. New southern schools accounted for much of the increase in the nation's supply of physicians during this period. The 1946 Hill-Burton Hospital Survey and Construction Act fostered the growth of institution-based, capital- and technology-intensive medicine in the South. Teaching hospitals represented about 20 percent of all Hill-Burton projects, including the burgeoning new academic medical centers at the state universities of Alabama, North Carolina, Texas, and Florida as well as the expansion of facilities at private medical schools such as Duke and Bowman Gray (now Wake Forest). Funding from the Veterans Administration and the National Mental Health Act also underwrote construction on southern medical school campuses as well as support for residency programs. At the state level, addressing the shortage and maldistribution of physicians and improving health care access for medically underserved rural and minority populations were the most common traditional justifications for founding new medical schools at public expense, but once established, schools like those at the University of North Carolina and the University of Florida had tended to abandon such priorities in favor of pursuing specialty training and clinical research. Rivalries between the larger, older flagship universities and newer institutions such as East Carolina University and University of South Florida contributed to political one-upmanship that sought to increase prestige and state budget lines by establishing medical schools. This tactic was facilitated by the populist fervor that overtook southern capitals following the Supreme Court's "one man, one vote" decision, which required southern states to comply with the Voting Rights Act of 1965 by redrawing racially gerrymandered voting districts.

In the context of the Great Society push for national health reform, the 1963 Health Professions Educational Assistance Act, Regional Medical Program (RMP) (1965), 1968 Health Manpower Act, and Area Health Education Centers (AHEC) residency program (1971) were particularly important in supporting the expansion of southern medical education as well as increasing the region's supply of primary care and minority physicians. AHEC, RMP, and other residency programs proved more successful than previous attempts to encourage MDs to consider general practice in rural and inner-city areas. These programs, along with the recruitment of numerous prominent faculty from outside the South to fledgling schools in Birmingham, Ala., or Gainesville, Fla., liberalized racial attitudes across campus and transformed southern medical schools from provincial outposts to modern health science centers. In 2000, Florida State University in Tallahassee established the first new allopathic medical school in the United States in over 20 years. Accredited in 2005, the school prepares physicians for community-based practice and emphasizes primary care, geriatrics, cultural diversity, and the needs of underserved populations.

KAREN KRUSE THOMAS
Johns Hopkins University

James O. Breeden, *Bulletin of the New York Academy of Medicine* (March/April 1976); Walter E. Campbell, *Foundations for Excellence: 75 Years of Duke Medicine* (2006); John Duffy, *The Tulane University Medical Center: One Hundred and Fifty Years of Medical Education* (1984); Timothy Jacobson, *Making Medical Doctors: Science and Medicine at Vanderbilt since Flexner* (1988); Kenneth M. Ludmerer, *Time to Heal: American Medical Education from the Turn of the Century to the Era of Managed Care* (1999); William W. McLendon, Floyd W. Denny Jr., and William B. Blythe, *Bettering the Health of the People: W. Reece Berryhill, the UNC School of Medicine, and the North Carolina Good Health Movement* (2007); Tennant S. McWilliams, *New Lights in the Valley: The Emergence of UAB* (2007); James Summerville, *Educating Black Doctors: A History of Meharry Medical College* (1983); Karen Kruse Thomas, *Journal of African American History* (Summer 2003).

Military Schools

For many reasons, Americans have long associated military schools with the South. None of the nation's four uniformed service academies is in the South, although Annapolis might demur. Yet popular culture loves southern military-school settings, as in the movie *Taps* (1981), Terence Fugate's 1961 novel *Drum and Bugle*, and Pat Conroy's *Lords of Discipline* (1980), which had as its thinly disguised locale his alma mater, the Citadel, in Charleston, S.C. The association may largely result from the popular perception of the South as America's Sparta, its most militaristic region. More important is British historian Marcus Cunliffe's argument that military academies have come to be regarded as a feature of "the idea of the South," whereas northern military schools are less visible in the culture. Finally, though, southerners have tended to be relatively enthusiastic in founding military schools and sending their sons to them.

The South has not been famed for its civilian preparatory schools, despite the existence of a few prominent ones. Military prep schools thrive, however, having withstood the reaction against them during the Vietnam War and despite the proliferation of private "segregation" academies in the South, which hurt military school enrollment in the same period. Although many military schools have gone coed, others are still staunch traditionalists. Alabama's Marion Military Institute is thriving; in 2006 it became state-supported and recognized as "The State Military College of Alabama." It joins Georgia Military College in

Milledgeville as one of only three or four military junior colleges in the United States. Southern military academies, such as Fishburne, Fork Union, and Hargrave in Virginia, Camden in South Carolina, Chamberlain-Hunt in Mississippi, and Riverside in Georgia continue to thrive. The Florida Air Academy in Lakeland and the Marine Military Academy in Harlingen, Tex., specialize in training for nonarmy military service. Virginia's Massanutten and Randolph-Macon academies are still military, but have coed day students. Some of the old standbys are gone, though—Mississippi's Gulf Coast Military Academy, Tennessee's Sewanee Military Academy, and Tennessee Military Institute. Georgia Military Academy became the civilian and coed Woodward Academy in 1966.

The enthusiasm for military schooling in the South began in the early 19th century, though military schools were initially a northern innovation. Capt. Alden Partridge, a member of the U.S. Military Academy's first graduating class of 1806, founded Vermont's Norwich University on the West Point model in 1819 as the nation's first private military college. He and his Norwich alumni popularized military schooling, founding private and public military academies, institutes, and colleges along West Point lines in the North and, even more prolifically, in the South.

Southerners, however, pioneered the idea of state-supported military colleges. By the time of secession every southern state either supported its own military colleges or extended state aid, including arms and accouterments, to private military schools. The federal government also provided assistance, as when the U.S. Army detailed a regular officer to teach military theory and tactics at St. John's College in Annapolis in 1824, at Norwich and Virginia Military Institute (VMI) in the 1830s, and at the University of Tennessee in 1840.

The nation's first fully state-supported military college, VMI, was founded in 1839, followed by South Carolina's two state institutions, the Citadel and the Arsenal, in 1842. These first public military colleges became better known than New England's Norwich and served as exemplars for other southern military schools. Col. Robert T. P. Allen, known affectionately to his cadets as "Rarin' Tarin' Pitchin' Allen," founded the Kentucky Military Institute (KMI) in 1845. Although it was a private school, that commonwealth's governor was designated its "inspector," and the state's adjutant general was a member of its board of visitors. It flourished until 1861, when its faculty and students marched off to war, some south and others north.

Maj. George Alexander founded the Arkansas Military Institute at Tulip in 1850, and it too flourished until its people went to war. Also in 1850, Mississippi's oldest chartered college, Jefferson, founded in 1802 near Natchez and attended by Jefferson Davis, resumed its military program earlier adopted in

1829 after the Alden Partridge plan. The state of Mississippi furnished it with muskets.

In 1851, West Pointer Arnoldus V. Brumby organized Marietta's Georgia Military Institute, which received state aid until Georgia bought it in 1857 and turned it into a state college. In Tennessee the Western Military Institute at Tyree merged with the ailing University of Nashville in 1855. Alabama provided particularly robust aid to state military education in the decade before the Civil War, extending generous support to two military academies at La Grange and Glenville and providing scholarships to two cadets from each county. Alabama also furnished arms and drill manuals to eight other military schools at various times in the decade of the 1850s and introduced compulsory military training into the University of Alabama in 1860. Texas called Col. R. T. P. Allen from KMI to found the Texas Military Institute at Bastrop. Florida provided arms to two private military academies, the West Florida Seminary and Quincy Military Academy.

At least 12,000 alumni of the antebellum South's public and private military colleges later served in the Confederate army, most of them as officers, and some of their faculty gained fame as Civil War generals. Bushrod R. Johnson, the military superintendent at the University of Nashville, became a Confederate major general. Maj. Daniel H. Hill, later a Confederate lieutenant general, opened the North Carolina Military Institute at Charlotte in 1859, and by the time Fort Sumter surrendered, 150 cadets were enrolled. Citadel cadets claim to have fired the first shots of the Civil War at Fort Sumter. In 1860 the first superintendent of the new Louisiana State Seminary of Learning and Military Academy, now LSU and still known as "the Old War Skule," was that future scourge of the South, William Tecumseh Sherman. The immortal Thomas "Stonewall" Jackson was teaching at VMI during John Brown's raid and commanded a company of cadets that stood guard over the courthouse and jail at Harpers Ferry during Brown's trial and hanging. Indeed, VMI furnished a total of 20 generals to the Confederacy, along with nearly 800 lower-ranking officers. Meanwhile, there was always a large southern representation at West Point, and many of its former cadets became Confederate leaders, the most famous being Jefferson Davis, class of 1828, and Robert E. Lee, class of 1829. The student bodies of several military schools, including VMI, the Citadel and the Arsenal, Georgia Military Institute, and the University of Alabama, served as units in the Confederate army and saw combat.

Some northerners in the Civil War era, and a few historians since, claimed that all this southern mania for military education was in fact part of the South's deliberate preparation for secession and war. It is true that much of the southern military school craze occurred in a period of growing sectional tension, and this tension occasionally provided justification for military education in the decade preceding secession. However, there were other factors at work. First, many southern parents were concerned about the unruly behavior of their sons and believed that military education would provide needed discipline and character development. Second, there seems to have been a regional consensus that militarism was easily reconciled with republicanism, that by training young men as good soldiers, educators could produce responsible, courageous, law-abiding, and self-disciplined citizens. Third, military school proponents successfully convinced state lawmakers that military schools could not only provide trained junior officers to the infamously ill-disciplined state militias, but also an affordable education to nonelite white youth. Thus, most state-supported military academies offered reduced or free tuition to cadets who agreed to teach in the state's schools for a predetermined number of years. In fact, most military school graduates never became officers in the regular army, and that was never the goal. The vast majority entered the civilian professions as teachers, engineers, or lawyers. One recent study has shown that the network of military schools and military educators in the South was a crucial element in the formation of a nascent middle class in the Old South.

After Appomattox, practically all southern military schools disappeared, except for VMI and the Citadel. However, during the Civil War, in 1862, the U.S. Congress had passed the Morrill Land Grant Act, which provided for federal land grants to fund the establishment of state agricultural and mechanical colleges that were also required to furnish military instruction. The act did not make such training mandatory, but all the white "aggie" schools of the South became military. When such colleges were founded in the defeated and impoverished South, they revived the military school tradition—at the University of Arkansas and North Georgia Agricultural College in 1871; at Auburn and the Virginia Polytechnic Institute in 1872; at Starkville, Miss., in 1878, where the first president was ex-Confederate Lt. Gen. Stephen D. Lee; at Raleigh, N.C., in 1887; at Clemson, S.C., in 1889; at the revived Louisiana State University; and above all, at Texas A&M, which by World War II had furnished more regular army officers than West Point. In addition to the land-grant institutions, some of the older state universities began to offer military instruction after the Reserve Officer Training Corps Acts of 1916 and 1920 extended ROTC to other than military institutes and land-grant colleges. At times it was compulsory, as at the universities of Mississippi and Alabama and at private colleges such as Davidson. Meanwhile, the southern military preparatory schools began reviving by the 1880s and became fashionable by the 1890s, especially in Virginia's Shenandoah Valley.

Black southerners have embraced military education as well. Hampton Institute, founded in 1868, required its male students, all African Americans and Native Americans, to join the corps of cadets and drill and wear uniforms daily. The same was true at the black land-grant colleges now known as Savannah State, South Carolina State, and Florida A&M. These last three schools were founded under the Second Morrill Act (1890), which made no mention of military training; yet leaders at these black colleges, much like white educators, wholeheartedly embraced military education as excellent preparation for responsible citizenship. Though living under military discipline, for several decades black cadets were rarely, if ever, allowed to carry rifles or actually study military tactics.

Some who argue for the existence of a peculiarly southern martial tradition suspect that it really came into its own after the Confederacy's defeat; by 1910, 90 percent of the U.S. Army's general officers had southern affiliations. Douglas MacArthur first donned a uniform at a Texas military institute; George Catlett Marshall graduated from VMI to lead the U.S. Army and Air Corps into victory in World War II; the U.S. Marine commander in the Pacific War against Japan, Holland M. "Howlin' Mad" Smith, started his martial career as an Auburn cadet; and Gen. William Westmoreland, commander of U.S. forces in Vietnam, attended the Citadel before receiving an appointment to West Point. During the Vietnam War, when public support for the military reached its nadir, military programs suffered less on southern university campuses than in any other part of America. At Chapel Hill an antiwar protest rally during the Cambodian invasion of 1970 fizzled out, and the following year enrollment applications at VMI and the Citadel rose from previous declines. ROTC programs continued to be maintained on southern civilian college campuses as well.

As the 20th century progressed, the southern land-grant colleges abandoned compulsory military education one by one, with Virginia Tech, Texas A&M, and Arkansas holding out until the 1960s. Military traditions at Virginia Tech and Texas A&M, however, remain dynamic and vibrant, as is the case with North Georgia College. Of the six military schools formerly recognized under federal law as "senior military colleges," five—VMI, the Citadel, Virginia Tech, North Georgia, and Texas A&M—are in the South (Norwich in Vermont is the sixth).

The original state military colleges, VMI and the Citadel, still retain their strict military orientation, but change has not bypassed them, either. Integration of African American cadets at VMI and the Citadel was not notably more traumatic than at other segregated southern colleges in the 1960s. Integration of female cadets in the 1990s, however, garnered national attention and proceeded only after long legal battles. In 1990 the Justice Department filed suit against VMI for its admission policy that excluded women. VMI won its case in U.S. District Court, but the Supreme Court ruled in 1996 that its all-male admissions policy was unconstitutional because it received public funds. The first female cadets matriculated at VMI in 1997. Meanwhile, the Citadel admitted its first female cadet, Shannon Faulkner, in 1995 after also having lost a lawsuit. Faulkner resigned and went home after only a few days as a "knob" (a reference to the shaved, bald heads of incoming freshmen cadets, which are said to resemble doorknobs), but four more women matriculated in 1997, two of them graduating in 1999. The transition from an all-male cadet culture has been difficult at times, but enrollment has not suffered at either school.

JOHN HAWKINS NAPIER III
Montgomery, Alabama

ROD ANDREW JR.
Clemson University

Bruce Allardice, *Civil War History* (December 1997); Rod Andrew Jr., *Long Gray Lines: The Southern Military School Tradition, 1839–1915* (2001); Laura Fairchild Brodie, *Breaking Out: VMI and the Coming of Women* (2000); James Lee Conrad, *The Young Lions: Confederate Cadets at War* (1997); Marcus Cunliffe, *Soldiers and Civilians: The Martial Spirit in America, 1775–1865* (1968); John Hope Franklin, *The Militant South: 1800–1861* (1956); Jennifer R. Green, *Military Education and the Emerging Middle Class in the Old South* (2008); Morris Janowitz, *The Professional Soldier: A Social and Political Portrait* (1960); Alexander Macaulay, *Marching in Step: Masculinity, Citizenship, and the Citadel in Post–World War II America* (2009); John Hawkins Napier III, *Alabama Historical Quarterly* (Fall–Winter 1967), *Alabama Review* (October 1980).

Political Activism among College Students

Southern college students do not have a national reputation for their political activism. Mainstream campus life has more often emphasized what writer Willie Morris once called "planned frivolity" over political involvement. Especially in predominantly white state universities, a frats-and-football subculture—at times apolitical, at times reactionary—has tended to set the tone for the campus. Nevertheless, the southern collegiate experience has never been entirely insulated from the political forces that have shaped the region and the nation. Indeed, segregation in southern higher education emerged in the mid-20th century as a central regional and national political issue. Moreover, despite the limits on political speech and corresponding self-censorship that plagued southern college campuses through much of the 20th century, beleaguered campus rebels at times emerged to challenge orthodoxies. The issues targeted by activist students in the South have ranged widely, but race relations often lay at the core when students mobilized. In the 1960s, African American collegians acting against racial subordination served as the vanguard of a southern student movement that helped reshape their own campuses, as well as regional and national politics.

When it occurred, student activism in the South grew from indigenous roots as well as broader national impulses. Thus, the first major political movement of southern college students in the 20th century—the black student revolts of the 1920s—was a manifestation of national postwar militancy among African Americans as well as a revolt against conditions and policies in the South's black colleges. Demonstrations occurred throughout the South, but the fullest flowering of this movement occurred at Fisk University in 1924 and 1925, with the active participation of W. E. B. Du Bois. In lectures as well as the pages of *The Crisis*, Du Bois opposed the restrictive policies at Fisk, including the shutting down of the student government association and newspaper and the denial of a request for a campus chapter of the National Association for the Advancement of Colored People. Student actions at Fisk and elsewhere included organized demonstrations and boycotts of classes. In a few cases, the black student revolts of the 1920s produced curricular changes and loosened the tight grip that the colleges had over the students' lives. In other cases, they resulted in the appointment of African Americans as college presidents.

The Great Depression and opposition to war helped create, during the 1930s, the largest student movement in American history before the 1960s. National student organizations such as the communist-led National Student League (NSL) and the socialist-led Student League for Industrial Democracy (SLID) occasionally ventured into the South, as in 1932 when the NSL sponsored a student delegation to the strike-torn coalfields of Harlan, Ky. Progress in the efforts to attract white southern students to this national movement was halting. Nevertheless, a small number of student radicals emerged at schools such as Tulane and Emory and the universities of Virginia and North Carolina, and the student Left found some support among religious radicals—Christian Socialists and left-leaning ministers, as well as members in the student YWCA and YMCA. The primary contribution of this handful of white southern activists was to challenge both Jim Crow and the interrelated limits on academic freedom that plagued southern higher education, as when an NSL chapter at the University of Virginia invited a prominent black socialist to speak on campus in 1934 and then publicly criticized the university for refusing to allow the speech.

Nationally, the student movement of the 1930s disintegrated with the advent of World War II, and postwar McCarthyism effectively limited student political mobilization throughout the nation and in the South, where demagogic southern politicians often conflated communism and support for civil rights for African Africans. Nevertheless, as legal decisions against segregated education increasingly focused attention on the South's dual systems of higher education, southern college students found themselves in the midst of the central domestic political question of the postwar period. The 1950s saw occasions of southern students mobilizing for and against the maintenance of segregation. In 1956 students at the University of Alabama were among those who rioted against the admission of an African American woman named Autherine Lucy, while students from Alabama State College in Montgomery and Florida A&M in Tallahassee participated in bus boycotts in those cities in the 1950s. But these examples of student political activity paled in comparison to the southern student movement that developed in 1960, when black college students throughout the South organized a movement against segregated public establishments that played a seminal role in a national student movement.

The sit-in movement began on 1 February 1960, when four students from North Carolina Agricultural and Technical College in Greensboro, N.C., sat down at the segregated Woolworth's lunch counter and refused to get up after being denied service. In the following days, other black students in Greensboro (along with a handful of white students) embraced this tactic of nonviolent direct action, and within weeks students in several other southern states, working with African American leaders in their communities, had initiated local sit-in movements targeting segregated lunch counters and other public establishments. In April a meeting in Durham, N.C., designed to coordinate these local activities, resulted in the founding of the Student Nonviolent Coordinating Committee. Student activists from Nashville, led by a 31-year-old African American graduate student at Vanderbilt University named James Lawson, were influential in drafting a founding statement that emphasized nonviolence not only as an important tactic but also as the core philosophical tenet of the new organization. Nonviolent direct action opened up a new avenue of politicization for black students throughout the South, and in 1960 and 1961 the movement enjoyed widespread support among students on black campuses, often attracting the participation not solely of campus rebels but also of traditional leaders. On some campuses—especially private institutions, which were more insulated from white, segregationist opposition—the sit-in movement took the form of a semisanctioned activity. The movement was strongest in the Upper South and larger cities in the Deep South. In public institutions, and in more repressive parts of the Deep South, the movement met with fierce and effective opposition from segregationist politicians and administrative boards. There, actual or threatened expulsions either quickly sapped the energy of local sit-in movements or prevented them from beginning at all.

The sit-in movement opened up new possibilities for political action for white students as well, though the dynamic that unfolded on predominantly white campuses was different in important respects. In some areas, small numbers of white students participated in sit-ins in the early 1960s. Their involvement generated opposition not only from conservative white students, but also at times from moderate whites who supported gradual desegregation but opposed the employment of nonviolent direct action to achieve it, arguing that such tactics produced disorder. On another major issue of the early 1960s desegregation era—continued segregation in higher education—moderate white students similarly opposed riots along the lines of the 1956 Autherine Lucy episode, though their opposition did not prevent violence involving students at the University of Georgia in 1961 and the University of Mississippi in 1962. Nevertheless, on predominantly white campuses, the political spectrum gradually expanded to make room for supporters of the civil rights movement, and these student activists began crafting an agenda that addressed not only rights for black people, but also other issues such as poverty and, especially after 1965, the war in Vietnam. The formation in 1964 of the Southern Student Organizing Committee (SSOC), a predominantly white group that embraced a number of left-liberal goals, was an indication of this broadening of the political spectrum.

Southern student politics in the second half of the 1960s revolved around three broad issues—Vietnam, Black Power, and student rights. The region's tendency toward militarism was reflected on its campuses, as prowar arguments found their voice in campus newspaper editorials and prowar organizing was visible on many campuses. For example, the South's first antiwar teach-in—held at Emory University in October 1965—was followed by a prowar rally, also organized in part by Emory students at Atlanta Stadium, that attracted more than 15,000 people. Nevertheless, an antiwar movement grew among southern college students. Regional and national organizations—SSOC and Students for a Democratic Society chief among them—provided some organization and intellectual rationale for the antiwar movement in the South. Usually, however, students organized around on-campus manifestations of the war, such as the presence of an ROTC program, recruitment by the military or its contractors, or military research on campus. By the late 1960s, antiwar demonstrations drawing participants in the hundreds, while not necessarily routine, were at least evident, even on Deep South campuses where little civil rights activity had been apparent in the early part of the decade.

Antiwar sentiment also was evident on the South's historically black campuses, but for black students in the South, Vietnam was often subsumed into the larger issue of Black Power and its application to higher education. The term "Black Power" came into common parlance in 1966 and generally reflected a rejection of nonviolence and racial integration in favor of advocating that African Americans take control of their own institutions and lives. Black Power sought to explore and celebrate the culture and history of African Americans while emphasizing cultural and political ties to Africa. In the South's approximately 100 historically black colleges and universities, Black Power was often manifested in trenchant criticisms of campus governance and curricula. The most radical student activists called for the region's Negro colleges to be transformed into "instruments of black liberation," and activist agendas generally combined calls for more student power and freedom on campus with calls for more curricular focus on the African American experience. Black Power was also evident on predominantly white campuses, where students called for full-fledged academic citizenship, including greater curricular attention to African American issues and more administrative attention to black students' needs. Demonstrations on historically black campuses were among the most explosive of the 1960s, meeting at times with violent resistance from police officers and state troopers. Protests at Texas Southern University in 1967, South Carolina State in 1968, North Carolina A&T in 1969, and Jackson State College in 1970 resulted in the deaths of students.

Whether protesting Vietnam or racism, the proximate issue for southern student activists in the late 1960s usually related in some way to the campus. At historically black and predominantly white schools alike, late-decade demands usually included calls for the end of parietal rules and curfews governing the nonacademic lives of students, greater involvement of students in the campus decision-making process, and changes in the curriculum to make coursework more relevant. Civil libertarian issues, including censorship of campus publications and regulations restricting the kinds of speakers who could visit campus, generated significant demonstrations at a number of schools, including the University of North Carolina at Chapel Hill, which in 1966 saw a dramatic challenge to a state law forbidding known communists or "fellow travelers" from speaking in state-supported schools. In addressing campus-related issues, the 1960s southern student movement perhaps achieved its most visible successes. As was true nationally, institutions in the South eliminated curfews (often applied more restrictively to women), appointed student representatives to campus governing bodies, and revised curricula to offer students more freedom of choice.

But perhaps the most significant accomplishment of the 1960s southern student movement, which was, on the whole, less radical and militant than its counterparts on more famous campuses on the two coasts and in the Midwest, was the opening to dissent on campuses where something akin to W. J. Cash's "savage ideal" (a violent intimidation of unorthodox ideas) had exercised enormous power. Thus, even as the southern student movement, like its national counterpart, dissipated in the early 1970s, pockets of activism continued to exist, which made it possible for southern students to play a part in subsequent national student movements. In the 1980s, for example, students in some southern institutions joined in demonstrations calling for universities to divest from financial interests in South Africa, still under apartheid. And in the late 1990s, southern students participated in a nationwide movement focusing on labor conditions in factories that produced apparel emblazoned with college and university logos. In neither case did these movements resemble their 1960s counterparts in breadth of participation, but these limits existed (sometimes to a lesser extent) in institutions outside the South as well. Campus rebels were now an accepted element of the student culture.

JEFFREY A. TURNER
St. Catherine's School, Richmond, Virginia

William J. Billingsley, *Communists on Campus: Race, Politics, and the Public University in Sixties North Carolina* (1999); Clayborne Carson, *In Struggle: SNCC and the Black Awakening of the 1960s* (1981); E. Culpepper Clark, *The Schoolhouse Door: Segregation's Last Stand at the University of Alabama* (1995); Robert Cohen, *When the Old Left Was Young: Student Radicals and America's First Mass Student Movement, 1929–1941* (1993); Gregg L. Michel, *Struggle for a Better South: The Southern Student Organizing Committee, 1964–1969* (2004); Robert Pratt, *We Shall Not Be Moved: The Desegregation of the University of Georgia* (2005); Doug Rossinow, *The Politics of Authenticity: Liberalism, Christianity, and the New Left in America* (1998); Joy Ann Williamson, *Radicalizing the Ebony Tower: Black Colleges and the Black Freedom Struggle in Mississippi* (2008); Raymond Wolters, *The New Negro on Campus: Black College Rebellions of the 1920s* (1975).

Politics of Education

In the years following the American Revolution, the young nation's leaders set about constructing a new vision for their infant nation. This new vision, of which education formed an integral part, helped define America. The Northwest Ordinance of 1787 gave primacy to education in the nation's infrastructure. It ensured the free exercise of religion, legislative representation, and the right to a jury trial while also prohibiting slavery. Along with morality and religion, education became central to the expansion of American freedom as defined by the nation's founders, many of whom hailed from the South. None other than Thomas Jefferson himself asserted, "It is absolutely necessary that knowledge of every kind should be disseminated through every part of the United States." In short, no nation could remain ignorant and maintain its freedom. The founders did not merely hold education in high esteem, they saw it as a means of cultural transmission and regeneration. If anything, the American Revolution was a literate revolt that implicitly enhanced the necessity of education.

In the century following the establishment of the new America, the nation saw the construction and dissemination of the American educational ideology, which took on local idiosyncrasies from region to region. In the South, it defended and even called for the expansion of slavery. It also fell under suspicion in the antebellum years by plain folk and poor farmers who questioned its value to everyday society. Plain folk saw little need for education, since it added seemingly little to everyday life and often produced arrogance and elitism. Southern elites, however, supported private institutions, or academies, or paid for private tutors in their homes. The early southern frontier, then, was a place where education, while held as an admirable goal by southern elites, had yet to permeate the minds of everyday southerners as a fruitful enterprise worthy of support. If school growth in the South lagged far behind that of the rest of the nation, it was steady. The South had 18,222 schools (public and private) in 1850, 20 percent of the national total of 87,257. By 1870, that figure had grown to 22,786 schools in the South, although the region's share of the nation's schools fell to 16 percent.

Reconstruction governments, dominated by newly registered freedmen and white Republicans, initiated a new direction in schooling in the South. The "Radical Republican" governments in the South increased school funding, established free public schooling, and raised the rate at which property was taxed in the South. An increase in the number of children attending schools soon followed, although schools remained segregated, and many southern children remain unschooled in the postwar period. But Reconstruction governments, in their greater attention to social needs, raised questions about the role of government with regard to schooling and social policy writ large, which Redemption governments, led by more conservative politicians, had to address when they returned to power after the end of Reconstruction.

The answer to such questions from the Redemption governments was to turn the state's attention away from the people and toward businesses, as revealed in redeemer tax policies and the redeemer's neglect of social issues facing southerners. To attract business, industry, and northern investment to the prostrate southern landscape, Redeemers lowered taxes on businesses, if they taxed them at all. State tax collections across the South fell precipitously, and the new order in the South had begun, one in which low taxes, disregard for social ills, and neglect of southern children would become the rule rather than the exception for the next 130 years. The establishment of segregation created additional school funding costs and divided already meager funds among black and white schools. Of course, having segregated schools was at once a cost burden and a cost-cutting tool, as white-dominated governments reduced funding for black schools as a way of keeping costs manageable. By 1900, the southern states with the highest per-pupil funding were Florida and Texas (only because they had fewer schools than other southern states), with around $1.46 per student compared to the national average of more than $8.00. The most southern schools could strive for in this environment was to stave off any increase in illiteracy, but surely not provide a full and free public education for the region.

Progressivism served as an able foe for redeemer political economy. By the early 1900s progressive southern educators, such as Walter Hines Page, Charles Dabney, and John Kilgo, pursued education reform through alliances with northern-based philanthropic groups and sympathetic southern governors. It was in this era that most southern states established fully operational statewide school systems. Of course this progressivism was carried out within the racial structure of the day, which included segregating schools by race and funding white schools at a much greater rate than black schools. The establishment of the Southern Education Board provided southern progressives with a tool for stimulating widespread interest in universal public education. Even within these social and racial strictures southern education progressed, including a decline in illiteracy rates, an increase in school attendance, and the emergence of educational reform and performance as a political issue. Also on the rise during this period was the southern university system. While each southern state had a college or two in the antebellum years, the roots of the modern southern university system were laid in the Progressive years. The flaw in the Progressive reform movement, at least in the South, was its paternalism, which southern poor whites resisted. Middle-class progressives tried to instruct poor whites how to be middle class, with no understanding or empathy for plain-folk life in the South. Thus, reforms during the era reflected the interests of and most benefited those in power who enacted them.

Educational "reform" continued in the pre–World War II years, and reform meant that funding saw a modest increase, more children received free text-books (in some states), teacher qualifications improved slightly, and the higher-education system grew incrementally. But training of public school teachers remained meager at best. Few teachers emerged from the South's colleges pre-pared to teach anything but the most basic of subjects, and many of them had little more understanding of or training in such subjects than their students possessed. In 1915, 70 percent of black teachers had little more than six years of elementary education, with the training for white teachers faring little better. If the quality of teacher preparation lagged behind other regions, the South did see solid growth in the quality and number of its universities, both public and private. Yet as remarkable as it was, this growth paled when compared to that of northern universities. For example, Idus Newby found that in 1927 "Harvard University spent more money for library books than the eleven state universi-ties of the Confederate South together, though the Harvard libraries already contained more volumes than the combined libraries of those universities." The region neither understood nor appreciated the role and purpose of universities, an attitude that prevails in the South in modern times. The Scopes "Monkey Trial" of 1925 illustrated a region at odds with itself, and with modernity, and served notice of a persistent sense of what Newby calls "intellectual confor-mity" that has plagued the course of higher educational history in the South ever since.

Between 1870 and 1940 America's population tripled, and school enrollment followed pace. Following World War II, education became more accessible as enrollments soared. Though the number of schools had greatly expanded through the first half of the century, one element of public education had not: federal funding. Federal assistance for schools had been proposed as early as the 1870s, but consistently had failed to pass for fears of government intrusion into states' rights. Only in times of national crisis did Americans consider ap-proval of federal monies for public schools. The issue came up during World War I when it was discovered that many draftees could not read. During the Depression, federal funds were proposed to ease the rash of closed schools and laid-off teachers. And after World War II a crisis in local education funding brought about another round of proposals for federal funding, all to no avail. It was not until 1957, when the Soviet Union successfully launched the Sputnik orbiter and America faced a crisis of the Cold War, that federal funding came.

The National Defense Education Act of 1958 injected massive amounts of federal money for grants, fellowships, and loans to foster the study of science, math, and foreign languages in an attempt to "catch up" educationally to the Soviet Union. The money also funded a massive increase in school construction.

But not all Americans enjoyed the same opportunities. Dominated by Jim Crow segregation, the South provided for dual economies, societies, and educational systems. Founded upon the principle of separate but equal, such dual systems were anything but equal. Southern white public schools received more money and had longer sessions, better-paid teachers, and better facilities than did black schools. In South Carolina in 1945 the number of black and white students in schools was nearly the same, but the state spent three times as much on white students as it did on black students. It also spent one hundredth of the money on busing black kids that it did on busing white kids to school. Mississippi acted similarly. In 1945 the state spent 4.5 times as much on white children.

It was a sad condition: black schools lagged far behind white schools in the South, as the white schools lagged far behind northern schools. In 1930, for every seven dollars spent on white school children in the South, two dollars went to black children. The effects of separate schools were easy to see. In 1940, 25 percent of southern whites had a high school diploma. Only 5 percent of blacks in the region had reached that level. In many ways, such ill-funded and ill-equipped black schools fit perfectly into the white-defined southern experience. Most southern whites discouraged blacks from doing or learning anything but a basic vocation and the etiquette of race. It was this condition that the NAACP sought to correct when it took on the *Brown v. Board of Education* case.

The U.S. Supreme Court's decision in *Brown* not only served as the death knell for racially split school systems and for segregation in the South, but also as a siren call for a new phase in the politics of race. If *Brown* was the vehicle used to create political change and social redemption in the South, and later in the rest of the nation, it also revealed how ambivalent education reformers had been about race in the past. The great education reform movements of the late 1890s and early twentieth century did little to address the racial situation in the South, or the rest of the nation for that matter. The fact that African Americans aggressively pursued an end to separate-but-equal schools reveals just how crucial education had become to the American mind in the pursuit of equality of opportunity and the promise of America.

If extremely slow, the dismantling of segregated schools followed a snail's pace because of the rise of massive social and political resistance in the South. Even before *Brown*, southerners had prepared for the day when their dual school systems might end. Leading the opposition were the White Citizens' Councils, first formed in Indianola, Miss. The councils planned to rid the South of "liberal" books and teachers and to prevent racial mixing. Soon after *Brown*, 101 southern congressmen signed the Southern Manifesto, pledging their determination to fight integration and to overturn *Brown*. Southern governors dusted off John C. Calhoun's principle of interposition, which held that states could nullify a federal law that stood in contradiction to their states' rights. Even religious leaders weighed in on the issue. A young minister from Virginia, Jerry Falwell, said that "if Chief Justice Warren and his associates had known God's word, I am confident that the . . . decision would never have been made." If blacks saw hope in *Brown*, they also saw a white South more determined than ever to prevent that hope from becoming a reality.

And it was in this era of desegregation and integration, of forced busing, and of the rise of antibusing, anti-integration leaders, such as Alabama governor George Wallace and Georgia lieutenant governor Lester Maddox, that the region underwent its greatest change. Massive resistance to integration turned into violent outbreaks against African Americans protesting for change and reform, which, in turn, led to the very thing that many southern whites had massively resisted: full voting rights and full integration of African Americans into the fabric of southern society, especially in education. This sea change in the southern racial order transcended schools and buses.

For a brief period, during the 1970s, the South came under the influence of a series of moderate governors, who were elected by educated, progressive, middle-class white voters and newly registered black voters. Reubin Askew, John C. West, Linwood Holton, Dale Bumpers, and James Holshouser led the class of "New South" governors who made education and education reform a central part of their administrations. During their terms, integration was completed (a highly debatable term) by 1972 and they turned their attention to the problem vexing most southern school systems today: funding. While federal district courts answered questions of school desegregation and integration, southern governors addressed funding these newly unified schools. The solution has been difficult to find, or to implement, for decades.

The problem for southern schools has long been the tax base on which they are supported. Combined with the codification of redeemer policies (at least in the political will of the southern statehouse), the overreliance of this tax base on highly volatile levies on consumption and property, which can ebb and flow in times of financial downturn, means that the South faces a great threat to education. But the solution to such issues often requires more political courage and selflessness than politicians and their constituents are willing to give. Several New South governors in the 1970s attempted to reform their states' tax structures with special attention to property taxation and assessment, but Redeemer policies, established by Redeemer governments a century before, were resilient as business and industrial interests and complicit legislators deflected any type of reform and defended the low tax base in the South, which, in turn, preserved educational mediocrity. The South today remains in a similar condition to that of the antebellum South: individualistic, available to only those who can afford it, whether that be in hiring private tutors in the home or establishing tuition-based academies. Education in the modern South has not moved far from that model, although more southern children have greater opportunity to attend school than ever before. When one examines funding disparity from county to county and from state to state, the pattern that was found in the antebellum South remains: those more affluent southern counties are better able to afford a stronger and more rounded education than their less affluent neighbors. In this sense, a wealthy elite, more white than black, are perpetuated in their affluence and education, while poorer whites and blacks fall farther behind.

GORDON E. HARVEY
Jacksonville State University

Thomas P. Abernathy, *The South in the New Nation, 1789–1819* (1961); Lawrence Cremin, *American Education: The National Experience, 1783–1876* (1980); Dewey Grantham, *Southern Progressivism: The Reconciliation of Progress and Tradition* (1983); Fletcher M. Green, *Democracy in the Old South, and Other Essays*, ed. J. Isaac Copeland (1969); Gordon Harvey, *A Question of Justice: New South Governors and Education, 1968–1976* (2002); Robert A. Margo, *Race and Schooling in the South, 1880–1950: An Economic History* (1990); I. A. Newby, *The South: A History*, (1978); George B. Tindall, *Emergence of the New South: 1913–1945* (1967).

Progressivism and Higher Education in the New South

Generally seen as a footnote in the tempestuous chronicle of the region after the Civil War, the history of higher education is now finding a more prominent place in the study of the New South. Recent research suggests that the chronically underfunded southern college provided a surprisingly vibrant microcosm of the cultural forces reorienting the postwar South. This research also suggests that southern universities contributed decisively to what would become the region's distinctive Progressive movement. Although students and faculty would indelibly shape the southern college, a new generation of reformers would singularly influence the direction those institutions would take in the new century. And while private colleges would spawn more than one intellectual renegade, the progressive impulse was most conspicuously manifest at the region's public universities.

Coming of age in the post-Reconstruction South, educational leaders at public colleges from Alabama to Virginia championed the values of the industrializing New South. Members of a fledgling middle class emerging in the urban South, these young reformers developed a critical temperament that set them apart from their antebellum predecessors. Instead of the ministry and politics, young professionals like Samuel Chiles Mitchell and Charles D. McIver turned to education as a vehicle of individual mobility and social reform. Often educated at northern universities and exposed to the intellectual currents then fostering a transatlantic progressive impulse, they found the provincialism of the South stifling and longed to bring the region into the coursing flow of modern development. That determination framed their vision of a system of higher education that would liberate the region from its economic disadvantages, procrustean politics, and cultural blight.

University progressives derived their ideas in large part from the New South Creed, the cause célèbre of journalists such as Henry Grady and Richard Edmonds in the 1880s. Grady and other boosters imagined that industrialization, agricultural diversification, and sectional harmony would liberate the South from its past and foster economic development. The South would overcome the legacy of slavery and the Civil War by modernizing and accommodating the North, albeit on southern terms. This transformation meant preserving existing racial hierarchies and paying homage to the Lost Cause.

Abiding by the creed's injunction to promote intersectional cooperation, southern reformers such as Edwin Alderman and Charles D. McIver actively cultivated links to northern philanthropists. Following the inauguration of the Conference for Education in the South in 1898, southern reformers joined northern business leader Robert Ogden to launch the Southern Education Board in 1902. The board became a coordinating agency for state-level education campaigns and a conduit of northern influence in the education movement. Most importantly, it provided a vehicle for southern progressives to disseminate their vision of social uplift through rational, modernized education.

At the head of state universities, they fostered the ideas of business efficiency and bureaucratic governance that gradually transformed the urban South in the 20th century. While no southern university came close to replicating the modernizing changes evident at northern schools, the impulse to streamline administration, professionalize instruction, and advance the agenda of academic specialization was abundantly evident in the early 20th century. Propelled by the region's economic woes and their own disdain for the classical instruction of the antebellum college, leaders of higher education promoted a utilitarian vision of university pedagogy that challenged the idea of the university as a sanctuary of liberal culture.

That vision of modernization through positivistic reform shaped the progressives' agenda of university extension and influenced the graduates who filled the South's new middle class. From the 1880s onward, southern progressive educators reached beyond their campuses, promoting programs of external outreach and social improvement. Reformist educators collaborated with progressives outside of higher education to promote better roads, public utilities, sanitariums, and improved elementary and secondary schools. They advocated for assistance to local chambers of commerce, YMCAs, state boards of health, agricultural experiment stations, and urban planning initiatives. Advocating for public funding, Chancellor Walter Barnard Hill of the University of Georgia invoked the image of the university as a public servant. Trained experts would help state and local governments to "adjust wisely their system of taxation, to solve municipal problems, and to improve the conditions of their penal institutions, reformatories, asylums, almshouses, tenement houses, and so forth. It is the function of the university to investigate," Hill argued.

University leaders dominated the southern education movement, the leading edge of Progressive reform in the region. Charles McIver of the North Carolina Normal and Industrial School for Women, Edwin Alderman, president of the University of Virginia, Charles Dabney, president of the University of Tennessee, and Hollis B. Frissell of the Hampton Institute were all original members of the Southern Education Board. Walter Barnard Hill of the University of Georgia and Samuel Chiles Mitchell of the University of South Carolina would eventually join them. Alderman, Mitchell, Hill, Dabney, and Edward Kidder Graham of the University of North Carolina actively supported educational reforms in their states. Coordinating elementary and secondary instruction and accrediting high schools were their highest priorities. George Winston of the University of Texas, Thomas D. Boyd of Louisiana State University, Robert B. Fulton of the University of Mississippi, and George Denny of the University of Alabama struggled to make the state university the arbiter of educational standards in their states.

The University of Tennessee's Summer School of the South embodied the pragmatic, service-oriented ethos that permeated the public college in the early-20th-century South. The school's leading advocate claimed that it would coordinate the "interests and forces of the whole movement for which the General and Southern Education Boards" stood. Yet it would also teach courses in sociology, economics, horticulture, and physiology, all in the interest of training teachers to "translate material appliances over into more abundant life and power and social efficiency." In their "Declaration of Principles," participants in the 1903 session announced that the "lines in the South must be both agricultural and mechanical: Our people must bring a trained brain and a trained hand to the daily labor. Education should be a means not of escaping labor, but of making it more effective."

The Summer School of the South exemplified the progressives' belief that education should be practical, socially beneficial, and hospitable to the interests of business. As Alderman explained, "Southern universities and colleges must do the work of social regenerative forces, reaching out directly into the life of the people, making known how much better light is than darkness, and how sweet it is for the eyes to behold the sun—ennobling the poor man's poverty and spiritualizing the rich man's gold." This drive to "ennoble" impoverished southerners would also dissuade them from being enticed by social movements like Populism, a source of considerable vexation for middle-class reformers. Troubled by the specter of class upheaval and racial conflagration in the 1890s, progressives promoted controlled modernization.

This commitment to education as a vehicle of social uplift was inextricably linked to a vision of ameliorating southern backwardness. Educational activists joined health reformers, municipal government critics, anti-child-labor activists, and railroad regulation proponents in an assault of southern stagnation. These "social efficiency" reformers, as historian William Link describes them, sought to eradicate southern isolation, illiteracy, and irrationality through expert leadership and rational governance. Educators led the way in the 1890s, organizing a region-wide campaign to improve rural schools and rationalize the educational system. Southern school reformers built on the contributions of northern philanthropists to black education during the Reconstruction period. The George Peabody Education Fund and the John F. Slater Fund had played a key role in establishing black colleges and grade schools.

Progressive educators simultaneously promoted change and accommodation to the social and political hierarchies of the New South. While they supported institutions of higher education for white women, most southern reformers promoted a brand of education that would not threaten male dominance. Male progressives preferred "coordinate" colleges, where women's institutions shared the resources of all-male universities but remained separate, to coeducation. Publicly funded women's colleges were operating in Mississippi, South Carolina, Georgia, North Carolina, Alabama, Texas, and Oklahoma by

1910. These state normal and industrial colleges emphasized the "domestic arts" and the training of teachers for an expanding school system. They also absorbed the progressive commitment to scientific agriculture that was institutionalized through federal legislation providing for the teaching of farming and domestic skills in the elementary schools.

Male administrators might have imagined that the vocational curriculum would preserve women's subordination, but female students considered it an instrument of self-actualization. The programs were so popular that even private women's colleges started adding technical and cultural studies to their traditional curricula. Moreover, reformers such as Charles D. McIver and P. P. Claxton of the University of Tennessee did espouse an ethic of social service to female college students, many of whom subsequently joined the crusade for southern educational reform. Women not only joined local campaigns for school improvement, but they also led them. For reformers like Elizabeth Avery Colton, a faculty member at Meredith College, responding to the progressive impulse meant working to improve the quality of women's higher education.

For all of the upward thrust of progressive rhetoric, reformers like Alderman and McIver had little interest in dismantling the Southern Lady's pedestal. What the Progressive movement did do, however, was improve the quality of the women's colleges, inadvertently cultivate a new generation of women educators who would expand the range of the separate sphere, and create opportunities for white women to gain experience and confidence in public life.

Progressives applied the same model of limited reform to African American education. While they championed education for social improvement, they carefully delineated the *kind* of education that would benefit whites and blacks. In so doing, they implicitly suggested the *degree* of social improvement that each race should achieve. Quite simply, white university progressives articulated a vision of education that simultaneously promoted economic modernization, class stratification, and black subordination. If white southerners were to be trained as both technical experts and skilled workers, African Americans would become more efficient agricultural laborers. Education would not, they insisted, deprive white planters of a landless and exploitable working class. White educators used the prestige of their institutions and the social prominence of their positions to advance the case for the Tuskegee-Hampton model of industrial education for blacks. They functioned as apologists for segregation and as conduits of donations from northern philanthropists. Those donations may have seemed "dangerous" to racial conservatives, but southern university progressives did everything in their power to channel them into institutions that reinforced racial control in an era of destabilizing economic change.

Southern educational progressives did more than mirror the larger movement transforming the South. Functioning as its intellectuals, promoters, and agents, they irrevocably linked the southern public university to its achievements and its many shortcomings.

MICHAEL DENNIS
Acadia University

Eric Anderson and Alfred A. Moss, *Dangerous Donations: Northern Philanthropy and Southern Black Education, 1902–1930* (1999); Michael Dennis, *Lessons in Progress: State Universities and Progressivism in the New South, 1880–1920* (2001); Dan R. Frost, *Thinking Confederates: Academia and the Idea of Progress in the New South* (2000); William Link, *The Paradox of Southern Progressivism, 1880–1930* (1992); Amy Thompson McCandless, *The Past in the Present: Women's Higher Education in the Twentieth-Century American South* (1999); Rebecca S. Montgomery, *The Politics of Education in the New South: Women and Reform in Georgia, 1890–1930* (2006); John R. Thelin, *A History of American Higher Education* (2004).

Quality of Education

Educational quality is a broad, complex concept characterized by various definitions and changing expectations over time. Traditional indicators of quality include the inputs of education (e.g., expenditures per pupil, qualifications of faculty, school characteristics) and system-level outcomes (e.g., high school dropouts and graduates). Newer definitions focus on the outcomes of the educational experience, specifically student-learning outcomes. Newer measurements include student achievement on standardized tests, performance of schools in yearly progress reports, and analyses of trends in college enrollment, retention, and graduation rates. Unfortunately, these data are often used to make comparisons of educational achievement within states, across states, by regions, and across countries, without consideration of the contextual differences that are strongly correlated with educational success.

At the turn of the 21st century, the southern region, as defined by the U.S. Census Bureau (which includes Texas, Oklahoma, Arkansas, Louisiana, Mississippi, Tennessee, Alabama, Kentucky, Georgia, Florida, South Carolina, North Carolina, Virginia, West Virginia, Delaware, and Maryland), claimed 36 percent of the U.S. population and led the nation in numerical growth, adding 14.8 million between 1990 and 2000 to become the nation's largest region at 100.2 million persons. The region not only grew during the last half of the 20th century, but the educational progress across the South increasingly mirrored the rest of the nation. In 1956 the SREB *Fact Book on Higher Education* reported that the southern region comprised 30 percent of the U.S. population, yet only 5 percent held bachelor's degrees. In 2000 the number of southerners 25 and older holding bachelor's degrees or above reached 22.5 percent, only slightly less than the national average of 24.4 percent. In 2000 the number of persons in the South enrolled in school, from nursery school through graduate or professional programs, totaled 26.5 million, the nation's largest enrollment. The large population growth in the South is not without challenges, however, as schools and colleges struggle to serve an enlarging and diverse student population. In 2008, Hispanics represented 15.0 percent of the population in the South as compared to 15.7 percent across the U.S.; blacks continued to be the largest minority population at 19.8 percent (as compared to 13.5 percent nationally). In every Southern Regional Education Board (SREB) state, nonwhite students were increasing their share of the school population, and by 2006 minority students were the majority in Florida, Georgia, Maryland, Mississippi, and Texas. Coupled with the increased demand for education in the South is the high level of poverty: 42.9 percent of the 51.9 million nationally who reside in poverty areas (places with rates of 20 percent or more poverty) live in the southern region. In 2006, 53 percent of students in public schools in the South received free or reduced-price lunches, with ranges from 70 percent in Mississippi to 33 percent in Virginia.

Not surprising, the region continues to lag behind the rest of the nation in per capita personal income (PCPI). In 2009, according to the Bureau of Economic Analysis, six southern states (West Virginia, Arkansas, South Carolina, Alabama, Kentucky, and Mississippi) were in the bottom quintile of PCPI, with Mississippi ranked 50th in both 1998 and 2008. The demographics of the South point to difficult challenges for educational progress, as minority students and students in poverty historically perform less well on standardized exams and are less likely to complete school and to enroll in college—primary indicators of educational quality across school systems and states.

In 2002 the SREB adopted 12 "Challenge to Lead" goals that set standards for student and institutional achievement. Subsequently, the southern states embraced the connection between school readiness and school success, and the region now leads the nation in providing access to state-funded prekindergarten for four year olds: 7 of the top 10 states nationally (in percent of four year olds served) are in the South. Access and quality, however, are not perfectly aligned, and many states fall short on quality in preschool education, as measured by the National Institute for Early Education Research. Impressively, North Carolina and Alabama hold the distinction nationally in meeting all 10 benchmarks for quality, while Florida and Texas each meet only 4 standards.

The impact of these two states on preschool education, however, can be seen in the absolute numbers: together, Florida and Texas serve approximately 328,000 preschoolers, 29 percent of those served in all states.

In 1969 the National Assessment of Educational Progress, administered by the U.S. State Department, began assessing the educational achievements of elementary and secondary students nationwide and reporting the findings in the *Nation's Report Card*. In the 1989 edition of the *Encyclopedia of Southern Culture*, Cameron Fincher noted, "Despite noticeable gains by students in the South, National Assessment findings tell an old and embarrassing story of educational deficits. A large proportion of public school students do not meet national expectations in basic learning skills or educational achievement." Since 1992 the percentage of fourth-grade students in the South who scored at or above the National Assessment of Educational Progress (NAEP) basic levels in reading and mathematics rose substantially and now closely matches the national average, yet the percentage of fourth graders in the SREB states at the proficient level in reading and math falls well below the national percentages. Nevertheless, between 2005 and 2007 many SREB states were successful in narrowing the performance gap between minority students and majority students, although achievement overall continues to lag behind white students in reading and mathematics. The relationship between poverty and educational performance is pronounced: fourth-grade students from low-income families across the South performed at the lowest levels on the NAEP assessments; it is small comfort that the gaps between low-income children and all other children on these assessments were smallest in the South.

Educational attainment in the middle school (eighth grade) is less promising. The 2009 SREB report *Keeping Middle Grades Students on the Path to Success in High School* states that "the SREB states have stalled in eighth-grade NAEP reading achievement for nearly a decade, and they have made little progress in eighth-grade NAEP math achievement." Variations within and across the states, however, are pronounced: three southern states (Delaware, Maryland, and Virginia) had a greater percentage of students scoring at the proficient level in reading than the average at the national level.

Large gains in high school graduation rates were achieved in the last half of the 20th century, when the number of high school graduates nationally grew from one in four in 1940 to four in five in 2000, and those with bachelor's degrees grew from one in twenty to one in four, respectively. The South mirrored this progress; yet, in the 2000 census the South continued to lead the nation in the percentage of high school dropouts (11.4 percent). Overall, in 2006 students living in low-income families were shown to be about 4.5 times more likely to drop out of grades 9–12 in a given year than peers from high-income families (9.0 percent vs. 2.0 percent). Yet, nationwide, between 1990 and 2000 considerable progress was made in lowering the percentage of 16 to 19 year olds not enrolled in high school from all racial and ethnic groups (e.g., from 10 percent to 8.25 percent for whites, 13.7 percent to 11.7 percent for blacks, and 21.8 percent to 21.1 percent for Hispanics). The lower retention rates among blacks and Hispanics, however, are particularly problematic in the South, which has a large and growing minority population.

The greatest improvement in southern high schools may be seen in the Advanced Placement (AP) exams. Between 2003 and 2008 all 16 states increased the percentage of seniors passing at least one AP exam, while five states exceeded the national average: Florida, Georgia, Maryland, North Carolina, and Virginia. Across the South, improvement in participation and success in AP exams was significant among Hispanic students: every state except one increased the percentage of Hispanic seniors who passed at least one AP exam.

In 2006 the South and the nation were at parity in the percentage of recent high school graduates who enrolled in college, at 61 percent, with 11 SREB states above the national average in college enrollment. The South made great strides over the decade in increasing the diversity of the college population. Although participation gaps remain, between 1997 and 2007 black student enrollment in the southern region rose by 49 percent, to 1.1 million students, and Hispanic enrollment grew to 611,900, a 72 percent increase. In 2007 the southern states comprised one third of the college enrollment nationwide.

In comparing the number of persons 25 and older with a high school diploma, several southern states were close to the national average. Nevertheless, in 2000 only four southern states (Delaware, Maryland, Oklahoma, and Virginia) exceeded the national average of 80.4 percent. Mississippi, at 73 percent, had the lowest percentage.

In 2007 approximately 27 percent of white southerners held a bachelor's degree or higher in comparison to 16 percent of black and 14 percent of Hispanic southerners. The importance of a college degree as a public good cannot be overstated. College graduates earn more money over a lifetime (and thus pay more taxes), and they serve their communities in important leadership positions in corporate, educational, nonprofit, and governmental positions. The region is home to a large number of prestigious research institutions, including such leading private universities as Duke, Johns Hopkins, Vanderbilt, Rice, Howard, and Emory, and leading public institutions such as the University of

Virginia, the University of North Carolina at Chapel Hill (first to hold classes in 1795), Georgia Institute of Technology, the University of Texas (Austin), and the University of Georgia (first chartered in 1785).

In conclusion, at the turn of the 21st century, educational progress was evident across all U.S. regions, and the South continued to make steady advances in achievement across all educational levels. It is important to note that selected comparisons show educational differences within states are often more pronounced than differences across states. Accordingly, the challenge to improve quality in the future will be to construct educational experiences within contexts that enhance the experience and probability of success in impoverished areas, by students in low-income families, and for minority and other first-generation students to bring these populations to parity. Importantly, the South made productive steps in education over the last two decades, and a rigorous focus on benchmarking educational activities, inputs, and outcomes will provide guideposts for continuing that progress into the next decade.

LIBBY MORRIS
University of Georgia

Steve Barnett, Dale Epstein, Allison Friedman, Judi Stevenson Boyd, and Jason Hustedt, *The State of Preschool, 2008* (2008); Kurt Bauman and Nikki Graf, *Educational Attainment: 2000* (2003); Alemayehu Bishaw, *Areas with Concentrated Poverty: 1999* (2005); Emily Forrest Cataldi, Jennifer Laird, and Angelina Kewal Ramani, *High School Dropout and Completion Rates in the United States: 2007* (2009); Jennifer Chesseman Day with Amie Jamieson, *School Enrollment: 2000* (2003); Crystal Collins, *SREB States Maintain Lead in Advanced Placement and International Baccalaureate Programs* (2009); Crystal Collins and Marilyn Thomas, *Set for Success: Improving Reading and Mathematics Achievement in the Early Grades* (2008); Frank Hobbs and Nicole Stoops, *Demographic Trends in the 20th Century* (2002); Jennifer Laird, Angelina Kewal Ramani, and Chris Chapman, *Dropout and Completion Rates in the United States: 2006* (2008); Marc J. Perry and Paul J. Mackun with Josephine D. Baker, Colleen D. Joyce, Lisa R. Lollock, and Lucinda S. Pearson, *Population Change and Distribution: 1990 to 2000* (2001); Marilyn Thomas and Crystal Collins, *Keeping Middle Grades Students on the Path to Success in High School* (2009); Marilyn Thomas and Joan Lord, *Ready to Start: Ensuring High-Quality Prekindergarten in SREB States* (2007).

Religion and Education

Religious institutions and individuals have used education to influence southern culture. Churches have established denominational schools and colleges, interdenominational academies, and theology schools. They have conducted weekly Sunday schools and Vacation Bible School classes every summer. All of these institutions have communicated the specific teachings and ways of their individual denominations, but they have typically also been standard-bearers of southern regional ways as well. They reflected the dominant evangelical approach of the region's numerically and culturally dominant Protestant groups. The ties between religion, education, and the broader culture were especially apparent in the role of religion in the public schools.

The Anglican Church established the College of William and Mary in 1693, and it remained the only religious college in the South until well into the 18th century. Religious groups in the colonial period trained ministers through apprenticeship programs. The number of denominational colleges, many of which also had theology schools, increased markedly in the late 1700s and early 1800s. Roman Catholics established the South's first school of theology—St. Mary's in 1791 in Maryland. By the early 1800s Catholics operated seminaries in Charleston, St. Louis, New Orleans, and Bardstown, Ky.

After the Great Revival at the turn of the 19th century, evangelical churches—especially the Baptists, Methodists, and Presbyterians—became increasingly prominent in the South and established their own schools. Many congregations and worshipers believed that education was less important than "the call" to the ministry, and many southerners since then have been suspicious of formally trained clergy, favoring religious zeal as the prime criterion for a successful preacher. Nonetheless, the southern churches have not been so anti-intellectual that they did not support educational institutions.

Presbyterians have a long tradition of supporting education, and this was reflected in the South. They established Hampden-Sydney in Virginia in 1776, with a seminary added in 1807, and the Union Theological Seminary in Richmond in 1812. They supported Transylvania University in Kentucky, the first college west of the Appalachian Mountains, but withdrew assistance in 1818. Centre College of Kentucky was a cooperative effort of the church and the state; in 1824 the school became fully affiliated with the Presbyterians. Davidson College, which was named for General William Lee Davidson, began near Charlotte in 1836.

In the 1830s the Methodists launched Randolph-Macon in Virginia, Emory in Georgia, Emory and Henry in Virginia, and Holston in Tennessee. The Baptists founded Furman in South Carolina in 1826, Mercer in Georgia in 1833, and Wake Forest in North Carolina in 1834. These were founded by state conventions or regional conferences and assemblies. The University of Richmond in Virginia (1832) was the first attempt of Baptists in the South to establish a school to train its preachers. The Southern Baptist Theological Seminary was set up in Greenville, S.C., in 1859, and moved to Louisville, Ky., in 1877. Some antebellum colleges began as denominational institutions but later became public schools—Auburn University in Alabama started as the Methodist-supported East Alabama Male College (opening in 1859), and the University of Kentucky traces its history back to Kentucky University (1865), a Disciples of Christ school.

The Civil War was as devastating to southern denominational schools as to other aspects of life in the region. The schools and their personnel had assisted in the religious justification of the Old South and offered institutional moral support to the Confederacy. After the war some religious schools became central institutions in tying Christian and southern values together. The University of the South at Sewanee, Tenn., was officially founded in the late 1850s, but it did not offer programs until its resurrection after the war. Washington College became forever identified with southern tradition when Robert E. Lee chose to spend his postwar years there as president, until his death in 1870; the school was soon renamed Washington and Lee.

Following the Civil War large numbers of religiously supported or affiliated black schools emerged. The American Missionary Association was a nondenominational (though mostly supported by Congregationalists) agency that worked among the freedmen during Reconstruction and after. By 1870 it helped to support 170 colleges. The African Methodist Episcopal Church, Zion, and other northern Methodist churches also played an important role in religious education in the South after the war. Schools dating from this period include Fisk in Tennessee, Hampton Institute in Virginia, Tuskegee and Talladega in Alabama, Atlanta University in Georgia, and Tougaloo and Rust in Mississippi. Baptists founded Roger Williams University in Nashville in 1863, and the Presbyterian and Reformed churches set up Biddle University in Charlotte, N.C., in 1867 and Knoxville College in Knoxville, Tenn., in the 1870s. Episcopalians established St. Augustine's in Raleigh, N.C., in 1867.

Church work, especially by evangelical groups, expanded during the late 19th and early 20th centuries as a part of the effort to impose religious values on the South. The Methodists had high hopes for Vanderbilt, which began as that denomination's central college in 1873. The church broke ties in 1914, after the school's governing board became increasingly independent. Emory, Southern Methodist University, and later Duke became important church-supported liberal arts colleges. The Disciples of Christ began financial assistance to the Add-Ran Male and Female College in 1889, and that assistance continued when the school became Texas Christian University in 1902. A closely related religious group, the Churches of Christ, emerged in the early 20th century and now operates 17 schools of higher education, mostly in the South, including David Lipscomb in Nashville, Tenn., Freed-Hardeman in Henderson, Tenn., Harding University in Searcy, Ark., Oklahoma Christian College in Oklahoma City, Lubbock Christian College in Lubbock, Tex., and Abilene Christian University in Abilene, Tex. These institutions are located in areas of the greatest strength of the Churches of Christ.

The South's financial resources could not always match the interest of its religious people in maintaining denominational schools. In 1874 the Methodist Episcopal Church, South, supported 50 colleges, but by 1902 the number had been reduced to 18. A Southern Baptist Convention committee insisted that the "disease of starting Baptist Colleges has been sporadic, endemic, and epidemic." Nonetheless, the churches were not abandoning educational work. Many former colleges were simply reclassified as secondary schools, still under church sponsorship at a reduced cost level. The Report of the Commissioner of Education, 1899–1900, to the federal government revealed that of 26,237 young people in educational institutions in the 11 former Confederate states plus Kentucky and Oklahoma, 13,859 were attending schools sponsored in some way by churches.

Denominational schools have continued to fulfill a number of vital functions for the churches in the 21st century. The evangelical groups are particularly concerned with missionary activity, and schools are a way to convey that interest to the young. Schools train lay people to work in counseling, publishing, and administration; they provide expertise in adult education, music, and recreational work. Faculties of these institutions are resources for local churches, offering workshops, institutes, and lectures.

The chief concern of denominational schools is the training of the clergy, and major church groups operate important theological schools. The southern Presbyterians maintain four seminaries: Union in Richmond (1823), Louisville in Kentucky (1901), Austin in Texas (1902), and Columbia in Decatur, Ga. (1928). The Cumberland Presbyterian Church has Bethel College, McKenzie, Tenn., and the Memphis Theological Seminary. The theological school at Baylor University (established 1901) evolved into the Southwestern Baptist Theological Seminary in Fort Worth (1908). The Baptists also sponsor the Southern Baptist Theological Seminary, which has been in Louisville, Ky., since 1877; the New Orleans seminary (1917); and Southeastern at Wake Forest, N.C. (1951). Important Methodist theological schools are the Perkins School at SMU, the Candler School at Emory, and the Duke Divinity School. The Protestant Episcopal Theological Seminary of Virginia is in Alexandria, and the Episcopal Seminary

Southern Baptist Theological Seminary, Louisville, Ky., 1931 (Photographic archives, University of Louisville [Kentucky])

of the Southwest is in Austin, Tex. St. Luke's School of Theology at the University of the South was the home to one of the South's most accomplished theologians, William Porcher DuBose.

Theological seminaries were rarely well endowed, and they had to face what historian Kenneth K. Bailey has called "a stifling popular distrust of scholarship." When scholarly findings revised traditional beliefs, "ancient myth was often acclaimed over present truth." A writer in the *Southern Methodist Review* in 1887 warned that requiring college training for itinerant preachers would "sound the death-knell of the Church." There were numerous celebrated attempts to remove professors at southern seminaries for teaching "dangerous" ideas—Alexander Winchell at Vanderbilt, James Woodrow at the Presbyterians' Columbia Seminary, Crawford H. Toy and William H. Whitsitt at the Baptist seminary in Louisville, and later, in the 1920s, John A. Rice at Southern Methodist University.

The Fundamentalist movement led to increasing questioning of the teachings of seminary professors during the 1920s. All southern white churches faced conflict over the issue, although the Presbyterian Church in the United States had fewer challenges than did the southern Methodists and the Southern Baptist Convention. Theological seminaries in the South have frequently faced challenges to their academic freedom, but their presidents and faculty have just as often stood up for free intellectual expression. They have represented religious humanism and ecumenism within denominations that have sometimes not championed those ideas in general.

The relationship between religion and education involves more than the training of preachers and the establishment of denominational schools. A good measure of the influence of southern religion on the overall regional culture is the importance of religion in public education. After the Civil War, southern churches and religious leaders crusaded to impose their moral values on society and also worked to insure religious influence in schools. At first the churches were suspicious of public education. The 1871 General Assembly of the southern Presbyterian Church insisted that education was "too dear, too vital to us as a Church, to be remitted to the State." Other church groups agreed, and the Methodists, especially, embarked on an ambitious plan to establish church boarding schools and other institutions for mass education. By the turn of the century the results were disappointing, because few such efforts were adequately supported financially.

The major denominations in the South came to champion the idea of public elementary and secondary schools; they worked to insure religious influences within public education. Vanderbilt University chancellor James H. Kirkland noted in 1910 that in the South "no unfriendly attitude has been shown to religion either in the lower schools or in the State universities. The Bible is generally read in the public schools, and often school is opened with a song and prayer." In the 1960s historian Francis Butler Simkins wrote that "the implementation of universal education by the southern states bids fair to be the means of making Christianity universal." Schools and colleges across the region "resound with daily prayers, hymns, and Bible reading." University faculty senates began their proceedings with prayers in some places through the 1970s, and sporting events often still begin with invocations (which sometimes are thinly veiled supplications to the gods for assistance to the home team).

Religion's place in public education has become an important issue in the contemporary period because of the church-state relationship. Although national in scope, the debate has focused especially on the South because of the region's tradition of close ties between religion and education. In the 1960 presidential campaign Democratic Party nominee John F. Kennedy spoke in Houston before a Protestant ministerial alliance, assuring the preachers that he would not support federal government funds for parochial schools; 20 years later southern fundamentalists were eager to receive tax credits for parents sending children to the Christian academies that increasingly dot the southern landscape.

Challenges to inclusion of prayers in public schools have come from the South. Madalyn Murray O'Hair was in the border South—Maryland—when she filed the lawsuit that led to the 1963 Supreme Court decision outlawing prayer in the public schools. She later moved to Austin, Tex., where she established an archive of the American atheist movement and continued to campaign against church-state ties. In the 1980s a black father in Alabama challenged that state's laws permitting moments of silence in the schools, and in the 1990s Pontotoc, Miss., became the focus of conflict between one mother who protested Christian school prayers and a larger community that saw majority rule thwarted by court decisions. The South's role in this controversy is complicated. The Southern Baptist Convention long advocated a strict separation of religion and public education and generally opposed government aid to schools as well as opposing school prayers. Baylor University was a leader in studying the issue and sponsored the *Journal of Church and State*. The Virginia-based Moral Majority, on the other hand, led the national effort to ratify a school-prayer amendment to the Constitution, and in the 1990s the Southern Baptist Convention, now controlled by fundamentalists, reversed its historic position and advocated school prayer.

Religious leaders and organizations have also played a major role in influencing textbook adoptions in the South. They have testified before state textbook commissions and persuaded many of them to exclude books discussing theories of evolution. Religious leaders and individuals were also prominent in efforts in the early and mid-20th century to adopt only textbooks that positively portrayed southern history and white supremacy. The intimate ties between region and religion were especially clear here. In the 1970s, independent Christian schools emerged in significant numbers in the South, reflecting concerns of many conservative Christians about secular influences in public schools, declining standards of educational discipline and instruction, and also the racial integration of public schools. Many were nondenominational expressions of fundamentalist antiestablishment sentiment.

Finally, the humble Sunday school deserves mention for its role in southern culture. It is neither uniquely southern nor even American. Robert Raikes, a printer and publisher in England, is normally considered the founder of the Sunday school movement, which caught on in the United States in the early 1800s. The first Sunday school in the South was apparently established in 1803 in the Second Baptist Church in Baltimore. Many religious people opposed the school idea at first as unbiblical, and Sunday schools were long a local congregational, lay effort more than an official tool of denominations. Sunday schools typically were regarded as missionary work—the Southern Baptist Convention at first included them as part of its Domestic Mission Board; that denomination's present Sunday School Board, headquartered in Nashville, was not set up until 1891. The major denominations embarked on campaigns after World War II to expand their Sunday school work so that it soon involved extensive organization, participation by adults as well as children, increased funding, and elaborate publications. The Sunday schools and related Vacation Bible Schools in the summer may not have been uniquely southern, but they have been fondly remembered institutions of regional life, effectively introducing children not only to the tenets of the region's dominant evangelical churches but also to the dominant cultural attitudes on race relations, child rearing, male-female roles, and countless other topics.

CHARLES REAGAN WILSON
University of Mississippi

Donald S. Armentrout, *The Quest for the Informed Priest: A History of the School of Theology* (1979); Kenneth K. Bailey, *Southern White Protestantism in the Twentieth Century* (1964); Ben C. Fisher, in *Encyclopedia of Religion in the South*, ed. Samuel S. Hill (1984); Thomas C. Hunt, James C. Carper, Charles R. Kniker, eds., *Religious Schools in America: A Selected Bibliography* (1986); Charles D. Johnson, *Higher Education of Southern Baptists: An Institutional History, 1826–1954* (1955); Lynn E. May, *Sunday School Leadership* (October 1980); Alan Peshkin, *God's Choice: The Total World of a Fundamentalist Christian School* (1986); Edward J. Power, *Catholic Higher Education in America* (1972); Joe M. Richardson, *Christian Reconstruction: The American Missionary Association and Southern Blacks, 1861–1890* (1986); T. Lane Scales, *All That Fits a Woman: Training Southern Baptist Women for Charity and Mission, 1907–1926* (2000).

Research Universities

Research universities in the South at the start of the 21st century stand literally and symbolically as "steeples of excellence" in the region's cultural and institutional landscape. Foremost are the nine southern universities among the 62 universities nationwide selected for membership in the prestigious Association of American Universities (AAU). The nine distinguished universities are, with parenthetical reference to year of selection, as follows: the University of Virginia (1904), the University of North Carolina at Chapel Hill (1922), the University of Texas at Austin (1929), Duke University (1938), Vanderbilt University (1950), Tulane University (1958), Rice University (1985), the University of Florida (1985), Emory University (1995), and Texas A&M University (2001).

The nine AAU member institutions are then joined by other universities in the South who, because of their records in obtaining sponsored research grants along with conferring Ph.D. degrees, are recognized as major research institutions. This tier includes Georgia Institute of Technology, Louisiana State University at Baton Rouge, the University of Georgia, the University of Kentucky, North Carolina State University, Virginia Tech University, the University of Tennessee, the University of South Florida, the University of Miami, Clemson University, the University of Oklahoma, Auburn University, the University of Mississippi, the University of Alabama, Mississippi State University, the University of Arkansas, and the University of South Carolina.

This group of 26 universities represents 13 states, suggesting a reasonable distribution of scholarly talent across the region. Most remarkable is the chronology of membership in the Association of American Universities. No university in the South was invited to be a charter member of the Association of American Universities in 1900. Only five southern universities were members at the end of World War II. One signal of the sustained ascent of research universities in the South is that four were selected for AAU membership since 1985, illustrative of an acceleration of academic research in the region in the late 20th century. In sum, although research universities may have developed relatively late in the South, their recent achievements have given the region a formidable presence in American higher education nationwide.

This growing presence includes the *collective* strength research universities in the South have demonstrated in recent decades. One example was the alliance of governors and university presidents to create the Southern Regional Education Board in 1946. Second was the interinstitutional and interstate cooperation to form the Southern Academic Common Market, with emphasis on doctoral and advanced professional degree programs. In 1982–83 the governors, U.S. senators, and university presidents in 14 southern states formed a consortium whose acronym was "SURA"—shorthand for the "Southeastern Universities Research Association." The landmark achievement of SURA was to win a major research grant in a nationally peer-reviewed competition sponsored by the U.S. Department of Energy's Office of Science. The focus of this collective grant application was to build and provide the scientific expertise for a demonstration of a relatively new branch of applied physics—a continuous electronic beam accelerator facility, or "CEBAF." Its home base was the Thomas Jefferson National Accelerator Facility in Newport News, Va. The historic feature was that SURA was selected in a high-level, nationwide scientific competition. The SURA proposal, for example, prevailed over the proposal submitted by the University of Chicago's Argonne Laboratories and a consortium of research universities in the Midwest.

The term "research university" understandably brings attention to the uppermost academic programs of these institutions—that is, Ph.D. programs whose projects, departments, and institutes emphasize advanced scholarship and sponsored research. The peak missions, however, may inadvertently mask the accompanying range of educational curricula that also are essential to research universities in the South. Typically, the southern research universities are large: in student enrollments, faculty, library holdings, as well as campus facilities and physical plant. Though most of these institutions report a total annual enrollment surpassing 20,000 students, the University of Mississippi, for example, has yet to reach that mark and the University of Florida exceeds it by 30,000. The number of full-time, tenure-track professors at each institution is approximately 4,000. The size of the research faculty and staff plus technical support personnel reflect that these institutions are both large and labor intensive. In many cases, the university represents the largest employer and landholder in its community. Nor does this only hold for large universities in small "campus towns," such as Charlottesville, Va., Gainesville, Fla., Oxford, Miss., Athens, Ga., and Chapel Hill, N.C. Even in large cities and metropolitan areas such as Atlanta, Nashville, Lexington, and Durham, the research universities are among the largest employers and real estate owners.

Related to their large size, research universities in the South often describe themselves as essential to the economic development of their host city or county—and in their state. As such they fulfill the University of California president Clark Kerr's 1963 image of universities as the "Knowledge Industry." Governors, mayors, and university presidents have referred to the research universities as "economic engines" for the state and region. This includes the obvious contributions of payroll and employer. Important for long-term regional development is the pioneering role of some research universities in the

South who dedicate substantial time and resources to partnerships with private industries and state governments to develop research parks. The North Carolina Research Triangle involving the University of North Carolina, North Carolina State University, and Duke University, widely acknowledged as the foremost model of a research park, has fostered numerous scientific inventions and patents and has brought to the cities and regions of the state exemplary innovation in high-tech industries.

This profile of research universities in the South implies a regional success story of sorts. However, these institutional achievements have been neither inevitable nor without conflicts. The end point of the contemporary "steeples of excellence" is preceded by episodes that make the universities integral to the social and political history of the South since about 1880. Universities in the South have been no less than "contested ground" in debates about what a university ought to be. Another caveat is that southern research universities have often fallen short in their promise to elevate southern states and to transform the more troublesome elements of state and regional culture. In various ways, many southern states top the lists of the nation's "worst." Although individual southern universities became nationally recognized for research, many southern states have lagged in competitive funding and have remained eligible for the National Science Foundation's Experimental Program to Stimulate Competitive Research (EPSCoR), to help them build a competitive scientific infrastructure.

Contrary to popular stereotypes, university leaders in the South during the late 19th century did not favor a nostalgic "moonlight and magnolia" notion of the southern campus. Instead, accounts of task forces and presidential conferences from 1870 to 1910 indicate they had an appreciation for progressive curricula and for the modernization of universities in the Northeast and Midwest. During the 1920s, Rockefeller-funded social scientists such as Howard Odum at the University of North Carolina, Chapel Hill, and Wilson Gee at the University of Virginia used such external funding to do research showing how regional deficits and problems such as the "talent drain" resulted from and contributed to the poor quality of life that kept southern universities from attracting and retaining accomplished scholars. By the 1930s a newfound regional identity among southern scholars had sparked new academic journals and scholarly associations, including the Southern Historical Society (1934) and the Southern Sociological Association (1935)—all of which gave impetus for new efforts in research. The challenge for reform-minded researchers was to persuade university presidents, legislators, and donors to provide ample, sustained funding for higher education and research, hand in glove with extensions of compulsory public schooling and endorsement of permanent taxation.

One enduring dilemma for research universities in the South has been to define and support coherent, academically strong undergraduate education. In general, the private or independent universities have fared better than the state universities in matters of selective admissions, high graduation rates, and distinctive curricular philosophy for the undergraduate course of study. Often located within rural or pastoral settings, southern state flagship universities, with a few marked exceptions, largely attract state residents. Within the boundaries of the particular state, degree attainment from the flagships has long affirmed rather than awarded elite social status, giving the undergraduate culture a conservative character. Thus, an overriding emphasis on social achievement rather than academic achievement sends many academically serious students elsewhere and keeps a preoccupation with fraternities, sororities, and intercollegiate athletics as a dominant feature of campus life.

Research universities in the South also have exhibited a strong association with big-time intercollegiate athletics. Research excellence and academic emphases at many southern universities often lag behind the attention given to high-profile revenue sports such as varsity football and basketball. A good way to capture this situation is to look at the alliances represented by intercollegiate athletic conferences. In the powerful Southeastern Conference, only two out of 12 institutions (Vanderbilt and Florida) are also members of the Association of American Universities. In contrast, the Big Ten conference of large Midwestern universities has all 11 of its institutions selected for membership in the academically elite AAU.

Racial exclusion also characterized the admissions and access to research universities in the South as late as 1970. Most conspicuous was the resistance to the enrollment of African American students at the University of Mississippi and the University of Alabama by the governors of those states. Yet state support for an expansive dual system of segregated universities and state-sponsored programs that exported graduate and professional students of color to universities in the North also stalled efforts to develop human and research capital. Elsewhere, racial desegregation usually was civil and orderly, albeit relatively slow to take place, and in recent years scholars have documented the avoidance, and in some cases strong objection, to racial integration at the nationally prominent private universities in the South—Vanderbilt, Tulane, Emory, Duke, and Rice.

As research universities in the South stand literally and symbolically as "steeples of excellence" in the region's cultural and institutional landscape, they also represent the problem of promises unfulfilled and the inability to harness the results of research to bring about complete social and cultural transformation. Largely constrained by the realities of southern politics, a reluctance to support public education at all levels, and social conventions relative to race, class, and gender, southern universities have persisted and achieved despite innumerable obstacles. Thus, as the southern landscape is marked by extremes, southern research universities as a group also exhibit a wide range of success on a national profile of research achievement.

JOHN R. THELIN
University of Kentucky

AMY E. WELLS
University of Mississippi

Thomas Kevin B. Cherry, *History of Higher Education Annual* (1994); Michael Dennis, *Lessons in Progress: State Universities and Progressivism in the New South, 1880–1920* (2001); Dan R. Frost, *Thinking Confederates: Academia and the Idea of Progress in the New South* (2001); Roger Geiger, *Research for Relevant Knowledge: American Research Universities since 1947* (1989); Melissa Kean, *Desegregating Private Higher Education in the South: Duke, Emory, Rice, Tulane, and Vanderbilt* (2008); Clark Kerr, *Uses of the University* (1963); Henry H. Lesesne, *A History of the University of South Carolina, 1940–2000* (2002); William A. Link, *William Friday: Power, Purpose, and American Higher Education* (1997); Clarence L. Mohr and Joseph Gordon, *Tulane: The Emergence of a Modern University* (2001); Amy E. Wells, *History of Higher Education Annual* (2001).

Teachers, Premodern

Any comprehensive analysis about the South's transition to modernity and the civil rights movement must include what teachers did, what they taught, how they taught it, and what they accomplished. During the 20th century, black teachers and white teachers, predominantly women, professionalized teaching, challenged political and social patterns of localism, and created a means for women to gain public authority. African American women contested measures that sustained unequal education. Through segregated teacher associations and activism, black and white teachers pushed southern states' public education systems into the modern era by working for improved funding, equalization, and better teacher certification standards. At the same time they taught modern values in the classroom in addition to academic subjects. Providing much of the backbone of middle-class leadership in communities across the

South, teachers changed the way southerners understood what it meant to be a citizen of the modern world and, most important, the meaning of equality, as they carried ideas about progress and civilization from the classroom into the community.

This tremendous shift in the world of southern culture that teachers made began during Reconstruction. Before the Civil War, states provided minimal funds for public education. Sons and daughters of the elite attended private academies and studied a classical curriculum. Some white teachers attempted instruction in the occasional community school, but attendance was sporadic and results minimal. Most teachers remarked that few parents saw the need for much learning. While a few blacks like Frederick Douglass and Susie King Taylor learned to read during the antebellum era, teaching a slave to read was illegal. To the freedpeople, literacy constituted part of the meaning of freedom. Assisted by the Freedmen's Bureau and the American Missionary Association (AMA), among others, blacks learned to read in almost any available location. Many of those who were literate, like Taylor, opened schools. Rural whites also hoped to gain from public funds provided for education by the early state constitutions. But most of these funds vanished after Reconstruction as powerful white Democrats and large landholders restricted their use for public education. In Georgia's 1877 constitution, for example, public funds were designated only for first through eighth grade. Now able to reassert power over landless blacks and poor whites, most white voters reaffirmed patterns of localism. This meant that funding for public schools was primarily determined by white trustees of the county or town.

How white trustees determined funds for public education depended on local circumstances. Schools in towns and cities received more revenue from taxes while rural schools earned far less. Attitudes about public education defined how teachers were to be trained. Because few whites cared about training black teachers or whether blacks were even educated, most black teachers relied on training from two sources: Some formal instruction from schools and universities funded by northern philanthropies like the AMA and later the General Education Board (GEB) or whatever they were able to glean from observing a local school, most of which rarely went past sixth grade. Future white teachers attended a normal school, a woman's college, a county training institute, or a high school. Because trustees controlled who taught at schools, states established few standards for teachers until the 1920s and 1930s. Salaries varied as well. In 1900 in Virginia, for example, white teachers' pay varied from $20 to $24 a month. Black teachers fared worse. Their salaries ranged from $8 to $14 a month. Women, who comprised at least 85 percent of all teachers in each state, earned barely enough to survive. Some worked extra jobs to be able to attend summer training schools. Most used their meager salaries to purchase extra supplies like books or pencils. To feign the appearance of ladies, they patched holes in dresses and the bottom of shoes.

Still, at the turn of the 20th century, black and white women, ambitious and dedicated, set their sights on improving the conditions of their communities as well as their own professional status. Most teachers came from small landholders, tenants, small business owners, or day laborers. Their families went to extraordinary lengths to ensure that the daughters attained an education and became teachers. Not only did these teachers come from families who recognized the social need and economic opportunities for women of the teaching profession, but many of these young women were determined to have a future beyond agricultural work or marriage. According to their respective race, teachers carried a commitment to improve their communities or uplift them to respectable middle-class standards that teachers learned during their training. Teaching afforded the possibility for rural women to gain professional status and some leadership opportunities. Completing their training was far from easy for most young women. To finish normal school, training school, or college, women scrubbed floors, cleaned houses, and did various jobs on campus. Few had the luxury of attending school without working. Some teachers, like Charlotte Hawkins Brown, Mary McLeod Bethune, and Martha Berry, eventually started their own schools. Regardless of their background, most teachers saw part of their work was a duty to educate communities about the changing cultural values swirling around them.

Black teachers, following the lead of Booker T. Washington, learned to rely on white philanthropic generosity by applying for funds from the Julius Rosenwald Fund or the GEB. Often, they attended training institutes established by the GEB and the John Slater Fund. As Booker T. Washington realized, the best way to gain financial support for education was to agree to follow an industrial curriculum that focused on teaching skills and crafts like masonry, carpentry, and sewing. Other black educators recognized Washington's success and cultivated relationships with white philanthropists to gain precious dollars that opened or maintained what few schools existed. But industrial education was not the only curriculum offered. Black students learned core academic lessons in English, black history, geography, arithmetic, and other subjects.

Part of teachers' efforts to create better, more viable public schools rested on their commitment to reform their communities. Making the school a central part of each community along with churches, family networks, and businesses, teachers taught more than ABCs. They reinforced evangelical Protestant values like abstaining from alcohol and dancing, practicing daily prayer, and reading the Bible. They insisted on certain attire, proper speech patterns, and personal habits for students in school. Just as many teachers wore uniforms during their training, so they contended that modest attire and shoes were part of what it meant to be a citizen in a modern state. Students washed their hands, scrubbed outhouses, and cleaned school grounds. To succeed in the modern world, black and white teachers taught their students they needed to know more than academics. These goals frequently merged with southern Progressive reformers' efforts to pass compulsory attendance laws and mandate longer school terms. Some teachers conducted drives for shoes and clothing so that students could come to school during the winter. Teachers met with parents and advised them about standards of cleanliness, sound nutrition, good manners, proper conduct, and the necessity of attending school, not to meddle in families' lives but to increase students' ability to obtain jobs and live healthy lives. Thus, teachers became cultural mediators between modernity's emphasis on individual success, consumption, and work habits and traditional rural culture's focus on evangelical Protestantism and interdependency.

For black teachers, being a Jeanes teacher included even more. Funded by Quaker philanthropist Anna T. Jeanes in 1907, Jeanes teachers traveled across districts to supervise other black teachers, instruct communities on health and moral standards, raise funds for schools, and organize parent and teacher associations. Overseen by white superintendents who often ignored them, Jeanes teachers represented the precarious position of black teachers. At times, they accomplished remarkable goals in communities and schools as they sustained underfunded black schools. At other times, they had to remember the boundaries that white school boards set about what they could do and how much money they could obtain. Through Jeanes teachers, blacks learned about actions of white state politicians, incidences of racist violence, and actions that the National Association for the Advancement of Colored People (NAACP) proposed.

By the 1930s, black and white teachers had established professional teacher associations, although their early efforts to improve teachers' salaries and schools made little impact. Black teacher associations faced additional obstacles of constantly trying to scrape together a few dollars more simply to keep some schools viable. In 1930, Georgia black teachers, for example, earned 47 percent of white teachers' salaries. A similar salary gap cut across most southern states. Still, most states had segregated professional teacher associations by the end of the New Deal. After facing persistent pay reductions and problems with student attendance as well as poor facilities in rural areas, teacher associations in the 1940s made demands for better pay, implementation of teacher certification standards, and higher standards for public education. If public education was important, then states had to provide more funds for schools. A combination of programs from the National Youth Administration and skills tests for World War II draftees indicated that southern blacks and whites lagged behind the rest of the nation in literacy standards.

Black teacher associations did more than seek increases in funding for appallingly unequal schools. Their association leaders in Georgia, Virginia, and other states encouraged them to pay their poll taxes and register to vote. Black teachers moved to the forefront of the struggle for equality in the 1940s. Beginning in Maryland in 1936, the NAACP's fight to equalize teachers' salaries swept across the South and included Virginia, North Carolina, Georgia, and Louisiana. North Carolina's government crafted an agreement with teachers to equalize pay beginning in 1937. Black teachers in Norfolk, Va., won their case for equal pay in 1940, although teachers in Newport News failed. As Virginia Teachers Association executive Luther P. Jackson noted, teachers may have won the equalization battle, but they still lacked equal pay. In some states like Georgia, teachers who challenged unequal pay were immediately fired. For all the costs, however, black teachers proved their extraordinary mettle by taking on white superintendents and politicians and challenging them to enforce equitable salaries.

Then came the United States Supreme Court decision in 1954 that changed black and white educators' lives—*Brown v. Board of Education*. Black teacher associations reluctantly supported the NAACP strategy of integration. Most knew that integrating schools meant that teachers and administrators would lose jobs. They knew that their ability to shape black children's lives by persistently reminding them that they were equal to anyone would be lost. What black teachers really sought was equal funding, a means to get new textbooks and buildings with indoor plumbing and roofs that did not leak. Few teachers, unlike Septima Poinsette Clark and Joanne Robinson, participated in public civil rights activities. After seeing the price of teacher equalization suits, teachers knew their very livelihood was at stake.

What was gained and what was lost because of *Brown* remains a debate among educators and historians. Clearly, some black teachers and administrators lost jobs. New schools for blacks were quickly deserted as black students transferred to white schools. Because of *Brown*, black communities lost some black schools that were centers of their community. It also closed some failed schools where little that resembled a solid academic foundation could be taught. Black teachers undoubtedly lost authority in communities and paid a price for *Brown*.

In the aftermath of *Brown*, African American and white teachers associations began to focus on integrating their separate associations. Not until 1951 did the National Education Association (NEA) recognize black teachers associations. It gave tepid support for *Brown*. As a result, black teachers who taught in white schools often faced harassment from white teachers—stony silences or threats of dismissal. In 1966 the NEA finally began the process of merging black and white teachers associations. Some were more successful than others. Georgia, North Carolina, Louisiana, and Alabama negotiated mergers that guaranteed black representation on executive boards and membership numbers for black teachers. After watching the merger results in South Carolina, Texas, and Virginia, black teachers associations were determined to ensure equitable representation. The NEA began to represent its members more effectively by gaining improved benefits and job security.

What teachers accomplished in their states and communities is no less than remarkable. By the 1950s, southern states were modernizing as teachers educated their students for the corporate, bureaucratized state and prepared communities for the transition from rural to industrial economies. Black teachers cultivated the groundwork for the civil rights movement. Because of their efforts to create modern public school systems, southern states faced the challenges of the modern state more effectively. Professional women who often said the least to promote themselves had accomplished much indeed.

ANN SHORT CHIRHART
Indiana State University

James D. Anderson, *The Education of Blacks in the South, 1860–1935* (1988); Ann Short Chirhart, *Torches of Light: Georgia Teachers and the Coming of the Modern South* (2005); Adam Fairclough, *A Class of Their Own: Black Teachers in the Segregated South* (2007); Louis R. Harlan, *Separate and Unequal: Southern School Campaigns and Racism in the Southern Seaboard States, 1901–1915* (1968); James Leloudis, *Schooling the New South: Pedagogy, Self, and Society in North Carolina, 1880–1920* (1996); William A. Link, *A Hard Country and a Lonely Place: Schooling, Society, and Reform in Rural Virginia, 1870–1920* (1986).

Technological Education

Along with the rest of the nation, the South has long been aware of technology and its impact. Automobiles, computers, and hydroelectric power represent three of the most obvious examples of revolutionary innovations brought about by technology. Only in recent decades, however, has southern technological education kept pace with these changes or evidenced a high level of achievement.

Southern higher education before and for some time after the Civil War was little different from that in the North. Focusing on the classical curriculum, a university education prepared the student for life as a cultured gentleman. Training in the sciences and practical fields such as engineering or agriculture had no place in the university experience. As Reconstruction ended, however, a growing awareness of the region's educational shortcomings emerged. When the American Association for the Advancement of Science met in Nashville in 1877, the local press emphasized the value of science and technology to the region's economic well-being. Editorials stressed the need for improved educational facilities to provide young southerners with the tools needed to prosper in the new, more technologically focused economy of the New South.

During the 1880s, therefore, the recovering South began to reevaluate the role of higher education. Classical coursework was supplanted by curricula designed to prepare the student for a place in the world of business, industry, and agriculture. Many southern states established schools to supply such education. Auburn (Alabama Polytechnic from 1899 until 1960), Georgia Tech (founded as Georgia School of Technology in 1885), Clemson (1889), Texas A&M (1876), and Virginia Polytechnic Institute (1872) all owed their existence or continuation to the "practical" mentality of state legislators and businessmen, as well as to federal support through the Morrill Act.

The cultural and intellectual change represented by these new schools, however, may have been more apparent than real. As historian Thomas D. Clark argued in 1965, southern agricultural and mechanical colleges were chiefly concerned with improving the farming community's way of life. By focusing on land policy and management, as well as agricultural and general engineering, these institutions represented a commitment to the region's agrarian society. Another example of cultural inertia in education may be found in the development of separate schools for African Americans during the late 19th and early 20th centuries. Both northern philanthropists (guided by the recommendations of George F. Peabody) and state legislators supported the idea of "industrial education" for blacks. Yet this education, even at George Washington Carver's famous experiment station at Tuskegee Institute (1881), was designed to train efficient and contented laborers for the semi-industrialized southern agricultural economy.

The first few decades of the 20th century witnessed only slight improvement in southern technological education. The number of institutions providing appropriate instruction grew to include Louisiana Polytechnic Institute, Tennessee Polytechnic Institute, Texas Technological College, and others, but few major improvements in curricula or equipment took place. The Great Depression hit state-supported institutions especially hard and further thwarted the growth of such schools.

The end of World War II signaled the beginning of a major change in technological education throughout the United States. The war had been a total technological endeavor, symbolized by the development and use of the atomic bomb. Students entering college after the war (with or without the GI Bill) naturally found engineering and science courses attractive. The war experience had also emphasized the practical value of government support for research and development. Defense-related research, whether performed in government or university laboratories, enjoyed generous federal funding during the early years of the Cold War. Because of their relative lack of expertise, however, southern schools received little of this federal largesse, preventing significant growth of the region's technological education base. Although large sums flowed from Washington to such southern outposts as Redstone Arsenal (Huntsville, Ala.) and Oak Ridge, Tenn., southern education received few of the benefits.

The national shock over the Soviet Union's successful launches of *Sputnik I* and *Sputnik II* in late 1957 precipitated another, and by far the most significant, change in America's educational history. For the next decade the nation focused on improving the scientific and technological base of American culture, with education receiving great attention and massive federal funding. Here, at last, the South began to enter the mainstream of technological and scientific development. The need for improved science education became immediately apparent, with southern schools at every level receiving federal funds to establish new programs and to improve existing ones. Recognizing another important regional need, the American Society for Engineering Education established its Historically Black Engineering Colleges Committee in 1964. Funded by such corporate donors as Standard Oil, IBM, General Electric, and others, this committee embarked on projects to improve the facilities and faculties at several such schools in the South. Aerospace research facilities, frequently cooperating with local universities, grew rapidly in Georgia, Florida, Alabama, Texas, and Louisiana. The University of Tennessee Space Institute was established in 1964, linking a graduate study program with research at the U.S. Air Force's Arnold Engineering Development Center. Schools such as the University of Alabama–

Huntsville, Florida Institute of Technology, and Rice University worked closely with the National Aeronautics and Space Administration to guide the Apollo program to its successful lunar landing in 1969.

The post-Apollo letdown, however, witnessed a dramatic decline in both funding for and interest in science and technology. The aerospace industry in the South, which had been the region's major path to its share in the technological renaissance of the Space Age, withered perceptibly, removing employment opportunities in many technical fields and placing the region's technological education in a precarious position.

Within a few years, especially as "Sun Belt" industries demanded technically proficient workers, southern schools again found themselves stressing technological education. With high salaries available to scientists and engineers with undergraduate degrees, universities found themselves deluged with applications. In the South the region's population growth further reinforced this trend, as shown by the 1980 establishment of Southern Polytechnic State University (originally Southern Technical Institute) in metro Atlanta as the 14th senior college in the Georgia University System.

During the last two decades of the 20th century, the American technological landscape changed in several ways, creating new challenges and opportunities for education. Concerns about American international competitiveness were reinforced by Japan's growing role in the world economy, made possible by that nation's emergence as a leader in consumer electronics. The 1983 publication of *A Nation at Risk: The Imperative for Educational Reform* focused public attention on weaknesses in American public education, emphasizing that schools were not meeting the need for a competitive workforce. Proposals for improvements in technological education were thus usually framed in terms of economic benefit, a perspective of special interest in the South where foreign automakers began to build assembly plants. Although generous state and local incentives and a nonunionized labor force played important roles in attracting these facilities, the existence of a postsecondary educational infrastructure was often used to recruit manufacturers. Automakers were soon established in Alabama (Honda, Mercedes-Benz), Kentucky (Toyota), South Carolina (BMW), and Tennessee (Nissan, Volkswagen). Dell Computer Corporation also found the South an attractive region for expansion. The Texas-based company established manufacturing facilities in Tennessee and North Carolina in 1999 and 2004, respectively, providing yet another technology-oriented addition to the region's economy.

State education systems recognized and responded to the new demands, usually focusing on their community and junior colleges as the sites for the required instruction. These schools had the added advantage of employing part-time instructors at lower salaries and minimum benefits, relieving stress on state budgets. The Mississippi State Board for Community and Junior Colleges, for example, not only oversaw the state's community college system, but it also had responsibility for the separate "Career/Technical Education" and "Workforce Education" divisions, both of which focused on technological education. Southern states also recognized the importance of a well-coordinated effort to integrate their technological education facilities with continued recruitment of high-tech economic ventures. In 1983, Arkansas established its Science and Technology Authority to encourage the state's research and development activities, business innovation, and education in the fields of science, mathematics, and engineering. The same year also witnessed the creation of the Tennessee Technology Corridor in the eastern part of the state. The agency to coordinate this activity hoped to draw high-tech businesses into the region by emphasizing existing facilities such as Oak Ridge National Laboratory and the University of Tennessee, both of which had well-established educational programs. Even more immediately accessible was the State Technical Institute at Knoxville, whose name was changed in 1988 to Pellissippi State Technical Community College, precipitating dramatic enrollment growth during the next two decades.

Because of its status as one of the premier science and technology facilities in the nation, Oak Ridge National Laboratory played a major role in the South's educational efforts. In addition to various partnerships with the region's universities, Oak Ridge pursued an extensive outreach program to improve science education at the precollege level. Such endeavors increased after the University of Tennessee joined Battelle as the managing contractor for Oak Ridge National Laboratory in 2000. Grants to Tennessee high schools upgraded science classrooms and laboratories in an effort to increase the learning opportunities for students interested in science and technology.

Indeed, as the 21st century dawned, increasing emphasis on improving science and technology education at the K–12 level characterized much educational reform discussion. Continued poor performance of American students in assessments of science and technology knowledge suggested a serious potential decline in American competitiveness and led to a growing interest in STEM (Science, Technology, Engineering, Mathematics) education at the state level. In the South, STEM centers often appeared on university campuses, geared toward improving public school teachers' instructional efforts. North Carolina established its Science, Mathematics, and Technology Education Center in 2002 to coordinate educational efforts throughout the state and to work with educational, industrial, and governmental agencies toward this end. The Arkansas Science and Technology Authority, founded earlier to encourage technological development in the state, established a STEM Coalition to provide support and funding for improvements in such education at the K–12 level. With NASA funding, the Alabama Mathematics, Science, and Technology Education Coalition drew leaders from business, education, and government in its effort to improve the state's science and technology education. Throughout the region, STEM activities became increasingly visible, often securing external funding from local businesses and government.

At every educational level, the focus on technological education was increasingly tied to economic concerns. In late 2008, despite a severe budget shortfall that forced massive cuts to higher education, the State of Tennessee provided more than $11 million for technological education programs and facilities to support a new billion-dollar semiconductor plant in Clarksville. Few observers questioned the importance of high-tech industries to the South's economy. The support of technological education to attract such industries similarly brought few complaints. In the face of dramatic budget cuts to other educational programs, however, the South's emphasis on technological education raised troubling questions concerning the region's commitment to a well-educated citizenry, rather than a well-trained workforce.

GEORGE E. WEBB
Tennessee Technological University

James D. Anderson, *History of Education Quarterly* (Winter 1978); Allan M. Cartter, *Southern Economic Journal* (July 1965); Thomas D. Clark, *Three Paths to the Modern South: Education, Agriculture, and Conservation* (1965); Eric Foner, *Reconstruction: America's Unfinished Revolution, 1863–1877*; Claudia Goldin and Lawrence R. Katz, *The Race between Education and Technology* (2008); Lawrence P. Grayson, *Engineering Education* (December 1977); Daniel S. Greenberg, *The Politics of Pure Science* (1967); Howard N. Rabinowitz, *The First New South, 1865–1920* (1992); *Rising above the Gathering Storm: Energizing and Employing America for a Brighter Economic Future* (2005); C. Vann Woodward, *Origins of the New South, 1877–1913* (1951).

Urban and Metropolitan Colleges and Universities (Post-1945)

From Richmond and Charlotte to Atlanta, Birmingham, Orlando, New Orleans, and Houston, public urban research universities stand as some of the most modernizing elements of the South. Karen DeWitt briefly probed this topic in the *New York Times* on 13 August 1991, but it is all the more compelling today. Unlike times past when the majority of southerners remained rural with a disproportionate lack of interest in higher education, today's southerners are increasingly urban: from 29 percent in 1920 to 73 percent in 2000. While the 2010 census will tell precisely how this trend has continued, there already are ample data showing that the fastest growing cities in America are below the Mason-Dixon line.

As part of this change, southerners are intensely focused on public higher education in cities. We do not yet have a full analysis of how Dixie's modern city folk found symbiosis with their urban universities. To encourage that understanding, however—an understanding essential to maximizing contributions of these institutions—here are some initial thoughts on the origins of public urban research universities in the South.

While urban higher education grew in the Northeast and Midwest in the years leading up to the Civil War, only one public university emerged in a southern city, the University of Louisville (Ky.). In 1846 this institution began to grow as part of a city perhaps more attuned to midwestern influences than to agrarian forces of the Old South not much interested in sophisticated city life. It was not until well after the Civil War that significant numbers of public urban universities appeared in Dixie. Different from their antebellum predecessors, white power structures of the New South under strong Yankee influence hungered for industry and finance in Birmingham, Atlanta, and other cities. Much like Thomas Jefferson, however, most could not see the transmitting of high culture for whites—public universities—as unfolding in any place but in isolated Old South villages such as Charlottesville, Chapel Hill, Tuscaloosa, and Oxford. Exceptions occurred in Columbia, S.C., Baton Rouge, La., and Knoxville, Tenn., where white state universities continued their development adjacent to towns of antebellum South origins. (This proclivity apparently did not apply to certain private higher-education developments, e.g., Queens College in Charlotte, N.C., and Birmingham-Southern College, both before and after the Civil War, where religious groups sought educational alternatives to the growing secular life in isolated university towns of the countryside.) At any rate, against this backdrop and the intensifying standards of Jim Crow, the initial wave of public higher education in southern cities occurred under the guidance of the only ones interested—black folks.

Aided significantly by the Morrill Act of 1890 the post-Reconstruction push for black education delivered a spate of city-located universities: Alabama A&M University (Huntsville, est. 1875), Jackson State University (Miss., est. 1877), and Alabama State University (Montgomery, est. 1878). This pattern persisted on up to the Great Depression—Southern University (Baton Rouge, est. 1880), Florida A&M University (Tallahassee, est. 1887), North Carolina A&T University

(Greensboro, est. 1891), Tennessee State University (Nashville, est. 1912), North Carolina Central University (Durham, est. 1925), and Norfolk State University (Va., est. 1935). The South still lagged far behind the Northeast in number and quality of well-developed public urban universities. But an ironic beginning was under way as traditional agrarian perceptions of place and race inadvertently permitted key modern steps toward sophisticated southern cities.

On that foundation other developments then occurred. With the Great Depression white southerners got more interested in urban life. In 1934 local business leaders in Houston, Tex., increasingly concerned about the future of their citizenry in economic crisis, donated crucial resources to develop a local two-year college into the University of Houston. Two years later, a lesser vision went to work in Alabama. In Tuscaloosa, 60 miles southwest of Birmingham, the Depression spun the University of Alabama downward. Many white families long able to pay for their children to go "away" to college no longer had the money to do so. Faced with plummeting enrollment and severe tuition losses, the University of Alabama opened an "extension center" in Birmingham and soon in other cities, where large pockets of unemployed qualified for federal assistance under the Second New Deal. As World War II brought major expansion to southern cities, similar urban operations produced even more revenues for some of these rural-based campuses through federally assisted engineering programs and later, for all of them, through federally supported education for veterans. In many southern states during the early postwar period total city-satellite enrollments actually surpassed those of the main campuses. In a few cases—notably, Atlanta—such historic enrollment growth led main campuses, reluctantly, to even more satellite offerings in a nascent strategy for public urban higher education. In other cases, such as Birmingham, the opposite occurred. With the return of sustained prosperity in the 1950s the University of Alabama's enrollments recovered. Its leaders no longer needed the income the satellites provided to support the main campus. Even more, they feared the growing attraction of going to college in the city would not only create new and competitive demands on public funding, but also threaten essentials of the Old Order of Alabama higher education. Potent "off-campus" support for this perception came from the dominant political and economic force in Birmingham, the United States Steel Corporation, which wanted nothing in town that might raise wages or create any other type of change. Nevertheless, a gradually growing group of civic elites in Birmingham crucially joined by a few others across the state, including several governors and indeed the medical dean in Tuscaloosa, thought otherwise. First they prevailed in moving the state medical college from Tuscaloosa to Birmingham. Then they grew the "extension center" into a vibrant Birmingham branch-campus of the University of Alabama, converting to their cause a newly arrived president in Tuscaloosa.

All across the South in the 1950s and 1960s such civic elites—rarely encountering what happened in Alabama—repeated this story. In retrospect they resembled earlier urban-education advocates in the American Northeast and Midwest in their crucial understanding that modern life includes cities with universities. They also harkened to the civic founders of late 19th-century British cities who developed public "civic universities" as key adjuncts for middle-class life emerging with industrialization. Much as British leaders pursued development funds from Parliament, some of the educational leaders of southern cities acquired massive, competitively awarded monies from the National Science Foundation and the National Institutes of Health. And their civic counterparts worked with them to be just as successful in capturing funds from Urban Renewal, the Appalachian Regional Commission, and other War on Poverty programs. Here, successes often could be traced to the same national political connections—senators and congressmen with longtime seniority—who had delivered the bulk of mobilization funds to the South during World War II. That the British movement and the southern movement occurred almost a century apart, however, accounts for two central differences. Unlike Britain's civic universities, the southern urban schools, in addition to classroom and civic engagement, vigorously embraced original research and other forms of creative activity as key components of faculty and student life. Likewise, in contrast to what happened across the Atlantic in the 1880s and 1890s, the southern-based civil rights movement of the 1950s and 1960s unfolded just as southern "urbans" took shape, leading racial equality to displace the historic white-only orthodoxy in their core civic values. The University of Louisville was the first of all southern public universities to throw out Jim Crow. It was desegregated in 1951, well before the civil rights movement gained serious momentum and before other southern universities, old and new, admitted blacks.

So, out of the Depression, World War II, and postwar developments in federal funding and civil rights, Dixie finally experienced a second wave of public-university growth in cities—this time under predominantly white influences, though influences well-connected to new black leaders in city politics. Historically rural-based universities whether intentionally or unintentionally were responsible for some of these new institutions. Georgia State University (Atlanta, est. 1955) was followed by Old Dominion University (Norfolk, Va., est. 1962). Then came the University of South Alabama (Mobile, est. 1963), the University of North Carolina at Charlotte (est. 1963), Auburn University at Montgomery (Ala., est. 1967), and the University of Tennessee at Chattanooga (est. 1968).

Three more gained institutional life in 1969: the University of Alabama at Birmingham, the University of Alabama at Huntsville, and the University of Arkansas at Little Rock. Those with direct Old Order lineage completed their appearance with George Mason University (Fairfax, Va., 1972) and the University of New Orleans (est. 1974).

Other southern urbans grew from the same mid-20th-century modernization but with little or no connection to rural-based main campuses. The University of Memphis (est. 1957) and the University of North Texas (Denton, est. 1961) evolved out of teachers colleges. The University of North Carolina at Greensboro (est. 1963) and James Madison University (Harrisonburg, Va., est. 1977) originated as women's colleges. Virginia Commonwealth University (est. 1968) grew from a private "professional institute" with strong social work and studio-art programs and—like the University of Alabama at Birmingham—a preexisting public medical college. The University of Texas at Dallas (est. 1969) arose after a private industry deeded its educational enterprise to the state. Then there was the unique case of Florida, where urban growth was so overwhelming from the mid-1940s to the late 1960s and resources so plentiful that civic elites and politicians simply created—i.e., without protracted evolution—*five* major new public urban universities: the University of South Florida (Tampa, est. 1956), the University of Central Florida (Orlando, 1963), Florida Atlantic University (Boca Raton, est. 1964), Florida International University (Miami, est. 1965), and the University of North Florida (Jacksonville, est. 1969). The only other place in the South where the "Florida phenomenon" seemed remotely replicated was in Atlanta with Kennesaw State University (est. 1963).

In some cases programs of southern urbans replicated those of the old campuses. The University of Louisville and the University of Houston, evolving at the same time as the University of Kentucky and the University of Texas respectively, offered a full array of doctoral programs. In response to radical expansion of their surrounding cities so did a few of the younger southern urbans: Florida International University, the University of South Florida, and Georgia State University. Otherwise, in response to a complex maze of forces—tradition, retarded state policies on all social services, and institutional turfdom alongside efficiency and societal need—most urbans did not offer the broad ranging doctoral programs of the main campuses. Instead, they focused on master's level education (in part to attract and retain research-oriented faculty for teaching undergraduates) and doctoral education in carefully targeted, rapidly developing professional fields—e.g., nursing, health administration, business management, and engineering. On the other hand, five had medical centers and related doctoral programs in the biomedical as well as social and behavioral sciences. As a result the University of Louisville, the University of Alabama at Birmingham, the University of South Alabama, the University of South Florida, Virginia Commonwealth University and, most recently, the University of Central Florida have stories of dramatic growth connected to grants from the National Science Foundation and the National Institutes of Health. Indeed, the Carnegie Endowment's 1986–90 analysis of "Per Capita Publications and R&D Funding Index for Research 1 Public Institutions" ranked the University of Alabama at Birmingham as No. 17 out of 32 such universities in the nation. Only four others were in the South: University of North Carolina at Chapel Hill (No. 12), North Carolina State (No. 16), University of Virginia (No. 21), and the University of Texas (No. 29). This led *The Rise of American Research Universities*, published by Johns Hopkins University Press in 1997, to report, "In no other American state [except in Alabama] has a new, urban campus . . . so surpassed the traditional flagship as a research university." By 2008 the Carnegie Endowment, using new categories, gave the University of Alabama at Birmingham a "very high research" classification (the only institution in Alabama with that rating) and the University of South Florida a "very high research" rating (along with the University of Florida and Florida State University). Three other urbans with medical centers—Louisville, Virginia Commonwealth, and Central Florida—received a "high research" classification, although the University of Houston, the University of North Texas, the University of Texas at Dallas, Jackson State University (Miss.), and George Mason University, despite not having medical centers, also fell into the "high research" category. Other urbans received Carnegie classifications of either "doctoral/research" or "large master's" offerings. The "economic impact" of these endeavors is difficult to assess with any specificity because of wide-ranging institutional formulae for "multiplier effect." Still, particularly in the case of institutions with medical centers and large amounts of federal funds translating into large payrolls, a cautious estimate is that every dollar of state funding invested in an institutional budget produced an eight-fold impact on local and state economies.

Though even more difficult to measure—and sometimes ignored for that reason—the "social impact" of these institutions through undergraduate education probably was just as striking. Long distinctive as a region with low family incomes, the South undoubtedly had an extreme problem with access to public baccalaureate-level education—"going away" to college was not affordable for millions—until the southern urbans emerged. A preliminary analysis of ACT data indicates that by 2007 in-state students seeking baccalaureate degrees "at home" in their cities generally had swelled the ranks of the urban-research universities. Granted, pockets of old alignments remained. Unless one considers the University of South Carolina an urban university because of its location in Columbia, which some might do, that state had no urban-research university. Likewise, Mississippi had only a small percentage of in-state citizens pursuing baccalaureate degrees on urban-research campuses. Yet the fastest growing in-state student population in Mississippi was in the city—at Jackson State University. Though much closer to parity and despite strong urban universities, Louisiana, Arkansas, and Kentucky still had more students at traditional campuses than in the city. Tennessee, however, reflected about equal numbers on the urban and traditional campuses. Likewise, Alabama—despite carefully orchestrated enrollment drives on the traditional campuses as well as several excellent nonresearch public universities—reflected urbans slightly ahead of "main" campuses.

Where urban life had developed the fastest, changes were more dramatic. Georgia reflected traditional-campus enrollments of some 7,000 students ahead of urbans. Atlanta's growth, however, was rapidly closing this gap. There, between 2000 and 2007, Georgia State University had a 26 percent increase in in-state undergraduate students, and nearby Kennesaw State University a whopping 59 percent increase. In North Carolina urbans had 39,550 undergraduates, the traditional campuses 34,000. In Texas traditional research institutions—the University of Texas at Austin and Texas A&M—enrolled 70,468 in-state students, the urbans chiefly of Houston and Dallas some 96,000. Then there was Florida. In 2007 the University of Florida and Florida State University had a combined in-state undergraduate enrollment of some 60,000. For the Florida research-urbans, however, led by the University of Central Florida and the University of South Florida, that figure was 117,000.

Certain public perceptions about these city students were true. Compared to the traditional campuses the urban institutions had older undergraduates—in 2007 an average age of full-time enrolled of about 23. More of the urban undergraduates commuted than lived in dormitories. Many worked while going to college. In 2007 this made for institutional graduation rates (those who completed baccalaureate degrees in six years or under) around 40 percent compared to approximately 63 percent at traditional institutions, where far fewer students worked. In line with national patterns, in 2007 the southern urbans averaged around 60 percent undergraduate female and the main campuses 50 percent. Moreover, even excluding traditional and historic black institutions of southern cities, urbans reflected some of the highest black enrollment in predominantly white research universities in America. In 2007 they averaged approximately 30 percent African American compared to a traditional-campus number of 20 percent. Similar diversity appeared with Latino students. Excluding traditionally or historically black southern urbans, which had virtually no Latino students, in 2007 they averaged 7.6 percent Latino compared to the main campuses' 3.7 percent. In short, as of 2009 when all projections about high school graduates in the South showed a rapidly declining percentage to be white males and an increasing percentage to be female, black, and Latino, it was interesting to ponder how the diverse learning environment of the southern urbans would further shift enrollment patterns in the region. Also, at a time when declining tax receipts and conservative political agendas brought funding cuts, and all public institutions had little choice about raising tuition rates, one wondered if an even larger percentage of southern students would elect to stay "at home" in their cities where they had better access to jobs to cover the rising costs of going to college.

On the other hand, certain perceptions about the new southern universities comprise little more than "urban myths." According to the ACT, in most cases, notably the University of Texas, the University of Virginia, the University of Florida, and the University of North Carolina, main campuses have higher admission standards than urbans. And, again according to the ACT, a few of the urbans have low admission standards, especially Norfolk State University and Alabama State University. In 2007, however, public myth to the contrary, none of the southern urban research universities had anything close to the "open admission" policies one appropriately finds at many public two-year colleges. In some states, for example Alabama, most of the urbans have admission standards right in line with main campus standards. Likewise, compared to main campus students the undergraduates of southern urbans as of 2007 were not disproportionately focused on business management and other professional education as opposed to arts and sciences education. What made arts-and-sciences education particularly strong at most southern urbans was extensive use of the surrounding city as a social laboratory for "hands-on" exploration of modern human issues — from prejudice and greed to philanthropy, economic development, art, and public culture. In those urbans with medical centers, arts and sciences undergraduates regularly engaged in research mentored by physicians and other health-care specialists. It was not uncommon, in fact, to find faculty in nursing, dentistry, or medicine team-teaching with philosophers and historians in undergraduate honors programs. Finally, there was the myth of crime on campus — something often associated with "city life" more than "college-town" life. According to data congressionally mandated and collected by the U.S. Department of Education, overall, the South's urban campuses had no greater propensity for violent crime than their main campuses. A 2007 snapshot — excluding data related to atypical tragedies at Virginia Tech —

reveals that violent crimes committed on campus and in dormitories averaged 0.59 actions per 1,000 students on the main southern campuses compared to 0.42 actions per 1,000 students on the urbans.

A region long struggling to balance tradition with change, the South's ultimate embrace of public urban research universities occurred only after the type of fight known to so many other elements of southern modernization. Granted, similar tensions in higher education occurred nationwide in the 1960s and 1970s. Older universities found themselves competing for students and resources with new universities—usually urban institutions but also nonurban universities evolving from teachers' colleges or two-year institutions into fuller institutional lives. Indeed, that older institutions at this time felt the need to start calling themselves *flagship* institutions—as if public higher education at the state level resembled a well-orchestrated armada under the direction of one main battleship—tells of the intensity and insecurity surrounding these national conflicts. Still, because of the South's unique history with race, antebellum values, and tortuous social change, how it experienced the modern higher education wars was arguably more intense than in other parts of the nation. When some historic universities withdrew their support for urban satellites right after World War II it only forecast what would happen on a larger scale over the next four decades. Powerful southerners still emotionally connected to certain antebellum ways were accustomed to higher education and other cultural achievement occurring only in historic college towns. Except for black higher education made nonthreatening in the context of Jim Crow, these traditionalists wanted New South cities tightly focused on industry and related business and finance. Libraries and perhaps museums were all right. Other southern whites of the new urban orientation thought differently. So in state capital after state capital—and cloistered boardroom after boardroom—as the rise of the southern urban universities helped shift the center of southern cultural life away from the country and into the city, visceral university issues of governance, money, and programs ignited warfare of Herculean proportions. A central irony in these southern higher-education wars was that from the 1930s through the 1960s many faculty and administrators of the older institutions obviously were among the most courageous and visionary of those urging southern modernization. Yet many of them balked when it came to supporting the most recent wave of southern modernization—sophisticated urban life through robust public urban higher education. They feared losing financial, programmatic, and stature advantages of the Old Order. For sure, increased state-level competition for public funds understandably exacerbated main campuses' perceptions of southern urbans as a "threat": a historically, chronically small pie would get cut into still smaller pieces. Still, southern main campuses had a chance to expand this pie for all and failed. In 1978 public urban research universities nationwide succeeded in getting Congress to pass the Urban Grant Act, which could have sent millions of development dollars to America's cities and their public urban research universities, much as the Morrill Act a century earlier provided dramatically effective stimulus funds for rural America through its universities. Although the Urban Grant Act of 1978 would have eased the competition for higher education resources in the South, not to mention advanced the modernization and general tax bases of southern states, main campus leaders did anything but lend a hand. Instead, they apparently sided with traditionalist brethren in control of the National Association of State Universities and Land-Grant Colleges in Washington, D.C., and made sure that the Urban Grant Act, which would have assisted only public urban universities, got next to nothing. As of 2009 the Urban Grant Act still awaited significant appropriation.

Already frustrated by state-level funding wars and taking tentative steps toward becoming more "traditional" as a new strategy for competing, many southern urbans saw the failure of the Urban Grant Act as a sure sign that national education policy like state policy would not modernize sufficiently for them to meet the needs of their expanding urban populations. So another strategy appeared. To solve their problem—to get more money—they began to "traditionalize" with wide-ranging programs to attract students from all across their states and indeed from all across the nation and the world. They dramatically expanded on-campus housing, student-life organizations, food services, weekend activities, study-abroad programs, residential honors programs. They cranked up bookstore and online offerings of baseball caps, umbrellas, backpacks, and sweatshirts bearing campus logos. They "greened" their campuses not just with trees, shrubs, flowers but entirely new quadrangles replete with bell towers and signature sculpture. Overnight, streets signs bearing "8th Avenue South" became "University Boulevard." Where possible, they changed athletic conferences and expanded NCAA programs—budgets and numbers of sports. By 2008 some 70 percent had initiated football programs. Indeed, a few who long had called themselves "urban institutions" dropped "urban" from mission statements and cancelled memberships in national associations dedicated to advancing urban public higher education, viewing such organizations as too weak to effect significant changes in state and federal educational development. However, these steps in no case signaled an end to the urban engagement responsible for their rise to prominence. Southern schools lacked the state funding and local philanthropy for urban activism available to urban universities in the Northeast and Midwest. Still, southern urbans remained energized about the city as a "real-life" tool for learning and teaching.

From the broadest perspective, by the start of the 21st century, southern urbans had evolved to a tripartite mission. They served certain needs of surrounding "living communities." Yet they also advanced the values of traditional-college communities as well as research standards of revered "disciplinary communities," such as the American Historical Association and the American Medical Association. In its complexity one hardly can imagine a more difficult approach to developing a university. But this strategy spoke strongly to the demands of modern life and of a region still in dire need of modernization. Within this complex formula, two icons of traditional southern university life—football and Phi Beta Kappa—symbolized the difficulty of remaking urban schools along traditional lines. The main campuses' Southeastern Conference football enjoyed evangelical-cult following among the masses of southerners. This left little room for others in any big-time (money-making) regional football market. Likewise, though well established on every main campus, Phi Beta Kappa—the most coveted of university honorary societies—existed in 2009 at only two of the South's urban institutions: University of North Carolina at Greensboro (which got its chapter in 1936 while still a woman's college) and Florida International University. Still, as America emerges from a recession with horror stories documenting the crucial nature of higher education for reasonable security in today's global economy, public urban research universities should thrive. They will not displace the badly needed "flagship" universities. Their growing demand in a now urbanized region, however, together with the international-level accomplishments of their faculty and students will make them as critical—in some instances more crucial—to future progress as the more historic research universities.

TENNANT S. MCWILLIAMS
University of Alabama at Birmingham

Thomas E. Bender, *The University and the City* (1988); Karen DeWitt, *New York Times* (13 August 1991); David R. Goldfield, in *A Companion to the American South*, ed. John B. Boles (2002); Hugh Davis Graham and Nancy Diamond, *The Rise of American Research Universities: Elites and Challengers in the Postwar Years* (1997); Arnold B. Grobman, *Urban State Universities: An Unfinished Agenda* (1988); David R. Jones, *The Civic Universities* (1988); Tennant S. McWilliams, *New Lights in the Valley: The Emergence of UAB* (2007); Merle E. Reed, *Educating the Southern Masses: The Rise of Georgia State University, 1913–1969* (2009); U.S. House of Representatives, Committee on Banking, Finance, and Urban Affairs, Serial No. 102-40 (28 October 1991).

Urbanization and Education

Scholars have given a variety of explanations for why education in the South differs from education in other regions of the United States. Some have emphasized geography as the causal factor, others economics, others ideology, others social structure, and still others some combination of these factors. Southern differences frequently are attributed simply to the rural nature of southern life. The urbanization of southern education took place mainly in the New South period and after (roughly 1875 to the present), and this fact provides one more angle from which the South's educational distinctiveness may be considered.

In broad outline, educational developments in southern cities were similar to those in other American cities. Southern cities experienced a progressive reform movement in education in the early 20th century, just as cities in other regions did; city schools in all regions were racked by the Great Depression of the 1930s as well as by the other economic gyrations of the 20th century; and educational institutions have grown more numerous and diverse in this century, both in the South and out of it. Since the 1954 *Brown v. Board of Education* decision of the U.S. Supreme Court, southern and nonsouthern school systems have been faced with the challenge of desegregation. Urban public universities in Charlotte, Birmingham, Tampa, Atlanta, New Orleans, and other southern cities have recently entered the competition for students and funds with nonurban southern public and private colleges and universities, just as newer public universities in Boston, Cleveland, Detroit, Chicago, and Milwaukee have begun to challenge the primacy of their regions' nonurban public universities and private colleges.

Yet, given this overall similarity from region to region, variations in the South's urban educational experience have distinguished it from the experiences of other regions. Changes regarded as innovations elsewhere have different meanings in the South. For example, the school system in Atlanta, Ga., in the late 19th and early 20th centuries selectively adopted educational innovations such as the introduction of technical subjects into the curriculum. Atlantans at first resisted the new subjects and then slowly accepted them, but only as new avenues of preparatory study for higher education. The reformist motive of providing true vocational education as an alternative offering was slow to be realized.

This hesitancy to embrace innovation wholeheartedly was characteristic of urban higher education as well. In the late 19th and the early 20th centuries, two of the region's urban institutions of higher education, Emory and Vanderbilt, were caught up in a struggle between utilitarian curricular reformers and traditional opponents of that reform. At Emory, which originally was in the small-town setting of Oxford, Ga., the conservatism of President Warren A. Candler (1888–98) undid vocational reforms achieved by his two immediate predecessors. Two decades later, Emory moved from Oxford to the urban setting of Atlanta, a move that was part of a plan by Candler, who by then was a Methodist bishop, to make Emory one of two universities closely tied to the Methodist Episcopal Church, South, and its traditional beliefs and values. Candler and his church had bitterly quarreled with its former affiliate university, Vanderbilt, which under the leadership of Chancellor James H. Kirkland chose secularism over Southern Methodism in order to receive a grant for its medical school from the Carnegie Foundation for the Advancement of Teaching.

At Vanderbilt, even after its divorce from the church and during several decades in which it was led by New South advocates like Kirkland and his successors, opposition to social and educational change was strong. A notable defense of traditional southern values came from the famous Vanderbilt Agrarians who published their manifesto *I'll Take My Stand* in 1930. Ironically, this defense of the values of the rural countryside came from one of the South's preeminent urban universities. One of the Agrarians, Donald Davidson, taught at Vanderbilt for over four decades from the 1910s to the 1950s, defending traditionalism in education and social life during that entire period. Davidson's rabid defense of segregation in the 1950s, however, showed the darker side of southern cultural traditionalism.

The urban South's experience with school desegregation since 1954 has run counter to the prophecies of doom made by Davidson and the anti-integration politicians. Desegregation has taken place with relative success in Florida's major cities—Jacksonville, Miami, and Tampa–St. Petersburg—as well as in other southern cities such as Charlotte, N.C., and Richmond, Va. Thus, by the 1970s most of the images of hate and fear that accompanied desegregation of urban schools came from such northern cities as Boston, Chicago, Buffalo, and Cleveland, rather than from the South. Explanations for this difference vary, but whatever the cause, the South's urban experience clearly contains something that has allowed it to meet the challenge of school desegregation without collapsing into spasms of hate. Nevertheless, the success of desegregation efforts must be interpreted in light of so-called white flight from urban public school systems. For example, in 1985 about 94 percent of the public school students in Atlanta and about 77 percent in Memphis were black. Although some school systems are successfully turning around such trends, the new patterns of segregation will persist in many locales in the foreseeable future.

These new patterns of segregation have been called resegregation by many, and Supreme Court decisions in the 1990s in urban areas in Oklahoma and Georgia, a border state and a Deep South state respectively, meant the diminution if not the end of mandatory efforts to desegregate public schools in much of the South. Following this trend, the Supreme Court–influenced abandonment of busing for desegregation in the Charlotte-Mecklenburg County schools was an enormously important reversal of successful desegregation, and a rather clear sanction of resegregation, undertaken this time with the weight of the law on the side of districting that proffered itself as nonracial, at the same time that it led to increased racial imbalance in many schools. Further litigation in the first decade of the 21st century, this time in the school districts of Louisville, Ky., and Seattle, Wash., meant more repudiation of attempts to desegregate urban schools, even those that replaced mandatory measures with voluntary policies.

Comparisons of the southern urban educational experience with that in other regions are almost always made with the Northeast or the Midwest, but southern cities, with the exception of Birmingham and a few others, have little in common with the industrial centers of those areas. As 21st-century commercial, regional, and governmental centers, most of the South's cities have more in common with western cities such as Los Angeles than they do with the older industrial centers. Fruitful results should emerge when southern urban educational development is compared to the situation in western urban centers, as well as to the Northeast and Midwest. Louisville and Seattle as the settings for two of the most recent landmark cases in school desegregation law may be significant indications of this trend.

WAYNE J. URBAN
University of Alabama

Mark K. Bauman, "Warren Akin Candler: Conservative amidst Change" (Ph.D. dissertation, Emory University, 1975); Charles Boger and Gary Orfield, eds., *School Resegregation: Must the South Turn Back?* (2005); John Kohler, "Donald Davidson, a Critique from the Losing Side: The Social and Educational Views of a Southern Conservative" (Ph.D. dissertation, Georgia State University, 1982); Kevin M. Kruse, *White Flight: Atlanta and the Making of Modern Conservatism* (2005); William E. Schmidt, *New York Times* (25 May 1985); Twelve Southerners, *I'll Take My Stand: The South and the Agrarian Tradition* (1930); Wayne J. Urban, in *The Age of Urban Reform: New Perspectives on the Progressive Era*, ed. Michael H. Ebner and Eugene M. Tobin (1977), in *Education and the Rise of the New South*, ed. Ronald K. Goodenow and Arthur O. White (1981).

Women's Higher Education

The higher education of southern women reflects the region's cultural, economic, and political history. Conceptions of gender, race, and class are intricately interwoven in the southern past. From the colonial era to the present, these factors colored educational policies and practices and contributed to the distinctive educational experience of women.

In the 18th and 19th centuries "higher education" encompassed all schooling beyond the primary level. The first school to offer advanced education to women was the Ursuline Academy in New Orleans. Founded by the Sisters of the Order of Saint Ursula in 1727, the academy is "the oldest, continuously operating school for girls and the oldest Catholic school in the United States." Salem Academy in Winston-Salem, N.C., founded in 1772 by the Moravians, was the first school established exclusively for girls in the British colonies. Throughout the 19th century Salem Female Academy offered primary and secondary courses to boarding and day students. In 1890 it began conferring baccalaureate degrees and in 1907 changed its name to Salem Academy and College. In the 18th century the Ursuline and Salem academies educated black, white, and occasionally American Indian girls in an integrated setting. But as racial policies became more restrictive, educational opportunities for nonwhite women became fewer. Although free women of color could attend private schools sponsored by various benevolent societies or religious organizations, enslaved women were denied even primary training by the slave codes of most southern states.

Gender segregation was the norm in the antebellum South. Academies had departments for girls and boys, and the curricula reflected the future prospects of the children. Girls were rarely prepared for trades or offered the classical subjects required for college. Because criteria for baccalaureate degrees varied tremendously, historians debate when collegiate education was first offered to women. Georgia Female College (renamed Wesleyan Female College in 1843), which was chartered in 1836, awarded its first baccalaureate degree in 1840 and claims to be the "first college in the world for women." The Tennessee and Alabama Female Institute (renamed Mary Sharp College in 1853) in Winchester, Tenn., required Greek, Latin, and calculus for its degrees and consequently considered itself the first "true women's college."

Southern colleges have been characterized as less rigorous than those in the Northeast, but Christie Anne Farnham contends that in the antebellum period elite southern women had greater access to the liberal arts than their northern counterparts. A classical education made future planters' wives better companions for their husbands and mothers for their sons, not competitors for jobs. In the North, women who sought the same education as men of their class were perceived as "mounting an attack on the sex segregation of the professions." For women whose families could not afford a private education, opportunities were limited. There was little teacher training available before the Civil War. When Christopher Memminger set up Charleston's public school system in the 1850s, he had to import teachers from New England.

The Civil War significantly impacted higher education. As Drew Faust notes, many parents saw residential colleges as refuges from slave uprisings or military actions. In Virginia, enrollments at Hollins Institute doubled during the war, and Farmville Female College advertised its remoteness from the battlefields as an attraction. Salem Academy became a haven for women from eastern North Carolina. But not all schools were isolated from the conflict. Mary Sharp closed when General Rosecrans occupied the town and made the college a hospital. Although it reopened in 1865, its enrollments never recovered and the school closed permanently in 1893. Columbia College shut down when Sherman's troops entered South Carolina's capital in 1865 and did not reopen until 1873.

The war transformed teaching into a profession for women. Most antebellum teachers were men, but by 1865 there were nearly as many women as men teaching in the classrooms. The demand for teachers was accompanied by an expansion of teacher education programs and by a change in attitudes toward women's employment. By 1880 more women than men were teaching in the region. Most of the private denominational colleges that sprang up throughout the South were coeducational, but several were single gender. Educational opportunities for black women expanded considerably after 1865. As Beverly Guy-Sheftall notes, every black women's college—Bennett, Spelman, Barber-Scotia, and Huston-Tillotson—originated in the postbellum South. Spelman, the oldest historically black college for women, opened in 1881 as the Atlanta Baptist Female Seminary and awarded its first college degrees in 1901. The name was changed to Spelman Seminary in 1884 and to Spelman College in 1924. In 2008 *U.S. News and World Report* ranked Spelman the nation's best historically black institution.

After the Civil War, southern states became eligible for Morrill Act land-grant moneys. Some states used federal funds to add vocational courses to the liberal arts curriculum of the state university; others created new institutions. Only Mississippi, South Carolina, and Virginia funded schools for blacks before the Morrill Act of 1890 required states to establish schools for both races. "Colored" land-grant colleges were all coeducational and until the 1920s provided the highest level of public education available to black women in the region. Aside from Howard University, chartered by the federal government in

1867, opportunities for black women to attend publicly funded liberal arts institutions were limited.

The first state-supported college for women was the Mississippi Industrial Institute and College for the Education of White Girls of the State of Mississippi in the Arts and Sciences (II&C), chartered in 1884. II&C offered vocational training and professional diplomas as well as liberal arts courses and baccalaureate degrees. In 1920 the name was changed to the Mississippi State College for Women and in 1974 to Mississippi University for Women. Publicly supported colleges for white women were subsequently established in Georgia (1889), South Carolina (1891), North Carolina (1891), Alabama (1893), Texas (1901), Florida (1905), and Oklahoma (1908). Students who promised to teach after graduation received free tuition.

Normal schools (from the French *école normale* or "model school") also offered teacher training. The 1907 Report of the U.S. Commissioner for Education listed 30 public normal schools for white students and 11 for blacks in the region. Whereas liberal arts degrees typically required a four-year course of study and were aimed at the elite, normal and industrial programs were shorter and catered to the middling classes.

The University of Mississippi admitted women students beginning in 1882, but other flagship universities were hesitant to admit women. In 1903 there were no women at the universities of Georgia, Louisiana, and Virginia and only three at the University of North Carolina. Some states established separate coordinate colleges for women. Mary Washington, the coordinate college of the University of Virginia, was miles away in Fredericksburg. But separate was seldom equal. At the turn of the 20th century, women's colleges, like black colleges, had poorer facilities, fewer programs, and inferior resources.

H. Sophie Newcomb Memorial College for Women in New Orleans was the exception to this "poor relation" status. Josephine Louise Newcomb founded the college in memory of her daughter in 1886 and eventually contributed $3 million to the institution. A coordinate college of Tulane University, Newcomb was the first degree-granting college for women established within an American university and served as a model for northern coordinate colleges such as Barnard and Pembroke. Newcomb was among the earliest schools awarded a "standard college" designation by the Southern Association of College Women.

World War II challenged traditional racial and gender views. Women became the majority on many campuses, and their contributions to the war effort earned them increased respect for their capabilities. The GI Bill brought additional changes in enrollment patterns. Columbia College opened classes to veterans and graduated its first male student in 1948. Florida made the state university in Gainesville and the state women's college in Tallahassee coeducational. Clemson, South Carolina's land-grant college, had temporarily enrolled women in engineering programs during the Great Depression and the Second World War; in 1954 the school opened all its programs to women. Institutions were slow to admit black women to their degree programs, however. A black woman received her master's degree from the University of Tennessee in 1954, but violence accompanied Autherine Lucy's attempt to enroll at the University of Alabama in 1956.

The connection between the politics of race and gender was apparent in the desegregation battles of the mid-20th century. The 1963 integration of Clemson led South Carolina state senator John D. Long to demand an end to coeducation at any historically white school that accepted black males. Integration, he argued, would threaten the purity of white womanhood and lead to the amalgamation of the races.

Integrationists employed racial and gender stereotypes to facilitate desegregation. Because black women were seen as less threatening than black men to white culture, and white women were perceived as less violent than white men, women were chosen to be plaintiffs in lawsuits seeking the integration of universities in Alabama, Florida, Georgia, and South Carolina. The men from North Carolina's A&T who organized the first sit-ins in 1960 were supported by women from Bennett and the Woman's College.

The civil rights and women's movements contributed to the demise of single-gender colleges. The Woman's College of North Carolina became coeducational in 1964 and changed its name to the University of North Carolina at Greensboro. Georgia College and State University admitted men in 1967. The University of Virginia became coeducational in 1970 and its coordinate college, Mary Washington, became a separate, coeducational institution in 1972. Winthrop University in South Carolina became coeducational in 1974. Mississippi University for Women opened its programs to men in 1982; Texas Woman's University (TWU), in 1995. The devastation of Hurricane Katrina in 2005 led Tulane to abolish H. Sophie Newcomb College and create a coeducational Newcomb-Tulane undergraduate division. Randolph-Macon Woman's College in Virginia announced its decision to become coeducational in 2006.

The last public universities to admit women were the Virginia Military Institute (VMI) and the Citadel. Both feared that coeducation would enervate the "adversative system" used to train the corps. Ignoring the *Brown* ruling against "separate but equal," VMI proposed a parallel Virginia Women's Institute for Leadership at Mary Baldwin, a private women's college. When Shannon Faulkner sued to be admitted to its corps, the Citadel proposed a women's program at Converse College. In *U.S. v. Virginia et al.* (1996) the Supreme Court ruled that neither the "goal of producing citizen-soldiers" or "adversative method of training" was "inherently unsuitable to women." The ruling resulted in the admission of women to the Citadel and VMI.

Women's higher education has changed dramatically over the centuries. The vast majority now attend racially integrated, coeducational institutions. Racial, ethnic, and social backgrounds are more diverse than ever, with Hispanic women the fastest growing minority group. Yet higher education still reflects the region's distinctive cultural, economic, and political history. The South boasts the top-rated historically black university or college in the nation (Spelman) and the "largest university primarily for women in the United States" (TWU).

AMY THOMPSON MCCANDLESS
The Graduate School of the College of Charleston (S.C.)

Christie Ann Farnham, *The Education of the Southern Belle: Higher Education and Student Socialization in the Antebellum South* (1994); Drew Gilpin Faust, *Mothers of Invention: Women of the Slaveholding South in the American Civil War* (1996); Lynn D. Gordon, *Gender and Higher Education in the Progressive Era* (1990); Frances Griffin, *Less Time for Meddling: A History of Salem Academy and College, 1772–1866* (1979); Beverly Guy-Sheftall, *Journal of Negro Education* (Summer 1982); Elizabeth L. Ihle, *Black Women's Academic Education in the South: History of Black Women's Education in the South, 1865–Present* (1986); Amy Thompson McCandless, *The Past in the Present: Women's Higher Education in the Twentieth-Century American South* (1999); *Mississippi University for Women et al. v. Hogan* 458 U.S. 718 (1982); Clarence L. Mohr, *Louisiana History* (Winter 2008); *United States, Petitioner v. Virginia et al.* and *Virginia et al., Petitioners v. United States*, 116 S.Ct. 2264 (1996).

Agrarians, Vanderbilt

In 1930, 12 southern intellectuals, most of whom were either teachers at, or graduates of, Vanderbilt University, published *I'll Take My Stand: The South and the Agrarian Tradition*, a collection of essays pugnaciously and defensively hailing the economy and culture of the South as an antidote to the evils of industrialism. "If a community, or a section, or a race, or an age, is groaning under industrialism, and well aware that it is an evil dispensation, it must find a way to throw it off," they declared in a jointly signed "Statement of Principles." "To think that this cannot be done is pusillanimous."

The warrant for an agrarian as opposed to industrial economy lay in the superiority of its culture, and, in fact, the majority of the symposium's essays were probing critiques, from a conservative viewpoint, of what the authors considered a flabby, deracinating, and often meretricious national culture. Chief among the instigators of Agrarianism were the Vanderbilt University professors John Crowe Ransom and Donald Davidson, both published poets, and their former student, Allen Tate, an aspiring poet who had already insinuated himself into New York literary circles. They managed to enroll in the symposium two southern literary figures of national reputation—John Gould Fletcher and Stark Young—as well as several of their associates, including the young poet and Vanderbilt alumnus Robert Penn Warren (who drew the unhappy task of defending segregation), the historian Frank L. Owsley, and the political scientist Herbert Clarence Nixon. Individual essays considered education, art, religion, and the notion of progress while others commented broadly and sometimes lyrically on southern cultural traditions and mores. There was relatively little economic analysis; the brief for southern agriculture was most compellingly an appeal for the pleasures of an imagined southern folk community. Although the writer Andrew Nelson Lytle scolded that the farm "is not a place to grow wealthy; it is a place to grow corn," in fact, it was spiritual, not material, wealth of southern folk life that animated his romantic command to the reader: "Do what we did after the war and the Reconstruction: return to our looms, our hand crafts, our reproducing stock. Throw out the radio and take down the fiddle from the wall."

Although widely reviewed at the time and a touchstone of southern studies ever since, the practical results of the Agrarian volume were nil. Critics depicted the Agrarians as "Twelve Canutes" attempting to resist the tides of change and guilty of mythologizing the southern past. ("Have they never been told that the obscenities and depravities of the most degenerate hole of a cotton-mill town are but pale reflections of the lurid obscenities and depravities of Southern backwoods communities?" wrote Gerald W. Johnson derisively.) In fact, the Agrarian project was complex: In part, the symposium was an act of filial devotion to the South, a proud and determined effort, in the midst of the profound changes produced in the South by modernization, to stay "reconstructed but unregenerate," as the title taken from the lyric to "Dixie" signaled. In part, it was of a piece with the cosmopolitan modernism of the 1920s. The Agrarians' ideas often tracked the Left's critique of industrial capitalism and its jejune popular culture: Ransom ascribed American cultural poverty to the pioneer tradition, Davidson called for an art that arose from folk culture, the psychologist Lyle Lanier warned of the "economic anarchy" resulting from corporate capitalism, and Tate neatly inverted progressive tropes of self-fulfillment through political action when he called on southern reactionaries to reestablish cultural traditions through "violence." In a decade characterized by contentious debates over the effects of modernity, the Agrarians struck a radical conservative note. They briefly pursued a decentralist economic program in the 1930s (contributing to an anthology edited by Tate and Herbert Agar entitled *Who Owns America? A New Declaration of Independence* in 1936), but it was their knowing manipulation of the symbol of the South that has inspired continued attention.

The Agrarians' own retrospective analyses of their movement differed; Ransom repudiated agrarian economics and embraced the New Deal, while Davidson embraced regionalism and a cultural and racial chauvinism that led to an intransigent defense of segregation in the 1950s. A generation of southern literary scholars, notably Cleanth Brooks, Louis Rubin, and Lewis Simpson, revered the Agrarians as the fathers of modern southern literary study; later neo-Agrarians such as Richard M. Weaver and M. E. Bradford interpreted the movement as an important inspiration for modern American conservatism.

PAUL V. MURPHY
Grand Valley State University

Paul Conkin, *The Southern Agrarians* (1988); Mark G. Malvasi, *The Unregenerate South: The Agrarian Thought of John Crowe Ransom, Allen Tate, and Donald Davidson* (1997); Paul V. Murphy, *The Rebuke of History: The Southern Agrarians and American Conservative Thought* (2001); Michael O'Brien, *The Idea of the American South, 1920–1941* (1979); Louis D. Rubin Jr., *The Wary Fugitives: Four Poets and the South* (1978); Daniel Joseph Singal, *The War Within: From Victorian to Modernist Thought in the South, 1919–1945* (1982); Twelve Southerners, *I'll Take My Stand: The South and the Agrarian Tradition* (1930).

Alabama, University of

Chartered in 1820, the University of Alabama opened in 1831 in Tuscaloosa, then a frontier town in the "Old Southwest." Founders modeled the school, both physically and academically, on the University of Virginia. Students routinely brought pistols and knives to campus and imbibed in alcohol obtained in town, flagrantly violating university rules. Violent student rebellions in which they assaulted each other and the faculty and terrorized university presidents ultimately led trustees to turn the university into a military academy by 1860. During the Civil War academic classes and military training continued until federal troops burned the university in April 1865.

When only one student registered in 1865, trustees decided to rebuild the

Denny Chimes, a 115-foot campanile named after the former university president George H. Denny (1912–36), is the University of Alabama's most recognizable landmark. (Zachary Riggins, University Relations Photography)

university before reopening in 1869. During Reconstruction, political turmoil paralyzed the university, resulting in frequent leadership changes, few students, and little money. When state appropriations rose in the mid-1870s, student numbers and faculty strength increased, although the school remained a military one. In 1880 Congress granted the university 40,000 acres of coal land in compensation for the 1865 burning of university facilities. Student unrest returned, now against the military system, which was discontinued in 1903. By the end of the 19th century the school had added women students, a chapter of Phi Beta Kappa, a flourishing Greek system, and an expanding athletic program.

The 20th century saw the university transformed from a small southern military college to a multidisciplinary university with several colleges. Programs such as law and medicine that had languished now flourished along with the new graduate school and extension centers. An integration effort in 1956 failed when a campus riot occurred. Segregation ended in 1963 with the enrollment of two African American students, despite Governor George Wallace's famous "stand in the schoolhouse door." In 2009, 3,379 African American students were enrolled. In 1969 extension centers at Huntsville and Birmingham became autonomous, and in 1975 university trustees merged those two campuses with that in Tuscaloosa to create the University of Alabama system. The national success of the athletic program in the 1970s overshadowed escalating faculty discontent with administrative neglect of academics. The president resigned after two "no confidence" votes of the faculty.

The university was now landlocked, unable to expand while the student population grew. In 1976 the university and the state mental health department agreed to swap land, with the university giving the mental health department property across town and receiving Bryce Hospital land adjacent to the campus. Now the university could more than double the size of its campus. Construction of new buildings began and has never stopped.

Until 1980 the University of Alabama was primarily a teaching university, with minimal emphasis on faculty research. That emphasis now changed, as university leadership encouraged its faculty to embark on research projects and to seek outside grants for support. As benefits, such research improved instructional quality at the university and assisted the state's economic development.

University leadership also instituted major academic improvements. Student admission and retention standards were strengthened, a comprehensive core curriculum was created, and an honors program was organized. To compete for superior students, the university launched successful financial campaigns among alumni to create scholarships in an era of declining state financial support. The results were dramatic, as the number of National Merit scholars grew along with enrollment.

The new emphasis on research stimulated attention to the university library. Manuscript holdings, already rich in personal papers, received voluminous political collections from Lister Hill, John Sparkman, Carl Elliott, and Tom Bevill. These gifts sparked other significant donations such as the Wade Hall southern collection and the Lupton collection of African American cookbooks. By 2009, the library contained nearly 3 million volumes and an estimated 1,700,000 government documents.

While the university's national academic reputation increased with faculty research, competition for legislative appropriations led the university increasingly to seek outside income. Faculty aggressively sought grants, and university leaders aggressively sought funds from alumni. Since 2000 both have been successful, especially multimillion-dollar gifts that have established such programs as the Blount Undergraduate Initiative. With the growth of the university's financial base, leadership has concentrated on attracting students of outstanding academic quality. In 2009 student enrollment was 28,807, including 388 National Merit scholars and 86 National Achievement scholars, and the university ranks 43rd among the top 50 public universities.

SARAH WOOLFOLK WIGGINS
University of Alabama

E. Culpepper Clark, *The Schoolhouse Door: Segregation's Last Stand at the University of Alabama* (1993); A. James Fuller, *Chaplain to the Confederacy: Basil Manly and Baptist Life in the Old South* (2000); Mary Chapman Mathews, *A Mansion's Memories* (2006); James B. Sellers, *History of the University of Alabama, 1819–1902* (1953).

Alabama, University of, at Birmingham

In 2009 the University of Alabama at Birmingham (UAB) existed as a public urban research institution spread across some 83 blocks of downtown Birmingham. The university's 2,050 faculty offered programs in the arts and sciences, business, teacher education, engineering, and wide-ranging health affairs to some 18,000 students, 10,650 of whom were undergraduates (32 percent African American). UAB's grants and contracts—excluding any state funds—totaled $480 million. It was the only university in Alabama classified by the Carnegie Endowment as a "very high research activity" institution. It also had Carnegie's "Civic Engagement" classification.

In 1936 the University of Alabama (UA), in Tuscaloosa, acquired New Deal funding to begin offering courses in a Birmingham ravaged by plummeting employment at U.S. Steel and other crises of the Great Depression. Located in an old house adjacent to the banking and municipal district, the Extension Center offered classes in the arts and sciences, teacher education, and engineering. In 1944 UA's Birmingham presence gained even greater profile when the UA Medical College moved from Tuscaloosa to Birmingham. The large pool of indigent patients found in a blue-collar and heavy-industry town encouraged such relocation. Even more, many powerful Alabama physicians—including the UA medical dean—wanted a four-year medical program developed in the relatively modern Hillman and Jefferson Hospitals, located some seven blocks south of the Extension Center. Such prospects generated intense political conflict. Many influential people of Alabama's antebellum centers—Mobile, Montgomery, Tuscaloosa—could not fathom something as culturally significant as a medical college developing in the state's new urban area, Birmingham (founded in 1871). Ironically, not even U.S. Steel, a key source of Birmingham's growth, was encouraging the move. The corporation feared a competing power structure and an enhanced payroll emerging in a city it had long held in colonial constraints. Further, a new urban elite in Birmingham might erode the "Big Mule" alliance that U.S. Steel and its management-class Birmingham colleagues had long had with rural elites of the old plantation counties—the controlling force in the Alabama legislature. Still, when key physicians statewide facilitated UA's gradual acquisition of Hillman and Jefferson hospitals, Gov. Chauncey Sparks used his considerable influence to seal the deal for Birmingham.

For some 25 years following World War II the UA Extension Center and the UA Medical College continued to grow, with Birmingham deans reporting to the president of UA in Tuscaloosa. Extension center enrollment in 1945 was 800; by 1963 it was 3,647. In 1947 a nursing school grew alongside the medical college, joined some 20 years later by the main nursing program, moved from Tuscaloosa to Birmingham. In 1948 a dental school took off. An incipient medical center was taking shape. Harking back to the fight over moving the medical college, however, the challenge this growth presented to Alabama's Old Order culture and higher education establishment, and to the state's finances, resulted in repeated conflicts with leaders of the Birmingham programs and their growing number of civic supporters. When the medical dean, Roy Kracke, and the dental dean, Joseph F. Volker, sought to get around obstacles of limited state funding and collaborated on a federal grant to build a facility bringing extension center programs physically adjacent to their own programs instead of continuing some seven blocks apart, the UA president feared the implications of such unity and blocked the move. When UA sought to require all Birmingham engineering students to complete their study in Tuscaloosa, it was only the threat of an Auburn University extension center in Birmingham that allowed continuation of the full Birmingham engineering program.

Still, out of the 1950s came changes ultimately permitting the emergence of a full institution in Birmingham. In 1953 Oliver C. Carmichael returned to his home state to be president of UA after having been chancellor of Vanderbilt University and then head of the Carnegie Endowment for the Advancement of Teaching, where he facilitated creation of the State University of New York (SUNY) system. Despite such experience he was quickly stymied in Tuscaloosa. In refusing to fight desegregation after the *Brown* decision he was too liberal for the UA Board of Trustees and most Tuscaloosa civic leaders, and in not pushing aggressively for desegregation he was too conservative for many Tuscaloosa faculty. Still, when the board effectively assumed control of UA's Tuscaloosa operations to block desegregation, the otherwise sidelined Carmichael began spending more time on Birmingham affairs. He approved plans to build a new facility for the extension center directly adjacent to the medical center. He recruited a new dean for the medical college. And he got to know much better the most dynamic leader among Birmingham affairs, dental dean and director of research and graduate studies, Joseph F. Volker. Carmichael encouraged Volker, a native of Elizabeth, N.J., to push ahead on high-profile federal funding opportunities for both the physical expansion and the programmatic growth of all Birmingham operations. By 1965 the extension center enrolled 4,572, and the medical center 1,023. He also did not discourage Volker's low-profile desegregation steps in these programs. Accordingly, by 1966 with the desegregation crisis essentially passed and Carmichael's successor, Frank Rose, equally interested in Birmingham, the UA board reorganized Birmingham programs—all medical center as well as extension center endeavors—to report up through the new position of vice president for Birmingham Affairs, and named Volker to this office.

By 1969, after several years of annual enrollment increases in Birmingham of around 30 percent, plus massive core grants from Urban Renewal and the Appalachian Regional Commission, and National Institutes of Health (NIH) and National Science Foundation (NSF) grants among the medical center faculty reaching $5 million, President Rose had reason to recommend even more autonomy for the Birmingham campus. What sealed his decision, however, had equally to do with developments down on the Gulf Coast. Mobile leaders asked for an expansion of their UA Extension Center along the lines of Birmingham affairs; Rose reacted oppositely by shutting down the Mobile center. In turn, Mobile's civic elite aided mightily by Gov. George Wallace—who needed the votes of the Mobile delegation in the legislature for his community college system—simply created a separate University of South Alabama, with a medical school. Stunned and fearing similar separatism closer to home, Frank Rose proceeded to convince the UA board that the Alabama political environment, not to mention "the Volker momentum" in Birmingham, called for creation of a UA system of three campuses: Tuscaloosa, Birmingham, and Huntsville (where extension center operations had grown alongside aerospace and defense endeavors). Few were surprised when Joseph F. Volker became the founding president of the University of Alabama at Birmingham (UAB).

Over the next five years President Volker consummated his long-developing plans: a public research university emphasizing interdisciplinary health science and clinical care, merged with an urban-civic university mixing part-time commuter students with gradually increasing numbers of traditional, full-time students in residence. He added schools of Public Health, Optometry, and Health-Related Professions. He developed doctoral programs in life sciences with interdisciplinary connections to those in health sciences. He hired faculty of international reputation, most notably heart-transplant surgeon John W. Kirklin. As he moved on to be founding chancellor of the UA system in 1976, Volker was succeeded in the UAB presidency by two he had long been mentoring: physician S. Richardson Hill (1976–86) and oral surgeon Charles A. ("Scotty") McCallum (1987–93). During these years, while developing a national profile as an urban university, UAB significantly increased numbers of full-time and dormitory-based students and added NCAA athletics under the leadership of basketball coach and athletic director Gene Bartow. Likewise by 1993, total enrollment reached 16,600 with 23 percent African American, and grants and contracts rose to $130 million. National accolades appeared. *U.S. News and World Report* profiled UAB as "the nation's number 1 up and coming university." The Carnegie Endowment's 1986–90 analysis of peer-reviewed publications and research funding ranked UAB as number 17 out of the top 32 "Research 1 Public Institutions" in America and the only Alabama institution in this category. Criticisms also appeared, as in the *Wall Street Journal*'s suggestion that UAB acted irresponsibly in accepting City of Birmingham bond-issue money to help build its football program when Birmingham city schools lacked appropriate support.

Despite short but intense discord inside and outside UAB over possible sale—"privatization"—of University Hospital, which ultimately did not happen, this growth continued on through the 1990s and into the early 21st century. Physician J. Claude Bennett became the last of the presidents who emerged from Volker's original leadership team. In 1996 he was succeeded by W. Ann Reynolds, who had been chancellor of both the California State University System and the City University of New York System. In 2002 she was succeeded by Carol Garrison, who had been provost and then acting-president of the University of Louisville. In 2009 President Garrison presided over a university still expanding its broad-ranging research, especially in biomedical and behavioral sciences, but also growing its campus—tree-lined avenues and quadrangles hosting an undergraduate population of some 74 percent full-time students, 20 percent of whom lived in new dormitories—with an endowment of $332 million.

TENNANT S. MCWILLIAMS
University of Alabama at Birmingham

Virginia Fisher, *Building on a Vision: A Fifty-Year Retrospective of UAB's Academic Health Center* (1995); Hugh Davis Graham and Nancy Diamond, *The Rise of Research Universities: Elites and Challengers in the Postwar Years* (1997); Tennant S. McWilliams, *New Lights in the Valley: The Emergence of UAB* (2007).

Alderman, Edwin A.

(1861–1931) EDUCATOR AND UNIVERSITY PRESIDENT.

Born in Wilmington, N.C., to James Alderman and Susan Jane Corbett Alderman, Edwin Alderman was an only son and the third of four children. His father was a timber inspector and a devoted officer in the First Presbyterian Church of Wilmington. His mother's family (of French ancestry) moved to Britain in the late 17th century. He married twice, first to Emma Graves in 1885. With her, he had three children, but all died in childhood, and Emma died in 1896. His second marriage, in 1904, was to Bessie Green Hearn in New Orleans, with whom he had one son.

Alderman received his early education in the private schools of Wilmington and at Bethel Military Academy in Warrenton, Va. In 1878 he enrolled at the University of North Carolina and was awarded his Ph.B. degree with honors in English and Latin, along with a prized oratorical medal, in 1882. He accepted a teaching position in the public schools of Goldsboro, N.C., temporarily, expecting to become a lawyer. But he never left education as a career. While in Goldsboro, he came under the influence of Edward P. Moses, whom he succeeded as superintendent of schools in 1885. In these years, he became an ardent advocate for public education in the southern Progressive tradition. In 1889 he and Charles Duncan McIver were appointed to conduct teachers' institutes to improve pedagogical techniques among teachers with limited training. This focus on primary and secondary education would prove a lifelong passion.

Beginning in 1892, Alderman began his career in higher education both as professor and administrator. For one year, he taught at the newly established State Normal and Industrial School for Women in Greensboro (now UNC Greensboro) where McIver had been named president. In 1893 he moved to the University of North Carolina at Chapel Hill as professor in the department of history and philosophy of education. Three years later, in 1896, he became president of UNC. The university grew in size and stature, but funding issues proved discouraging.

In 1900, Alderman moved to a private university as president of Tulane University in New Orleans. He continued his interest in building primary and secondary education in the South and enhanced the reputation of the university. By this point, Alderman was recognized as a formidable leader in the movement to strengthen public education. He was a founding member of the Southern Education Board, established in 1901, which with help from northern philanthropists advocated for free, tax-supported school systems throughout the South. Alderman remained active with the organization until it disbanded in 1914.

In 1904 Alderman was selected to become the first president of the University of Virginia (UVA), previously administered by a chairman of the faculty and board of visitors. He served in this position for 25 years. His tenure as president was transformative for the university. He developed professional schools (law, medicine, education, and engineering), secured larger state appropriations, raised admissions standards for students while increasing enrollment, built a large endowment, oversaw the admission of women to professional and graduate schools (but ultimately bowed to alumni pressure to avoid the creation of a coordinate college or full coeducation), reorganized the undergraduate curriculum, increased the size of the faculty sixfold, grew the student body fivefold, and promoted the "democratization" of educational opportunity. He established the *Virginia Quarterly Review*, still in publication, in 1925.

Alderman embraced the southern Progressive agenda. He claimed that he wanted to move the University of Virginia from "the ideals of Oxford to the ideals of Wisconsin; to transform it from an aristocratic University to a democratic University." He did so by supporting educational reform in public schools throughout the state, to encourage enrollment in the university from this sector. The Curry School of Education developed close ties to state superintendents, and Alderman appointed Charles Payne to focus on primary and secondary educational reform. He also developed an extension program (under Charles Maphis and George Zehmer) to bring lectures from UVA faculty to areas well beyond Charlottesville. Alderman was an active supporter of Woodrow Wilson, and in 1924 he was called upon to deliver a memorial address before the U.S. Congress. By then, his reputation as a national educational leader was at its peak.

Yet, like many southern Progressives, he was blind to the needs of African Americans and other disadvantaged groups. He had ties to the Aristogenic Association, a group that believed in white survival and Anglo-Saxon superiority. During his tenure, eugenics research became a major focus within the Biology Department and School of Medicine, and Ivey Foreman Lewis, a leading eugenicist, influenced both faculty hires and the nature of the student population for decades.

Plagued by ill health for several decades, Alderman spent two years at a sanatorium at Lake Saranac (from 1912 to 1914) to receive treatment for tuberculosis of the larynx and complications in both lungs. He largely ran the university from a distance, relying increasingly on the help of John Lloyd Newcomb, who would succeed him as president. Edwin Alderman died of a stroke in 1931, while traveling to deliver an address at the inauguration of the president of the University of Illinois. Despite his long-term illnesses, he was a powerful and highly respected southern Progressive educational leader.

PHYLLIS K. LEFFLER
University of Virginia

Edward Ayers, *The Promise of the New South: Life after Reconstruction* (1992); Michael Dennis, *Lessons in Progress: State Universities and Progressivism in the New South, 1880–1920* (2001), *Virginia Magazine of History and Biography* (January 1997); Gregory Michael Dorr, *Journal of Southern History* (May 2000); Dewey Grantham, *The Regional Imagination: The South and Recent American History* (1979); Dumas Malone, *Edwin A. Alderman: A Biography* (1940); Presidents Papers, Harrison-Small Special Collections Library, University of Virginia.

American Missionary Association Colleges

The American Missionary Association (AMA) strongly believed that emancipated blacks should become full citizens and have access to all levels of education. It chartered Atlanta University, Hampton Institute, Fisk University, Talladega College, Tougaloo College, Straight College (now Dillard University), Tillotson College (Huston-Tillotson), and LeMoyne College (LeMoyne-Owen). Hampton Institute quickly became an independent industrial school, and the AMA focused on liberal arts training. The curriculum was similar to that in a majority of contemporary liberal arts colleges. Since few former slaves were prepared for higher education, the colleges also taught primary, secondary, normal, and college preparatory classes. Initially, a majority of students were in the lower grades. Fisk University accepted its first college students in 1871, but had an enrollment of only 33 by 1883. Talladega did not accept its initial college class until 1891. In 1908 the AMA taught 10,593 elementary students, 1,166 secondary, 1,169 special students, 147 theological, and 159 college students. The colleges were small, underfunded, and understaffed but offered the best opportunity for black youth to achieve higher education. The colleges continued their secondary and normal training and provided thousands of teachers for black public schools.

All black colleges struggled to survive in the early 20th century. Their students were poor, and southern whites were indifferent or hostile; collections for black education were declining in the North, and appeals to northern philanthropy fell on deaf ears unless requested for industrial education. The only growth in funds came from blacks themselves. Despite poverty and discrimination, tuition payments made by black students to AMA schools rose by 50 percent between 1900 and 1910. Poverty and neglect did not prevent a steady, if uneven and slow, improvement of the colleges. In 1918 the number of elementary students had declined to 4,624 while the secondary students had increased to 3,039 and college students to 351, a natural progression of students since 1908. In that same year Fisk granted 28 bachelor's degrees. Talladega awarded 16, Atlanta University 11, and Straight and Tillotson one each.

AMA colleges experienced rapid growth and improvement between 1915 and 1930. The curriculum was modernized, with greater attention given to the social and natural sciences and less on the classics. The course of study differed little from that of white colleges except for more emphasis on black history and literature, and racial uplift. AMA schools always instilled racial pride and stressed the responsibility of students to assist their less fortunate brethren. During this period the AMA increased its appropriations by five times, and northern philanthropists began to support black colleges. The number of black college students increased eightfold. Nearly 3,000 students were enrolled in AMA colleges in 1940, and the number increased significantly after the war.

Though occasional students such as W. E. B. Du Bois hailed from the North, a majority of the early students came from southern AMA schools. Most were from poor, uneducated families. Nearly all took summer jobs, many as teachers, and enrollment was small in the fall because students were picking cotton. As late as 1900 some Tougaloo women still followed the plow during growing season so they could pay tuition. Northern teachers marveled at both students' and parents' willingness to sacrifice for education. By the turn of the century the student profile began to change. In 1903, 24 children of alumni enrolled at Talladega. There were 30 high school valedictorians in the 129-member Talladega freshman class of 1934, and similar quality students enrolled in the other colleges. A large percentage of AMA college graduates attended professional or graduate school. Of course, many students were still impoverished, the first in their families to attend college, and suffered educational deficiencies. Among parents of Tillotson College students in 1943–44 were 39 common laborers, 79 domestic servants, and 31 unemployed. The colleges consistently raised standards, but always attempted to minister to all segments of the black population.

Faculty improvement paralleled that of students. In the early years, most faculty taught both secondary and college classes, and many were more fitted for the former. Nevertheless, Du Bois, who graduated from Fisk University in 1888, found the faculty "inspiring and beneficial." In 1889 he enrolled at Harvard, where he found not better teachers, only teachers better known.

All AMA colleges had interracial faculties, though at first most college instructors were white. As more blacks earned degrees, they joined the college ranks. The AMA on principle insisted upon interracial staffs in all its colleges. Given the state of race relations at the time some friction between black and white faculty was inevitable. A Tougaloo nurse was released in 1911 because she grew to take "the southern attitude" toward her black colleagues, and some blacks resented white faculty. Fortunately, hostile blacks and patronizing whites were in a minority. In 1943 Chicago *Defender* reporter Enoch P. Waters described Talladega College as "an oasis of racial democracy in a desert of racial segregation and prejudice." He found no racial distinctions and saw whites and blacks "mingling freely and with equality." Other AMA campuses were similar to Talladega.

As the number of black faculty increased so did the quality. A 1932 U.S. Office of Education study deplored the lack of research and publication in black colleges, a charge relevant to most AMA schools in the 1920s. Low salaries, library deficiencies, heavy teaching loads, no research funds, and segregated educational societies contributed to these shortcomings. Still, all AMA colleges made gains in scholarship and number of Ph.D.s on the faculty. Fisk University, under the leadership of sociologist Charles S. Johnson, became a genuine center of scholarship in the 1930s. Sixteen Talladega faculty published books or articles in the mid-1930s, and in 1935 Dillard faculty had published more than 100 articles, musical compositions, monographs, and books. Accreditation validated the enhanced quality on AMA campuses. Accrediting associations ignored black colleges until the Southern Association of Colleges and Secondary Schools began to evaluate them in 1928. Fisk received an "A" rating in 1930, and Talladega in 1931. All AMA colleges were eventually awarded an "A" rating.

No matter the quality of faculty, students, and facilities, the relationship with the surrounding white communities ranged from grudging acceptance, to indifference, to active hostility. A few southern whites always supported black colleges, but their numbers were small. When in the 1920s the AMA rejected the demand of Austin, Tex., whites that all white teachers at Tillotson be removed, the Ku Klux Klan wrote a threatening letter and visited campus. White staff who ventured off AMA campuses often met with cold civility at best, and blacks encountered segregation, discrimination, suspicion, and occasional violence. President Buell Gallagher boasted that during his 10 years at Talladega only one shot was fired at his house. The Tougaloo entrance sign was constantly riddled with bullets. In 1925 a Tougaloo student lost an eye escaping from four hooded white men who brutally beat her boyfriend. Hollis Price, black president of LeMoyne College, lamented in 1943 that it took all his ingenuity to live peaceably with Memphis whites "while still holding to any principles." In 1942 trainmen assaulted several Talladega students on the L&N Railroad, the Klan visited campus in 1948 and 1949, and in 1950 Talladega students asked the WHTB radio announcers not to "refer to Negroes as 'niggers'" in its newscasts.

The AMA saw its colleges as providing "Education for Liberation," and they played a significant role in the struggle for equality. The AMA's interracial faculties by their very presence defied the South's racial code. Colleges protested blatant discrimination and injustice and formed NAACP chapters. More overt action began in the 1930s with interracial conferences on several campuses, and World War II accelerated defiance of segregation. Student NAACP chapters became more aggressive. President Gallagher of Talladega, with threat of federal intervention, pressured local companies to employ blacks. At Tillotson, President Mary E. Branch insisted on mixed seating for all college programs, sponsored interracial meetings, and became president of the Texas branch of the NAACP. When in 1946 Tougaloo staff and students tried to vote, they were driven from the polls and one member was badly beaten and thrown in jail. Students at all the colleges engaged in sit-ins, and the colleges often served as headquarters for voter registration drives.

Desegregation, so long fought for by faculty and students, seriously damaged the very colleges that produced many of the civil rights leaders. In an effort to maintain the fraud of separate but equal, all southern legislatures had increased funding of black public colleges. These colleges were not only cheaper, but offered attractive scholarships to the best high school students and outbid private schools for faculty. Moreover, white colleges were employing black faculty and offering scholarships to exceptional students who traditionally attended AMA institutions. The succeeding decades were fraught with peril for AMA colleges, but all survived, and most maintained their normal enrollment. In 1979, Fisk had 1,527 students, Dillard 1,117, LeMoyne-Owen 905, Tougaloo 783, Huston-Tillotson 696, and Talladega 500. They continue to struggle to balance budgets, nurture a broad spectrum of students, retain adequate faculty, train leaders, and steadily chisel away at discrimination. AMA colleges have graduated only several thousand students, but their impact is incalculable. They gave several generations of black youth hope, pride, knowledge, confidence, and opportunity. During the dark days of segregation, lynching, social and economic discrimination, and political powerlessness, the colleges never wavered in their belief in black intellectual equality and insisted that black Americans should and eventually would become first-class citizens. The colleges "functioned as multifaceted institutions" providing educated African American teachers, ministers, physicians, dentists, attorneys, and social, political, business, and professional leaders for the black community.

JOE M. RICHARDSON
Florida State University

Fred L. Brownlee, *New Day Ascending* (1946); Clarice T. Campbell and Oscar A. Rogers, *Mississippi: The View from Tougaloo* (1979); H. Paul Douglass, *Christian Reconstruction in the South* (1909); Henry N. Drewry and Humphrey Doermann, *Stand and Prosper: Private Black Colleges and Their Students* (2001); Patrick J. Gilpin and Marybeth Gasman, *Charles S. Johnson: Leadership beyond the Veil in the Age of Jim Crow* (2003); Maxine D. Jones and Joe M. Richardson, *Talladega College: The First Century* (1990); Joe M. Richardson, *Christian Reconstruction: The American Missionary Association and Southern Blacks, 1861–1890* (1986), *A History of Fisk University, 1965–1946* (1980); Chrystine I. Shackles, *Reminiscences of Huston-Tillotson College* (1973).

Arkansas, University of

The University of Arkansas, located at Fayetteville in the northwest corner of the state, was created by the legislature in 1871 as the state's first public university and its first land-grant college, authorized by Congress in the Morrill Act of 1862. In addition to agricultural and mechanical skills, the university provided education in the liberal arts, sciences, and humanities as well as training in the military arts for men when the university opened for classes to women and men in early 1872. The school's early years were marked by adversity as it struggled to survive inadequate financing, caused in part by the anti-intellectualism pervading Arkansas politics in the 1880s. The university grew slowly, mostly as a result of its role as a normal school, training teachers.

As part of its land-grant status, the University of Arkansas developed research and public service components at the turn of the century to augment its teaching mission. An agricultural experiment station was created in 1888 and an agricultural extension service in 1914. These programs proved to be greatly beneficial to the state's agricultural economy. Likewise, the university also established programs at the state capital, Little Rock, beginning with a medical school (now the University of Arkansas for Medical Sciences) and then a law school (now the Bowen School of Law at the University of Arkansas at Little Rock). Separate colleges of agriculture, education, engineering, and arts and sciences were established by 1912. In the mid-1920s a business college, an engineering experiment station, and a law school at the Fayetteville campus were added. Graduate instruction was initiated in 1927, and a broad range of programs is now offered leading to master's and doctoral degrees.

In the early 20th century the university began to receive greater support from the citizens and more generous funding from the legislature. Its newfound status, though, caused some legislators to try to move the university or various parts of it, such as the agriculture college, to central Arkansas. Meanwhile, students also became more vocal as their numbers increased. They started a campus newspaper in 1906 and staged a successful strike against the university in 1911 to force changes in what they perceived to be onerous policies.

The school's "middle period" of development—during the tenures of presidents John C. Futrall, J. William Fulbright, and Arthur M. Harding—was characterized by growth in enrollment, strengthening of the faculty, expansion of the physical plant, and broadening of the curriculum. Enrollment boomed soon after World War II as a result of the GI Bill. State and federal allocations followed, and the number of academic fields of study was enlarged. In 1948 the University of Arkansas became the first southern university since Reconstruction to integrate without litigation when Silas H. Hunt enrolled in the School of Law.

Partnering agreements with other campuses in Arkansas were established in the 1950s and 1960s, and the University of Arkansas System was created to oversee the member campuses. Four-year campuses included those at Fayetteville, Pine Bluff, Little Rock, and Monticello, as well as the Medical Sciences school at Little Rock. In the 1980s and 1990s community colleges were added to the system, including Phillips and Cossatot Community Colleges, as well as those at Hope, Batesville, and Morrilton. A new campus, the University of Arkansas at Fort Smith, was added in 2001, and the Clinton School of Public Service was created in 2004. By 2009 the system also oversaw the Arkansas School for Mathematics, Sciences, and the Arts; the Division of Agriculture; the Arkansas Archeological Survey; the Arkansas Criminal Justice Institute; the Winthrop Rockefeller Institute; and Garvan Woodland Gardens.

Student population again rose during the 1960s as the baby boom generation came of age and more students enrolled in college to avoid being drafted into the Vietnam War. A division of continuing education was established at the end of the decade. In the 1970s the Fayetteville campus added a professional school of architecture whose first dean was the renowned architect Fay Jones. Schools of social work and nursing were added later. In tandem with the increased emphasis placed on research and scholarly publication, poet Miller Williams founded the University of Arkansas Press, the chief academic publisher in the state.

In the early 21st century, the Walton Family Charitable Support Foundation gave $300 million to the university, then the largest single gift to a public institution of higher education, to endow an honors college and its graduate school. Presently, the Fayetteville campus offers degrees in more than 120 fields of study, including agriculture, human environmental sciences, arts, physical and biological sciences, business administration, education, health professions, engineering, architecture, law, and premedical sciences. In the 2009–10 academic year, more than 3,700 undergraduate and graduate degrees were awarded—2,494 bachelor's, 946 master's, 160 doctoral, and 122 professional degrees. Total enrollment at the Fayetteville campus was nearly 20,000 at the beginning of the fall 2009 semester.

WILLIAM FOY LISENBY
University of Central Arkansas

CHARLES YANCEY ALISON
University of Arkansas

Robert A. Leflar, *First 100 Years: Centennial History of the University of Arkansas* (1972); John Hugh Reynolds and David Yancey Thomas, *History of the University of Arkansas* (1910).

Atlanta University Center

The Atlanta University Center (AUC) began in 1929 as a consortium of three African American institutions of higher learning—Atlanta University, Morehouse College, and Spelman College. All began after the Civil War, with Atlanta University founded by the American Missionary Association (1865), Morehouse College founded at a Baptist church in Augusta, Ga. (1867), and Spelman College beginning as Atlanta Baptist Female Seminary (1881). The Methodist Episcopal Church launched Clark College in 1867, and it joined AUC in 1957, the same year that Morris Brown College became an AUC affiliate. Morris Brown, which the Methodists began in 1881, left the consortium in 2002 but has since rejoined. Four historically black seminaries merged to create the Interdenominational Theological Center (ITC) in 1958, and it became an AUC member the following year. The Morehouse School of Medicine became a separate institution in the early 1980s and joined AUC in 1983. Two AUC affiliates, Atlanta University and Clark College, merged in 1988.

Each of the AUC institutions is independent, with separate governing boards, presidents, students, faculty, staff, and facilities. They have differing missions: as liberal arts undergraduate colleges (Morehouse for men, Spelman for women), as a coeducational institution granting undergraduate and graduate degrees (Clark), and as a professional medical school (Morehouse School of Medicine). All the members of AUC are physically located in the West End Historic District in Atlanta, facilitating the sharing of resources and services that defines the consortium. The AUC coordinates collaborative projects and administers programs available to the institutions. The consortium created a career placement center in 1966, a computer science department in 1967, and a dual-degree engineering project in 1969 and has provided cross-registration services for half a century. The Robert W. Woodruff Library supports the institutions with information services and a research center containing a rich collage of archival materials on African American life, including extensive materials on Martin Luther King Jr.

CHARLES REAGAN WILSON
University of Mississippi

Marilyn T. Jackson, in *The New Georgia Encyclopedia*, online; www.aucenter.edu.

Auburn University

Auburn began as a Methodist liberal arts college, chartered as the East Alabama Male College by the Alabama legislature over Gov. John A. Winston's veto on 1 February 1856. Winston had questioned the creation of a second Methodist college since the legislature had just chartered Southern University at Greensboro, which had the support of the Methodist Conference. Both institutions opened in 1859. Auburn had a faculty of six, a student body of 80 men, and a board of trustees of 51. Closed during the Civil War, Auburn reopened in 1866, but by 1872, with no money to operate the school, the Methodist Church transferred ownership to the state, and Auburn became the Agricultural and Mechanical College of Alabama, the first land-grant institution in the South. From this point there was internal conflict between the traditional and land-grant philosophies. Another continuing problem was the meager and inadequate financing from the state, a situation common in the South following the Civil War and, later, in the Great Depression.

Two early presidents, Isaac Taylor Tichenor and William Leroy Broun, led in the development of Auburn's physical plant, scientific curriculum, agricultural education, and experiment stations, but Broun's greater contribution was to recruit a core of brilliant young faculty who shaped the university for 50 years after his death. Two of these dynamic men were George Petrie, a young Johns Hopkins Ph.D., who first came to Auburn in 1887 and who served the university as a history and Latin professor, academic dean, and football coach; and L. N. Duncan, who became president in 1935 and guided the university out of debt to financial stability. Women were admitted in 1892 and were allowed to pursue baccalaureate degrees. In 1899 the school's expanding academic program influenced the legislature to rename the college the Alabama Polytechnic Institute, and in 1960, in recognition of the name by which it had been commonly known and to emphasize the diversity and breadth of its academic programs, the school officially became Auburn University.

An account of Auburn University's accomplishments must begin with its agricultural research and extension service contributions, which have improved the economy of the state of Alabama and helped to feed people everywhere, especially in Third World countries. Its pioneer efforts in domestic farming of catfish attracted a large number of foreign graduate students. Auburn's superior ROTC program has produced many outstanding officers, and its School of Engineering has graduates all over the world, particularly in the aerospace industry.

A second campus was created by the legislature in 1967 in Montgomery, and by the 1980s the Auburn campus had more students than any other university campus in Alabama. Auburn's athletic teams compete as "Tigers" to a cheer of "War Eagle," and the student newspaper is *The Plainsman*—a reference to the name "Auburn," which came from a line by the poet Oliver Goldsmith, "Sweet Auburn, loveliest village of the plain." Although Auburn has attracted a large group of foreign and out-of-state students, the majority remain Alabamians with conservative political views. The first black student enrolled in 1964; yet despite a vigorous minority recruitment program and scholarships, blacks remain a small but well-integrated part of the student body and make up a high percentage of the athletes. Harold Melton was elected in 1987 as Auburn's first black president of the Student Government Association and was followed the next year by Cindy Holland, the first female president.

Historically, Auburn has enrolled a much larger number of male students than female, but although the numbers vary, gender enrollment has been about equal in the 21st century. Gender equity regarding faculty and deans has improved, including a female provost and five female deans as of 2009. Early in the technological revolution, Auburn made a strong commitment to instructional technology, and the nature of classroom instruction changed. The campus is wired to the Internet, e-mail is an official form of communication between faculty and students, and registration, fee payments, and grade posting are done online. Auburn has moved to a pedestrian central campus.

Auburn has increased student housing on campus and in 2009 opened a new student village with amenities not found in the older dorms. A new student center opened in 2008. The university's hotel and restaurant on campus have provided quality experiences for the hotel and restaurant management classes. The College of Veterinary Medicine opened a new, state-of-the-art, large-animal teaching hospital in 2003.

In order to coordinate the university's research with private investments, Auburn University Research Park opened with a new gold-certified Leadership in Energy and Environmental Design (LEED) building in 2009. The traditional land-grant extension commitment remains strong and includes a liberal arts outreach program, the Caroline Marshall Draughon Center for the Arts and Humanities.

In 2000 Auburn shifted from the quarter system (which had been adopted as a World War II measure) back to a semester system, which required curricula revisions at all levels. Auburn has applied a cap on enrollment in order to maintain the quality of its academic programs and admits about 4,000 freshmen each year. As a result, the average ACT score and grade point average have gradually risen. By student enrollment, the College of Engineering and the College of Liberal Arts are the two largest colleges on campus. International programs and study abroad opportunities for students have increased, an area encouraged by Jay Gogue, who became president in 2007. The fall 2009 enrollment was 24,602 students.

LEAH RAWLS ATKINS
Auburn University

Leah Rawls Atkins, *Blossoms amid the Deep Verdure: A Century of Women at Auburn, 1892–1991, with Additional Material, 1992–2007* (2008); Ralph B. Draughon, *Alabama Polytechnic Institute* (1954); Mickey Logue and Jack Simms, *Auburn: A Pictorial History of the Loveliest Village* (1996); Malcolm McMillan and Allen Jones, *Auburn University Bulletin* (May 1973); R. G. Millman, *The Auburn University Walking Tour Guide* (1991).

Barnard, Frederick A. P.

(1809–1889) EDUCATOR AND SCIENTIST.

Born in Sheffield, Mass., Frederick Augustus Porter Barnard spent half of his professional life in the South. Barnard received his A.B. degree from Yale in 1828 and, suffering from increasing deafness, he taught mathematics and geography at institutions for the deaf from 1831 to 1837. In 1838 he accepted a teaching position at the University of Alabama, where he hoped to pursue his developing interest in the sciences, especially astronomy, and higher mathematics.

Barnard taught mathematics, natural philosophy, and chemistry at Alabama. He was instrumental in the establishment of an observatory at the university, although he had to struggle with the board of trustees, the administration, and the state government for the funds. While in Alabama, Barnard cultivated an interest in early photographic techniques. He learned daguerreotypy from Samuel F. B. Morse and opened a gallery in Tuscaloosa in 1841. He maintained a scientific interest in photography and published articles in photographic journals throughout his career. During the years 1853–54 Barnard opposed a reorganization of the Alabama curriculum that would have implemented the same type of broad elective system used at the University of Virginia and Brown University. Barnard favored retaining a traditional discipline-oriented system in which the student would be allowed a few elective courses. The board of trustees, as well as Basil Manly, the president of the university, supported the Virginia plan and it was adopted. Barnard refused to work under the new system and resigned in 1854.

Barnard then went to the University of Mississippi, which had opened in 1848. The university badly needed instructors, and Barnard taught courses in mathematics, chemistry, physics, civil engineering, and astronomy. An ordained Episcopal minister, he also accepted a job as rector of the Oxford church. In 1856, only two years after his arrival, Barnard became president of the university. As president, his work was hampered by local residents, who saw no practical purpose for the university and regarded it with varying degrees of suspicion and dislike. Barnard was somewhat successful in his efforts to improve instruction and to acquire more sophisticated equipment for the school. His main interest at the University of Mississippi, as at Alabama, was the sciences, and his critics charged that he emphasized the study of science too heavily, to the exclusion of more traditional studies. As sectional differences intensified, suspicion of Barnard's northern roots pursued him. In March 1860 he was tried by the board of trustees on the charge of being "unsound on the slavery question." His supporters rallied behind him, however, and Barnard was cleared of the charges. Although Barnard was increasingly unhappy with his situation and attempted several times to secure positions elsewhere, poverty kept him from leaving Mississippi.

After Mississippi seceded from the Union early in 1861, university business was interrupted by the enlistment of many students in the military. Barnard left Mississippi in late 1861 and relocated in Norfolk, Va., which Union troops captured in May of 1862. Confederate president Jefferson Davis offered to hire Barnard to conduct a survey of the natural resources of the Confederacy, but Barnard refused because of his Union sympathies.

After the war, Barnard spent two years with the U.S. Coastal Survey and was then elected president of Columbia College, now Columbia University, in New York City. During his 25 years at Columbia (1864–89), Barnard instituted standard entrance exams, introduced the concept of elective courses, and strengthened and enlarged the graduate and professional schools. His interest in science continued, and he was instrumental in founding the National Academy of Sciences in 1863. Barnard College, an official women's college of Columbia University, was established after his death and named in his honor.

Although Barnard later said that his years in Mississippi were among his worst, he seems to have genuinely loved the South and its people. His influence at the southern universities where he worked was felt long after his departure, especially in the area of the sciences, and his hopes for upgrading the quality of education at Alabama and Mississippi were eventually fulfilled.

KAREN M. MCDEARMAN
University of Mississippi

William J. Chute, *Damn Yankee!: The First Career of Frederick A. P. Barnard* (1977); John Fulton, *Memoirs of Frederick A. P. Barnard* (1896).

Barr, Stringfellow

(1897–1982) EDUCATOR.

Stringfellow Barr stands as the foremost advocate of the neoclassical curriculum in American colleges and universities during the first half of the 20th century. The enduring, organic monument to this distinctive educational commitment is his leadership in conjunction with colleague Scott Buchanan in revitalizing and reforming St. John's College of Maryland according to the principles of a "Great Books" course of study. It combined rhetoric and analytic skills acquired via serious study of Latin and Greek along with careful reading of selected, influential works in English and other vernacular languages.

A native of Virginia, Barr was born on 15 January 1897 in Suffolk, south of the James River. Although he matriculated at Tulane University in 1912, he eventually returned to his home state and transferred to the University of Virginia where he concentrated in history and completed his B.A. degree in 1916 and his M.A. in 1917. Following his service with the U.S. Army Ambulance Service and the Surgeon General's Office in World War I, Barr remained in Europe to pursue advanced studies. This included receiving the diploma from the University of Paris in 1922, followed by additional advanced studies as part of a fellowship in history at the University of Ghent in Belgium.

After having completed his graduate studies on the Continent, Barr accepted an appointment as assistant professor in modern European history at his alma mater, the University of Virginia. During the period 1924 to 1937 his achievements there included serving as advisory editor and, later, as editor of the *Virginia Quarterly Review*. He was promoted to associate professor in 1927 and to professor in 1930. In 1936 he collaborated with philosophy professor Scott Buchanan to draft a proposal for a "great books" honors program within the University of Virginia. Their proposal was not accepted—a disappointing decision that prompted Barr and Buchanan to leave the University of Virginia in 1937 in order to teach and work on curriculum reform as part of the Committee on the Liberal Arts at the University of Chicago. In concert with the educational philosophies of President Robert Maynard Hutchins and Associate Professor of Law Mortimer Adler, Barr and Buchanan focused on the interesting task of creating and implementing a course of study that provided coherence and significance as an alternative and antidote to what they viewed as the lack of discipline and substance that characterized the nationwide drift toward reliance on the elective system and option for a departmental major.

Barr's tenure at the University of Chicago was intense yet short. After a little more than a year there, the trustees of St. John's College of Maryland, having heard of the distinctive curricular work he and Buchanan had been pursuing, invited the two colleagues to come to the historic campus in Annapolis, where Barr would serve as president and Buchanan as dean. Their administrative appointments were also an invitation to implement their plans for a neoclassical "Great Books" program at this financially beleaguered college, which also had lost its accreditation. Barr was a visible, effective president of St. John's College from 1937 to 1946. During his tenure the college regained financial solvency, experienced an enduring increase in enrollments, maintained high academic requirements for admission, and acquired a favorable reputation and respected following for its liberal arts program, which emphasized rigorous study and avoided the conventional American undergraduate institution's predilection for intercollegiate athletics.

Barr left the college's presidency in 1947 to pursue a multifaceted role as a public intellectual. This pursuit included serving as president of the Foundation for World Government from 1948 to 1958 and appointments as a professor of humanities at Newark College of Rutgers University from 1955 to 1964 and as a fellow at Robert Maynard Hutchins's Center for the Study of Democratic Institutions in Santa Barbara, Calif., from 1966 to 1969. During these decades he was a prolific author of historical works as well as a novel about academic life. He understood the importance of communication media and relied on a widely broadcast radio show to promote a public forum on international relations and world affairs. He retired in 1969 and died in Alexandria, Va., in 1982.

JOHN R. THELIN
University of Kentucky

Stringfellow Barr, *Change* (May 1974); Gerald Grant and David Riesman, in *The Perpetual Dream: Reform and Experiment in the American College* (1978); Arthur Levine, in *Handbook on Undergraduate Curriculum* (1978); John R. Thelin, in *American National Biography* (1999).

Baylor University

Chartered by the last Congress of the Republic of Texas on 1 February 1845, Baylor University is the oldest institution of higher education in Texas and the world's largest Baptist university. Eponym and one of the chief founders was District Judge Robert Emmett Bledsoe Baylor, who also was an ordained minister. Twenty-four young men and women comprised the opening class of the school at Independence, Tex., on 18 May 1846. The first president, Henry Lee Graves, resigned in 1851 and was followed by Rufus C. Burleson, whose 10-year tenure saw 55 students graduate, including the first graduate, Stephen Decatur Rowe, in 1854. The Civil War years were naturally lean for Baylor, especially during the two-year administration of George W. Baines, great-grandfather of U.S. President Lyndon B. Johnson. Baines was followed by William Carey Crane, who led the institution from 1864 until his death in February 1885.

The Baptist State Convention voted in 1886 to consolidate Baylor and Waco universities at Waco, with the new home to be Baylor University at Waco. Rufus C. Burleson was named president of the unified school, and Reddin Andrews became vice president. Burleson opened the new Baylor University in the facilities of the former Waco University, but within two years new facilities were constructed on a 23-acre site given to the institution by the City of Waco. At first the university's degrees for females, who pursued a slightly different curriculum from males, carried the title of "maid" while the men received "bachelor's" degrees. Before the turn of the century all courses were offered to both sexes and all undergraduate degrees were designated "bachelor." Graduate degrees were also available by 1894.

Samuel Palmer Brooks assumed operational control of the university in 1902. A former faculty member and a graduate of both Baylor and Yale, Brooks initiated programs to move the university from its regional parochial level to a complete university status. During Brooks's 29 years as president, several different schools were established as well as a college of arts and sciences. In addition, the university opened a theological seminary (which moved to Fort Worth in 1910 to become Southwestern Baptist Theological Seminary) and began to offer medical degrees through a college of medicine. That college was given independent status in 1969.

Upon Brooks's death in 1931, Pat M. Neff, a former Texas governor (1920–24), was elected president. The Depression caused numerous hardships on the faculty and staff, but the stringent operational measures of Neff enabled the institution to emerge from the period debt free. In 1948 Neff was replaced by William R. White, who immediately embarked upon a building program to meet the post–World War II boom. This work was continued and greatly enlarged with the coming of Judge Abner V. McCall to the helm of the institution in 1961. During McCall's 20-year administration, Baylor's campus expanded from 40 acres to 350 acres and the number of physical structures increased to total more than 50. In June 1981 Dr. Herbert H. Reynolds became president and presided until 1995, after which he became chancellor of the university until his retirement in 2000.

Through efforts to fulfill the founders' vision of a university to meet the needs of all the ages to come, the university continues to pursue initiatives such as ensuring a low student-faculty ratio, offering smaller class sizes, increasing research opportunities for undergraduates, and providing the best facilities for learning and living. The current 14,000-student population represents all 50 states and more than 80 countries. The vibrant campus atmosphere, with 260 student organizations, is enhanced by Baylor's participation as the only private university in the competitive Big 12 Conference for NCAA Division I athletics. The market value of endowment exceeded $1 billion for the first time in May 2007. In October 2009 Baylor and a group of state, county, and city governments and organizations and higher educational institutions in Central Texas announced the creation of the Central Texas Technology and Research Park and the park's first project, the Baylor Research and Innovation Collaborative.

Baylor, one of the select 10 percent of universities with a Phi Beta Kappa chapter, offers 151 baccalaureate, 76 master, 30 doctoral, and juris doctor degree programs. The present academic system includes the College of Arts and Sciences, Hankamer School of Business, School of Education, School of Engineering and Computer Science, Graduate School, Honors College, Law School, School of Music, Louise Herrington School of Nursing, George W. Truett Theological Seminary, and School of Social Work. The university also conducts graduate programs with the U.S. Army Academy of Health Sciences in San Antonio and West Point. Baylor consistently ranks in the top 100 national doctoral-granting universities by *U.S. News and World Report* and as a "Best Buy" by *The Fiske Guide to Colleges.*

EUGENE W. BAKER
BRENDA TACKER
Baylor University

Eugene W. Baker, *Nothing Better than This* (1985), *To Light the Ways of Time: An Illustrated History of Baylor University, 1845–1986* (1987); Eugene W. Baker and Lois Smith Murray, *Baylor at Independence* (1972); James Milton Carroll, *A History of Texas Baptists* (1923); Kent Keeth, *Looking Back at Baylor: A Collection of Historical Vignettes* (1985); *The Story of Baylor University at Independence, 1845–1886* (1986).

Berea College

In 1853, Kentucky politician Cassius Marcellus Clay and others persuaded abolitionist John Fee to preach a series of sermons in the foothills of Madison County, Ky. The following year, Fee built a home there on a ridge he called Berea, after the town cited in Acts 17:10. The next year, a one-room school, which doubled as an antislavery church, was built. Fee planned to create a college there that would educate "all colors, classes, cheap and thorough." Some neighbors resented and feared far-sighted egalitarian leaders such as Fee, and that fear, combined with the widespread inflammatory effect of John Brown's raid, caused armed men to drive Fee and the other Berea leaders out of the state in 1859. However, the intrepid group returned after the Civil War and incorporated Berea College. The college resumed classes in 1866, and the Reverend Henry Fairchild of Oberlin became its first president in 1869. For the remainder of the 19th century, Berea's student body was almost equally divided between recently emancipated African Americans and whites from the southern mountains. That changed when the Kentucky Day Law, passed in 1904, forbade interracial education. The school remained segregated until 1950.

Succeeding President Fairchild's tenure (1869–89) were William B. Stewart (1890–92), William G. Frost (1892–1920), William J. Hutchins (1920–39), Francis J. Hutchins (1939–67), Willis D. Weatherford Jr. (1967–84), John B. Stephenson (1984–94), and Larry Shinn (1994–). Berea College has emerged as an institution with major commitments to educating poor Appalachian youth, to providing a liberal arts education in a nonsectarian atmosphere of Christian service, to maintaining the early founders' goals of interracial education, and to continuing a labor program that allows all students to work their way through school. Berea's educational philosophy has paid rich dividends to southern Appalachia. Although the school has produced Nobel Prize winners and citizens of national accomplishment, almost half of Berea's graduates have returned to their mountain homeland to provide significant service as hard-working teachers, nurses, social workers, agricultural agents, journalists, and community leaders.

The Berea College Country Dancers, a traveling demonstration team formed in the 1930s, illustrates Berea College's commitment to educate students within the context of their Appalachian culture. In July 1970, Berea College intensified that commitment by establishing an Appalachian Center and hiring alumnus Loyal Jones as director. Under Jones's leadership, the Appalachian Center became a model of excellence in Appalachian research and service. It sponsors the annual Weatherford Award for the best Appalachian book of the year, and it reaches out across the region with an excellent newsletter and *Appalachian Heritage*, a literary quarterly. Other significant endeavors have been the Appalachian Museum, the Brushy Fork Institute, the Celebration of Traditional Music, a series of four Humor Festivals, and the New Opportunity School for Women. Helen Lewis served as interim director of the Appalachian Center after Jones's retirement in 1993, and Gordon McKinney served as director from 1995 to 2006, when Chad Berry was appointed director. In 2009, Berea renamed the Appalachian Center the Loyal Jones Appalachian Center.

Through the Appalachian Center, Berea College has achieved one of its greatest accomplishments: an annual summer workshop in Appalachian history and literature that has trained several generations of high school and college teachers to work with people throughout southern Appalachia to shape a more prideful identity. Workshop participants have received graduate credit through the University of Kentucky and studied under an all-star faculty that included Richard Drake, Loyal Jones, Billy Best, Wilma Dykeman, Leonard Roberts, Jim Wayne Miller, Gurney Norman, James Still, Ron Eller, Harry M. Caudill, and Cratis Williams.

Today, under the leadership of President Shinn, Berea College remains one of the most successful liberal arts colleges in America. It is nationally recognized for its innovative curriculum that stresses environmental concerns and service learning, and the college continues to be a leader in using endowment funds to help students, across lines of gender, race, and nationality, work their way through college.

JAMES M. GIFFORD
Jesse Stuart Foundation

Richard B. Drake, *One Apostle Was a Lumberman: John G. Hanson and Berea's Founding Generation* (1975); E. Henry Fairchild, *Berea College: An Interesting History* (1875); William Goodell Frost, *For the Mountains: An Autobiography* (1937); Elizabeth Peck, *Berea's First Century, 1855–1955* (1955); John A. R. Rogers, *Birth of Berea College* (1903); Richard D. Sears, *A Utopian Experiment in Kentucky: Integration and Social Equality at Berea, 1866–1904* (1996); Shannon H. Wilson, *Berea College: An Illustrated History* (2006).

Bethune, Mary McLeod
(1875–1955) EDUCATOR.

On 10 July 1875 educator, federal government official, and club woman Mary McLeod Bethune was born near Mayesville, S.C. She was one of 17 children born to former slaves and farm workers, Samuel and Patsy (McIntosh) McLeod. In 1882 Bethune abandoned many of her farm chores to attend the newly opened Presbyterian mission school for blacks near Mayesville. Aided with a scholarship, she left South Carolina in 1888 and continued her education at Scotia Seminary (later Barber-Scotia College) in Concord, N.C., completing the high school program in 1892 and the Normal and Scientific Course two years later. Hoping to become a missionary in Africa, she studied at the Moody

Bible Institute in Chicago, but in 1895 the Presbyterian Mission Board turned down her application for a missionary post.

A disappointed Mary McLeod returned to her native South Carolina and began her first teaching job at Miss Emma Wilson's Mission School, where she had once been a student. Shortly thereafter, the Presbyterian board appointed her to a teaching position at Haines Normal and Industrial Institute, and later transferred her to Kindell Institute in Sumter, S.C.

Following her marriage to Albertus Bethune in May 1898, she and her husband moved to Savannah, Ga., where their only child, Albert McLeod Bethune, was born in 1899. Later that year, the family relocated to Palatka, Fla., where Mary McLeod Bethune established a Presbyterian missionary school. Five years later, after separating from her husband, Bethune pursued her lifelong ambition to build a school for black girls in the South and with her son moved to Daytona Beach, Fla., where, in October 1904 the Daytona Literary and Industrial School for Training Negro Girls opened with Bethune as its president. Like most black educators in the post-Reconstruction South, Bethune emphasized industrial skills and Christian values and appealed to both the neighboring black community and white philanthropists for financial support. As a consequence of Bethune's unwavering dedication, business acumen, and intellectual ability, the Daytona Institute grew from a small elementary school to incorporate a high school and teacher training program. In 1923 Bethune's school merged with Cookman Institute, a Jacksonville, Fla., college for men, and became the Daytona-Cookman Collegiate Institute. Six years later, the school's name was changed to Bethune-Cookman College in recognition of the important role that Mary McLeod Bethune had played in the school's growth and development.

As an educator in the South, Bethune had concerns that extended beyond campus life. In the absence of a municipally supported medical facility for blacks, the Daytona Institute, under Bethune's guidance, maintained a hospital for blacks from 1911 to 1927. During much of this same period she also operated the Tomoka Mission Schools for the children of black families working the Florida turpentine camps. Ignoring threats made by members of the Ku Klux Klan, Bethune organized a black voter registration drive in Florida, decades before the voter registration drive of the 1960s. As a delegate to the first meeting of the Southern Conference for Human Welfare, Bethune voiced her opposition to degrading southern racial customs.

Bethune joined and held official positions in a number of organizations, but she is best known among club women and the public at large for her monumental work with the National Council of Negro Women, which she founded at age 60 in 1935. Bethune served as its president until 1949. Dedicated to meeting the myriad needs of blacks in all walks of life, the council grew under Bethune's leadership to become the largest federation of black women's clubs in the United States.

Headquartered in Washington, D.C., and with chapters located throughout the country and abroad, this association published the *Aframerican Woman's Journal*, established health and job clinics throughout the South, and educated a number of black youths from poor families in the South.

In 1935 President Franklin D. Roosevelt appointed Bethune as one of his special advisers on racial affairs, and four years later she served as the director of black affairs for the National Youth Administration. In May 1955 at the age of 79, one of the South's most well-known women died. The unveiling of a statue of Bethune in a federal park located in the nation's capital in 1974 and the opening of the Mary McLeod Bethune Museum and Archives for Black Women's History in Washington, D.C. in 1979 are lasting testaments to Bethune's intelligence and determination.

SHARON HARLEY
University of Maryland

Joyce Ann Hanson, *Mary McLeod Bethune and Black Women's Political Activism* (2003); Rackham Holt, *Mary McLeod Bethune: A Biography* (1964); Aubrey Thomas McCluskey and Elaine M. Smith, eds., *Mary McLeod Bethune: Building a Better World, Essays and Selected Documents* (1999) Barbara Sicherman and Carol Hurd Green, eds., *Notable American Women: The Modern Period: A Biographical Dictionary* (1980); Emma Sterne, *Mary McLeod Bethune* (1957).

Birmingham-Southern College

Birmingham-Southern College traces its lineage to two 19th-century Alabama institutions of higher learning founded with primary funding from the Methodist Church. The first was Southern University, chartered in 1856 and located in Greensboro by the Church's Alabama Conference. Officially opening in October 1859, Southern University had barely begun before the Civil War severely disrupted its mission to promote "literature, science, morality and religion." The second school began in 1898 as the North Alabama Conference College on a hilltop in Owenton, a wooded suburb just west of Birmingham. Its name was formally changed to Birmingham College in 1906 in an effort to attract non-Methodist students.

Over the next two decades both schools struggled with enrollment and funding. World War I challenged the viability of both campuses, as they experienced significant enrollment declines and mounting debts. In 1918, the two schools merged, adopting the name of Birmingham-Southern College (BSC) and locating the campus on the Owenton hilltop. Southern University alumnus and president C. Cullen Daniel became the new college's first chief executive.

Daniel's uneventful tenure was brief, and he resigned in January 1921. His successor, Guy E. Snavely, would serve for 17 years and have a greater impact on the college's academic and institutional life than any other president over the next half-century. Snavely's achievements were numerous and grew more impressive over time: winning accreditation with the Southern Association of Colleges and Schools; securing a chapter of Phi Beta Kappa, one of only two in Alabama; overseeing expansion of the campus to 125 acres and the construction of many new buildings, including a new library, a preparatory school, an administration, a women's facility, a presidential residence, and an athletic field and stadium. From a graduating class of only 13 in 1921 enrollment grew to more than 2,165 students at its peak. By 1938 a faculty of 12 grew to 55, including 24 with doctorates. Significantly, Snavely had demonstrated a successful strategy of not relying on Church funding by tapping the resources of the surrounding Birmingham community, where wealth had been sustained despite the Great Depression.

This same strategy was employed by his immediate successors—Raymond Paty (1938–42) and George R. Stuart (1942–55)—and helped the college survive World War II and meet the increasing demands for higher education in its aftermath. However, even greater challenges were ahead as Birmingham became the focal point of racial conflict in the 1950s. In this period (1954–65) the college's wealthy benefactors became stalwart supporters of Jim Crow segregation, mounting a hard-line resistance to racial change.

Dr. Henry King Stanford (1957–62) soon became a victim of this tumultuous racial climate. A Georgian, Stanford understood the stakes, yet courageously advocated that BSC desegregate voluntarily. He also defied trustees and community leaders and refused to expel students who openly expressed support and sympathy for civil rights demonstrators. When Stanford opposed the city's 1962 decision to close its parks rather than obey a court order to desegregate, "Bull" Connor bellowed, "Doctor, I don't give a good goddamn what you want for Birmingham. I'm just gonna tell everybody I know not to send their children to Birmingham-Southern." Six months later, Stanford resigned to accept the presidency of the University of Miami, where he built a thriving institution over the next 20 years.

His successor, Howard Phillips (1964–68), reaped the benefits of much that Stanford had initiated in campus expansion. Notably he also obtained a $2.2 million Ford Foundation grant that recognized BSC as a national "center of educational excellence." However, before matching funds could be fully raised, Phillips resigned suddenly in February 1968, citing poor health. His departure left a critical leadership vacuum that would not be fully filled until 1976.

In this interim, Birmingham-Southern was governed by three different administrators: trustee Robert F. Henry (1968–69), Charles Hounshell (1969–71), and Ralph Tanner, an alumnus and faculty member (1972–75). With four presidents in less than 10 years, the college was daunted by a sense of drift, confusion, and malaise. Active discussions even arose about relocating to a more pastoral ridge south of Birmingham, which created even more uncertainty.

Finally in late 1975, the college turned to dynamic, young leadership. Neal R. Berte became the college's

11th president on 1 February 1976, arriving from the University of Alabama, where he was dean of the New College and vice president for educational development. In nearly three decades of unprecedented leadership, and exceeding Snavely's tenure by 12 years, Berte restored fiscal confidence, confirmed the college's commitment to its Birmingham hilltop, and substantially transformed and modernized the campus. During Berte's tenure, the endowment grew from under $11 million to more than $136 million at its peak. The annual operating budget increased from $3 million to nearly $57 million, allowing for higher faculty salaries. At the same time, the number of faculty increased by nearly 70 percent, and the student-to-faculty ratio was lowered to 12 to 1. Enrollment more than doubled to 1,500 even as the quality of the student academic profile strengthened, maintaining BSC as an academic leader among state institutions.

Increases in private gifts and grants to the college were dramatic and sustained, beginning with $2 million a year in 1976 and reaching a record $22.3 million in 2003. With this level of financial support, Berte expanded the campus to 192 acres, constructed more than 25 new facilities, and completed substantial additions or renovations to venerable older buildings.

In October 2003, Berte announced his retirement as president and was appointed chancellor until his formal retirement in 2006. G. David Pollick, the president of Lebanon College, a Methodist-affiliated school in Pennsylvania, succeeded Berte as the 12th president of Birmingham-Southern in July 2004.

ROBERT CORLEY
University of Alabama at Birmingham

Donald Brown, *Forward, Ever: Birmingham-Southern College at Its Sesquicentennial* (2005); G. Ward Hubbs, *Guarding Greensboro: A Confederate Company in the Making of a Southern Community* (2003); Joseph H. Parks and Oliver C. Weaver Jr., *Birmingham-Southern College, 1856–1956* (1957).

Black Mountain College

Thoroughly southern in its origins, though less so in its style, Black Mountain College was founded in 1933 by the volatile South Carolina classics scholar John Rice. The college began in buildings rented from the Blue Ridge Assembly of the Baptist church three miles outside Black Mountain, N.C.; in 1941 it moved a few miles to its permanent site at Lake Eden, N.C. Black Mountain became one of the least orthodox but most influential institutions in American educational history—influential out of all proportion to its short life and the size of its enrollment, which never went above 75. The history of the college breaks down into three periods: the first concluding with Rice's resignation in 1940; the second concluding with the 1949 departure of the painter Josef Albers, a powerful figure in the college after 1933 and especially so after Rice left; the third concluding with the closing of the college in 1956. Many documents charting this history are preserved in the state archives in Raleigh, N.C.

Prophetic of many of the experimental social and educational communities of the 1960s, Black Mountain College from its beginning broke with tradition. The community was largely self-supporting, performing much of its own labor and raising its own livestock and crops. The arts occupied the center of a curriculum of unprecedented flexibility; the college had no requirements, minimal bureaucracy, and never received accreditation. Contrary to the legalized segregation of the 1940s and 1950s, it admitted blacks. The Black Mountain community was probably more diverse than historian Martin Duberman's description of it as "a Yankee island in a Southern sea" suggests, but the college community's members were outside the mainstream of both national and regional culture and politics because of their lifestyles and views of education.

Black Mountain College saw its most creative years, those for which it is best known, under the direction of the poet Charles Olson. Between Olson's arrival in 1951 (after a short visit in 1949) and the school's closing in 1956 because of falling enrollment, lack of faculty, and financial problems, Black Mountain had as students or instructors people who have since become recognized as major innovators in virtually every art: Olson, Robert Creeley, Robert Duncan, and Edward Dorn in poetry; Merce Cunningham in dance; John Cage and David Tudor in music; Robert Rauschenberg in painting. The school also sponsored one of the most important avant-garde literary journals of the post–World War II period, the *Black Mountain Review*, of which seven issues appeared between 1954 and 1957. Black Mountain College survived only 23 years—in late 1954 its enrollment had plunged to nine students—but its impact on the arts in America is still being felt and measured.

ALAN GOLDING
University of Mississippi

Fielding Dawson, *The Black Mountain Book* (1970); Martin Duberman, *Black Mountain: An Exploration in Community* (1972); *OLSON: A Journal of the Charles Olson Archives* (Spring 1974–Fall 1978).

Bob Jones University

Located in Greenville, S.C., Bob Jones University (BJU) is the self-proclaimed "world's largest fundamental Christian school," attracting over 4,000 students from all 50 states and over 40 countries around the world. Begun in 1927 in Panama City, Fla., by the evangelist Bob Jones (1883–1968), the lineage of the school is firmly rooted in the turmoil of the fundamentalist-modernist controversy that wracked American denominations in the 1920s and within the larger cultural dislocations experienced by the United States in the same decade with rapid urbanization, mass immigration, and the resulting increased religious and ethnic diversity of the country. Preaching a stock sermon entitled "The Perils of America," Jones traveled Scopes Trial–era America decrying the inroads made by theological modernists in churches, in denominational and state universities and colleges, and in the larger culture. Frustrated in his evangelistic work with "leading boys and girls to Jesus Christ and then seeing them attend educational institutions which shake their faith," Jones resolved to build his own educational institution. Bob Jones College opened its doors in Panama City, Fla., on 14 September 1927.

Although buffeted by the Great Depression—the college relocated in 1933 from Florida to Cleveland, Tenn., in part because of the economic pressures of the era—Bob Jones College experienced great growth. During the years in Cleveland, Bob Jones College expanded to include educational offerings from kindergarten through graduate school. It was also during the 1930s that evangelist Jones's son, Bob Jones Jr. (1911–97), emerged as his father's successor and the most ardent proponent of what would become the school's hard-line, militant separatism. Trained as a historian, Bob Jones Jr. grew the college's academic offerings, added programs in drama and opera, and built one of the southeastern United States' most noted museums of Baroque art, collecting works by Botticelli, Tintoretto, Rubens, and Rembrandt. Assuming the title of president in 1947, he also led the school to achieve university status and to move to its present location in Greenville, S.C., as the college outgrew its Cleveland campus. As president, Jones led the school to make a sharp break with such noted evangelical leaders as Billy Graham (who had attended Bob Jones College for one semester in the 1930s) and other Protestant institutions such as Moody Bible Institute over questions of associating with theological moderates, liberals, or Roman Catholics. The younger Jones actively embraced politicians such as George Wallace, Barry Goldwater, and Billy James Hargis, as well as holding annual "Americanism" conferences. On one occasion he added to his harsh, pugnacious persona by asking God, from the pulpit of the university chapel, to "smite" one American cabinet officer (Secretary of State Alexander Haig) "hip and thigh, bone and marrow, heart and lungs."

Bob Jones University embraced a cultural conservatism rooted in the post–Civil War American South, that forbad the admission of African Americans until 1971 and any interracial dating until 2000, when Bob Jones III (b. 1939), then president, announced a policy change. Jones III assumed the presidency in 1971 as his father transitioned to the role of chancellor. He continued his father's hard-line theological and cultural conservatism and defied the revocation of the school's tax exemption over its interracial dating policy all the way to the U.S. Supreme Court in 1983. Upon losing the case, Jones III ordered flags on campus lowered to half-mast and declared that "churches and Christian schools will only be tolerated if they serve the purposes of the government." When the visit of candidate George W. Bush to the campus in the spring of 2000 once again focused national attention on the interracial dating ban, erupting into another firestorm of controversy, Jones III appeared on national television to announce the dropping of the ban because "I don't want to hurt the church of Jesus Christ." In later years, Bob Jones University issued a public apology for its stance on race, stating that, "we failed to accurately represent the Lord and to fulfill the commandment to love others as ourselves. For these failures we are profoundly sorry."

Bob Jones III became chancellor of the university in 2005, passing the presidency on to his son, Stephen Jones. The younger Jones lacks the pugnacious style of his forebears and admitted to one writer that he had been embarrassed by some of the vitriolic comments made over the years. He also led the university away from his grandfather's strict conviction that the university should not seek regional accreditation on separatist grounds. In 2005, Bob Jones University received full accreditation from the Transnational Association of Christian Colleges and Schools.

MARK TAYLOR DALHOUSE
Vanderbilt University

David O. Beale, *In Pursuit of Purity: A History of American Fundamentalism since 1850* (1986); Mark Taylor Dalhouse, *An Island in the Lake of Fire: Bob Jones University, Fundamentalism, and the Separatist Movement* (1996); Camille Kaminksi Lewis, *Romancing the Difference: Kenneth Burke, Bob Jones University, and the Rhetoric of Religious Fundamentalism* (2007); George Marsden, *Fundamentalism and American Culture* (1980); Bob Nestor, *Bob Jones University* (2008); Daniel Turner, *Standing without Apology: The History of Bob Jones University* (1997).

Bond, Horace Mann
(1904–1972) COLLEGE ADMINISTRATOR AND EDUCATOR.

Horace Mann Bond was a well-known figure within the black community for much of the 20th century. Although many outside the black community might not have heard of him, he was the father of Julian Bond, a noted leader of the student and civil rights movements of the 1960s, the first black member of the Georgia legislature, and the 21st-century leader of the National Association for the Advancement of Colored People. Horace Bond himself had a productive career as an academic researcher and as the leader of two black colleges. Born in Nashville, one of five children of James and Jane Bond, Horace Mann Bond was named for the abolitionist-leaning Horace Mann, a president of Antioch College who was better known, at least to posterity, as the father of the common-school movement. Horace Bond's father was a preacher who moved his family around the South. Bond lived in Tennessee, Alabama, Kentucky, and Georgia while growing up. He was influenced by his maternal grandmother, who inculcated him with a love of education, a quality that was approved of and intensified by both of his parents.

Bond's mother taught school, and she began the young Horace's education by taking him with her to her classroom when he was a toddler. Bond excelled in school wherever he attended. He obtained his undergraduate degree from Lincoln University in southeastern Pennsylvania, arguably the oldest college for African Americans in the United States He earned master's and doctoral degrees from the University of Chicago, studying sociology with Robert Park and education with Newton Edwards. His doctoral dissertation, "Negro Education in Alabama: A Study in Cotton and Steel," was published in 1939 by Carter G. Woodson's Associated Publishers. It is still in print, most recently in a paperback edition from the University of Alabama Press. Bond's academic career prospered with help from Park and philanthropies such as the Rosenwald Fund and the General Education Board. He was a faculty member at Alabama State University, a faculty member and department head at Fisk University, and a dean at Dillard University, before being chosen as the president of Fort Valley (Ga.) State College in 1939. In 1945 he was chosen as the first black president of his alma mater, Lincoln University. He held this position for 12 years, resigning under some political pressure in 1957. Bond had successes in his college presidencies, but he also ran into substantial opposition, at Lincoln particularly, from older white faculty and their allies among alumni. After leaving Lincoln, he took a position in the School of Education at Atlanta University, then the graduate center for the federated institutions in the Atlanta University Center.

Bond was widely known because of his presidencies and because of the links he forged between Lincoln and leaders in Africa such as Kwame Nkrumah in Ghana and Nnamdi Azikiwe in Nigeria. Both of these men had studied at Lincoln and, through them, Bond sought meaningful ties between Lincoln and Africa. Bond was also a founder and leader of the American Society of African Culture (AMSAC). In addition to his administrative and international accomplishments, Bond sought to establish himself as a leader in African American scholarship. In addition to his dissertation, he published four books, including a textbook on black education written in the 1930s, a volume on black scholars, and (posthumously) a history of Lincoln University. He also published many articles on topics such as intelligence testing, various aspects of black higher education, and in the areas of history and sociology of education. If Bond did not attain the scholarly eminence in his lifetime that he sought, the longevity of his dissertation, the thoroughness of his other books, and the richness and comprehensiveness of his articles mean that his scholarly reputation has, if anything, been enhanced since his death in 1972.

WAYNE J. URBAN
University of Alabama

Horace Mann Bond, *Black American Scholars: A Study of Their Origins* (1969), *Education for Freedom: A History of Lincoln University* (1976), *The Education of the Negro in the American Social Order* (1934), *Negro Education in Alabama: A Study in Cotton and Steel* (1939, 1994); Wayne J. Urban, *Black Scholar: Horace Mann Bond, 1904–1972* (1992).

Bradford, Melvin E.

(1934–1993) EDUCATOR, SOCIAL COMMENTATOR, AND POLITICAL ACTIVIST.

Melvin E. Bradford proclaimed himself an eighth-generation Texan, who, proud of his Confederate ancestry, dedicated his career to the perpetuation of southern, white, and elite values rooted in the Civil War era. Although generally styled by others a conservative, he preferred a stronger self-identification. Bradford deemed himself a reactionary. "'Reaction' is a necessary term in the intellectual context we inhabit late in the 20th century," he reflected in 1990. "Merely to conserve is sometimes to perpetuate what is outrageous."

From his posting as a professor of English literature at the Jesuit-affiliated University of Dallas (1967–93), he emerged as a leader of a coterie of white academicians focused on the reversal of nearly 50 years of civil rights progress. Bold and consistent in his views, Bradford condemned faith in human equality while articulating the case for an ordered society premised upon the supposed innate inequality of mankind. He grounded his belief system in a grand historical paradigm that melded his comfortable conviction of white superiority with a distinctive interpretation of the ideological dynamics of both the American Revolution and the Confederate crusade. He authored scores of cogent articles scattered across both popular and professional journals that were eventually collected into seven thick volumes, and, as an accomplished orator, he spoke with equal eloquence to crowds gathered in support of presidential candidate George Wallace and to college and university assemblages throughout the United States and Europe.

Bradford's path to prominence began as a young student in a Fort Worth school system whose curriculum had been long overseen by the United Daughters of the Confederacy and like-thinking patriotic societies. Entering the University of Oklahoma in 1952, he possessed an intense love for the southern culture of his upbringing blended with an acute awareness of the gathering pressures for civil rights reform and other challenges to the traditional entitlements of the region's white elites. The undergraduate Bradford found solace in the anthology *I'll Take My Stand* (1930) published by the Nashville Agrarians, a loose association of 12 intellectuals dedicated to "a Southern way of life against . . . the American or prevailing way." He later reflected upon his satisfaction at finding in their work "a voice for the deepest sentiments of the people I have known best . . . [the] wisdom of the world 'where I was born and raised.'" In 1959 he entered Vanderbilt University anxious to earn his doctorate in English literature, where he was mentored by Donald Davidson, the last of the Agrarians residing in the Tennessee capital.

Under Davidson's influence, the Vanderbilt English Department had a well-deserved reputation as a bastion of "plantation" thought. A powerful voice opposed to civil rights reforms in Tennessee, Davidson taught that the founding fathers never intended the phrase "all men are created equal" to apply to nonwhites and encouraged his students to see both the Declaration of Independence and the Constitution as conservative scriptures designed to shield society from the anarchy of democracy. Enamored of his professor's values, Bradford proclaimed in the late 1980s that he had "not changed my mind since I was a graduate student at Vanderbilt. Not my mind or my method for arriving at such conclusions, the way in which I reason with regard to political abstractions."

Across an academic career that spanned just a quarter century, Bradford secured a dedicated following of noteworthy academicians appreciative of his "political abstractions" that consistently criticized the modern affection for human equality. While he early secured a niche as a William Faulkner critic, in 1971 Bradford moved beyond the limited confines of literature to launch an attack on Abraham Lincoln. The brash assault upon this icon of American civil religion proved pivotal to his career. It projected him into ideological circles beyond narrow academia and established his credentials as an intellectual leader among those white southerners set on reversing the tide of civil rights reforms.

Bradford candidly admitted to a visceral hatred for the Great Emancipator, seeing in his quest to free the slaves a radical and harmful misinterpretation of the Declaration of Independence clause "all men are created equal." Neither Thomas Jefferson nor any of the other Revolution War patriots intended that phrase as a general dictum applied to all humanity, he averred. It was a specific statement defining the relationship of Englishmen in their home country to other Englishmen in America. This distortion of the Declaration of Independence, Bradford lectured, became Lincoln's "lasting and terrible impact on the nation's destiny."

Bradford's love of "political abstractions" easily melded into more practical expressions of his intensely held values. In 1972 he found a hero in presidential candidate George Wallace. Crusading throughout the Dallas area, Bradford organized Wallace followers, ushered them into local Democratic Party caucuses, and in turn was elected by them to the Democratic state committee. From 1972 to 1974 he proved an embarrassment to party centrists, who longed to disassociate themselves from their party's segregationist past. Bradford crusaded for Republican Ronald Reagan in 1980, becoming a member of the newly elected president's transitional team. Impressed by Bradford's intellectual acumen, Reagan nominated him to head the National Endowment for the Humanities (NEH), but the Texas professor's open expression of racist beliefs doomed his candidacy. Appearing before students at Michigan's highly conservative Hillsdale College, Bradford proclaimed his distaste for the NEH's Fellowship for College Teachers, a program he contemptuously termed "grants for second-rate scholars" because they amounted "to a hidden quota for minorities of various categories who have shown no academic promise but who have the right politics." Responding to the inevitable outcry from liberal journalists, progressive academicians, and civil rights advocates, the president rescinded Bradford's nomination, replacing him with the more acceptable conservative William Bennett. Nonetheless, Reagan retained his admiration for the Dallas scholar, appointing him head of the Board of Foreign Scholarships, which administers the Fulbright Program, a posting that did not require United States Senate approval.

Bradford soon faded from the national scene, but not from the consciousness of his conservative admirers. Together they pronounced that the left-wing opposition to his leadership of the NEH made him a martyr sacrificed in their war against the forces of liberalism and cultural anarchy. Thereafter Bradford returned to his love of writing tightly focused essays whose themes had large cultural and intellectual applications, and he was in much demand as a speaker providing an alternative voice to the more dominate cultural crusade for equal rights. In his later years, Bradford pleasured in his association with the contributors to the *Southern Partisan*, a small, controversial journal that projected an idealized image of the 19th-century Confederacy and offered it, along with the Old South it protected, as a viable alternative to the Yankee-dominated South of their own era. He contributed to its first and subsequent issues and shortly before his passing became its editor in chief.

Bradford longed for a South freed from what he defined as the oppressive forms of northern egalitarianism and bound once again by a glorious Anglo-Saxon order to the exclusion of all other races. Perhaps a clue to that desire exists in his presentation of his academic self. Like any good scholar, the Dallas professor carefully listed those organizational memberships that defined his professional persona: the Modern Language Association of America, the American Political Science Association, the Southwestern American Literature Association, and, of course, the Sons of Confederate Veterans.

FRED A. BAILEY
Abilene Christian University

M. E. Bradford, *Against the Barbarians, and Other Reflections on Familiar Themes* (1992), *A Better Guide than Reason: Studies in the American Revolution* (1979), *From Eden to Babylon: The Social and Political Essays of Andrew Nelson Lytle* (1990), *Generations of the Faithful Heart: On the Literature of the South* (1983), *Original Intentions: On the Making and Ratification of the United States Constitution* (1993), *Remembering Who We Are: Observations of a Southern Conservative* (1985), *A Worthy Company: Brief Lives of the Framers of the United States Constitution* (1982); Clyde N. Wilson, ed., *A Defender of Southern Conservatism: M. E. Bradford and His Achievements* (1999).

Branscomb, B. Harvie

(1894–1998) CHANCELLOR OF VANDERBILT UNIVERSITY.

Bennett Harvie Branscomb, a New Testament scholar who served as chancellor of Vanderbilt University from 1946 to 1963, was a pivotal figure in that school's evolution. A formidable, energetic man of keen intelligence, sharp wits, and first-rate political sense, Branscomb set Vanderbilt firmly on the road to becoming a nationally important center of research and education.

Branscomb was born in Huntsville, Ala., in 1894. He grew up in several rural Alabama towns where his father, a Methodist minister, led congregations. As a young man he attended Birmingham College (later Birmingham-Southern). Branscomb graduated in 1914 and then spent three years at Oxford as the second Rhodes Scholar from Alabama, earning a distinguished M.A. in biblical studies. After Oxford he worked with Herbert Hoover's Belgian Relief Commission, returned to the United States in 1917, and served briefly in the military, although World War I ended before he saw combat. In 1919 Branscomb began teaching philosophy and theology at the infant Southern Methodist University in Dallas, remaining until 1925 when he left to take a teaching job at the Duke University Divinity School. He stayed at Duke for 21 years, with a year at Columbia to finish his doctoral degree in 1927. He became dean of the Divinity School in 1944 and two years later he assumed the chancellorship of Vanderbilt University, a position he held until his retirement in 1963.

In his 17 years as chancellor of Vanderbilt, Branscomb orchestrated a dramatic transformation of the Nashville school. He inherited an institution in desperate financial straits, strongly local in character, and swollen with returned veterans. He immediately grasped, however, that the combination of postwar economic and social changes in the South and the massive outpouring of federal and philanthropic funds for research and education gave him the opportunity to create at Vanderbilt a top-tier national university. A brilliant fundraiser, Branscomb positioned Vanderbilt with federal agencies and private philanthropies as the most "progressive" of the southern universities. For example, he delicately coaxed the conservative Vanderbilt board into a gradual course of desegregation, beginning in 1953 with the graduate program in the School of Theology, always making sure that the small changes were known in national educational circles. This strategy not only made Vanderbilt a favorite of grantors but also helped attract outstanding faculty who were beginning to avoid segregated institutions. Branscomb misstepped badly in 1960, though, in his reaction to the involvement of a black divinity school graduate student, James Lawson, in the lunch counter sit-ins that began in Nashville that spring. Branscomb's expulsion of Lawson at the behest of the Vanderbilt trustees fueled a very public crisis that included the resignation (later retracted) of nearly the entire Divinity School faculty. The damage from this embarrassing incident was contained, however, and Branscomb never lost focus on his main goal—the pursuit of academic excellence.

When Branscomb retired in 1963, Vanderbilt was a fundamentally different institution from the one he arrived at in 1946. Its faculty had more than doubled, there were 31 new buildings, the endowment had expanded two and a half times, and library holdings increased from 470,000 to 840,000 volumes. Most important, Branscomb dramatically improved the institution's quality of teaching and research by astutely and aggressively raising standards for hiring and admissions. National in character, with a growing reputation, and on sound financial footing, Vanderbilt was positioned for even greater growth in the next decades.

MELISSA KEAN
Rice University

Harvie Branscomb, *Purely Academic: An Autobiography* (1978); Paul K. Conkin, *Gone with the Ivy: A Biography of Vanderbilt University* (1985).

Brown, Charlotte Hawkins
(1883–1961) ACTIVIST AND EDUCATOR.

Regarded as the "First Lady of Social Graces," Charlotte Hawkins Brown spent more than 50 years guiding the education and social habits of southern black youth at her Palmer Memorial Institute in North Carolina. The descendant of slaves, Brown was born Lottie Hawkins on 11 June 1883 in Henderson, N.C. Lottie's grandmother, Rebecca Hawkins, descended from English navigator Sir John D. Hawkins. At an early age, Brown witnessed the importance of education and cultural aspirations as envisioned by her mother and grandmother. Lottie's 18-member family moved to Cambridge, Mass., in 1888 for better social, economic, and educational opportunities. At Cambridge, the young Brown attended the Allston Grammar School and cultivated a friendship with Alice and Edith Longfellow, children of Henry Wadsworth Longfellow, who lived in her neighborhood near Harvard University. Demonstrating early proclivities for leadership, Brown, at age 12, organized her church's Sunday school kindergarten department. At Cambridge English High School, moreover, she proved herself an excellent scholar and artist, having rendered several crayon portraits of classmates. Considering "Lottie" too ordinary, she changed her name to Charlotte Eugenia Hawkins upon graduation. Having observed Brown in 1900 reading Virgil while babysitting two infants, Alice Freeman Palmer, humanitarian and president of Wellesley College, assumed the role of her benefactor.

Influenced by educator and power broker Booker T. Washington, Brown sought to teach blacks in the South. To further this goal, she enrolled, with the help of Palmer, in the State Normal School at Salem, Mass., in the fall of 1900. Having been approached by a field secretary of the American Missionary Association, a white-led group that administered and financed southern black schools, Brown eagerly accepted an invitation to teach in her native state. Barely 18 years old, Brown emerged from a Southern Railway train in the fall of 1900, where she was confronted with the unfamiliar terrain of Guilford County, N.C. Suspending her junior college education at State Normal School, she began her first teaching job at Bethany Institute in Sedalia—a small, dilapidated, rural school for African Americans. Securing money from northern friends and donations from the Sedalia community, Brown soon raised funds to erect a campus with more than 200 acres and two new buildings. Alice Freeman Palmer Institute, named in honor of her benefactor, opened on 10 October 1902. It was later renamed the Alice Freeman Palmer Memorial Institute upon Palmer's death.

Distinguished among its contemporaries, Brown's private finishing school for rural African Americans provided college preparatory classes for upper-level high school students. Such instruction fitted the school's dual ambitions: to undo common assumptions of African American inferiority and to provide an expansive education beyond vocational studies. At Palmer, classes included art, math, literature, and romance languages.

In addition to academic training, Brown outlined an exacting program of racial etiquette, involving lessons in character and appearance, for black boys and girls. Brown expected her students to abide by a strict code of Victorian moral conduct. She worked to smooth "the rough edges of social behavior" by producing graduates who were educationally sound, religiously sincere, and "culturally secure." This cultural regime, in part, took the form of small discussion groups for boys and girls. Led by an adult male and female counselor, respectively, students received individual attention in matters of etiquette. In one boys' session, discussion centered on the best manner in which to obtain "culture" along with clean minds and bodies. Students also participated in "wholesome" fitness activities designed to nurture habits of self-reliance, self-control, and fair play. Palmer girls played basketball and volleyball. The young men's sports repertoire was more expansive, including basketball, football, baseball, and track and field.

Perhaps Brown's most noted contribution to her students' cultural education was her etiquette manual, *The Correct Thing to Do—to Say—to Wear*. In it, she succinctly defined good manners for boys and girls at home and outside it. Proper introductions, boy-girl relationships, and dress are also addressed. Palmer's curriculum and Brown's writings mirrored her race philosophy, which sought a holistic education for black youth based on the uplift of the individual. Charlotte Hawkins Brown and fellow black educators Mary McLeod Bethune and Nannie Helen Burroughs became collectively renowned as the "Three B's of Education," stressing liberal arts and cultural training for racial uplift. The school's political and cultural legacy largely hinges on Palmer's credo, "Educate the individual to live in the greater world." Brown's shepherding of Palmer, which survived a major fire in 1917, ended in 1952. She died in 1961 and was buried on the Palmer campus, which is now a state historic site.

ANGELA HORNSBY-GUTTING
University of Mississippi

Charlotte Hawkins Brown, *The Correct Thing—to Do—to Say—to Wear* (1941); Colonel Hawkins Jr., in *The Heritage of Blacks in North Carolina*, vol. 1, ed. Philip N. Henry and Carol M. Speas (1990); Tera Hunter, *Southern Exposure* (September/October 1983); Marsha Vick, in *Notable Black American Women*, ed. Jessie Carney Smith (1992); Charles Weldon Wadelington, *Charlotte Hawkins Brown and Palmer Memorial Institute: What One Young African American Woman Could Do* (1999), *Tar Heel Junior Historian* (1995).

Burroughs, Nannie Helen
(1879–1961) EDUCATOR AND SOCIAL ACTIVIST.
As a church and organization leader, school founder and educator, women's advocate and race champion, Nannie Helen Burroughs was a pragmatic warrior and outspoken public intellectual who defied conventional female confinements of her era. Through her newspaper commentary, speeches, and writings she inserted herself into the male-centered discourse on race advancement. Her work paralleled that of better-known black women predecessors and contemporaries including Annie Julia Cooper, Mary Church Terrell, and Mary McLeod Bethune, and her accomplishments and zeal for racial uplift were just as impressive. Burroughs brought into the public sphere a deep concern for the black working class who lacked "social or economic pull" and a belief in self-help that caused people to compare her with Booker T. Washington. Burroughs, however, was more like W. E. B. Du Bois in her belief that blacks must demand their full rights, including woman suffrage, and must keep agitating for justice. "Hound dogs are kicked, not bull dogs," she wrote.

Burroughs's unique contribution to black female empowerment was in her understanding that black women needed both "respectability"—sometimes oversimplified by scholars as a middle-class notion—and economic self-sufficiency. In her view, one was not possible without the other. Her school, the National Training School for Women and Girls in Washington, D.C., was the realization of her dream of providing a practical education that would make black women economically self-sufficient and place them beyond spiritual and moral reproach. It was founded in 1909 with the help of the Women's Auxiliary of the National Baptist Convention, where Burroughs was the long-serving corresponding secretary. Graduates were expected to become community-minded wage earners who would counter the prevailing negative stereotypes of the black race—particularly its women. Burroughs's grand vision was reflected in the fact that in naming the school she left out "Baptist," although she was supported by that denomination, and included "National" to announce the school's nonsectarianism and her own independence. Women wrote to Burroughs from across the nation seeking admission for themselves or their daughters and expressing delight in the prospect of living in such a protective enclave and reaping its many benefits.

Burroughs believed that women were the linchpins of race progress, and the curriculum stressed Christian-inspired precepts about the dignity of all work. By training black women to be skilled workers and "professionalizing" their work, including domestic work, she sought to raise women's self-esteem, race pride, and wages. Her school offered a mandatory black history course, courses in music, public speaking, secretarial skills, the Bible, and hygiene, plus nontraditional courses in shoe repair and printing. Using student labor, successful commercial ventures such as the Sunlight Laundry were launched. The school's creed, the three B's—"the Bible, the Bath, and Broom, clean life, clean body, clean house"—was infused into every aspect of school life. So was Burroughs's defiant certitude about black female education that is captured in the famous declaration that became the school's motto: "We specialize in the wholly impossible."

In establishing the National Training School for Women and Girls (renamed the National Trade and Professional School for Women and Girls in 1939), Burroughs bucked the male leadership of the National Baptist Convention, who were wary of women leaders, and Booker T. Washington, who opposed locating black schools outside of the South for fear of losing support from white northerners. Burroughs realized the importance of having a black female presence in the nation's capital and used that visibility to attract a national and international student body. In addition to her long tenure as founder and principal of the National Training School for Women and Girls, Burroughs helped to organize the National Association of Wage Earners in 1921 to support better wages and living conditions for domestic workers.

Following her death in 1961, the school was renamed in her honor and continues as a kindergarten-through-sixth-grade Christian day school on that same Washington, D.C., hillside from which Burroughs looked out into the world and sought to change it.

AUDREY THOMAS MCCLUSKEY
Indiana University

Nannie Helen Burroughs Papers, Library of Congress Manuscript Division; Sharon Harley, *Journal of Negro History* (Winter/Autumn 1996); Evelyn Brooks Higginbotham, *Righteous Discontent: The Women's Movement in the Black Baptist Church, 1880–1920* (1993); Audrey Thomas McCluskey, *Signs* (Winter 1997); Victoria W. Wolcott, *Journal of Women's History* (Spring 1997).

Campbell, John C.

(1867–1919) EDUCATOR.

John Charles Campbell was born in LaPorte, Ind., 14 September 1867. He attended Williams College and Andover Newton Theological Seminary, graduating from the latter institution in 1895. That same year he married Grace Buckingham and moved to Joppa, Ala., where he headed a mountain academy. After serving there three years, he taught in the public schools of Stevens Point, Wisc., and then in 1900 moved to Tennessee, where he served as principal of the Pleasant Hill Academy. From 1901 to 1907 he was superintendent of secondary education, dean, and president of Piedmont College, Demorest, Ga. In 1905, during his tenure at Piedmont, Campbell's wife died. Two years later, in 1907, he married Olive A. Dame of Medford, Mass., and spent several months traveling with her in Sicily and Italy.

In 1908 Campbell attended a meeting of the National Conference of Charities and Correction in Richmond, Va., one session of which was devoted to benevolent work in Appalachia. This led directly to the work for which he is now best remembered. Inspired by a paper at the conference, Campbell approached Mary Glenn, a prominent figure in social work circles, with a proposal to conduct a survey of the social, industrial, educational, and religious problems of the Appalachian mountaineers, which would aid in ascertaining what resources were needed or available. Campbell's proposal was presented to the trustees of the Russell Sage Foundation on 25 May 1908. Funding for the survey was approved annually until October 1912, when he was appointed secretary of a newly established Southern Highland Division of the foundation. Campbell then began to carry out his plans for Appalachia. In an effort to foster cooperation among agencies working in the region, he helped organize the Conference of Southern Mountain Workers (later known as the Council of the Southern Mountains) and for many years served as the group's leader. At Campbell's suggestion the southern Presbyterian Church centralized its school work in the mountains and formed the Synod of Appalachia in 1914—the first formal acknowledgement by that denomination that Appalachia formed a natural, distinctive unit of organization.

Campbell worked for years on a book utilizing the information gathered in his survey of mountain problems, but *The Southern Highlander and His Homeland* (1921) did not appear until two years after his death. Although polemical, it is generally considered the best early study of Appalachia. Campbell's greatest difficulty in finishing the volume was that Appalachia was not a coherent region with a uniform culture and a homogeneous population, but was instead a complex part of America that could not be easily simplified or reduced to generalizations.

Campbell died in Asheville, N.C., 2 May 1919. With his passing the Russell Sage Foundation's work in the mountains came to an end, although for several years the organization continued to fund the annual meeting of the Conference of Southern Mountain Workers. Campbell's widow, herself a major figure in Appalachian cultural work, helped establish the John C. Campbell Folk School at Brasstown, N.C., in honor of her husband, who was one of the early American advocates of the Scandinavian folk school as an alternative to the traditional rural school. This school is still operating.

W. K. MCNEIL
Ozark Folk Center
Mountain View, Arkansas

Isaac Messler, *Mountain Life and Work* (April 1928); Henry D. Shapiro, *Appalachia on Our Mind: The Southern Mountains and Mountaineers in the American Consciousness, 1870–1920* (1978); David E. Whisnant, *All That Is Native and Fine: The Politics of Culture in an American Region* (1983), *Modernizing the Mountaineer: People, Power, and Planning in Appalachia* (1979).

Campus Ministries

Campus ministries have become the primary locus for student religiosity at both public and most private southern universities and colleges. Although it began in 1844 in London, England, by the late 1800s the Young Men's Christian Association's (YMCA) Student Department had spread throughout the United States. Robert E. Lee, president of Washington College in Virginia, endorsed the formation of a YMCA at his institution, believing the organization would "do much to fix the attention of the students upon the subject of religion and to cultivate moral and religious sentiments in the community." The YMCA student work was relatively weak in the South, however, perhaps because of the strong denominational character of many universities and colleges and some cultural resistance to organizations from outside the region. Still, significant numbers of southern students attended the YMCA's summer conferences, creating a student volunteer movement that promoted "the evangelization of the world in this generation" through foreign missions. Student chapters at predominantly African American institutions were organized by the YMCA's "colored work department."

As enrollments at public universities began to dwarf those at denominational institutions, denominations responded by establishing their own campus ministries in the early 1900s. In the Methodist Episcopal Church, South, the collegiate department of the Epworth League—"All For Christ" its motto—promoted discipleship and evangelism, both at Methodist institutions like Vanderbilt and Emory as well as at state universities. In the 1920s, as the YMCA declined in significance, the Southern Baptist Convention created chapters of the Baptist Student Union at many public institutions. In the early 1900s, Newman Clubs and Hillel Foundations were established at institutions with significant Catholic and Jewish minorities, respectively.

By midcentury, the unofficial establishment of Protestant Christianity had waned at public universities, if somewhat less slowly in the South. Moreover, many denominational institutions had largely shed their sectarian character, as progressively fewer schools required religious practices such as chapel attendance. As the public life of universities and colleges became more secular, the locus of campus religiosity shifted from chapels and classrooms to denominational and parachurch campus ministries. The significance of denominational Protestant ministries peaked in the first two decades after the Second World War, as Protestant denominations—often with the encouragement of university administrations—built campus centers, planted churches adjacent to campuses, and hired campus ministers. In the 1960s some mainline Protestant campus ministries offered support to the civil rights movement and expressed discontent with the war in Vietnam.

During the 1950s and 1960s evangelical campus ministries—including InterVarsity, Campus Crusade for Christ, the Navigators, and the Fellowship of Christian Athletes—expanded to the South but achieved limited success due to the relative strength of Baptist and Methodist ministries. With the exception of the Baptist Student Union, however, most mainline campus ministries declined in influence, as evangelical organizations more rapidly adapted to changes in popular culture and benefited from the antiestablishment ethos of the late 1960s and early 1970s. Today, evangelical campus ministries form the most visible religious presence at most public and private universities and colleges in the South and have achieved particular success among members of athletic teams. Typically dissenting from regnant attitudes toward sex and alcohol use, evangelical students form a partially countercultural minority on many campuses.

Despite the visibility of evangelical campus ministries, the religious offerings at most southern institutions of higher education have become markedly more diverse in recent decades. Hillel Foundations and Newman Clubs maintain a large presence at some southern universities and colleges, and as the enrollment of international students has increased, the formation and rapid growth of Muslim Student Associations has been one of the most significant developments in campus religiosity in recent decades. The vitality of student religious life, from locker-room prayer sessions to dormitory Bible studies to halal and kosher meals, belies the notion of a thoroughgoing secularization of the American university.

JOHN G. TURNER
University of South Alabama

C. Howard Hopkins, *History of the Y.M.C.A. in North America* (1951); George M. Marsden, *The Soul of the American University: From Protestant Establishment to Established Unbelief* (1994); Douglas T. Rossinow, *The Politics of Authenticity: Liberalism, Christianity, and the New Left in America* (1998); John G. Turner, *Bill Bright and Campus Crusade for Christ: The Renewal of Evangelicalism in Postwar America* (2008).

Center for the Study of Southern Culture

Established in 1977 at the University of Mississippi with funding from the National Endowment for the Humanities (NEH), the Center for the Study of Southern Culture was initially proposed by two faculty members, Robert Haws, a history professor, and Michael Harrington, a philosophy professor, as a center where scholars could study the literature, history, and music of the South with a specific focus on race relations. Vice Chancellor for Academic Affairs Art DeRosier and Chancellor Porter L. Fortune Jr. supported the proposal, and folklorist William R. Ferris, a native of Vicksburg, Miss., became the Center's founding director, serving from 1978 to 1998. Charles Reagan Wilson followed Ferris as director until 2007, when Ted Ownby took over as interim director and then became permanent director the following year.

The Center began its work in 1977 with a Eudora Welty Symposium that featured the Mississippi author in person. An interdisciplinary program working with university departments and faculty, including anthropology and sociology, English, history, literature, and political science, offers over 60 courses covering life, culture, and heritage in the American South. Although it began with a focus on southern U.S. culture and history as a microcosm of the American experience, the Center has broadened its scope to encompass the future of southern culture, the global South, and challenges to long-held conceptions of what is southern. The Center found a physical home on the university campus in the historic Barnard Observatory, built in the late 1850s and renovated 1989–91.

One of the first regional centers in the nation, the Center for the Study of Southern Culture, with a grant from NEH, developed a bachelor of arts program in Southern studies that enrolls about 40 undergraduates and a master of arts program that accommodates about 24 students each year, attracting them from around the world. The Gray and Coterie awards are presented to undergraduates for excellence in research papers on the South, the Lucille and Motee Daniel Award is given to a notable graduate research project, and the Peter Aschoff Prize is awarded for an accomplished paper on music, especially the blues. In addition, the Center presents the Eudora Welty Awards for Creative Writing to high school students for distinguished short stories and poetry. It has a strong specialty in documentary studies, directed by David Wharton. The Gammill Gallery in Barnard Observatory displays the work of students and teachers as well as visiting collections from across the nation. Much of the Center's research is housed in the university's Special Collections and Archives, including the Southern Media Collection, now housed in the library's visual archive, and the Blues Archive, the largest public blues collection in the world.

The Center's work has led to the creation of several affiliated institutions, such as the Southern Foodways Alliance, which holds its annual Southern Foodways Symposium on the university campus each fall, and the William Winter Institute for Racial Reconciliation. It publishes the periodicals *Mississippi Folklife* and *Living Blues*, a magazine devoted to blues musicians and the culture that produced them, since 1983. The Center helped establish the radio programs *Thacker Mountain Radio*, a live community radio broadcast in Oxford, Miss., and *Highway 61*, a blues program first hosted by William Ferris on Mississippi Public Radio. Wilson and Ferris edited the *Encyclopedia of Southern Culture* (1989), which won the Dartmouth Prize from the American Library Association as best reference work of the year of its publication. Other publications include Dorothy Abbott's multivolume *Mississippi Writers* (1985–91) and the scholarly book series New Directions in Southern Studies (published by the University of North Carolina Press).

The Center is widely recognized for its symposia and conferences that occur across the world, including Faulkner conferences in Paris and Moscow, but mostly on the University of Mississippi campus, including the Faulkner and Yoknapatawpha Conference, the Porter L. Fortune Jr. History Symposium, the Oxford Conference for the Book, the Future of the South Conference, the Blues Today Symposium, and the weekly Brown Bag lecture series. Major funding for the Center's many projects has come from the NEH, the Ford Foundation, the Phil Hardin Foundation, and the Friends of the Center. An advisory committee has assisted the work of the Center since its beginning.

ANNA F. KAPLAN
Columbia University

Marie Antoon and Tom Rieland, *The Center for the Study of Southern Culture* (film, 1984); Center for the Study of Southern Culture Web site, www.olemiss.edu/depts/south; David Sansing, *The University of Mississippi: A Sesquicentennial History* (1999).

Chautauqua

From its start in 1874 at a Methodist Sunday school assembly in Lake Chautauqua, N.Y., this adult-education movement had a southern flavor, and its felicitously packaged blend of entertainment, semiclassical culture, popular religion, and self-improvement was widely welcomed in the Bible Belt. One cofounder, John Heyl Vincent, a Methodist minister born in Tuscaloosa, Ala., hailed the Chautauqua as a way to "mitigate sectional antipathies" in the post–Civil War years.

Although the circuit or tent Chautauquas still made their rounds of the southern hinterlands until the early 1930s, the independent Chautauquas, which met annually at the same site, had the most lasting influence. Independent Chautauquas were founded at Hillsboro, Va., 1877; Purcell, Va., 1878; Mountain Lake Park, Md., 1883; Monteagle, Tenn., 1883; DeFuniak Springs, Fla., 1884; Siloam Springs, Ark., 1886; Lexington, Ky., 1887; and the Piedmont Chautauqua at Lithia Springs (then Salt Springs), Ga., 1888. The spectacular Piedmont Chautauqua was the brainchild of Henry W. Grady, who called it the "Saratoga of the South." With the assistance of Marion C. Kiser and the Atlanta business community, an 8,000-seat tabernacle, two Italian Renaissance style hotels, and a summer college building were constructed in about a month by an army of workers. In its heyday, the Piedmont Chautauqua's Summer College was headed by W. R. Harper, dean at Yale College, and included faculty from Harvard, Johns Hopkins, and the University of Virginia.

The circuit Chautauquas began in the Midwest in 1903 and soon spread to the South, where two systems, Alkahest of Atlanta and Radcliffe Attractions of Washington, D.C., handled most of the bookings. Alkahest, boasting that it "covered Dixie like the dew," had a principal, seven-day circuit that played 40 towns per year. Radcliffe had three circuits that were scheduled for weeks and split weeks in well over 200 towns. The onset of the Depression and the popularity of radio combined to bring on the demise of the circuit Chautauqua.

The programs in both the independent and circuit Chautauquas were similar, offering something for all tastes and ages. Most popular were the inspirational addresses by such well-known speakers as Russell H. Conwell and William Jennings Bryan, but also widely enjoyed were the dramas, marching music, symphonic concerts, lectures on science, Gilbert and Sullivan operas, Cossack choirs, and magic shows. Many southerners remember the tent shows fondly for first bringing "culture" and entertainment to rural areas.

BENJAMIN W. GRIFFITH
West Georgia College

Victoria Case and Robert O. Case, *We Called It Culture: The Story of Chautauqua* (1948); Benjamin W. Griffith, *Georgia Review* (Spring 1972), *Georgia Historical Quarterly* (Summer 1971); Theodore Morrison,

Chautauqua (1974); Hugh A. Orchard, *Fifty Years of Chautauqua* (1923).

Chavis, John

(1763–1838) TEACHER AND PREACHER.

John Chavis was the first African American to receive a college education in the South. Originally Chavis hoped to serve as a Presbyterian minister, but he primarily worked as a teacher. After 1807, he operated a small school in the various North Carolina counties he lived in—Chatham, Granville, Wake, and Orange. Some of his students were black; others were members of prominent white families, including the sons of North Carolina's chief justice Leonard Henderson, Charles Manly, who later served as the state's governor, and Abram Rencher, who became governor of New Mexico. Perhaps his most notable student was North Carolina Whig senator Willie P. Mangum.

Little is known of Chavis's early life, but he identified himself as freeborn and claimed to be a Revolutionary War veteran. During the early 1790s—a period when race relations were still more fluid than they would become during the 19th and 20th centuries—Chavis studied for the ministry. It was not uncommon for evangelical churches to call free blacks to the ministry of evangelizing slaves. Around 1790 he began to study with President John Witherspoon of the College of New Jersey (later Princeton University), who often tutored free blacks and American Indians. Witherspoon was an orthodox theologian who vehemently opposed slavery. When Witherspoon died in 1795, Chavis became a student at Liberty Hall Academy (later Washington and Lee University) in Lexington, Va., which had been founded by Presbyterian clergymen in 1749.

Chavis's arrival at Liberty Hall marked the first time a free black would enroll in a southern white institution of higher learning, and it was probably possible because both Chavis and the school's rector, Rev. William Graham, had studied under President John Witherspoon. Yet Chavis's relationship with Graham is a paradox because Graham had developed a scriptural defense of slavery that he included in lectures to his senior classes and evidently feared the consequences of emancipation. Graham's views about slavery differed sharply from those of Witherspoon. Chavis disliked slavery but did not favor abolition because he, too, feared the consequences of emancipation. In spite of their differences, mutual respect between the two men would have been essential to Chavis's success at Liberty Hall. Chavis and Graham lived and worked together during a time when Americans were struggling with the concept of a new republic that proclaimed liberty for white men while denying it to black slaves. The fiery political rhetoric of the 1790s politicized some blacks, and it profoundly influenced Chavis's views about social relations and politics.

Upon completion of Chavis's academic studies, the Lexington, Va., Presbytery examined and certified him as a licentiate. This was a notable accomplishment for a free black, yet it occurred just as southern race relations became less fluid and the future for free blacks became more bleak. One catalyst for that change was the 1800 slave conspiracy of Gabriel Prosser in Richmond. Virginia's legislative response to Gabriel's attempt to seize the Richmond armory and subsequently free the state's slaves adversely affected the liberty of John Chavis and other free blacks. He had to register with the Clerk of the Rockbridge County Court in 1801 in order to obtain certification of his free status. Around 1804 he moved to North Carolina, where he worked as an itinerate preacher, but mostly as a teacher of children.

Chavis became a patriotic citizen of North Carolina, a state in which blacks had the franchise until 1835. Surviving handwritten letters to Senator Willie Person Mangum provide a small glimpse of Chavis's political views. He identified himself as a Federalist and strong supporter of Henry Clay's American System—a protective tariff, internal improvements, and the Bank of the United States. In 1831 he expressed strong disapproval of President Andrew Jackson, and he denounced the nullification plan of South Carolina's John C. Calhoun. On the more troubling issue of slavery, Chavis wrote, "That slavery is a national evil no one doubts. All that can be done, is to make the best of a bad bargain. I am clearly of the opinion that immediate emancipation would . . . entail the greatest earthly curse upon my brethren . . . that could be conferred upon them." No one understood the plight of free blacks during the antebellum period better than Chavis. In light of harsh laws that southern states enacted after Nat Turner's insurrection, the Orange, N.C., Presbytery advised him to stop teaching or preaching. Subsequently, his only income was an inadequate pension paid by the presbytery. Severely limited by new law, Chavis died in poverty at age 75.

THEODORE CARTER DELANEY
Washington and Lee University

Ted Carter DeLaney, in *American National Biography* (1999); Douglas R. Egerton, *Gabriel's Rebellion: The Virginia Slave Conspiracies of 1800–1802* (1993); John Hope Franklin, *The Free Negro of North Carolina* (1943); Elizabeth Fox-Genovese and Eugene D. Genovese, *The Mind of the Master Class: History and Faith in the Southern Slaveholders' Worldview* (2005); Henry Shanks, ed., *The Papers of Willie P. Mangum*, vols. 1–5 (1950–56).

Citadel

Located in Charleston, S.C., the Citadel remains a southern institution steeped in American history. In 1842 the South Carolina legislature approved a bill creating the South Carolina Military Academy, designating the guard duties at the arsenal on Marion Square in the center of Charleston be combined with a system of military education in the sciences and liberal arts for "poor but deserving boys of the State." Citadel students and graduates have participated in every military action since the college's founding. Some claim that on 9 January 1861, three months before the firing on Fort Sumter, Citadel cadets fired the first shots of the Civil War when a battery of cadets stationed on Morris Island fired upon the U.S. steamer *Star of the West*, which was attempting to supply Fort

The South Carolina Corps of Cadets during a Friday afternoon military dress parade on Summerall Field on the Citadel campus (Russell K. Pace/The Citadel)

Sumter. Many of the school's graduates served with distinction in the Confederate Army. When the war ended, the school became the headquarters for the 21st United States Colored Regiment. Federal occupation of the college ended in 1879, and in 1882, after a concerted effort by powerful alumni, including the governor, the school resumed its training of "citizen-soldiers."

The Citadel would eventually outgrow its location in the center of Charleston, relocating in 1922 to a 100-acre site on the banks of the Ashley River. Like most public institutions, the college scraped by during the Great Depression, surviving on public funding from both the South Carolina legislature as well as federal New Deal programs. During World War II, many cadets enlisted or were drafted, significantly dwindling the Corps of Cadets. The Citadel Class of 1944 is known as the "Lost Class" because all members of the class left the college to serve in the military.

The Citadel rebounded economically after the war as federal defense dollars and jobs flowed southward. At the same time, a national Cold War ethos that emphasized conformity, anticommunism, and military preparedness boosted the college's image. Meanwhile, the school grappled with the social and political forces unleashed by World War II. In the wake of the 1954 *Brown v. Board of Education* decision, the Citadel and its new president, General Mark W.

Clark, stood in staunch opposition to school desegregation. It was not until 1966, the year after Clark retired, that Charles Foster would enroll as the first African American cadet at the Citadel.

It was also during this time that the all-male school became deeply embroiled in the culture wars that grew out of the Vietnam era. While certain members of the corps of cadets began growing their hair longer and flouting authority, school officials touted the college as an "oasis of order" in a chaotic world. By the mid-1970s, the Citadel benefited from national pundits' promotion of the South as the "New America," a trend that elevated white southern "good ol' boys" to the status of national icons. The institution continued to thrive during the macho age of Ronald Reagan and Rambo while falling prey to the same racial tensions that marked this era. In 1986, the hazing of a black cadet by five upperclassmen dressed as Klansmen propelled the college's problems into the national spotlight. Six years later, following widespread coverage of another racially charged campus incident, Citadel officials banned the waving of "unofficial banners," including Confederate flags, at sporting events and began looking to replace "Dixie" as the college's fight song.

These decisions attracted much less attention than they might have, since by this time the Citadel was engaged in a much larger battle over its single-sex admission policies. In 1992 the Citadel's admissions office inadvertently approved the application of Shannon Faulkner, a woman from upstate South Carolina. When they rescinded their acceptance, Faulkner sued. Over the next few years, Citadel officials tried several methods of preserving an all-male corps of cadets. They toyed with the idea of becoming a private institution and won legislative support for what they hoped would qualify as a "parallel" military program for women at Converse College, a private, all-female school in Spartanburg, S.C. In the end, such efforts failed, and on 12 August 1995 the Citadel complied with the appellate court's order and admitted Faulkner into the Corps of Cadets. On 28 June 1996, two days after the United States Supreme Court's decision in *United States v. Virginia* ended Virginia Military Institute's all-male admissions policy, the Citadel's governing board voted unanimously to remove a person's gender as a requirement for admission. In May 1999, Nancy Mace, the daughter of a Citadel graduate, became the first female to graduate from the corps of cadets.

ALEX MACAULAY
Western Carolina University

Rod Andrew, *Long Gray Lines* (2001); O. J. Bond, *The Story of The Citadel* (1936); Nancy Mace, *In the Company of Men* (2001).

Clemson University

Clemson University, South Carolina's 1862 land-grant college, is based on three distinct charters. First, the will of Thomas Green Clemson, the founder, who had been married to John C. Calhoun's daughter Anna, conveys the Calhoun-Clemson home Fort Hill, 814 acres, and Clemson's wealth to South Carolina, on the condition that it place the institution under 13 trustees: seven life trustees, named in the will, with full power to fill vacancies, and six term trustees to be selected by the legislature. Signed by the governor (27 November 1889) and ratified by the state supreme court chief justice, the Act of Acceptance is the second charter. The legislature then committed the Morrill land grant (1862) and the Hatch (1887) acts' endowments to Clemson's trustees, forming Clemson's third charter.

The trustees soon named Virginia mathematician Henry Strode the first president of the Clemson Agricultural College of South Carolina (its name until 1 July 1964) and J. S. Newman to oversee the Agricultural Experiment Station, where research began quickly. Then the trustees set about erecting faculty homes, classroom buildings, and one barracks. The trustees decided that the student body should all be male and military. Clemson's teaching mission began 6 July 1893, with 446 white South Carolinians, aged 14 to 22, although the will made no gender, racial, or other such restrictions. The first class, about half divided between agriculturalists and engineers, graduated December 1896. Very shortly, the trustees added textiles (1898) and architecture (1912). Almost from its beginning, Clemson began a traveling, on-site extension program. Through a life trustee, Congressman A. Francis Lever (S.C.), the Smith-Lever Act of 1914 added service to the missions.

By 1895, Clemson enrolled its first out-of-state students and in 1896 began playing intercollegiate athletics—baseball first and then football. The 1896 football team selected the Tiger from Princeton as its mascot. Female professionals joined the faculty in 1905, Asian students in 1912, female graduate students in 1946, female undergraduates in 1955, and male and female African American students in 1963. Of these events, the only one that drew national attention was in 1963 when national journalists and photographers crowded the area and had nothing to report. Clemson has awarded 102,484 bachelors, 426 associates, 28,221 masters, 350 educational specialists, and 3,014 doctors' degrees (as of 2007).

The four-year military requirement was eliminated in 1954 and all such requirements in 1971, although strong ROTC programs are still part of the school's offerings. Alumni and students have served in every armed conflict and participated in overseas reconstruction and aid from the Spanish-American War to the present. Nearly 500 have given their lives in active military service.

Given the breadth of its student body, the quality of its faculty, and the levels of degrees offered, Clemson's name was changed to Clemson University on 1 July 1964. The faculty is noted for teaching, research, and service in such fields as communications, architecture, history, bioengineering, astrophysics, materials science, agriculture, and recreational therapy. That research has led to grain enrichment, replacement body parts, and new understandings of human endeavor through history, architecture, and literature.

Clemson's landholdings measure 33,000 acres, and its physical plant is currently valued at $627 million. Library holdings are in excess of one and a half million titles plus industrial, scientific, and agricultural documents, photographs, and papers of political leaders since 1825.

JEROME V. REEL JR.
Clemson University

Ernest M. Lander Jr., *The Calhoun Family and Thomas Green Clemson: Decline of a Southern Patriarchy* (1983); Donald McKale and J. V. Reel, eds., *Tradition: A History of the Presidency of Clemson University* (1998).

College of William and Mary

In 1693, King William III and Queen Mary II of England granted a royal charter to establish the College of William and Mary, the second oldest college in British North America. The charter called for the school to provide instruction in divinity, philosophy, languages, and other arts and sciences. The all-male liberal arts college would consist of three schools: grammar, philosophy, and divinity. It would provide an education for the sons of Virginia gentry and educate young men for the ministry. The Reverend James Blair served as the first president of the college (1693–1743).

The grammar school opened in 1694; the main building, Wren Building, was completed in 1700. After Williamsburg became the capital of the colony in 1699, the college served as the temporary headquarters of the colonial government, beginning in 1700. The college also established its Indian school about the same time. Professors of natural philosophy, moral philosophy, and divinity offered a curriculum modeled on the British university systems.

The College of William and Mary established the first chair in law and the first instruction in modern languages among the early American colleges. Phi Beta Kappa was founded at the college in 1776. In 1779 it was the first American college to become a university. George Washington served as the school's first American chancellor (1788–99). Future presidents Thomas Jefferson, James Monroe, and John Tyler attended the college. Chief Justice John Marshall studied briefly under George Wythe, a signer of the Declaration of Independence and the first professor of law at the school.

The history of William and Mary always involved a struggle for adequate funding. At the end of the American Revolution, the college lost its royal support. The school closed from 1780 to 1782 as British, French, and American troops occupied college buildings. The relocation of the Virginia capital and its legislature to Richmond in 1780 was a serious financial blow to both Williamsburg and the college.

As Williamsburg shrank to a small village in the 19th century, the college suffered a decline in funding and enrollment. Lack of income and students and an accumulation of debts plagued William and Mary for decades. Although enrollment grew under the leadership of President Thomas Roderick Dew (1836–46), student numbers plummeted in the 1850s. The Civil War brought more tribulations. Northern troops set fire to Wren

College of William and Mary, Williamsburg, Va., c. 1840 (University Archives, Swem Library, College of William and Mary)

Building in 1862. The building, which had endured fires in 1705 and 1859, became a scorched shell. In 1865 President Benjamin Ewell (1854–88) reopened the school, closed it in 1868, and then opened it again in 1869. But a severe lack of funds forced Ewell to close the college from 1881 until 1888.

Between 1888 and 1919 the college underwent three major transformations that probably saved it from extinction. The first came in 1888 when President Ewell finally persuaded Virginia's General Assembly to provide an annual appropriation to the college to train young men to become public school teachers. The college reopened to offer two educational tracks for its students, liberal arts or teacher training, which brought young men back to the college and provided a steady source of revenue.

President Lyon G. Tyler (1888–1919) succeeded President Ewell. During his tenure, Tyler led the school in two additional crucial transformations. To permanently secure state appropriations, Tyler led the school to relinquish its private status in 1906 and become a public institution. President Tyler's greatest plan materialized in 1918. College enrollment had fallen from 244 in 1905–6 to 149 in 1917–18 because of World War I. Fearful of further reductions, President Tyler boldly requested that the college accept women students. In 1918 the General Assembly passed an act to change the all-male William and Mary into Virginia's first public coeducational liberal arts college.

After Tyler retired, Julian Alvin Carroll Chandler (1919–34) succeeded him and became renowned for the changes he brought about. In 1918–19, student enrollment, including its first 24 women, had fallen to 131. By 1932–33, however, enrollment soared to 1,602 students; just over half were women. Chandler transformed the student body, quadrupled the size of the faculty, and added additional women deans and faculty. He expanded the curriculum in liberal arts, teacher education, and law and offered numerous new preprofessional training programs. Chandler built a magnificent campus with new dorms, classroom buildings, and numerous additional facilities. He established college divisions in Richmond and Norfolk, which later grew into Virginia Commonwealth University and Old Dominion University. The total value of the college buildings, grounds, and endowment soared.

After a slowdown during the Great Depression and World War II, William and Mary continued its upward spiral. The college slowly began racial integration in the 1950s. Another great expansion in students, curriculum, research, and buildings in the 1960s led to the creation of "New Campus" as well as to the authorization of new doctoral programs in history, education, physics, and marine science under the leadership of President Davis Paschall (1960–71). New schools of law, education, business administration, and marine science have flourished alongside arts and sciences. In 1993 the College of William and Mary celebrated its 300th birthday, having become a modern university and one of the most highly respected public institutions in the nation. Today there are 5,700 undergraduates and 1,900 graduate students studying in more than 40 programs in the College's five undergraduate and graduate schools.

JAMES P. WHITTENBURG
CAROLYN S. WHITTENBURG
College of William and Mary

College of William and Mary, *Vital Facts: A Chronology of the College of William and Mary* (1997); Susan H. Godson, Ludwell H. Johnson, Richard B. Sherman, Thad W. Tate, and Helen C. Walker, *The College of William and Mary: A History*, 2 vols. (1993); Carolyn Sparks Whittenburg, "President J. A. C. Chandler and the First Women Faculty at the College of William and Mary" (Ed.D. dissertation, College of William and Mary, 2004).

Commonwealth College

Commonwealth College, the South's most notorious attempt at radical education, was established in 1923 at New Llano Cooperative Colony near Leesville, La. Its founders were Kate Richards O'Hare, her husband, Frank, and William E. Zeuch—all radical socialists and followers of Eugene V. Debs. All three were firmly convinced that a new era was at hand and it would be governed by a revolutionary social class, the industrial worker. The example of Ruskin College in Florida, where they had met, convinced them that higher education for workers could be best realized by locating their college in a cooperative community. New Llano Colony seemed to be the perfect fit for this experiment. However, strong personalities and conflicting aims between college and colony soon made collaboration impossible, and it was clear by the spring of 1924 that Commonwealth had to find a new home.

The college eventually relocated to western Polk County, Ark., where mountain vistas were beautiful and land was cheap. Here the Commoners—students, faculty, and staff—labored to carve a campus out of a virtual wilderness while carrying on with schooling and tending crops. Only the generosity of Roger Baldwin and the American Fund for Public Service kept the struggling experiment alive. As buildings were completed and a lifestyle emerged, Director Zeuch strove to isolate Commonwealth from the rough and tumble of the labor movement as well as avoid local controversy. However, Zeuch's low-profile policy was devastated in 1926 when the Arkansas American Legion charged the school with Bolshevism, "Sovietism," free love, and communism. Calling for an immediate investigation, the legion pressed for a full disclosure of school policy, lifestyle, and pedagogy. After months of unwanted publicity, the college was cleared by J. Edgar Hoover, who denied any Federal Bureau of Investigation record of subversive activity. Nevertheless, as far as public opinion was concerned, the college was forever "Red."

Zeuch's utopian vision for the struggling school was completely destroyed in 1931 when a revolt, headed by longtime Commoner Lucien Koch, seized the college and displaced the director and his supporters. Activists, both as union organizers and strike supporters, took students and faculty to various labor hotspots throughout the country. The new Commonwealth soon found the activities of the recently formed Southern Tenant Farmers Union (STFU) in eastern Arkansas irresistible. Though union leaders H. L. Mitchell, Howard Kester, and Gardner Jackson wanted no part of the "Red" school, the community of interests between the two was overwhelming. The union soon became the college's sole preoccupation, but by 1936 the relationship had become so acrimonious that the STFU's national supporters, including Norman Thomas and Roger Baldwin, demanded a total reorganization of the college. Though Commonwealth accepted the ultimatum, its administration minimized the changes by selecting radical Presbyterian minister Claude Williams as director. STFU leaders were terrified of Williams's apparent communist sympathies, but for nearly two years, the reformed college worked well with the union. Union president J. R. Butler became an instructor at the school as well as a Williams supporter.

But the earlier fears came true in August 1938, when a document surfaced purporting to be a plan by the communists at Commonwealth to "capture" the union. The plot apparently had Williams's approval. The STFU quickly severed its ties with the college, leaving Commonwealth without a viable purpose. The resulting estrangement from organized labor, along with shattered finances, a dilapidated physical plant, and poisoned relations with its neighbors, forced the school to consider drastic changes. Rejecting proposals to close or merge with Highlander Folk School at Monteagle, Tenn., the Commonwealth College Association decided to make the school into a radical labor drama center. This was too much for local residents. Charges of anarchy, failure to fly the American flag during school hours, and displaying the hammer and sickle emblem of the Soviet Union were filed against the college, and it was hauled into Polk County Court. Found guilty, the school was forced to close and liquidate its property to pay its fines. By the end of 1940, Commonwealth College was gone.

While the Commoners were involved in an ongoing series of ideological disputes within and frequent crises from outside, the day-to-day routine of schooling and self-maintenance never varied. Though the school's curriculum was geared to the interests of the available faculty, it always contained a strong worker's perspective of the liberal arts. Eliminating all "bourgeois claptrap" from their campus, the school strove to be a self-sufficient "educational commune" by requiring 20 hours of labor per week from each staff member and student in return for subsistence and, in the case of students, instruction. Faculty members received no pay and were expected to participate in every campus activity, including farmwork, maintenance, or anything else necessary to escape from "bourgeois interests." Women worked in the kitchen, the library, the laundry, and the school office, while men toiled on the wood crew, carpentry crew, farm crew, masonry crew, or hauling crew. Self-sufficiency was never achieved; the Commoners could, at best, produce 70 percent of their needs. The continuing deficit had to be satisfied by constant fundraising and grants from radical sources like the American Fund for Public Service.

Classes began at 7:30 each morning and were usually held in the instructor's cottage. The unvarying format was group discussion, often heated. Commonwealth gave no grades, conferred no degrees, and had no class attendance requirement. Classes seldom exceeded six students, and the total student body never numbered more than 55. The only entrance requirements were intelligence, a sense of humor, and dedication to the labor movement. Commonwealth's most famous student, Orval Faubus, said that he had "never been with a group of equal numbers that had as many highly intelligent and smart people as there were at Commonwealth College." These "smart people" certainly produced a rich legacy of powerful labor leaders, influential folk and literary icons, and prominent musicians and dramatists. Commonwealth and its Commoners also provided the civil rights movement with much in the way of evangelical recruiting and meeting techniques.

WILLIAM H. COBB
East Carolina University

American Fund for Public Service Records, Rare Books and Manuscripts Division, New York Public Library, New York City, New York; William H. Cobb, *Radical Education in the Rural South: Commonwealth College, 1922–1940* (2000); Raymond Koch and Charlotte Koch, *Educational Commune: The Story of Commonwealth College* (1972); Southern Tenant Farmers' Union Papers, Southern Historical Collection, University of North Carolina, Chapel Hill; St. John Collection of Commonwealth College Papers, Special Collections, University of Arkansas Libraries, Fayetteville.

Couch, William Terry
(1901–1988) PUBLISHER.
Editor and director of the University of North Carolina Press, William Terry Couch had a profound effect on southern intellectual life from the 1920s until the end of the Second World War. Born in Pamplin, Va., he was the son of a country Baptist preacher, John Henry Couch, and a schoolteacher, Sallie Love Terry. His father gave up the ministry in 1917 and returned to farming near Chapel Hill, N.C., where he had grown up. William worked on the farm and also took a job at a generating plant of the Southern Power Company. From such humble circumstances, he gained a genuine appreciation for the conditions of the southern white working classes and refused to romanticize them.

In 1920, Couch entered the University of North Carolina but then dropped out to join the U.S. Army. He served two and a half years, rose to the rank of sergeant, but twice failed the physical for admission to West Point. Upon his return to college at Chapel Hill, he began to attract notice as editor of the *Carolina Magazine*. Louis Round Wilson, university librarian and director of the fledgling University of North Carolina Press, hired him as a part-time assistant director in 1925.

Wilson told Couch that the press could never publish books on such contentious subjects as race, religion, or economics, but Couch had other ideas. Although he did not formally become director of the press until 1932, Couch moved quickly to establish the University of North Carolina Press as the preeminent publisher of critical studies on the South. Of the 450 titles published under his tenure, 170 were devoted to the South.

Combative, pugnacious, and sometimes tactless, Couch courted controversy. He demanded facts, detail, and unflinching honesty. Saying he "had been for the New Deal before there was a New Deal," Couch published books on lynching, public relief for the poor in North Carolina, income and wages in the South, cotton mill workers and their villages, Negro child welfare in North Carolina, strikes, and unionization. Couch once told William F. Buckley that because of such publications he had been labeled a "communist." Couch edited two books himself: *The Culture of the South* (1934), a collection of essays on southern society, and *These Are Our Lives* (1939), originally a Federal Writers' Project to record the experiences of southern working people in their own words.

Couch's southern liberalism had its limits, however. Despite his sympathy for the plight of southern blacks, he remained an ardent segregationist. The clash between his liberal credo and his segregationist views climaxed with the publication of *What the Negro Wants* (1944), edited by historian Rayford W. Logan. In it, leading black intellectuals such as W. E. B. Du Bois, Gordon B. Hancock, and A. Philip Randolph demanded an end to segregation. Stunned by their demands, Couch insisted that Logan change the book's emphasis. Logan refused and threatened legal action. Couch published the book but inserted a "Publisher's Introduction" that argued for white superiority and unapologetically asserted black inferiority. Segregation must be maintained, he contended, and southern liberals applauded his stand.

In 1945, Couch left Chapel Hill to become director of the University of Chicago Press, but President Robert M. Hutchins dismissed him from that position in 1950. Couch believed that his termination resulted from publication of a shocking book about Japanese internment during World War II, and he considered his dismissal a violation of academic freedom.

During the 1950s and 1960s Couch served as editor in chief of *Collier's Encyclopedia* and *Yearbooks* and editor of the *American Oxford Encyclopedia*. His political views continued to shift sharply to the right. In 1963–64, he briefly established the Center for American Studies, a research organization financed by the William Volker Fund. The purpose of the center was to promote "a revival of conservative principles in America," but when negotiations to merge with the Hoover Institute at Stanford University failed, the center closed. Couch also corresponded with such conservative commentators as Russell Kirk, Robert Welch (head of the John Birch Society), and James J. Kilpatrick. In addition to being an inveterate anticommunist, Couch bitterly opposed the civil rights movement, and he once stated that the *Brown* decision (1954) had created "the greatest possible antagonism between the races." By then his views were far removed from the southern liberalism that characterized his directorship of the University of North Carolina Press.

Couch retired to Chapel Hill in 1968 and died in Charlottesville, Va., in 1988.

JEFFREY J. CROW
North Carolina Department of Cultural Resources

W. T. Couch, interviewed by Daniel J. Singal, Southern Oral History Project Collection, University of North Carolina, Chapel Hill (1972); William Terry Couch Papers, Southern Historical Collection, University of North Carolina, Chapel Hill; Kenneth R. Janken, *North Carolina Historical Review* (April 1993); Karen Lisa Posser, in *The North Carolina Century: Tar Heels Who Made a Difference, 1900–2000*, ed. Howard E. Covington Jr. and Marion A. Ellis (2002); Daniel J. Singal, *The War Within: From Victorian to Modernist Thought in the South, 1919–1945* (1982); University of North Carolina Press Records, University Archives, Chapel Hill.

Curry, J. L. M.

(1825–1903) EDUCATOR, MINISTER, AND POLITICIAN.

A transitional figure between Old South and New, Jabez Lamar Monroe Curry displayed elements of both cultural traditions in his versatile public career. Born into a socially prominent, economically secure family and steeped in John C. Calhoun's constitutional doctrines, Curry studied law at Harvard. Horace Mann's example impressed upon him the value of universal education, and from his first term in the Alabama legislature in 1847 to his final role in the Conference for Education in the South at the end of his life, Curry forcefully articulated the essential social, moral, and political functions of public education.

Elected to the U.S. House of Representatives in 1857, Curry resigned to defend secession and to serve in the Confederate Congress, but after 1865 he accepted emancipation when he embraced the racial paternalism of the New South. An ordained Baptist minister, he briefly assumed the presidency of Howard College in Alabama before joining the faculty of Virginia's Richmond College. In 1881 the Peabody Fund, established through the generosity of George Peabody of Massachusetts, named him general agent for its southern education campaign. Except for a three-year period (1885–88) as U.S. minister to Spain, Curry held the position until his death and became the incomparable orator-administrator of the late-19th-century education awakening.

Prodigious traveler, prolific correspondent, and author of numerous reports, he repeatedly addressed southern legislatures and citizens' groups to appeal for tax-supported schools. After 1890 he also represented the Slater Fund, endowed by John F. Slater of Connecticut to educate southern blacks. Because he defined universal education to include blacks and women, Curry championed coeducation, industrial education, teachers' institutes, and normal schools for teacher training.

In spite of his states' rights principles, Curry advocated enactment of the unsuccessful Blair education bill, a measure sponsored in the 1880s by Senator Henry Blair of New Hampshire to appropriate federal funds to fight illiteracy. Curry artfully identified enhanced literacy with the promotion of personal independence, the preservation of limited government, and the protection of individual liberties. Although he remained committed to black advancement, he grew increasingly pessimistic about it, and his inherent white-supremacist racism triumphed over his sense of noblesse oblige. More derivative than original in his ideas, Curry personified southern implementation of northern philanthropy and energetically crusaded for education as the paramount force of social and cultural stability.

BETTY BRANDON
University of South Alabama

J. L. M. Curry Papers, Manuscripts Division, Library of Congress and Alabama Department of Archives and History, Montgomery; Merle Curti, *The Social Ideas of American Educators* (1935); Jessie Pearl Rice, *J. L. M. Curry: Southerner, Statesman, and Educator* (1949).

Desegregation (College) in Louisiana

In antebellum Louisiana, higher education was a tenuous proposition. The College of Orleans (1805), Centenary College (1805), the Medical College of Louisiana (1834), and the Louisiana State Seminary of Learning and Military Academy (1860) all were small, struggling, segregated institutions. Members of Louisiana's substantial population of *hommes du coleur libre* (free people of color) desiring higher learning had to look elsewhere. Louisiana did experience brief, limited college desegregation during Reconstruction. Straight University, founded in 1869 by the American Missionary Association to promote black education, was perhaps Louisiana's first integrated college; three of its first eight law graduates were white. In

1874 the legislature chartered integrated Louisiana Agricultural and Mechanical College (A&M) in New Orleans after the State Seminary, renamed Louisiana State University (LSU) in 1870, resisted desegregation. However, in 1877 a new legislature transferred A&M's assets to Baton Rouge, merging it with practically defunct but segregated LSU, thus ending Louisiana's dalliance with racially mixed higher education.

The state colleges created thereafter were uniformly segregated, beginning in 1880 with Southern University, a black land-grant school. To train teachers, the Louisiana legislature chartered the all-white State Normal School (Natchitoches) in 1884. Louisiana Tech University (1894) grew out of a legislative desire for "a first-class Industrial Institute and College for the education of white children." In 1896 the Supreme Court enshrined racial separation in *Plessy v. Ferguson*, mandating only that separate facilities be substantially equal. By 1901, as white-only Southwestern Louisiana Industrial Institute (Lafayette) and the Colored Industrial and Agricultural School (later Grambling) first met classes, the state funded four public colleges for whites and Southern for black Louisianans.

Large disparities in funding favoring white colleges magnified educational inequities, which in turn mirrored the larger injustices of de jure segregation. African Americans relied on a few private colleges for postprimary education because, as of World War I, there were no black public high schools in Louisiana. Graduate and professional schooling were simply unavailable. Grambling's eventual inclusion in state funding offered little relief as new, white, state junior colleges in Hammond (1925), Monroe (1931), Lake Charles (1939), and Thibodaux (1948) joined the competition for resources and quickly developed four-year programs.

Gradually, black Louisianans challenged this inequality, seeking admission to programs unavailable at Grambling and Southern. Hurchail Jackson's LSU Law School application was denied in 1938, as were the 1946 applications of Charles Hatfield and Viola Johnson to the law and medical schools, respectively. When they sued, a federal judge ruled that Southern University should provide such programs. Nonetheless, eight more African Americans applied, unsuccessfully, to LSU's schools of engineering, medicine, and law in 1950. Finally, in 1951, Amos Lutrill Payne was admitted to LSU's graduate school. However, undergraduate programs statewide remained unaffected.

Two years later, Alexander P. Tureaud Jr., son of Louisiana's preeminent civil rights attorney, sought admission to LSU's undergraduate program. Though he finally prevailed in court, Tureaud opted to remain at Xavier University in New Orleans. The breakthrough for undergraduates came at the all-female College of the Sacred Heart (Grand Coteau, La.), which admitted two African American girls in 1953. Then, a month before the May 1954 *Brown* decision, a federal court found for four plaintiffs in *Constantine v. Southwestern Louisiana Institute*, ruling that white regional state colleges in the absence of similar black institutions violated *Plessy*'s "separate but equal" clause. Eighty African Americans enrolled at SLI that historic fall; about three-quarters of them were women. It was the earliest, most substantial undergraduate desegregation of a public college in the Deep South, preceded in the entire region only by Virginia Tech's 1953 admission of a single black undergraduate. Using *Constantine* as precedent, federal district courts ordered McNeese State College (Lake Charles) and Southeastern Louisiana College (Hammond) desegregated in 1955.

Then a panoply of racist legislation stalled further desegregation, neutralized the NAACP's Louisiana operations, and authorized new, segregated branches of LSU and Southern in New Orleans. A federal court order desegregated LSUNO prior to its 1958 opening, while SUNO was built, despite African Americans' objections to yet another Jim Crow campus. And a 1955 suit to desegregate Northwestern State College collapsed when local racists pressured the plaintiffs to abandon their litigation.

Several more years elapsed before Nicholls State College experienced court-ordered desegregation in September 1963. SUNO succumbed in 1964, as did LSU's undergraduate division. The last citadels of legal segregation collapsed in 1965 when a federal judge took 10 minutes to open Northwestern State and Louisiana Tech to black students. A friendly suit two months later produced Grambling's first white student, a veteran civil rights activist. In 1966 Southwestern Louisiana broke the color barrier in Deep South basketball, propelling the school to national prominence in the sport and withering scrutiny from the NCAA. Evidence of Louisiana's educational past would remain in the form of a long-running suit to erase remaining vestiges of segregation and, ironically, in the early 21st century continuance of three governing boards for the state's universities—the LSU system, the state universities, and the Southern University system.

MICHAEL WADE
Appalachian State University

Roger Fischer, *The Segregation Struggle in Louisiana, 1862–1877* (1974); *Negro Education: A Study of the Private and Higher Schools for Colored People in the United States* (1916); Charles Vincent, *A Centennial History of Southern University and A&M College, 1880–1980* (1981); Michael Wade, in *Higher Education and the Civil Rights Movement*, ed. Peter Wallenstein (2008).

Dodd, William E.

(1869–1940) HISTORIAN AND DIPLOMAT.

Born 21 October 1869 near Clayton, N.C., William Edward Dodd was the son of John D. and Evelyn Creech Dodd. As the scion of a hard-scrabble farmer, he developed an animosity toward those social and economic elites he believed oppressed the common folk. He particularly resented the southern aristocracy typified by his maternal great-uncle Ashley Horne, a wealthy Clayton merchant and political figure.

Largely educated in local common schools, the teenage Dodd briefly attended Clayton's small private academy where he developed a taste for things intellectual. Short-term teaching assignments in rural North Carolina funded his matriculation at Virginia Polytechnic Institute at Blackburn, where he earned his bachelor's diploma in 1895 and a master's degree in 1896. Stilling his pride, Dodd secured a loan from Samuel Horne, Ashley's brother, and entered German's Leipzig University to further his interest in history. In Dodd's absence, his father lost his small landholding to the Horne family, which further inflamed the budding scholar's animus toward southern elites.

In Germany, Dodd identified the Prussian Junkers with the despised aristocrats of his native South. Such ideas were reinforced by Leipzig University's Karl Lamprecht, whose concept of *Kulturegeschichte* (cultural history) persuaded Dodd that the "common man" should be a "guiding force in society" and "the aristocratic portion of the country should occupy only a part of the pages of history." Awarded his doctorate in 1900, he returned home longing for a democratic hero and finding one in Thomas Jefferson.

First at Randolph-Macon College in Ashland, Va. (1900–1908), and then at the University of Chicago (1908–33), Dodd emerged as a nationally respected proponent of Jeffersonian democracy and a severe critic of southern planters and northern capitalists alike. Such themes permeated his major works: *The Life and Times of Nathaniel Macon* (1903), *Jefferson Davis* (1907), *Statesmen of the Old South* (1911), *The Cotton Kingdom* (1919), *Woodrow Wilson and His Works* (1920), *Lincoln or Lee: Comparison and Contrasts of Two Great Leaders in the War between the States* (1928), and *The Old South Struggles for Democracy* (1937). Popular as the first American graduate professor to emphasize southern history, Dodd influenced a generation of scholars including Avery O. Craven, Frank Lawrence Owsley, Henry C. Nixon, and Walter Prescott Webb. The American Historical Association recognized Dodd's stature, electing him president in 1933.

As a southerner and a historian, Dodd was drawn to Woodrow Wilson, the first southern-born United States president since Reconstruction. Considering Wilson a second Jefferson, he authored a eulogistic biography of him, edited an extensive collection of Wilson correspondence, and, throughout the 1920s, spread the message of Wilsonian internationalism in lectures across the United States. Dodd's Leipzig education, his stature as a Wilson scholar, and his fervent faith in democracy prompted newly inaugurated President Franklin D. Roosevelt to designate him ambassador to Adolf Hitler's Germany in June 1933.

Although it valued him as a symbol of American democracy in the mist of Nazi totalitarianism, the State Department considered Dodd severely flawed as a diplomat, one who offended the German government and frustrated his embassy staff. The Hitler administration grudgingly tolerated Dodd's official protest of persecutions aimed at Jews, Christian ministers, and university professors, even as it took umbrage at his open distaste for Hitler, his public disdain for Nazi symbols, and his symbolic boycotts of the annual Nuremberg Party Rallies. Dodd received little support from his own embassy officials, who found their mundane tasks made more difficult by a retaliating German government. By nature a southern plebeian, Dodd disliked the patrician bearing of career Foreign Service officers, which further complicated his work as ambassador. Suspicious of his own secretary's loyalty, he dictated to his daughter his most private letters to Roosevelt and the State Department, unaware that she shared his missives with her paramour in the Soviet embassy. Nonetheless, Dodd, the observant historian, early recognized the resurgence of the German war machine and warned of Hitler's lust for European conquests. If Hitler's armies "broke into Leningrad," Dodd predicted in 1936, "we should have such horrors that one can hardly imagine the consequences."

Responding to State Department pressures, Roosevelt recalled Dodd in December 1937. Upon his arrival in the United States, he commenced an extensive tour throughout the country, prophesying the coming European conflict. Exhausted by his European experiences and his lectures across America, his health collapsed and he died on 9 February 1940.

Throughout the odyssey of Dodd's life, he maintained a powerful sense of class consciousness. From his youthful experiences he developed a bitterness toward the aristocracy of his native soil, and from his adult observations he fashioned a resentment toward all privileged classes—southern patricians, northern industrialists, Prussian Junkers, German Nazis. He preached the egalitarian ideas he believed embodied in Thomas Jefferson and the internationalist vision of Woodrow Wilson. Had the South won in 1865, he once wrote, it would have meant the "repudiation of the Declaration of Independence and . . . the explicit recognition of social inequality." The planters would have formed "a State in which the laboring class should be the property of the capitalists," and in which "every man should have a place and should keep his place." Yeoman born, Dodd found that vision intolerable.

FRED A. BAILEY
Abilene Christian University

Fred A. Bailey, *North Carolina Historical Review* (July 1989), *William Edward Dodd: The South's Yeoman Historian* (1997); Robert Dallek, *Democrat and Diplomat: The Life of William E. Dodd* (1968); Wendell H. Stephenson, *The South Lives in History: Southern Historians and Their Legacy* (1955).

Duke University

Duke University in Durham, N.C., traces its origins to a local academy organized by a group of Methodists and Quakers under the leadership of Brantley York in Randolph County, N.C., in 1838. Known initially as Union Institute, it was reorganized in 1851 for the training of teachers and named Normal College before it became affiliated with the Methodist Church in North Carolina and was renamed Trinity College in 1859. Continuing to operate during the harrowing years of the Civil War, the college, long presided over by Braxton Craven, acquired a northern-born, Yale-trained president, John F. Crowell, in 1887. In 1892, inspired by generous support offered by Durham Methodists grown prosperous

Chapel at Duke University, Durham, N.C. (Duke University Archives)

in the tobacco industry, particularly Washington Duke and Julian S. Carr, Trinity College moved to Durham.

A spellbinding Methodist preacher and dynamic administrator, John C. Kilgo, succeeded Crowell as president in 1894 and greatly increased the interest of the Duke family in Trinity. In 1896 Washington Duke offered an endowment of $100,000 provided that Trinity admit women "on equal footing with men," and the college, which even earlier had some women students, quickly accepted the offer. Other gifts from the Duke family followed, with Benjamin N. Duke, Washington Duke's son, serving as a leading benefactor and the principal liaison between the college and the family.

Thanks to support from the Dukes and to an able, relatively young, and ambitious faculty recruited from the new graduate schools at Johns Hopkins, Columbia, and other northern universities, Trinity College had developed by the time of World War I into one of the leading liberal arts colleges in the South. Despite the clamor of powerful Democrats in North Carolina, the trustees of the college refused in 1903 to oust historian John Spencer Bassett, who had publicly deplored the racist politics of the "White Man's Party." Trinity thus achieved one of the pioneering victories for academic freedom in the United States and strengthened its belief in and reputation for independent thought and scholarship.

Dreams of a university organized around Trinity College dated back to Crowell and the 1890s, but President William Preston Few launched a serious effort to realize the dream in the early 1920s. Because Benjamin N. Duke was in failing health after about 1915, Few began with Duke's blessings and assistance to focus his efforts on James B. Duke, Benjamin Duke's younger brother and by far the richest member of the family. In 1919 and again in 1921 Few sketched out his plans to James B. Duke and proposed that, because several educational institutions in the United States were already named Trinity, if and when funds became available to enlarge the institution in Durham it should be named Duke University. James B. Duke was not ready to go along in 1921, but by December 1924, he was.

Naming Duke University as one of the prime beneficiaries of the perpetual philanthropic foundation he then established as the Duke Endowment, James B. Duke also provided around $19 million for the rebuilding of the old Trinity campus, for the creation of a new campus with Tudor Gothic buildings, and for the acquisition of some 8,000 acres of adjoining forest land. In 1930, when the first buildings on the new campus were completed, the old Trinity campus became the site of the coordinate Woman's College, which in 1972 was merged back into Trinity College as the liberal arts college for both men and women. Training in engineering was available in Trinity College after 1903, and in 1939 a separate School of Engineering was organized (renamed the Pratt School of Engineering in 1999). In addition to divinity and law schools, the medical school and hospital were opened in 1930 and a school of nursing in 1931. What eventually became the Nicholas School of the Environment was established in 1938, and the Fuqua School of Business in 1969. The Sanford School of Public Policy became Duke's 10th school in 2009.

Duke's leaders have included Terry Sanford (1917–98), who had served as governor of North Carolina from 1961 to 1965 prior to serving as president from 1969 to 1985. His experience in leading the state proved beneficial to

Duke, and the school flourished during his tenure, adding more than 25 buildings and undertaking a successful fund-raising campaign. In 1993 the trustees hired the president of Wellesley College, Nannerl O. Keohane, to be Duke's eighth president. At the time, she was only the second woman ever to lead a major private research university. Under her leadership Duke has enjoyed growth in endowments, facilities, academic programs, and the diversity of the faculty, staff, and student body. In 2004 Richard Brodhead, former dean of Yale College and the A. Bartlett Giamatti Professor of English at Yale University, became Duke University's ninth president and the 14th person to lead the institution since its founding as Union Institute in 1838. Since arriving at Duke, in addition to emphasizing the importance of academic freedom and free speech in a democratic society, Brodhead has focused much of his leadership on enriching the undergraduate experience of Duke students and expanding the university's financial aid endowment to ensure that a Duke education is accessible to qualified students regardless of their family's financial circumstances. He has called for Duke to become an international center in addressing health care inequities through a major global health initiative involving faculty and schools across the university and has championed Duke's efforts to bring the fruits of faculty and student research through a translational process to serve society.

With 6,400 undergraduate students and 7,262 graduate and professional students enrolled as of the 2009–10 academic year, Duke University continues by choice to be one of the smaller, voluntarily supported, major universities in the nation.

ROBERT F. DURDEN
TIMOTHY D. PYATT
Duke University

Nora C. Chaffin, *Trinity College, 1839–1892: The Beginnings of Duke University* (1950); Robert F. Durden, *The Launching of Duke University, 1924–1949* (1993); Earl W. Porter, *Trinity and Duke, 1892–1924: Foundations of Duke University* (1964); University Archives, Duke University Library.

Emory University

Emory University began as Emory College in Oxford, Ga. Chartered in 1836 as an all-male school under the auspices of the Georgia Methodist Annual Conference, Emory admitted its first students in 1838. The school was named for John Emory, a Maryland Methodist bishop known for his dedication to education.

When the General Conference of the Methodist Episcopal Church, South, severed its ties with Vanderbilt University in 1914, Bishop Warren A. Candler, a former Emory president, persuaded the church to make Emory College the new focus of its educational efforts. The bishop's brother, Asa, founder of Coca-Cola, provided a million-dollar endowment and a 75-acre tract of land in Druid Hills, a new northeast suburb of Atlanta. Chartered in 1915, Emory University first opened theology, law, and medical schools, followed by schools of business and graduate arts and sciences (1919); nursing (1922); librarianship (1925–88); dentistry (1944–90); and public health (1990). The original campus became the site of a nationally recognized two-year institution, Oxford College. Between 1922 and 1953, Emory also had a junior college at Valdosta, Ga.

Throughout its existence, Emory's history has followed, and sometimes led, some of the most important debates about racial diversity. Emory's founding denomination, the Methodist Episcopal Church, had an international reputation in the 18th century as an antislavery denomination. But in the 19th century, the northern and southern United States branches of the church increasingly diverged over slavery. The final split occurred over the ownership of an enslaved woman known as Kitty, by an Emory trustee, Bishop James O. Andrew. The Methodist Episcopal Church and the Methodist Episcopal Church, South, remained apart until 1939. Following the Civil War, Atticus Haygood, Emory president 1875–84, was a leader in the New South movement, which argued for racial tolerance towards African Americans while maintaining segregation and white supremacy. The limits of New South tolerance were tested by Andrew Sledd, a Latin professor whose stance against lynching in a 1902 article in the *Atlantic Monthly* led to his forced resignation.

As part of the missionary efforts of the Methodist Episcopal Church, South, Emory faculty, students, and alumni journeyed to China, Korea, and Latin America, establishing schools and Christian churches in those regions and inviting students from those areas to attend Emory College and Candler School of Theology. Even as Emory solidified its reputation as a Methodist institution, the school became know nationally for its relative openness to Jewish students and still maintains a strong Jewish presence among its undergraduate population.

In 1953 Emory officially admitted women to its undergraduate student body; a few women had matriculated as special students before 1953 and had been a presence on campus in the nursing school and to a lesser degree in the other professional schools. In 1962 Emory won a state Supreme Court lawsuit, overturning a Georgia law that took away the nonprofit tax status of private educational institutions if they desegregated. In 1963 Emory's first African American students graduated from the School of Nursing.

The changing student body led to changes in the curriculum. In response to student protests, Emory established the first black studies program at a higher education institution in the Southeast in 1971. In 1989 Emory became the first university in the United States to offer a Ph.D. program in women's studies. In 1999 the establishment of the Tam Institute for Jewish Studies solidified nearly 30 years of support for the field at Emory. Interdisciplinary programs in African studies, Middle East and South Asian studies, and others also joined traditional disciplinary departments.

These changes came from an ethical standpoint and were designed to transform Emory from a regional school into a world-class institution. The sciences, the professional schools, and particularly the health sciences also expanded their focus to include a wider range of interdisciplinary and cutting-edge efforts. Emory's healthcare system is now the largest in Georgia. Relationships with the Jimmy Carter Presidential Library and the Centers for Disease Control have solidified Emory's expansion of international research efforts in the health sciences, public policy, and other fields, and attracted faculty, staff, and students from around the world.

In 1979 Robert and George Woodruff advanced Emory's efforts by donating $105 million to the university, at the time the largest single donation to an institution of higher education. On the basis of its research success, Emory was invited to membership in the Association of American Universities in 1995. Between 1994 and 2009 Emory University ranked among the top 20 universities in the country according to *U.S. News and World Report*.

LESLIE M. HARRIS
Emory University

Henry M. Bullock, *A History of Emory University* (1936); Gary Hauk, *A Legacy of Heart and Mind: Emory since 1836* (1999); J. Willis Hurst, *The Quest for Excellence: The History of the Department of Medicine at Emory University School of Medicine, 1834–1986* (1997); Melissa Kean, *Desegregating Private Higher Education in the South: Duke, Emory, Rice, Tulane, and Vanderbilt* (2008); Terry L. Matthews, *Journal of Southern Religion* (December 2003); Joseph C. Moon, *An Uncommon Place: Oxford College of Emory University, 1914–2000* (2003).

Fisk University

Fisk University, a leading black educational institution for more than a century, opened in Nashville, Tenn., in 1866. A private, coeducational, liberal arts school, it offers the bachelor's and master's degrees. Fisk, founded by the American Missionary Association, was designed to supply desperately needed, qualified black teachers and ultimately to become a first-class college giving black youth the same educational opportunities and advantages enjoyed by whites. Initially, all students were in primary grades, but a normal class was enrolled in 1867. In 1871 four students were accepted into the college department, but the absence of adequate public schools caused the college preparatory and college classes to remain the smallest in the school for several years. By 1883 there were 33 college pupils and 48 in college prep classes. Fisk awarded 15 B.A. degrees in 1885.

The period 1870 to 1915 was critical for Fisk. Black poverty, white indifference, and the popularity of vocational education threatened Fisk's aspiration of becoming a major liberal arts college. However, with small annual collections, tuition, and the $150,000 earned by the Fisk Jubilee Singers, President E. M. Cravath, supported by a determined faculty and loyal students, constructed a new campus, improved the faculty, and built a solid college department. By 1915 Fisk was widely assumed to be the premier black college in the country.

When students joined alumni in 1925 to oust Fayette A. McKenzie, a white president whom they considered dictatorial and too friendly to local whites, a new era began in Fisk history. Under the leadership of President Thomas E. Jones and noted scholar Charles S. Johnson, who was to become Fisk's first black president in 1946, the university experienced unprecedented growth. By 1940 it had become an outstanding center for the study of black life and culture, and it continued to grow in reputation and financial support. In the 1950s it had an endowment of several million dollars, boasted the nationally acclaimed Alfred Stieglitz Collection of Art, the Carl Van Vechten music literature collection, a good library, and outstanding students. Faculty members Charles S. Johnson, James Weldon Johnson, Aaron Douglas, Arna Bontemps, John W. Work Jr., and others had achieved international recognition in their fields. In 1952 Fisk became the first predominantly black college awarded a Phi Beta Kappa chapter.

One mark of a great university is the degree to which its students are equipped to cope with the demands of life. Fisk alumni have distinguished themselves in almost every field of endeavor. Hundreds of Fiskites have become physicians, college presidents, professors, writers, statesmen, and community leaders. Scholar-activist W. E. B. Du Bois, historian John Hope Franklin, Congressman John Lewis, and poet-professor Nikki Giovanni are just a few of the famous graduates of Fisk University. Between 1875 and 1963, approximately one-fifth of Fisk's undergraduates earned advanced degrees.

From its origin, Fisk defied southern racial codes by maintaining an interracial faculty and advocating equal rights. Beginning in 1943, it housed the American Missionary Association's Race Relations Department, which hosted such civil rights advocates as Thurgood Marshall and Martin Luther King Jr. and vigorously contested segregation and discrimination. It trained numerous civil rights leaders, supported student sit-ins, and persistently struggled for black equality. Unfortunately, desegregation, which Fiskites fought so valiantly to achieve, seriously undermined the school. Formerly segregated white institutions now competed for black students and faculty. This trend combined with increased competition from public black colleges, rapid diversification, increased expenditures for faculty and students, rising costs, and inadequate funding, pushed the school to the brink of insolvency by the late 1970s. Many friends thought Fisk might fold, but persistence, sound leadership, devoted students, faithful alumni, and generous donors such as Camille and Bill Cosby returned Fisk to prominence. By the 1990s, Fisk again was flourishing. It was approaching a balanced budget, and between 1991 and 1995 Fisk ranked first among all colleges and universities whose African American students continued their studies in the 13 most productive doctoral granting schools. A recent National Science Foundation study revealed that Fisk alumni earned more doctorates in the physical sciences than African American graduates of any other school in the nation. Adequate funding remains a problem for all private African American colleges and universities, but on 25 June 2008 President Hazel R. O'Leary announced that Fisk had raised $9.23 million during the fiscal year. This achievement ended nine years of budget deficits and qualified the university for an Andrew Mellon Foundation matching grant. Fisk students enjoy a financially stable institution, an excellent faculty, sufficient facilities and library, and a tradition of excellence.

JOE M. RICHARDSON
Florida State University

Chronicle of Higher Education (21 May 1986); L. M. Collins, *One Hundred Years of Fisk University Presidents, 1875–1975* (1989); Patrick J. Gilpin and Marybeth Gasman, *Charles S. Johnson: Leadership beyond the Veil in the Age of Jim Crow* (2003); Lester C. Lamon, *Journal of Southern History* (May 1974); *New York Times* (29 April 1986); Gustavus D. Pike, *The Jubilee Singers, and Their Campaign for Twenty Thousand Dollars* (1873); Joe M. Richardson, *A History of Fisk University, 1865–1946* (1980); Richard Robbins, *Sideline Activist: Charles S. Johnson and the Struggle for Civil Rights* (1996).

Florida, University of

The University of Florida is a publicly funded land-grant university located in Gainesville. It was the first southern public institution to be admitted, in 1985, to the Association of American Universities. The university traces its origins to the Seminary Act of 1851, which endowed state schools for east and west Florida. The East Florida Seminary opened in Ocala in 1853 (the year on the university seal) and moved to Gainesville after the Civil War. The seminary achieved success as a regional preparatory school but never attained the status of a college. The seminary was later abolished and its endowment assigned to the university.

Florida had chartered a land-grant college as early as 1870, but it was 1884 before it opened in Lake City as the Florida Agricultural College. A research unit, the Florida Agricultural Experiment Station, was established in 1888. The college and station subsisted largely on federal funds. State funding gradually increased, and in 1903 the college became the University of Florida. Lake City's bid to be the site for the new state university was rejected, though, and the university's faculty, administration, library, and equipment relocated to Gainesville. There was a flurry of building construction shortly before passage of the Buckman Act of 1905, which allocated federal land-grant funds to the university.

As a land-grant institution, agriculture and engineering figured prominently in the university's curriculum. After Buckman, greater emphasis was placed on liberal arts, sciences, and professional degrees. A School of Pedagogy, now the College of Education, opened in 1906. A law degree was first offered in 1909. Architecture, business administration, and journalism were added in the 1920s. Fine arts were added after World War II and expanded in the 1970s.

The College of Pharmacy opened in 1924, but a full-fledged medical program awaited the creation of the J. Hillis Miller Health Center in 1957. A teaching hospital opened the following year and became Shands Hospital in 1965. Clinical services were privatized in 1980. Shands HealthCare now manages academic medical centers in Gainesville and Jacksonville as well as specialty and community facilities throughout northeast and central Florida.

In 1913 the university launched a summer school. The summer school was coeducational, and coursework could be applied to a degree. In this way, the university had its first female graduate in 1920. After 1925 women of a "mature" age were admitted to specific degree programs. However, female enrollment during regular sessions never exceeded 20 in any year prior to World War II. Gender divisions ended entirely in 1947. Female enrollment has exceeded male at the university since 1998.

The first African American was accepted in the College of Law in 1958, but black undergraduates were not admitted until 1962. At the end of the 1960s only 156 black students were enrolled. Campus protests and the sudden exodus of one third of the black student body in the spring of 1971 became the catalyst for an effective affirmative action plan. In 2008 minority students constituted approximately 28 percent of the nonalien student population. The university also claims the highest concentration of Jewish students outside Israel.

The Institute of Food and Agricultural Sciences (IFAS) was organized in 1965 to serve as the umbrella organization for the university's agricultural units, including the College of Agricultural and Life Sciences, county extension and Florida 4-H, and the Center for Tropical Agriculture. IFAS also includes a statewide network of research and education centers. The Citrus Research and Education Center in Lake Alfred, founded in 1917, is the largest research facility devoted to a single commodity.

The graduate school was organized in 1909 and awarded the first doctorates in 1934. The first nonagricultural research units, the Bureau of Economic and Business Research and the Institute of Inter-American Affairs, now the Center for Latin American Studies, were established in 1930. The Engineering and Industrial Experiment Station opened in 1941 and played a key role in the expansion of applied research. Gatorade, the world's first sports drink, was developed by a medical team led by Robert Cade in 1965. In the environmental sciences, Archie Fairly Carr's work with sea turtles and Howard T. Odum's wetlands research achieved international recognition. William Maples, founder of the C. A. Pound Human Identification Laboratory, won fame for his breakthroughs in forensic anthropology. In 2009 the university's research and scholarship ranked 58th in the Academic Ranking of World Universities.

The school colors, orange and blue, were adopted sometime around 1910, and the alligator became the mascot in 1911. Florida is a Division I NCAA school and a founding member of the Southeastern Conference. Between 1991 and 2009 Florida garnered the SEC all-sports trophy in every year but one. Beginning in 1968 with men's golf, the Gators have won 22 national team championships including football championships in 1996, 2006, and 2008 and back-to-back men's basketball titles in 2006 and 2007.

CARL VAN NESS
University of Florida

Carl Van Ness and Kevin McCarthy, *Honoring the Past, Shaping the Future* (2003); Samuel Proctor and Wright Langley, *Gator History* (1986).

Franklin, John Hope

(1915–2009) HISTORIAN.

John Hope Franklin stood in the first rank of professional historians and also in the first rank of those blacks who have worked actively on behalf of the modern civil rights movement. Born in Rentiesville, Okla., in 1915, Franklin embodied the ethnic and racial complexities of the South: his family was part Cherokee and part black, and some of its members served as slaves to the Cherokees in the antebellum decades. His father, Buck Franklin, became a successful lawyer in Tulsa and saw his legal offices destroyed in one of the antiblack riots after the Armistice of 1918. Buck Franklin quietly rebuilt his legal practice, for a time actually operating inside a tent, and this experience became vital to the spirit of John Hope Franklin's own protests and achievements.

Given the chance to attend college, young Franklin studied at Fisk (A.B., 1935) and then entered the Harvard graduate program (A.M., 1936; Ph.D., 1941) at a time when there were few black historians in the country. Between 1942 and 1992 he taught at Fisk University, Howard University, Saint Augustine's College, Brooklyn College, the University of Chicago, and Duke University. In the field of civil rights, Franklin was instrumental in integrating the Southern Historical Association, the American Historical Association, and the Mississippi Valley Historical Association (now the Organization of American Historians), all of which he eventually served as president; he also contributed background research for the National Association for the Advancement of Colored People in the campaign to integrate the public schools, culminating successfully in the legal case *Brown v. Board of Education* (1954).

In the study of black history Franklin published four major works among scores of edited and special studies. *From Slavery to Freedom: A History of African Americans* (1947; 8th ed., 2000) was an encyclopedic mapping of the path of black progress in America, optimistic in its style. *The Militant South, 1800–1861* (1956) was a bolder, more pessimistic interpretation, which traced both a self-destructive urge among the antebellum southern leaders who produced the Civil War and a continuing tendency to violence after the war. *Reconstruction after the Civil War* (1963) was one of the early efforts to revise the mythic white view of the horrors of Reconstruction, as embodied in historian William A. Dunning's works, and to focus on black participation and achievement in the post–Civil War period. And *Runaway Slaves: Rebels on the Plantation* (with Loren Schweninger, 1999) was a very sophisticated quantitative analysis of data concerning slave resistance to oppression, which like his entire oeuvre, emphasizes at once the glorious idea of equality and the sordid facts of inequality even in the best of southern and national venues.

In 1992 Franklin became emeritus professor of legal history at Duke University, but he in no sense retired, publishing a number of scholarly studies, revising earlier studies, and helping to recruit African American scholars in all fields of study to teach at the school. He remained a public figure of importance, serving in the Clinton administration as chairman of the advisory board to the president's initiative on race. In that post, he took occasion, much as he had when far younger, to lecture federal officials, not excluding President Clinton himself, about the continuing failure of the United States to provide adequate educational or job opportunities for black youth. Through the long decades, Franklin retained a scholar's dignity and a humanist's respect for the opinions of others while working as diligently as any other activist advocate for racial justice in the South and the nation.

JOHN HERBERT ROPER
Emory and Henry College

John Hope Franklin, *Free Negroes in North Carolina, 1790–1860* (1943), with John Whittingham Franklin, *My Life and an Era* (2000); Earle E. Thorpe, *Black Historians: A Critique* (1971); interviews with John Hope Franklin, August Meier, C. Vann Woodward, and LeRoy Graf, typescripts in Southern Historical Collection, University of North Carolina, Chapel Hill.

Friday, William C.

(b. 1920) UNIVERSITY PRESIDENT AND EDUCATIONAL STATESMAN.
William Clyde Friday was born in Rapine, Va., the son of David Nathan and Mary Elizabeth Friday. Growing up in the cotton textile manufacturing center of Gaston County, N.C., in the town of Dallas, Friday attended Wake Forest College for one year (1937–38) and then transferred to North Carolina State College in Raleigh, where he graduated with a degree in textile engineering in 1941. During his senior year at State College, Friday met Ida Howell, an undergraduate at Meredith College, and they were married in May of 1942. Friday then served as an ordnance officer at the Naval Ammunition Depot (NAD) at St. Julien's Creek, near Norfolk, Va. Mustered out in 1946, he and Ida moved to Chapel Hill, where he enrolled in the University of North Carolina School of Law.

Finishing his law degree in 1948, Friday began a rapid ascent up the UNC administrative ladder, as a protégé of UNC system presidents Frank Porter Graham and Gordon Gray. When Gray resigned in 1955, the UNC Board of Trustees chose the 35-year-old Friday as acting president. Performing well in that capacity, Friday was appointed president in 1956 and inaugurated at William Neal Reynolds Coliseum at State College in 1957. During Friday's career as UNC president, which lasted three decades until his retirement in 1986, he faced a series of challenges that were central to post–World War II American higher education. In May 1961, after Friday learned that three N.C. State players had admitted shaving points during the Dixie Classic, a large basketball tournament held annually in Raleigh, he acted to reform UNC intercollegiate athletics programs, which were careening out of control, by cancelling the tournament on 22 May 1961, although his decision was extremely unpopular.

Friday faced an even more serious challenge in 1963 when a General Assembly hastily enacted legislation barring any "known" communist or person who had invoked the Fifth Amendment from speaking at any of the state's public colleges or universities. The passage of the speaker ban was directed not so much at communists—few of whom visited UNC campuses—as it was at the supposed "threat" of civil rights activists, who were leading a statewide revolt against segregation that year. Only after student radicals challenged this law in 1966, by inviting outside speakers Herbert Aptheker, a Communist Party member, and Frank Wilkinson, an activist who had taken the Fifth Amendment, did the speaker ban come to an end. In 1968 a three-judge federal district court in Greensboro declared the speaker ban an unconstitutional restriction of the First Amendment's protection of free speech.

Friday led the University of North Carolina during a period of growth, reorganization, and restructuring. During the 1960s the UNC system expanded from three to six campuses with the addition of new campuses at Charlotte in 1965 and Wilmington and Asheville in 1969. Higher education underwent further change during the late 1960s and early 1970s, culminating in a wholesale restructuring. Much of the pressure came from an alliance of the former state teachers' colleges that formed an effective political alliance. East Carolina University conducted a successful campaign to establish a state-supported medical school in Greenville. With UNC trustees opposed to any major restructuring of the system, a fight erupted in the legislature. The result, determined in a special session in 1971, was compromise—the creation of a revamped 16-campus system, but the continuing influence of UNC administrators and trustees over the new system.

Friday's greatest challenge as a university president was how to deal with the heritage of racial segregation in higher education. Until the 1950s, the UNC campuses excluded African Americans, and this all-white system coexisted with publicly supported, all-black institutions at Greensboro, Durham, Fayetteville, Winston-Salem, and Elizabeth City, along with a historically Native American college at Pembroke. Between 1973 and 1981, federal officials in the Department of Health, Education, and Welfare, and, after 1980, the Department of Education, waged an on-again, off-again campaign to desegregate North Carolina public higher education. Where the thinking of Friday and that of federal officials opinions diverged had less to do with whether or not desegregation should occur but about how it should occur. While federal officials favored applying the same model used in elementary and secondary education—primarily pupil assignment and other compulsory measures—Friday and other UNC officials argued for an aggressive program of incentives to encourage students to attend minority institutions. This disagreement, which led to a lawsuit filed by UNC in federal court in 1979, resulted in a consent decree in 1981 affirming UNC's approach.

WILLIAM A. LINK
University of Florida

William J. Billingsley, *Communists on Campus: Race, Politics, and the Public University in Sixties North Carolina* (2003); Arnold K. King, *The Multicampus University of North Carolina Comes of Age, 1956–1986* (1987); William A. Link, *William Friday: Power, Purpose, and American Higher Education* (1995).

Furman University

Furman University is a highly selective, coeducational liberal arts college in Greenville, S.C., distinguished by an academic program rooted in engaged learning, competitive Division I athletics, and a conservatory-quality music program. Established in 1826 by a group of South Carolina Baptists, the Furman Academy and Theological Institution was named to honor Baptist leader Richard Furman. On 15 January 1827, 10 students began classes in Edgefield, S.C. In 1829, Furman moved to the High Hills of the Santee in Stateburg, S.C., and dedicated its mission solely to ministerial education. Over the first decade of its existence, Furman struggled financially with consistently low enrollments, even failing to hold classes in the 1835–36 academic year while state Baptist leader Nicholas Ware Hodges aggressively pursued funding. In 1836, the chair of the board of trustees, Reverend Jonathan Davis, in consultation with his son-in-law James Clement Furman, purchased 557 acres in Winnsboro, Fairfield County, and moved the campus yet again. After a brief experiment with a curriculum that included manual labor, Furman continued to have difficulty attracting enough students to maintain financial viability.

In 1850 Furman trustees decided to move the college yet again to Greenville, an upcountry village attractive for many reasons. Vardry McBee, known by many as the "Father of Greenville," had wooed Furman by offering land near the banks of the Reedy River for less than half of its appraised value, and local Baptists had a decades-long history of supporting boys' and girls' academies. With Furman's move to Greenville, the boys' academy in the town closed and the girls' academy evolved into the Greenville Baptist Female College.

The match proved fertile, and Furman thrived in Greenville throughout the 1850s. In 1859 the institution assumed the appellation of Furman University and named longtime professor James C. Furman, a son of Richard Furman, as its first president. That same year, the Southern Baptist Theological Seminary was established as an outgrowth of the Furman Theological Department and located in downtown Greenville until 1877, when it moved to Louisville, Ky.

During the Civil War, Furman closed, as most of its student body volunteered for service in the Confederate Army, and some of Furman's faculty and administrators went to work at the Greenville Baptist Female College. After war's end, Furman reopened its doors but struggled financially. Nonetheless, a dedicated administration and faculty persevered. When pressed by acquaintances to abandon the university, President Furman is said to have replied, "No, I have nailed my colors to the mast, and if the ship goes down, I will go down with it."

Through the tenacious efforts of Charles Judson, a professor at the university and treasurer of the board of trustees, Furman achieved financial stability in the late 19th century. Indeed, during Judson's tenure as treasurer, an important precedent was established, giving the board, and not the South Carolina Baptist Convention, control over Furman's budget.

In 1924 Furman achieved accreditation by the Southern Association of Colleges and Schools, and it joined the Southern Conference in athletics several years later. A fortuitous meeting between President Ben Geer and James Buchanan Duke resulted in the naming of Furman as a Duke Endowment beneficiary; this funding helped the university survive the Great Depression and remains a valuable component of the university's annual budget. Furman gradually increased coordination with the Greenville Woman's College (GWC), and in 1938, the two institutions united under the Furman board, with GWC absorbed into Furman University.

As a result of the G.I. Bill, Furman experienced rapidly expanding enrollments in the postwar years. Dilapidated facilities, overcrowded classrooms, and geographically segregated men's and women's campuses led the Furman trustees to move the university some five miles north of downtown Greenville. After breaking ground on the new campus in 1953, the first students began residing on the new campus in 1958. By 1961 the full complement of male and female students moved onto the new campus, making Furman a truly coeducational institution.

Furman experienced much growth and progress during the 1960s and 1970s, particularly under the leadership of President Gordon Blackwell. In 1963 trustees approved a racially blind admissions policy and Furman's first African American undergraduate student entered in 1965. In 1968, study-abroad programs began, and five years later, Phi Beta Kappa bestowed a charter to the university.

After decades of increasing strife, Furman's board of trustees took the extraordinary step of severing the university's ties to the South Carolina Baptist Convention. Over the period 1990–92, President John E. Johns, himself the son of a Baptist minister, adroitly guided Furman through the process of separation. Today, Furman does not maintain formal relationships with any religious body, yet the motto of the university, remains *Christo et Doctrinae* (For Christ and Learning).

In 1994, David E. Shi assumed leadership of the university and focused his considerable energies on improving the quality of Furman's student body, campus facilities, and long-term financial position. Within a decade and a half, the university was ranked in the top 10 among universities nationwide for the percentage of alumni giving, the endowment had increased 400 percent, applications had increased 75 percent, and 29 major construction projects were completed.

Furman's national reputation has also improved dramatically during President Shi's tenure. Aggressively promoting the concept of engaged learning, "a problem-solving, project-oriented, experience-based approach to liberal arts," Furman was ranked fourth in the nation in undergraduate research by the middle of the first decade of the new century. In recent years, Furman has also proven itself a national leader in environmental sustainability. President Shi was a charter signatory on the American College and University Presidents' Climate Commitment addressing climate change and pledging to contribute to climate neutrality, and the university dedicated the David E. Shi Center for sustainability in March 2010.

In 2010 Furman University inaugurated Rodney Smolla as its 11th president.

COURTNEY L. TOLLISON
Furman University

Judith T. Bainbridge, *Academy and College: The History of the Woman's College of Furman University* (2001); Archie Vernon Huff Jr., *Greenville: History of the City and County in the South Carolina Piedmont* (1995); Al Reid, *Furman University: Toward a New Identity, 1925–75* (1976); Courtney Tollison, *Furman University* (2004).

General Education Board

After a tour of southern black schools led by Robert C. Ogden, John D. Rockefeller Jr. convinced his father to make a financial contribution to education in the South. The following year the Rockefellers pledged $1 million to be spent over a 10-year period and created the General Education Board (GEB). Chartered by the U.S. Congress in 1903 for "the promotion of education in the United States of America, without distinction of race, sex, or creed," the GEB by 1964 appropriated more than $325 million, approximately 20 percent of which was earmarked for black education.

At the turn of the 20th century the poverty of the post–Civil War period still restricted education in the South, and the region supported two school systems—one for black children and one for white. Because many rural areas were without schools, the GEB designated much of its initial support to developing rural schools. One of its first grants was to Berea College, located in an impoverished area of Kentucky. Berea was also the recipient of the GEB's last appropriation when, in 1964, the board contributed to the establishment of a Special Student Aid Program. The GEB funded training in agricultural economics and community development, believing that the southern economy had to improve before educational advancements could develop.

The GEB worked nationally to raise teachers' salaries, to support natural science and humanities studies, to provide research fellowships, and to improve medical school facilities and staffs. Its continuing focus, however, was on the South, and from 1940 to 1964 the GEB concentrated its work there. Universities such as Atlanta, Duke, and Tulane benefited, as did black students aspiring to teach and black educators who received GEB fellowships for further training.

The GEB strengthened black education enormously. Historically black colleges and universities such as Fisk and Dillard received millions of dollars in GEB grants. Rather than attacking the South's system of school segregation, the board tried to improve the quality of education by working through the predominantly white structure. Because the GEB was a northern institution, its members believed they had to proceed cautiously if their efforts were to succeed. The GEB raised the level of education for both blacks and whites by fighting the inequality of education, not between the races, but between the South and other regions of the United States.

JESSICA FOY
Cooperstown Graduate Programs
Cooperstown, New York

Raymond B. Fosdick, Henry F. Pringle, and Katharine D. Pringle, *Adventure in Giving: The Story of the General Education Board* (1962); *General Education Board: An Account of Its Activities, 1902–1914* (1915); *General Education Board Review and Final Report, 1902–1964* (1964).

Georgia, University of

Nearly every review of the history and status of any American university begins with the obligatory recitation of the institution's accomplishments and its standings. In 2010, the University of Georgia (UGA) scarcely resembles its predecessor institution of 50 or 60 years ago. Today UGA has 35,000 students, 2,800 faculty members, and a budget of more than $1 billion annually (in 1945 enrollment stood at 2,297, there were approximately 350 faculty members, and the budget was slightly over $4 million). UGA consistently ranks in the top 20 public universities in the United States according to *U.S. News and World Report*. Its students come mainly from Georgia, although they represent every state and more than 100 foreign countries. Its libraries are magnificent, and its sponsored research record, in terms of dollars, is impressive. It has 17 colleges, and its students rank ninth in the United States in numbers of those who study abroad. Its charter, issued in January 1785, rang with Revolutionary rhetoric and places the university among the oldest state universities.

Until only six or seven decades ago, UGA was definably and exclusively a Deep South university lagging in virtually every category in American higher education. Most obviously, until 1961, it was for whites only. Like other southern universities, it began to change and improve in the early 1960s, pushed ahead by courageous civil rights leaders and a set of able university presidents and progressive governors of Georgia. By 2010, it was not entirely clear whether the identity of the university as a "southern" university deeply embedded in regional culture was any longer of primary importance to the vast majority of the faculty, undergraduate students, or graduate students.

Many of the cultural currents that affect the University of Georgia are as much national as they are regional. In nearly every respect, from faculty and student recruitment through competition for research dollars, the university operates in competitive national and international contexts. Ironically, however, issues of southern identity sometimes work against the institution as it seeks to recruit and retain faculty members. Nevertheless, many of UGA's primary challenges and issues directly stem from a culture that was clearly and historically southern.

In the 50 years since desegregation began, the university has struggled to increase the number of African American students to a level that is

Arch and Holmes-Hunter Academic Building, University of Georgia, Athens. As the traditional entrance to the university, the arch serves as a gateway between the north campus and downtown Athens. Its three columns represent wisdom, justice, and moderation. (Paul Efland, UGA Photographic Services)

more nearly proportional to their representation in the state's population. Numerous factors have made this difficult, including skyrocketing standards for admission related to the university's increasing national reputation and the enormous growth of the state's population. Various court challenges to university policies thought to favor minorities have also been impediments to recruitment of such populations. Many argue that the university's climate is not hospitable to minority students, particularly African Americans. The presence on campus of a significant number of black professors (UGA is a national leader in this respect) helps to alleviate such concerns, but the persistent, near-total segregation of the fraternity and sorority system does little to encourage black students to attend the institution.

Intercollegiate athletics, a campus fixture since before 1900, became a major public-relations tool for the university beginning in the 1910s. By the 1950s, after a brief questioning of the role of big-time football, athletics administrators began to act more and more independently of the university through the independent Georgia Athletic Association, established in 1929. By the first decade of the 21st century, largely because of the success of football and the adoption of sophisticated marketing techniques, athletics had become immensely profitable with nearly all of the profits flowing back into athletic coffers, which support numerous athletics teams as well as a football stadium that seats more than 90,000 spectators.

The relationship between athletics and the university has often been tense. Differing academic standards for admission by scholarship athletes and occasional scandals involving those standards have tested the academic/athletics relationship. Most notably, the so-called Kemp affairs of the late 1980s led to the resignation of the university president and severely damaged the university's reputation just as it was being considered for membership in the elite Association of American Universities.

The expansion of women's athletics, first under the provisions of Title IX and later as an established policy of the university, has offered some positive balance. Like many American universities, UGA has seen the number and percentage of women students grow dramatically in the past few decades. UGA steadfastly refused to admit women until 1919 and for decades, with the exception of the World War II years, their numbers remained relatively stable. By the fall semester of 2009, however, they constituted 55 percent of the 35,000 students, consistently out-competing male counterparts for admission to the institution.

To understand the University of Georgia culturally and historically, it is worth knowing that it stands as the capstone of the University System of Georgia, comprised of 35 institutions of higher education with nearly 300,000 students. It competes and actively collaborates with the Georgia Institute of Technology and Emory University, both AAU members, through the Georgia Research Alliance. Collectively, the three institutions control an enormous talent pool and make a very large economic and cultural impact upon Georgia, now the ninth most populous state, more than half of whose residents were born outside its borders.

Pondering at length the question of the university's place in southern culture would not seem to be a profitable exercise for UGA administrators, yet they have to be constantly aware of such matters as they deal with an increasingly conservative band of state officials. In recent years, the state-provided percentage of the university's budget has been in steady decline and as of 2010 is threatening to dip below 30 percent, although the university's budget is still much higher than many state universities on the national stage. It seems unlikely that this trend will reverse, particularly since the extremely strong support Georgia politicians gave to higher education from the 1960s through the 1990s has diminished. If the transformation of the University of Georgia and higher education in Georgia since World War II is not yet complete, it is nonetheless profound.

THOMAS G. DYER
University of Georgia

Robert Preston Brooks, *The University of Georgia under Sixteen Administrations* (1956); Thomas G. Dyer, in *The American South in the Twentieth Century*, ed. Craig S. Pascoe, Karen Trahan Leathem, and Andy Ambrose (2005), *The University of Georgia: A Bicentennial History, 1785–1985* (1985); Robert A. Pratt, *We Shall Not Be Moved: The Desegregation of the University of Georgia* (2002).

Georgia Institute of Technology

Georgia Tech was chartered in 1885 by the Georgia state legislature and admitted its first freshman class in 1888. Interest in a school of technology in Georgia had been stimulated by the campaign for southern industrialization led by men like Henry W. Grady, editor of the *Atlanta Constitution*. In 1883 a legislative committee settled on the Worcester Free Institute in Massachusetts as an appropriate model for Georgia's new school. Worcester had pioneered the "commercial shop" system of technical education, in which students shared time between academic studies and work in the shops producing goods for sale.

When Georgia Tech opened in Atlanta in 1888, it offered degrees only in mechanical engineering. The first professor of that subject, John Saylor Coon, was a founding member of the American Society of Mechanical Engineers. The rapid addition of programs in electrical and civil engineering, industrial chemistry, and textiles reflected both the development of modern engineering practice in America and the economic needs of the state. After the turn of the century, architecture and commerce were added to the curriculum. Although the commercial shop system was scrapped in the 1890s, Georgia Tech retained a heavy emphasis on practical application.

Georgia Tech first won national recognition in engineering in 1930 when it received one of six awards made by the Guggenheim Foundation—and the only one in the South—to support a program in aeronautical engineering. World War II radically transformed Georgia Tech, as it did other colleges. Under the leadership of President Blake Van

Leer, Tech responded to the need for a more science- and mathematics-based engineering and for postgraduate training by shifting its curriculum decisively away from the shop approach, by strengthening programs in the sciences and mathematics, and by establishing its first Ph.D. programs. In 1948 its name was changed from Georgia School of Technology to the Georgia Institute of Technology. It remained part of the state-controlled University System of Georgia. Georgia Tech officially began admitting female students in 1952, and in 1961 it became the first major state university in the Deep South to admit African American students without a court order.

The post–World War II era also witnessed the growth of applied research, particularly in the electronics field, with most of the work being done through the Engineering Experiment Station (renamed in 1984 the Georgia Tech Research Institute). Research and development in electronics have in more recent years provided a base for high-tech "spin-off" firms in and near Atlanta. Other research fields at Georgia Tech have also grown considerably: In 1999 the new Georgia Tech Regional Engineering Program extended its instruction to other students in southeast Georgia, and in 2005 Georgia Tech's biomedical engineering joint doctoral program with Emory University received national recognition as one of seven Centers of Cancer and Nanotechnology Excellence.

As of the fall of 2009 Georgia Tech's total enrollment was 20,545 students. It now offers 100 undergraduate and graduate degree programs in colleges of architecture, computing, engineering, management, sciences, and liberal arts. The Georgia Tech campus has grown to a 400-acre site near downtown Atlanta. This campus was used as Olympic Village during the 1996 Olympics, held in Atlanta.

Georgia Tech's football program began to play a major role in the school's existence in 1904, when the college hired its first full-time coach, John Heisman, whose famous trophy has honored college football's best players since 1936. Under Heisman and his successors, W. A. Alexander and Bobby Dodd, Tech enjoyed a reputation as a national powerhouse for over half a century and has claimed four national championships since the program began. Other sports at Georgia Tech include men's basketball, baseball, golf, tennis, indoor and outdoor track, cross country, and swimming and diving as well as women's basketball, softball, tennis, indoor and outdoor track, cross country, swimming and diving, and volleyball.

Among Georgia Tech's alumni are numerous presidents of major corporations and leading practitioners in Tech's areas of expertise. President Jimmy Carter attended Georgia Tech before enrolling in the Naval Academy and received an honorary doctorate from the institute in 1979.

ROBERT C. MCMATH JR.
Georgia Institute of Technology

MARY AMELIA TAYLOR
University of Mississippi

Marion L. Brittain, *The Story of Georgia Tech* (1948); Georgia Institute of Technology Web site, www.gatech.edu (2010); Robert C. McMath Jr. et al., *Engineering the New South: Georgia Tech, 1885–1985* (1985); Robert B. Wallace Jr., *Dress Her in White and Gold: A Biography of Georgia Tech and of the Men Who Led Her* (1969).

Gildersleeve, Basil

(1831–1924) CLASSICAL SCHOLAR. Born 23 October 1831 in Charleston, S.C., Basil Lanneau Gildersleeve became the most renowned American classicist of the late 19th century. Founder of the *American Journal of Philology* in 1880, Gildersleeve taught classics at Johns Hopkins for almost four decades and became a central figure in the professionalization of Greek and Latin studies in the American university.

Gildersleeve grew up in a home of pronounced southern loyalties. His father, Benjamin, was a northerner by birth but adopted the southern antebellum sectional cause with enthusiasm. A Presbyterian minister and editor of a denominational paper, Benjamin Gildersleeve supervised his son's early education and introduced him, somewhat unsystematically, to the classics. Basil Gildersleeve went on to attend the College of Charleston, Jefferson College in Pennsylvania, and Princeton, where he graduated in 1849. He taught classics at a private academy in Richmond, Va., and then spent 1850 to 1853 in Germany at Berlin, Göttingen, and Bonn, before taking his Ph.D. at Göttingen. After three years in Charleston writing and teaching, he became a professor at the University of Virginia in 1856. Except for his service in the Confederate army, which left him with a crippling leg injury received in the Shenandoah Valley campaign, he remained at Virginia until he took a position at Johns Hopkins in 1876. He died 9 January 1924.

Gildersleeve's *The Creed of the Old South* (1915) was a work celebrating the antebellum South. Southerners after the war produced many rationalizations for the romanticized plantation society, but Gildersleeve's stood out for its perspective on southern history. Although proud of the South's wartime heroism and unquestioning of southern ideals, he did not portray the South as the center of the universe. He did compare the Civil War to the Peloponnesian War—the North was Athens, the South, Sparta—but he knew the ultimate judgment of southern history would come far in the future. His long perspective on history enabled him to escape the anger and bitterness so prevalent in the first generation of southern intellectual life after the war.

Gildersleeve was also significant as a representative of southern intellectual ties with German culture. He inherited a dislike for British culture, stemming from family memories of the British occupation of Charleston during the War of 1812, and his reading of the Scottish historian Carlyle reinforced Gildersleeve's aversion to the English and pointed him toward an interest in Goethe. Gildersleeve called the German author "the most important of all the teachers I ever had." He studied Goethe endlessly for a time in his youth. "This was the era of my Teutomania," he recalled later. His youthful interest in Germany proved to be enduring. German philology—and that nation's system of university education and scholarly research—became his model for the United States. He hoped, particularly, to give studies of Greece and Rome a new vigor through application of rigorous scholarly methods pioneered in Germany.

CHARLES REAGAN WILSON
University of Mississippi

Basil Gildersleeve, *Forum* (February 1891), *Selections from the Brief Mention of Basil Lanneau Gildersleeve*, ed. C. W. E. Miller (1930); Fred Hobson, *Tell about the South: The Southern Rage to Explain* (1983); C. W. E. Miller, *American Journal of Philology* (January 1924).

Graham, Frank

(1886–1972) EDUCATOR AND STATESMAN.

Professor and president of the University of North Carolina, U.S. senator, and United Nations mediator, Frank Porter Graham was born in Fayetteville, N.C., in 1886. He received both undergraduate and law degrees from the University of North Carolina and a master's degree from Columbia, afterwards studying at the University of Chicago, the London School of Economics, and elsewhere. He left a position as instructor in history at the University of North Carolina for service in the Marine Corps during World War I but returned to rise to the rank of professor by 1927.

Frank Porter Graham, president of the University of North Carolina (1930–49) (Southern Historical Collection, University of North Carolina, Chapel Hill)

In 1930 Graham became president of the University of North Carolina; and in 1932, when that institution was consolidated with the North Carolina College for Women and North Carolina State College, he became president of the larger institution, the Consolidated University of North Carolina. Graham worked diligently during the Great Depression to increase the university's scholarship funds for needy students and often was involved in intense controversy over political, social, and economic policies. All the while he defended the freedom of the university to seek, learn, believe, speak, and publish. Sometimes he was the object of personal attacks for his support of unpopular causes or persons, yet he never wavered in his faith in the young and in the future of a free, democratic society.

Beyond the university, Graham was concerned with the needs of the poor and underprivileged, and he supported racial justice. Twice he was president of the North Carolina Conference for Social Service, and at President Franklin D. Roosevelt's appointment he served on federal boards and commissions, including the National Advisory Council on Social Security, of which he was chairman. During World War II he served on the National Defense Mediation Board and the National War Labor Board. President Harry Truman appointed him to the President's Committee on Civil Rights, for which Graham made a historic report on the country's racial problems and presented proposals for their solution. At Truman's request he served as the representative of the United States on the United Nations committee on the Dutch-Indonesian dispute. He also helped organize, and was the first president of, the Oak Ridge Institute of Nuclear Studies. In 1949 he was appointed by the governor of North Carolina to fill an unexpired term in the U.S. Senate, but in a bid for nomination for reelection he failed to win a majority in the primary. In a second primary the racial issue was injected to Graham's disadvantage, and he was rejected by his party.

Service on the President's Committee on Civil Rights and his well-known commitment to human rights and association with liberal causes contributed to Graham's defeat. Nevertheless, he continued his public service: as defense manpower administrator for the U.S. Department of Labor, as United Nations representative to mediate the dispute between India and Pakistan over Kashmir, and as assistant secretary general of the United Nations. Graham, a deeply religious man, worked diligently for human betterment not only at home but also throughout the world. He died in Chapel Hill, N.C., in 1972.

WILLIAM S. POWELL
University of North Carolina at Chapel Hill

Frank P. Graham Papers, Southern Historical Collection, University of North Carolina, Chapel Hill.

Hampden-Sydney College

A private liberal arts college enrolling some 1,100 students, Hampden-Sydney is situated on a large rural campus in Virginia's tobacco-growing Southside, that part of the Old Dominion that has appeared to some observers as most reminiscent of the Old South. The college has been in continuous operation since January of 1776 and is the nation's tenth-oldest institution of higher learning. Hanover Presbytery founded the college "as a southern replica of Princeton," according to historian Lawrence A. Cremin, intending to nurture both an educated commitment to public service and to promote the Presbyterian faith in the heavily Scotch-Irish population of south-central Virginia. The name Hampden-Sydney was apparently chosen as symbolic proclamation of the founders' commitment to the principles of political and religious liberty for which John Hampden and Algernon Sydney had struggled in 17th-century England. The college's first board of trustees included such revolutionary luminaries as Patrick Henry and James Madison.

The school colors, garnet and gray, derive from a uniform of purple hunting shirts (dyed with the juice of pokeberries) and gray trousers, which the student militia company wore while helping to defend Williamsburg and Petersburg during the late 1770s. At the outbreak of the Civil War the student body organized another company of militia, and the "Hampden-Sydney Boys" fought for the Confederacy in a losing effort at Rich Mountain on 10 June 1861. The Union Theological Seminary, now located in Richmond, had been founded at the college in 1812. In 1838 the college's medical department established the Medical College of Virginia, which later also moved to Richmond and is today the MCV Campus of Virginia Commonwealth University.

Hampden-Sydney continues to draw a decided majority of its students from Virginia and the neighboring states of the Upper South. The college remains most distinguished for an ambience that blends latter-day preppiness with gentlemanly traditions that strike some observers as elitist or anachronistic. A visitor in 1985 noted "the prevalence on campus of late-model BMWs and crudely laundered khakis." About 99 percent of the students are men, and the college is one of only four liberal arts colleges in the country committed to remaining effectively all-male. Although about 1 percent of the students are female, generally from faculty and staff families, a popular bumper sticker identifies Hampden-Sydney as a place "Where men are men and women are guests." Yet in the spring of 2007 the anonymous wife of a faculty member, herself an attorney, praised the college on the Web site "College Confidential" for offering "a classical liberal arts education in a supportive environment where lasting friendships will be built." She reported having "attended a major Ivy League university for college where I received none of the devotion and attention that my husband and his colleagues give their students." In August of 2008 Forbes.com ranked Hampden-Sydney as number 50 among "America's Best Colleges."

Hampden-Sydney has clearly repudiated the racialist legacy of its past. The second Rhodes scholar in the college's history, selected in December of 1985, was a black student from Southside Virginia, who also served as president of student government. In December of 2008 the college announced its first African American president, Christopher Howard, a 1991 graduate of the Air Force Academy who studied at Oxford as a Rhodes scholar.

SHEARER DAVIS BOWMAN
University of Kentucky

Herbert C. Bradshaw, *History of Hampden-Sydney College, Volume I: From the Beginnings to the Year 1856* (1976); Lawrence A. Cremin, *American Education: The Colonial Experience, 1607–1783* (1970), *American Education: The National Experience, 1783–1876* (1980); Zöe Ingalls, *Chronicle of Higher Education* (18 September 1985).

Hampton Institute

In 1863 the 200-acre grounds of a former plantation in Elizabeth City County, Va., called "Little Scotland," became the campus for what would become the Hampton Normal and Agricultural Institute, one of the permanent educational institutions for free blacks

A class in mathematical geography studying the earth's rotation around the sun, Hampton Institute, Hampton, Va., 1899 (Frances Benjamin Johnson, Library of Congress [LC-USZ62-62376], Washington, D.C.)

established by northern missionary teachers in the mid-1800s. The first southern reading of the Emancipation Proclamation occurred on the plantation site, beneath the branches of the aptly named Emancipation Oak. Classes began there, under the shade of that oak tree and the tutelage of Mary Smith Peake, the daughter of a freed slave. In 1868 former Union general Samuel Chapman Armstrong formalized these classes by establishing the Hampton Normal and Agricultural Institute with funding from the American Missionary Association and the Freedmen's Bureau. As the son of missionary parents, Armstrong grew up in the Sandwich Islands (now Hawaii) and observed the success of the Hilo Manual Labor Institute there, where students paid their tuition and board by working at housekeeping, gardening, masonry, and carpentry jobs.

Armstrong desired that Hampton be such a vocational institution, and, indeed, its students helped construct many of the school's early buildings. The first classroom building was completed in 1870, and in the same year Hampton received its official charter, which allowed it to receive funding from the state and federal governments. The school's elementary- through college-level students received training in agriculture and skilled trades, and many pursued teaching careers in black schools, though opportunities were limited. The school's mission emphasized commitment to moral virtues, respect for discipline in the military tradition, and compromise and accommodation toward whites. Booker T. Washington, an 1875 graduate of the Hampton Institute, adopted this approach in his vocational education philosophy at Tuskegee Institute in Alabama. Such an approach, however, clashed sharply with the growing demand in the 1890s for black liberal arts programs; the rift between W. E. B. Du Bois and Washington stemmed in large part from Washington's dedication to the traditions of Hampton Institute.

By the 1920s, Hampton Institute had gradually phased out its elementary and secondary programs and deemphasized its vocational component; it began offering courses for a bachelor of science degree in 1922. By 1933 the school received accreditation as a four-year college, and its graduate programs began in 1956. Weathering the strife of a white-supremacist "racial purity" campaign in Virginia in the 1920s and 1930s, the institute finally obtained black leadership under Alonzo G. Moron's presidency from 1947 through 1959. The institute became Hampton University in 1984.

For many reasons, Hampton University is recognized, according to Mary F. Berry and John W. Blassingame, as "one of the most influential schools in the history of black education." Hampton Institute was one of the first colleges to invite African students and to accept American Indians; in 1878 it accepted 17 American Indian prisoners of war from Fort Marion, Fla., and by 1899, 135 of the school's 1,000 students were American Indians. The university has also produced world-renowned choirs, a dance company focusing on black traditions, research projects to preserve black folklore, training programs in Africa, and a variety of publications and conferences on issues important to African American history and culture. Its library houses an outstanding collection of materials on black history. In January 2010 Hampton received an $8 million grant to build a biomedical research center on its campus to expand its research programs. The private, coeducational, independent institution offers technical, liberal arts, preprofessional, professional, and graduate degree programs.

Hampton University, an NCAA Division I member of the Mid-Eastern Athletic Conference (comprised of 12 historically black colleges on the Atlantic coastline), offers a variety of men's and women's sports and has trained several players for the NFL and NBA: Donovan Rose, Alonzo Coleman, and Rick Mahorn, to name a few.

Both the faculty and student body of Hampton University are interracial and intercultural; the school currently has students enrolled from 49 states and 35 territories and nations. In 2005 the university's black, non-Hispanic enrollment was 5,568, its white, non-Hispanic population was 591, and its "foreign/other" population was 140. Its 2004–5 enrollment was 6,309 students.

Notable graduates of Hampton University include Booker T. Washington, Alberta Williams King (mother of Martin Luther King Jr.), comedian

Wanda Sykes, Septima Poinsette Clark (often called the "Grandmother of the American Civil Rights Movement"), Spencer Christian (former weather forecaster for ABC's *Good Morning America*), and Vanessa Gilmore (U.S. District Court judge for the South District of Texas).

SHARON A. SHARP
University of Mississippi

MARY AMELIA TAYLOR
University of Mississippi

Samuel Chapman Armstrong, *Twenty-Two Years' Work of the Hampton Normal and Agricultural Institute* (1893); Mary Frances Berry and John W. Blassingame, *Long Memory: The Black Experience in America* (1982); W. Augustus Low and Virgil A. Clift, eds., *Encyclopedia of Black America* (1981); August Meier and Elliott Rudwick, *From Plantation to Ghetto* (1966); Carol Ann Poh, *National Register of Historic Places Inventory/Nomination Form: Hampton Institute* (1974); Alrutheus A. Taylor, *The Negro in the Reconstruction of Virginia* (1926); Raymond Wolters, *The New Negro on Campus: Black College Rebellions of the 1920s* (1975).

Head Start

Often noted as the most successful of President Lyndon Johnson's Great Society programs, Head Start has held a distinguished place within the American culture. Periodically, politicians have tried to alter the program, but it has been difficult to make drastic changes to its original mandate—a comprehensive child-development program offering education, health, nutrition, and social services for impoverished children. When the Office of Economic Opportunity (OEO) launched Project Head Start in the summer of 1965, however, it was not warmly embraced in the South.

Head Start grew out of the Community Action Program operated by OEO. As a component of Community Action, Project Head Start had to follow legislative regulations that required the participation of the poor in the planning and implementation of its programs. Just like other Community Action Programs, local communities organized and administered Project Head Start. Parents were essential for a successful venture—working as teachers' aides, taking special courses to improve the home environment, or advising in the development and administration of programs. In most cases, OEO covered 80 percent of the cost for a Head Start program, and the local community funded the balance. Eventually, Head Start grew to include summer sessions for children aged five and six; a full year for those three, four, and five; parent and child centers for children up to two years old; and a school follow-through program for children six to eight.

Funding for Project Head Start came directly from Washington, bypassing state control, which led many southern state and local politicians to worry that it harbored the potential to accelerate the progress of public school desegregation and further black political empowerment. OEO issued guidelines that clearly indicated the agency would fund only those projects that did not racially discriminate. These regulations included all aspects of the program—the location of the Head Start Center, the eligibility of participants, and the recruitment and placement of staff, transportation, and publicity. As a result, in many southern cities and towns OEO often mediated between rival factions—those who held political and economic power and those seeking resources to improve their communities that had long been neglected.

The first inspector general of OEO, William Haddad, created a special Head Start task force to investigate complaints of discrimination. OEO's General Counsel's Office also became involved in setting policy to ensure that Head Start programs complied with the Civil Rights Act of 1964. To avoid a long hearing process, OEO's attorneys focused on the hiring policies of Head Start faculty, targeting discrimination that violated the student's rights as a beneficiary instead of the teacher's rights as an employee. The agency's legal staff also sought to end de facto segregation in OEO-sponsored programs even where no deliberate local policy of segregation existed. Finally, the General Counsel's Office interpreted the separation of church and state to the benefit of OEO programs. Congress allowed the antipoverty agency to offer "special, remedial and non-curricular educational assistance." Under these terms, OEO could support programs operated by parochial schools, an interpretation that had special significance in the South. When a school district refused to sponsor a Head Start program or when OEO denied a school system funds because it refused to comply with its nondiscrimination requirements, parochial schools often stepped in to fill the void. For example, in Mobile, Ala., the Catholic Charities office operated Head Start centers throughout the region under Archbishop Toolen's Antipoverty Committee. After the public schools refused to comply with OEO's antidiscrimination guidelines, the Head Start programs sponsored by the Catholic Church were the only integrated public education programs operating in the area. The Most Pure Heart of Mary, located in the heart of the black business district, housed a Head Start program, and it also became the site of weekly mass meetings for Neighborhood Organized Workers, a grassroots effort that challenged the slow pace of Mobile's desegregation process in education, housing, and employment.

One of the earliest Head Start Programs in the South also revealed the political weaknesses of the OEO. The Child Development Group of Mississippi (CDGM) launched a statewide Head Start program in May 1965 with 85 centers in 45 counties enrolling 6,000 children. That summer OEO's grant to CDGM totaled almost $1.5 million. U.S. Senator John Stennis of Mississippi charged that CDGM was a front for the Mississippi Freedom Democratic Party and that it geared its programs exclusively toward poor African American children. The CDGM's leaders were proud of their civil rights activism, and they viewed this OEO program as an opportunity to provide education to poor children while advancing the civil rights movement. During the ensuing two-year battle, OEO issued funds, retracted support, and then helped create a second organization to operate the

Head Start program in Mississippi. It was not one of OEO's finest hours, and the agency received justifiable criticism for its handling of this project.

In 1973 President Richard Nixon dismantled OEO and spun off many of its programs into the existing federal bureaucracy. Head Start got absorbed into the Department of Health, Education, and Welfare. More than 20 million young people have been touched by this antipoverty effort; in 2008 it served almost 900,000 children at a cost of $7 billion.

SUSAN YOUNGBLOOD ASHMORE
Oxford College of Emory University

Susan Youngblood Ashmore, *Carry It On: The War on Poverty and the Civil Rights Movement in Alabama, 1964–1972* (2008), in *The New Deal and Beyond: Social Welfare in the South since 1930*, ed. Elna Green (2003); John Dittmer, *Local People: The Struggle for Civil Rights in Mississippi* (1994); Michael L. Gillette, *Launching the War on Poverty: An Oral History* (1996).

Highlander Folk School
(1932–1961)
Highlander Research and Education Center
(1961–)

The Highlander Research and Education Center (formerly named Highlander Folk School) is an education center for social change located in east Tennessee. Highlander has been in the forefront of social justice organizing in the South and nationally, playing a vital role in the southern labor movement, the civil rights movement, the environmental justice movement, and the global justice movement, among others.

Highlander Folk School began in 1932 on the Cumberland Plateau in Grundy County, Tenn. Highlander's founders, Myles Horton and Don West, were both from the South and had been inspired by the social gospel movement and the Danish Folk Schools. They decided to build a school for adult education in the South. Dr. Lilian Johnson had land and a community house outside Monteagle where she had been working to teach local people about cooperatives, and she wanted someone to take over her work, so she agreed to let Horton and West try out their new ideas for a year. After that year, she turned the site over to them to use for the long term.

The new school's first efforts in helping the local Appalachian community included setting up a nursery school, construction of a cannery, and offering a variety of educational programs. As labor organizing increased in the region, Highlander responded by conducting labor-organizing training sessions, working with local Works Progress Administration employees and with miners in the Davidson-Wilder community and Grundy County. Highlander branched out to serve workers in the growing textile industry, which was organizing throughout the South. The staff offered labor-organizing education at the school and in locals throughout the region. Highlander facilitated and hosted workshops that focused on enhancing organizing skills needed for union organizing.

Zilphia Johnson Horton, Myles's wife, was committed to also incorporating culture as an important part of workshops, so square dancing, music, and drama became part of the curriculum. This tradition of integrating culture with social action is a strong thread in Highlander's educational model that continues today.

In the 1940s, Highlander staff made the decision that workshops would be integrated, believing that economic justice could not be achieved as long as black and white workers were segregated. And in the 1950s Highlander became increasingly involved in the civil rights movement, offering workshops on school desegregation and the *Brown v. Board of Education* decision.

In the mid-1950s, Septima Clark, a teacher from Charleston, S.C., became education director at Highlander and worked with Esau Jenkins and Bernice Robinson to develop the Citizenship Schools on John's Island, one of the South Carolina Sea Islands. The Citizenship School model became a vital part of the civil rights movement by teaching thousands of African Americans to read and write, resulting in black students being able to pass literacy tests required to attain the right to vote. The Citizenship School model of education, based on people's needs and experiences, was then replicated throughout the South.

Highlander supported work on school desegregation and hosted the first gathering for the student leaders of the southern sit-in movement in April of 1960. Highlander continued to serve as a meeting site for Student Nonviolent Coordinating Committee (SNCC) members and their adviser, Ella Baker. Other leaders also met at Highlander, including Bernice Johnson Reagon, Fannie Lou Hamer, Rosa Parks, Anne Braden, and countless others who helped shape and move the civil rights movement forward.

From its very beginning, Highlander faced harassment from powerful economic and political forces who wanted to squelch labor and civil rights organizing in the South. In 1961 Tennessee revoked Highlander Folk School's charter and confiscated the 200-acre site, including 13 buildings. The charges included holding integrated gatherings.

The Citizenship School Program then joined the Southern Christian Leadership Conference (SCLC), to ensure its continuance, and Highlander changed its name to the Highlander Research and Education Center and relocated to Knoxville. It continued hosting civil rights gatherings but also began working again with groups in Appalachia, where there was a resurgence of activity in labor organizing in response to growth in the mining industry and the federal War on Poverty.

In 1971, Highlander Research and Education Center moved to a farm on Bays Mountain in Jefferson County, Tenn., and built a workshop center, library, offices, and staff housing. Work in the 1970s and early 1980s concentrated on efforts to reduce poverty, improve health and environmental conditions, and enhance democratic institutions in Appalachia. Staff worked to support health clinics built by the United Mine Workers of America and their efforts to organize against the devastation caused by strip mining for coal. Highlander worked with the Appalachian Alliance in 1979 and 1980 on a participatory research project that focused on land ownership in Appalachia, documenting both the vast areas owned and controlled by corporations and the low tax base resulting from this pattern of ownership. Highlander became part of an international organization, the Participatory Research Network, which worked to challenge the hierarchical view that "knowledge" was what was learned in a formal education setting and to focus instead on the knowledge of ordinary people to inform research and serve as researchers in determining solutions to their own issues.

In the 1990s, Highlander recognized the region's changing demographics and the need to develop new leaders for social justice. The school developed new programs for immigrants and youth and supported lesbian/gay/bisexual/transgendered groups organizing in the region. Economic work also continued at Highlander, focusing on deindustrialization in the region and opposition to free trade agreements such as the North American Free Trade Agreement. Highlander supported the creation of two statewide networks, the Tennessee Industrial Renewal Network, begun in 1989, and the Tennessee Immigrant and Refugee Rights Coalition, begun in 2002.

Highlander's work changes as the needs and organizing work of groups in the South and Appalachia change, but the core methodologies of popular education, cultural organizing, and participatory research continue. The school maintains its core beliefs that social change should be led by people directly affected by issues and that everyone has access to knowledge that is important in addressing injustice within their communities.

SUSAN WILLIAMS
Highlander Research and Education Center

Frank Adams, with Myles Horton, *Unearthing Seeds of Fire: The Idea of Highlander* (1975); John M. Glen, *Highlander: No Ordinary School* (1996); Myles Horton, with Herbert and Judith Kohl, *The Long Haul* (1997); Eliot Wigginton, ed., *Refuse to Stand Silently by: An Oral History of Grass Roots Social Activism in America, 1921–1964* (1991).

Homeschooling

Prior to the mid-19th century, "schooling" in the United States was an activity that took place at home, led mainly by parents. Yet, in the wake of the common-school movement and the Industrial Revolution, home education lost legitimacy and, subsequently, legal status. The transition from homeschooling to formal schooling was slower in the South as a result of slow urbanization and a dominant agrarian culture that kept children close to home during planting and harvest seasons. Nonetheless, by 1918 every state in the country had compulsory attendance laws that mandated parents to send their children to "formal" schools or risk serious legal consequences. Thus, most children ages 6 to 12 were involved in some sort of formal schooling by 1930.

Interest in homeschooling resurfaced in the late 1950s and gained even greater support during the1960s and 1970s. Its popularity increased in response to the rise in antigovernment sentiment and related educational reforms, a focus on the child, and removal of religious education from public schools. Despite the legal ramifications, some families chose to take their children out of schools, public or private. As homeschooling practices increased, so did pressure on the government to recognize parental rights to educate their own children. In 1972 the U.S. Supreme Court decision in *Yoder v. Wisconsin* legalized homeschooling by granting parents permission to opt out of compulsory school attendance laws on religious grounds. It charged states with the task of balancing parental rights to educate their children and the government's interest in ensuring access to education for all children. Consequently, issues like instructor certification, length of day/instruction, appropriateness of curriculum, and forms of assessment became subject to state regulation. Thirty-seven states overall have adopted homeschool legislation. Of the southern states, eight have homeschooling statutes/regulations: Arkansas (1985), Florida (1985), Georgia (1984), Louisiana (1984), North Carolina (1988), South Carolina (1988), Tennessee (1985), and Virginia (1984).

Oklahoma is the only state in the country with a constitutional amendment that guarantees the right to homeschool. Alabama, Florida, South Carolina, Tennessee, Texas, and Virginia, instead, make provisions that protect parents' right to homeschool. These states passed Religious Freedom Acts, or Religious Freedom Restoration Amendments (RFRAs), which protect citizens' rights to exercise religion in all areas, including education. If parents' free exercise of religion is significantly hindered by having to comply with state regulations for homeschooling, parents may use the RFRA to justify homeschooling practices. As a result of the Religious Freedom Acts, homeschooling in the South has been minimally regulated in regard to curriculum, length of instruction, teacher qualification, and assessment when compared to other regions.

In 2007 approximately 1.5 million American children were homeschooled, a 36 percent increase from 1999. State estimates show that rises in homeschooling rates in the South parallel nationwide trends. Because of low regulation and the prominence of conservative social attitudes, the modern homeschool movement has strong roots in the South. Homeschooling occurs mostly in families that self-identify as conservative and Christian, white, with a traditional gender division of labor (two parents, one working), and three or more children. In these families the parents generally choose to homeschool to provide their children with religious scholarship and avoid curricula that include topics such as evolution and sex education. Proponents who do not identify with conservative rationales for homeschooling contend that public school curricula should include a diverse focus that reflects the multicultural heritage of the United States. Other proponents, specifically racial minorities, believe that homeschooling is essential to addressing the persistent educational achievement gap. Despite differing reasons, both conservative- and liberal-minded parents agree that the public school system is failing and that parents are ultimately responsible for educating their children. As a result, homeschooling remains an important option for many parents.

CELESTE LEE
CADDIE PUTNAM RANKIN
Emory University

Milton Gaither, *Homeschool: An American History* (2008); Christopher J. Klicka, *Homeschooling in the United States: A Legal Analysis* (2001); J. Gary Knowles, Stacey E. Marlow, and James A. Muchmore, *American Journal of Education* (February 1992); Tal Levy, *Journal of Black Studies* (July 2009); Mitchell Stevens, *Kingdom of Children* (2001); U.S. Department of Education, Institute of Education Sciences, National Center for Educational Statistics, "Parent and Family Involvement in Education Survey" (2007).

Jackson State University

Founded in Natchez, Miss., as a private church school by the American Baptist Home Missionary Society in 1877, Jackson State University was established "for the moral, religious, and intellectual improvement of Christian leaders of the colored people of Mississippi and the neighboring states." Twenty students were enrolled when the school opened on 23 October. Its first president, Charles Ayer of New York, resigned in 1894, and Luther G. Barrett succeeded him. In the same year the school relocated to Jackson, and it became Jackson College in 1899. In 1903 the college moved to its present location in the heart of the city.

Zachary Taylor Hubert of Atlanta became the institution's first black president in 1911. His administration broadened the course of study and awarded the first college-level degree (B.A.) in 1924 to Annie Mae Brown Magee. Major educational activities of the college during this time were directed toward teacher education. The Home Missionary Society withdrew its support of the institution in 1938, and the college joined the state system of higher education. Initially, the state assumed support of the college for the purpose of training rural and elementary schoolteachers, and in 1942 the board of trustees raised the curriculum to a four-year teacher education program. The college added a division of graduate studies and a program of liberal arts in 1953 and became Jackson State College in 1956.

On 2 March 1967 John A. Peoples Jr. became the sixth president and the first alumnus to serve in that capacity. The university expanded its academic program and reorganized its curriculum under his tenure, adding a graduate school and schools of liberal studies, education, science and technology, and business and economics. Margaret Walker became director of the Institute for the Study of the History, Life, and Culture of Black People in 1968. Since that time the institute has sponsored distinguished lectures, readings, and symposia on the black experience.

Jackson State had its own share of the civil rights movement of the 1960s and 1970s. Jackson State students were involved in cafeteria sit-ins and other civil rights demonstrations through the 1960s, and in 1961 Jackson State student James Meredith left the school after his first semester to begin the landmark desegregation of the University of Mississippi. Jackson State itself received national publicity on 14 May 1970 when two students were killed and 12 wounded on campus as local authorities and national guardsmen confronted students during a riot (the culmination of civil rights demonstrations, Vietnam protests, and harassment by white motorists on nearby Lynch Street) on campus. The incident occurred 10 days after the killing of students at Kent State University.

In 1974 the college gained university status and became Jackson State University. In 1979 it was officially recognized as the Urban University of Mississippi. Jackson State University's special mission as an urban university has since prompted the faculty to increase involvement in services to the community; the university now serves the citizens of Mississippi with a broad array of public services, continuing education, and research programs. The university's Mississippi Urban Research Center aids students in researching and analyzing "pressing urban issues" like public health, violence and crime, drug and alcohol abuse, and urban education and offers conferences, workshops, and contractual services to share ideas and resources with local businesses, schools, and community outreach organizations. While Jackson State offers a variety of curricula, many of its degree programs specifically address fields relevant to urban life, such as public health, business, education, engineering, and public administration.

In 2002 Jackson State University was part of a 29-year-old desegregation lawsuit settlement, which ended the disproportionately small amount of funds distributed to historically black colleges and universities in Mississippi. The settlement distributes $503 million over 17 years to three historically black state universities in Mississippi—Jackson, Mississippi Valley, and Alcorn. In November of 2009, however, as a result of the state's budget crunch, Gov. Haley Barbour proposed that the state's three historically black universities merge into Jackson State to save the state money. Not unexpectedly and after statewide protest, by February 2010 Barbour's proposed merger had died in the state legislature.

Jackson State offers 43 bachelor's, 36 master's, 11 doctoral, and three specialist-in-education degree programs. Unique academic centers on campus include the English as a Second Language Institute, the Institute for Educational Renewal, and the Mississippi e-Center, which provides information technology and a conference center for developing businesses and researchers. The university's fall 2009 enrollment was 8,783 students.

Numerous alumni of the university's sports teams have continued to play for professional basketball (Lindsey Hunter, Chicago Bulls), football (Lem Barney, Detroit Lions), and baseball (Dennis Ray "Oil Can" Boyd, Red Sox) teams; other notable Jackson State graduates include Cassandra Wilson, jazz singer and musician, and Rod Paige, U.S. secretary of education for the George W. Bush administration.

LELIA G. RHODES
Jackson State University
MARY AMELIA TAYLOR
University of Mississippi

Jackson State University, www.jsums.edu (2010); Mississippi e-Center, www.msecenter.com (2009); Lelia G. Rhodes, *Jackson State University: The First Hundred Years, 1877–1977* (1978); Tim Spofford, *Lynch Street: The May 1970 Slayings at Jackson State College* (1988).

Journal of Southern History

When 18 men and women scholars met in Atlanta on 2 November 1934 to organize the Southern Historical Association (SHA), the organizers hoped to publish a journal, although financial support was uncertain. But when Wendell Holmes Stephenson reported that his home institution, Louisiana State University, would fund such a scholarly periodical under his editorship, the idea became reality, and that December the first board of editors met and decided the quarterly periodical should be titled the *Journal of Southern History* (JSH). After much discussion between SHA organizers and Stephenson, it was determined that while the annual meeting of the SHA would include sessions on world history and U.S. history in general, the JSH would publish articles, documents, and book reviews only on the history of the South. The first issue was published in February 1935, and it contained four articles, one edited document, reviews of 16 books, a brief section entitled "Historical News and Notices," and a directory of the article contributors. All the contributors were academic historians. The JSH established its scholarly reputation in the first issue. The February 1936 issue contained an article summarizing the annual meeting of the SHA held the previous fall, and beginning in 1937 there was an annual report by the SHA secretary-treasurer. The journal format remained unchanged for almost three decades. The initial editorial board was all male, but one of the authors in the first year was a woman, and one article dealt with women; three articles treated some aspect of African American history.

Fred C. Cole, who had served as editorial associate for five years, replaced Stephenson as editor for volume 8, in 1942, and the following year the JSH editorial offices moved to Vanderbilt University under the editorship of William C. Binkley. Although Ella Lonn had in 1941 become the first woman scholar to serve on the board of editors, the range of topics covered changed very little. The editorial offices moved again in late 1948, this time to the University of Kentucky, and beginning with the February 1949 issue (volume 15), Thomas D. Clark served as managing editor. Kathryn A. Hanna served on the board of editors for 1945–48, and Nannie Mae Tilley for 1949–50, but it would be more than 20 years before another woman scholar, LaWanda Cox, was named to the editorial board for 1972–75. The JSH remained at the University of Kentucky through 1958, although in 1953 former editorial associate J. Merton England replaced Clark as managing editor. In 1959 the JSH editorial offices moved to Rice University, where it continues to this day. William H. Masterson served as managing editor for two years, then William W. Abbot edited the journal for 1961–63, followed by Philip F. Detweiler for 1963–65. Longtime editor Sanford W. Higginbotham took the helm in 1965 and served for 18 years, retiring in the summer of 1983, after which John B. Boles became managing editor. His title was changed to editor in 2006, and Randal L. Hall was named managing editor.

A series of minor changes have occurred in the format over the past two decades. The report on the annual meeting ceased being published in the 1993 issue, and by the 1980s it was exceedingly rare for documents to be reprinted. Beginning with the May 1964 issue and continuing thereafter, the JSH staff compiles a very complete listing of articles on southern history published in a wide variety of other journals. This "Southern History in Periodicals" covers the prior year, although items missed are entered the following year with proper notation. The board of editors is now more diverse; the first African American board member was appointed in 1983, and women now represent half or more of the members. In 2008, for example, five of the eight members were women, and two were African Americans. In subject matter too the JSH now reflects quite accurately the variety of topics and methodologies that characterizes modern scholarship. The JSH is also now available electronically via JSTOR, with the normal five-year moving wall behind print publication.

For many decades the JSH has been edited with unusual care. Articles are selected via the process known as double-blind review (neither author nor referees know each other's name), with three to six readers for submissions. The acceptance rate varies, but generally about 15 percent of submissions are eventually accepted. In the editing process, every footnote, statement of fact, and quotation is checked, and much care is given to grammar, style, and vigor of argument. The JSH staff, which now consists of an editor, managing editor, associate editor, and office manager, is supplemented by four to six graduate student editorial assistants, who do most of the initial fact-checking. Approximately 300 books are reviewed annually. The SHA pays the printing costs and provides Rice University with a sizable annual subsidy, but Rice underwrites most of the editing expenses. This allows the JSH to maintain its reputation as a rigorously edited journal at the same time it keeps its subscription cost far less than other major history journals. With SHA members and subscribers around the world, the JSH is the flagship journal for southern studies and a leading journal of U.S. history.

JOHN B. BOLES
Rice University

Bethany Leigh Johnson, "Regionalism, Race, and the Meaning of the Southern Past: Professional History in the American South, 1896–1961" (Ph.D. dissertation, Rice University, 2001); *Journal of Southern History* (1935–2008).

Kappa Alpha Order

Kappa Alpha Order, a national social fraternity for men, preserves in its basic principles and traditions the southern ideal of character its early members feared might perish with the society that existed in the South prior to the Civil War. Founded in the immediate aftermath of war, on 21 December 1865 at Washington College (now Washington and Lee University) in Lexington, Va., Kappa Alpha Order began to refine its ideals in 1866 at the urging of founding member Samuel Zenas Ammen, later editor of the *Baltimore Sun*, who thought they were too vague and weak. In an effort to establish a strong foundation for the continuing existence of Kappa Alpha Order, the members under the guidance of Ammen began a reformation and elaboration of the order's principles that resulted in a clearly southern-oriented fraternity.

The order's outlook drew on the idea of the southern gentleman. The ideal of a gentleman, wrote Ammen, is "that of the chivalrous warrior of Christ, the knight who loves God and country, honors and protects pure womanhood, practices courtesy and magnanimity of spirit, and prefers self-respect to ill-gotten wealth." Ammen and other early members considered these virtues and graces to be distinctively southern. And they perceived Gen. Robert E. Lee, who was president of the college during the order's formative period (1865–70), to be the perfect expression of the southern gentleman and the spiritual founder of Kappa Alpha Order.

In perpetuating southern traditions of gentlemanly conduct, Kappa Alpha

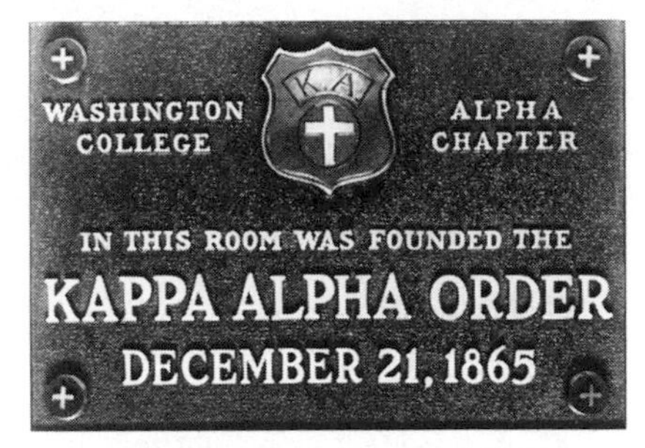

Plaque commemorating the founding of the Kappa Alpha Order, Washington College, Lexington, Va., 1865 (William Garver, Kappa Alpha Order, Lexington, Va.)

Order distinguishes itself from all other college social organizations and appeals to men across the nation. Although at first the order preferred to remain exclusively in the South, today it includes 114 undergraduate chapters on university and college campuses from coast to coast, with about 100,000 members initiated since its founding. On some college campuses Kappa Alpha Order celebrates its southern heritage in spring festivities known as Old South, which includes a week of parties, cookouts, movies, parades, lawn parties, and the annual Old South Ball. The celebration of the Confederate heritage has become muted and less public in recent years.

NEWELL TURNER
New York, New York

Samuel Z. Ammen, *History of the Kappa Alpha Fraternity, 1865–1900* (1900); William K. Doty, *Samuel Zenas Ammen and the Kappa Alpha Order* (1922); Gary T. Scott, *The Kappa Alpha Order, 1865–1897: How It Came to Be Southern* (2009).

Kentucky, University of

Founded in 1865 in Lexington, the state's land-grant agricultural and mechanical college was at first an uneasy component of the Disciples of Christ's Kentucky University. The college was separated in 1878 from the faction-torn university, and in 1882 James K. Patterson, president since 1869, led students and faculty across town to the new campus donated by the city. Patterson persuaded a divided legislature to retain a state property tax for the college.

In 1908, noting the coeducational enrollment of 500, the legislature renamed it State University, Lexington, Ky., thereby initiating a collegiate infrastructure, including arts and science, agriculture, law, three engineering colleges, and the existing Agriculture Experiment Station. His mission accomplished, Patterson resigned in 1910, and Judge Henry Stites Barker left the bench to become president. Renamed the University of Kentucky in 1916, the institution underwent an investigation that demanded drastic reforms and replacement of Barker. In August 1917 Frank LeRond McVey, an experienced outside academic, accepted the presidency though he was warned about Kentucky's "damnedest politics." He retired in 1940 from an academically improved university with 6,000 students, 500 staff, and an annual income of $3 million. The university awarded 791 degrees in that year. Morale was good despite discouragements suffered during the Depression.

After World War II a large influx of veterans put great pressure on the university to provide classroom and living space, but desegregation became the most significant change during the postwar years. Following a successful legal challenge to segregation by Lyman T. Johnson in 1949, UK rejected massive resistance plans and accepted African Americans into the graduate school. By the 1950s, the undergraduate classes were integrated and UK began its gradual evolution into a more diversified campus.

The opening of the Chandler Medical Center in the 1950s accelerated UK's research mission while providing much-needed medical training and care for Kentucky's citizens. In the 1960s, UK experienced rapid enrollment growth and unprecedented expansion of statewide influence. This was due in part to a community college system administered by UK that ultimately provided educational opportunity across the commonwealth.

Otis A. Singletary began his 18-year tenure as president in 1969, through a period of sustained growth despite strict budgetary limitations. The physical expansion program included Commonwealth Stadium, the Agricultural Sciences Center, the Tobacco and Health Research Institute, the Warren Wright Medical Plaza, the College of Nursing, the Morgan Biological Sciences buildings, and the Singletary Center for the Arts. New academic initiatives included the Markey Cancer Center, the Gaines Center for the Humanities, the Maxwell Gluck Equine Research Center, the Institute for Mining and Minerals Research, and the Sanders-Brown Research Center on Aging. President Singletary's development efforts resulted in over $140 million in private funding and the university's first central development office. Booming enrollments matched campus growth. Even after instituting a more restrictive admissions policy, enrollment climbed to a record 46,550 by the end of Singletary's term.

During the administration of Charles T. Wethington Jr., a concerted effort was made to increase research. The legislature's creation of the Research Challenge Trust Fund resulted in the allocation of $110 million for such endeavors. A new School of Public Health, the opening of the Advanced Science and Technology Commercialization Center, and the development of the Coldstream research campus exemplified this effort. Moreover, university faculty secured record funding for research contracts, grants, and gifts. In 1999–2000 the school ranked 14th among land-grant institutions for licensing and patent income. Wethington's hallmark, however, was the new, $58 million William T. Young Library built without state funding. By the end of his term, the UK libraries' book endowment ranked first among public universities.

President since 2001, H. Lee Todd Jr. has led his alma mater to a greater level of national prominence. He launched UK's Top-20 Business Plan, providing quantitative measures for UK to achieve its state-mandated goal of becoming a top-20 public research university. Todd's reforms have led to a 13 percent enrollment growth while increasing student quality. Since 2001, UK's research expenditures have more than doubled from $159.9 million to $337 million in 2008. While pushing for higher standards and expanded research, Todd has reminded Kentuckians that as UK strives for national recognition it must make service to the commonwealth its highest priority.

TERRY L. BIRDWHISTELL
University of Kentucky

ERIC MOYEN
Lee University

CARL CONE
Lexington, Kentucky

James Franklin Hopkins, *The University of Kentucky: Origins and Early Years* (1951); Charles G. Talbert, *The University of Kentucky: The Maturing Years* (1965).

Key, V. O., Jr.

(1908–1963) POLITICAL SCIENTIST.
V. O. (Valdimer Orlando) Key Jr. was born on 11 March 1908 in Austin, Tex., and was one of the early pioneers in the behavioral movement in American political science for his studies of the American electorate, public opinion, and voting behavior.

Key received his undergraduate education at McMurray College and then at the University of Texas at Austin, where he received his B.A. degree in government with high honors in 1929 and his M.A. degree in government in 1930. He spent the next four years studying in the political science department at the University of Chicago, where he earned a doctorate in 1934, with his dissertation titled "The Techniques of Political Graft in the United States." That same year he married another political scientist, Luella Gettys, in Chicago.

Key took his first teaching position in the fall of 1936 at the University of California at Los Angeles (UCLA). While teaching there Key started a study on the initiative and referendum in California. Coauthored with fellow UCLA professor Winston W. Crouch, the study was published in 1939 as *The Initiative and the Referendum in California*.

In 1936 Key left his teaching job at UCLA when he was invited to join the staff of the Social Science Research Council in Chicago. Working for the council and at the behest of the Social Security Administration, he produced a report entitled *The Administration of Grants to States*. In 1937 Key went to work for the National Resources Planning Board in the U.S. Department of the Interior.

In 1938 Key was hired as an assistant professor of political science at Johns Hopkins University. While teaching at Johns Hopkins, Key continued to publish many important articles in academic journals and in 1942 his first textbook, *Politics, Parties, and Pressure Groups*, which examined the relationship between political parties and interest groups. During World War II, he was employed by the Bureau of the Budget on the Committee on Records of War Administration under the direction of Professor Pendleton Herring. The committee's work was published as the *United States at War* in 1946.

In 1946 professor Roscoe Martin persuaded Key to undertake a study of the electoral process in the southern United States at the University of Alabama, which was financed by a $40,000 grant from the Rockefeller Foundation. Key oversaw the southern electoral study while two young scholars, Alexander Heard and Donald Strong, traveled around the various southern states doing the initial research for it. In 1949 all of this research culminated in the writing of Key's seminal book, *Southern Politics in State and Nation*. The work was a systematic study, state by state, of the southern electoral process based on many interviews with prominent southerners and statistical analysis of southern electoral results.

In 1949 Key accepted the Alfred Cowles Chair of American Government at Yale University and became the chairman of the department of political science there. Key's tenure at Yale, between 1949 and 1951, was tumultuous and resulted in his accepting a long-standing offer to become a faculty member in the department of government at Harvard University in 1951.

While teaching at Harvard in 1954 Key published a how-to textbook for students on research techniques entitled *A Primer of Statistics for Political Scientists*. In 1956 he followed up his *Southern Politics in State and Nation* with a study of all of the states north of the Mason-Dixon Line entitled *American State Politics: An Introduction*. Key also acted as the political science editor for the Alfred A. Knopf publishing house and continued to publish many important articles in major academic journals throughout his years at Harvard. He also served as the president of the American Political Science Association in 1958 and 1959.

Hoping to advance his statistical and survey skills, Key spent the 1959–60 academic year at the Survey Research Center at the University of Michigan, and his studies there resulted in another influential work entitled *Public Opinion and American Democracy*. In April of 1963 Key became seriously ill and was hospitalized, dying on 4 October 1963 at Beth Israel hospital in Brookline, Mass. Prior to his death, Key's research focused on how voters rationally choose which candidates to vote for in elections, and the work was posthumously published in 1966 as *The Responsible Electorate*.

ANDREW LUCKER
Case Western Reserve University

Andrew M. Lucker, *V.O. Key Jr.: The Quintessential Political Scientist* (2001).

Kirkland, James H.

(1859–1939) EDUCATOR AND ADMINISTRATOR.

James Hampton Kirkland was the second chancellor of Vanderbilt University, in Nashville, Tenn. He was elected in 1893, at the age of 33, and remained until 1937, thus becoming one of the longest-serving university leaders in U.S. history. During his administration Vanderbilt came to spearhead the "university movement" in the South.

Kirkland was born and raised in Spartanburg, S.C., the youngest of eight children of William Clark, who died in March 1864, and Virginia Lawson Galluchat Kirkland. Kirkland entered Wofford College in his native Spartanburg in 1873. He encountered there two young faculty members who had recently returned from their student days in Europe: Charles Forster Smith and William Malone Baskervill. They ultimately inspired him to embark on a European study tour himself. Having saved enough money as an instructor in Greek at Wofford, Kirkland traveled to Leipzig, Germany, where he registered at the university for the fall 1883 semester. He remained there until 1885, earning a Ph.D. degree in Old English. His mentors at Leipzig included the Greek scholar Georg Curtius and Richard Wülker, professor of English. Kirkland moved on to study in Berlin and eventually traveled to Geneva in the summer of 1885, where he hoped to learn French. But his health broke down, and from then until the following spring, he slowly recovered, traveling also to Italy and visiting Leipzig, Paris, and London.

Upon his return to the United States, Kirkland was appointed professor of Latin at Vanderbilt University, a position he held until his election as chancellor in 1893. Kirkland was ambitious and focused. Already during his student days he had economized his time and money, a quality that would prove to be a great asset to him as chancellor. He understood that a great university education can only be achieved when one bridges the gap between local customs and national standards rather than imposing foreign concepts, emblematic of his sensitivity to the southern cultural context. He also understood that a great university cannot exist without excellent preparatory schools, which is why in 1895 he got actively involved in creating the Association of Colleges and Secondary Schools of the Southern States. Moreover, he was not a proponent of a purely utilitarian educational concept but urged his students to follow their own inclinations rather than picking a school merely for career considerations.

As a practicing Methodist at a university that was denominational at that time, Kirkland fought his toughest battle as a university administrator in the first decade of the 20th century, which ultimately resulted in a break with the Methodist Church in 1914. This "battle of the bishops" came about because the Methodists did not provide sufficient funding, while northern philanthropists such as Andrew Carnegie typically refrained from giving to denominational colleges in the South. When Kirkland had to choose between running a low-profile school under Methodist control or developing Vanderbilt into a foremost research university without the church's support, he decided in favor of the latter, though throughout his life he remained a devout Methodist.

After his break with the church, Kirkland was rather successful in securing funding from the Carnegie and Rockefeller foundations. One of his greatest achievements was the remodeling of the Vanderbilt Medical School in the mid-1920s. His friendship with, among others, Abraham Flexner helped in the undertaking. Both men had vacation houses near Ahmic Lake in Ontario, where they had spent the summers with their families since the 1910s.

In 1895, Kirkland met Mary Henderson of Knoxville, Tenn., who, after a brief courtship, became his wife in November of that year. It was a very happy marriage, judging from the numerous letters they exchanged from the first day of their acquaintance until his death. They had one daughter, Elizabeth, born in February of 1898, who studied at Wellesley College and married the Greek scholar Benjamin Meritt. Among his other interests, Kirkland was a passionate gardener who cultivated iris, the Tennessee state flower.

ANJA BECKER
Vanderbilt University

Anja Becker, *Journal of Southern History* (November 2008); Paul K. Conkin, *Gone with the Ivy: A Biography of Vanderbilt University* (1985); Edwin Mims, *Chancellor Kirkland of Vanderbilt* (1940).

Louisiana State University

The Louisiana State Seminary of Learning, forerunner of Louisiana State University, opened on 2 January 1860 near the central Louisiana village of Pineville and admitted only male students. Its first superintendent was William Tecumseh Sherman, of later Civil War fame, who reluctantly departed for the North after Louisiana's secession in 1861. After several abortive attempts were made to keep the institution open, classes were suspended for the duration in 1863 as federal forces approached during an invasion of the Red River valley. The seminary reopened in 1865 under the superintendency of David French Boyd, a prewar faculty member and ex-Confederate colonel who was to remain at the helm for 17 of the next 21 years.

Despite financial stresses typical of the Reconstruction era, the seminary was beginning to flourish when fire destroyed the main building in October 1869 and brought it close to extinction; Boyd presided over its transfer to Baton Rouge, where the seminary shared space in a large structure with the State Institute for the Deaf, Dumb, and Blind until 1869. In early 1870 the seminary was renamed Louisiana State University. During his long tenure David Boyd presided over two watershed events: the legislatively mandated merger in 1877 with Louisiana A&M College, previously located in New Orleans (becoming Louisiana State University and A&M College in the process); and the move in 1886 to the former grounds of the U.S. Arsenal in Baton Rouge—LSU's first permanent home in 17 years and the springboard for its eventual development into a large modern university.

David Boyd's younger brother, Thomas Duckett Boyd, was elected president in 1896 and his 31-year tenure—longest of any LSU president—was to encompass several further historical landmarks: the admission of women to the student body in 1906; the utilization by the state of oil severance taxes during the 1920s to provide the university with a solid, permanent support base; and the move to the present campus, beginning in 1925 and pointing the way to the university's most spectacular period of growth. During the decade of the 1930s Governor, later Senator, Huey P. Long adopted LSU as a pet project and channeled state funds into construction and faculty expansion at a time when most universities were retrenching; one result was a quadrupling of enrollment before World War II, making LSU at the time the second largest university in the former Confederate states. The university became a major center of southern literary and scholarly activity in the 1930s, focused on the *Southern Review*, which was established by Robert Penn Warren and Cleanth Brooks in 1935.

During the post–World War II era LSU expanded into a statewide system, including eight separate administrative entities in five cities, with the "flagship" campus in Baton Rouge attaining an enrollment of more than 30,000 students before leveling off in the mid-1980s. (Its 1984–85 enrollment was 28,979 students.) Court-ordered desegregation brought the first black graduate student to LSU in 1950, and all levels have been desegregated since the 1960s. Research began to be emphasized by the mid-1960s and by the end of the decade, LSU, long known for research in agriculture and chemistry, won acclaim from the National Science Foundation for other sciences such as physics, astronomy, mathematics, and geology. In 1978 LSU was awarded status as a sea-grant university, matching its land-grant status of long standing, and became a space-grant university in 2005. As of 2009 only 21 universities nationwide held land-, sea-, and space-grant designations.

The 1980s was a difficult decade for LSU. The decline in oil prices, upon which Louisiana's economy was based, caused budget cuts and reductions in the number of programs, and building maintenance was put on hold. Despite these problems, LSU was designated a Research I institution by the Carnegie Foundation in 1987. By the mid-1990s,

Louisiana's financial situation had improved, and cuts from the previous decade began to be restored.

As of 2009–10, LSU had a student population of just over 28,000 from all 50 states and 110 foreign countries and offered over 200 undergraduate and graduate degrees. The university's governing body, the LSU System, was established in 1965 and as of 2009 comprised 10 campuses in five cities, 10 public teaching hospitals in 10 cities, the LSU Agricultural Center, the Hebert Law Center, and the Health Sciences Center. The system's governing body is the 16-member board of supervisors. Since 2007, Dr. John V. Lombardi has served as president of the LSU System, and in 2008 Dr. Michael V. Martin became chancellor of the main campus in Baton Rouge.

JACK FISER
BARRY COWAN
Louisiana State University

Vergil L. Bedsole and Oscar Richard, eds., *Louisiana State University: A Pictorial Record of the First Hundred Years* (1959); Germaine M. Reed, *David French Boyd, Founder of Louisiana State University* (1977); Thomas F. Ruffin, Jo Jackson, and Mary J. Hebert, *Under Stately Oaks: A Pictorial History of LSU* (2002); Louisiana State University, Office of Communications and University Relations, *General Catalog, 2009–10* (2009).

Lovett, Edgar Odell

(1871–1957) UNIVERSITY PRESIDENT. When William Marsh Rice, a wealthy Houston, Tex., merchant, called a group of friends together in 1891 and drafted a charter to establish the William Marsh Rice Institute for the Advancement of Literature, Science, and Art, that document was frustratingly vague. Rice specified that nothing was to be done until he died, but even after his murder on 23 September 1900 it took several years to settle his estate; then the trustees he had chosen had to try to determine exactly what his institute should be. Luckily they decided they should hire a capable educator both to decide the function of the proposed institute and to set it under way. After an elaborate search, they chose a young Princeton professor of astronomy and mathematics, Edgar Odell Lovett, who officially accepted the appointment on 18 January 1908. He proved to be a fortuitous choice, both because of his education, experience, and vision and because of his administrative skills. Blessed with trustees who trusted him and followed his guidance, Lovett transformed the vague founding charter—which hinted of a mere vocational school—into a blueprint for building a research university. Lovett understood what an opportunity the combination of an imprecise charter, a munificent endowment, and cooperative trustees represented: drawing on educational innovations at home and abroad, he could create from this mix a model private university.

Lovett was well equipped for his task. Born in Shreve, Ohio, on 14 April 1871, he graduated in 1890 from Bethany College. After teaching for two years at West Kentucky College, he entered graduate school at the University of Virginia, where he earned a doctorate in astronomy in 1895. Then Lovett traveled to the University of Leipzig in Germany, earning a doctorate in mathematics in 1896. He returned to the United States and spent the spring of 1897 teaching at Johns Hopkins University and the University of Virginia, and after a summer lecturing at the University of Chicago, he joined the faculty of Princeton University in the fall of 1897. He rose quickly through the ranks, becoming professor of mathematics in 1900 and professor and chair of astronomy in 1905. When Lovett accepted the presidency of what was then called the Rice Institute, the trustees asked him to take a fact-finding trip to Europe (which Lovett expanded to a round-the-world trip) inspecting universities, laboratories, and research institutes and interviewing academicians about the newest developments and best practices in universities. Accompanied by a private secretary and his wife, Lovett traveled for nine months, both intriguing the world of scholarship about his plans in Texas and getting an inspired idea of what might be accomplished in the then small city of Houston.

Upon his return, the Rice trustees accepted Lovett's vision: hire first-rate faculty from the best universities in the world, promote research as well as teaching, attract the most capable students possible, and build an architecturally consistent and distinguished campus, with Ralph Adams Cram chosen as architect. Lovett's plans came to fruition in September 1912 when the university opened. He celebrated this event with a major academic convocation on 10–12 October 1912, and before an international audience Lovett spelled out his entire vision: undergraduate and graduate work, an honor system, eventually residential colleges, rigorously high academic standards—"no upper limit" to the university's ambition. Initially the university would focus on science and engineering, but as the city of Houston grew, the university would expand programs in the humanities, the social sciences, and ultimately a range of professional schools. Lovett then spent more than three decades leading the Rice Institute through two world wars and the Great Depression. He never wavered from his basic ideas, and he shaped the institution according to his founding vision.

Lovett was internationalist in perspective and sought to bring scholars and visiting faculty from abroad to Rice, but he also believed that universities must adapt themselves to the needs of their immediate locale. As with many Progressive era educators, Lovett strongly believed that universities should serve their state and nation. The university charged no tuition and was coeducational, but, a creature of its time, it did not accept African American students (barred by the charter) until 1966, although Asian and Hispanic students were admitted almost from the beginning. The university was religiously diverse and unusually free from political or clerical interference. Lovett served as president until March 1946, and he remained involved in university affairs almost until his death on 13 August 1957. Far more than its namesake, Edgar Odell Lovett shaped the character and ethos of the Rice Institute, whose name change to Rice University in 1960 represented the progress made toward fulfilling his expansive founding vision of 1912. Rice is, in everything but name, Lovett's university.

JOHN B. BOLES
Rice University

John B. Boles, *University Builder: Edgar Odell Lovett and the Founding of the Rice Institute* (2007).

Mays, Benjamin Elijah

(1894–1984) CIVIL RIGHTS ACTIVIST, WRITER, AND COLLEGE PRESIDENT. Benjamin Mays was born in South Carolina outside of Rambo (now Epworth), the youngest of eight children to Hezekiah Mays and Louvenia Carter, former slaves turned tenant farmers. Growing up in the rural South at a time when African Americans were disfranchised by law, Benjamin E. Mays experienced firsthand a climate of hate where lynching and race riots were common. In fact, Mays's first memory was the 1898 Phoenix riot where his cousin was murdered by whites.

Early in life Mays had developed an "insatiable desire" for education, but racial inequality and prejudice severely handicapped his opportunity for it. Struggling against his limited education, his family's poverty, and his father's insistence that he remain on the farm, Mays enrolled at the high school of the black South Carolina State College. Four years later, in 1916, Mays graduated at the top of his class and became engaged to fellow student Ellen Harvin.

Mays looked to continue his education at a northern college. Rejected from his top choice, Holderness School in New Hampshire, because of his race, Mays enrolled at Bates College in Lewiston, Maine, where he graduated with honors in 1920. Following graduation, Mays briefly returned home to South Carolina to marry Harvin, who had been teaching home economics at Morris College in Sumter, S.C. Benjamin and Ellen Mays moved to Chicago, where Mays enrolled at the University of Chicago to study divinity. After three semesters at Chicago and a personal invitation from John Hope, president of Morehouse College in Atlanta, Ga., Mays took a teaching position at Morehouse, where he taught algebra and mathematics from 1921 through 1924 and served for a year as acting dean. During his tenure at Morehouse, Mays was ordained in 1921 and served as the pastor of the Shiloh Baptist Church. The experience allowed Mays to grow in his spiritual faith and helped him cope with the loss of his wife, Ellen, who died in 1923.

Shortly after the death of his wife, Mays left Morehouse to continue his graduate work at the University of Chicago, where he earned an M.A. in 1925. Although he considered pursuing his Ph.D., Mays instead returned to South Carolina State to teach English. There he met and married Sadie Gray, and the couple moved to Florida to work with the National Urban League to improve housing, employment, and health care for African Americans. A few years later, in 1928, expecting to be fired for challenging segregation, the Mayses resigned from their jobs and moved to Atlanta, where Benjamin took a position with the National YMCA, working to integrate that organization in the North and the South. In 1930 Mays left the YMCA to conduct a study of black churches with fellow minister Joseph W. Nicholson. The study, which focused on 609 urban congregations and 185 rural congregations, was published in 1933 as *The Negro's Church*.

In 1931 Mays returned to the University of Chicago School of Religion to finish his Ph.D., which he received in 1935. In 1934, as he was finishing his doctoral program, he accepted an appointment as the dean of the School of Religion at the prestigious Howard University in Washington, D.C. In this position Mays traveled overseas to visit world leaders such as Mahatma Gandhi of India. After six years at Howard, Mays accepted an offer to become president of Morehouse College in Atlanta. For 27 years Mays worked tirelessly at Morehouse, collecting for the college $15 million in donations, overseeing the construction of 18 buildings, and conducting weekly Tuesday-morning talks with students. One student whom Mays particularly impressed was Martin Luther King Jr., who often stayed late to discuss theology with him. King and Mays became lifelong friends. In 1968 Mays delivered the eulogy at King's funeral.

In 1967 Mays retired as president of Morehouse College and took the position of chairman for the Atlanta public school board, where he worked to correct racial inequalities in the school system. During this time, in 1970, Mays finished his autobiography, *Born to Rebel*, which has stood as a valuable contribution to the study of American race relations. In the end, the life of Benjamin E. Mays was celebrated and respected. He was awarded with 49 honorary degrees and, in 1984, was inducted into the South Carolina Hall of Fame.

ORVILLE VERNON BURTON
Coastal Carolina University

Lawrence Edward Carter, ed., *Walking Integrity: Benjamin Elijah Mays, Mentor to Martin Luther King Jr.* (1998); Randal M. Jelks, *AME Church Review* (July–September 2002); Benjamin E. Mays, *Born to Rebel: An Autobiography* (2003).

Mercer University

Founded as Mercer Institute in 1833, Mercer University is today a comprehensive institution with campuses in Macon, Atlanta, and Savannah, Ga., and regional academic centers statewide. The school offers degrees in such diverse fields as engineering, law, medicine, pharmacy, theology, music, business, education, and liberal arts. In the 2009–10 academic year, more than 8,000 students attended Mercer, the second largest Baptist-affiliated institution worldwide.

The conception of Mercer University began with the 1828 death of Savannah jeweler and silversmith Josiah Penfield. He bequeathed $2,500 to the Georgia Baptist Convention for educational use, provided that matching funds were raised. At the convention's 1829 meeting, the required amount was pledged immediately. Convention moderator and influential pastor Jesse Mercer contributed $250, the first of his many financial gifts. The convention selected a 450-acre farm just north of Greensboro, Ga., as the site of the school. The area was later named Penfield in honor of the school's initial benefactor.

The convention appointed a committee to found the school, which voted unanimously to name it in Jesse Mercer's honor, and appointed five trustees. On 14 January 1833 Mercer Institute, a manual labor school for young men, opened with 39 students. Billington Sanders was named principal and steward. Sanders and his wife, Cynthia, housed 26 of the original students in their home. In December 1837 the state legislature granted a charter changing the institution to Mercer University and naming Sanders its first president.

In 1841 Mercer graduated its first class of three students. The eponymous Jesse Mercer passed away that September, and though his will indicated substantial gifts of bank stock and other assets for the university, his relatives contested it. The will stood, but the school's financial resources were still limited. In December 1844 the university's trustees voted to abolish the manual labor program, citing its high cost and minimal benefit. At the same time, a crisis emerged in Baptist life: the issue of slavery divided northern and southern Baptists. In response to this growing schism, at the 1845 Georgia Baptist Convention meeting, Mercer's trustees called for a stronger emphasis on theology "so as to meet the present necessities of the Denomination at the South."

As early as 1850 convention delegates debated the possibility of moving the school away from Penfield. The proposals were vetoed, and the school remained in Greene County. During the Civil War, Mercer was the only university in Georgia that remained open, even as many of its students enlisted. During the convention meeting in 1866, it was reported that the trustees were unable to pay the faculty "even so much as a considerable fraction of their salaries."

After the war, Georgia Baptists again pushed for Mercer's removal from Penfield, and the school was moved to Macon in 1871. Law classes were added in 1874, and the campus's landmark administration building was completed. In January 1892 Mercer played the University of Georgia in the state's first football game. Today the school boasts Georgia's only NCAA Division I athletics program at a private university.

Throughout the 20th century, Mercer continued to grow, merging with the Southern School of Pharmacy in 1959 and the Atlanta Baptist College in 1972. Course and degree offerings were also expanded, with the School of Medicine beginning classes in 1982 and the School of Engineering in 1985. The year 1986 saw the merger of Tift College, a Georgia Baptist women's school, with Mercer. The Georgia Baptist College of Nursing joined the Atlanta campus in 2001, and the medical school expanded its four-year program to Savannah in 2008.

In 2005, conflicting views about the purpose of Baptist higher education led the Georgia Baptist Convention and Mercer to end their relationship. A revision of the university's charter officially closed this long chapter in the school's history in 2006. The university continues to embrace its Baptist roots, however, and sponsored the New Baptist Covenant gathering in Atlanta in 2008. Mercer has been honored for its service-learning emphasis, being named to the President's Higher Education Community Service Honor Roll and recognized by the Clinton Global Initiative University. Today Mercer University is expanding into new areas both geographically and programmatically, promoting intellectual freedom, and providing high quality undergraduate, graduate, and professional education.

LAURA BOTTS
Mercer University

C. Ray Brewster, *Branches from Jesse's Tree: Sketches from the Life and Times of Jesse Mercer* (2008); Will D. Campbell, *The Stem of Jesse: The Costs of Community at a 1960s Southern School* (1995); Spright Dowell, *A History of Mercer University, 1833–1953* (1958); Bartow Davis Ragsdale, *Story of Georgia Baptists*, 3 vols. (1932–38).

Millsaps College

Millsaps College was founded in 1890 by the Mississippi Methodist Church after Maj. Reuben Webster Millsaps, a native Mississippian, Confederate veteran, and Harvard Law School graduate, pledged $50,000 to begin a "Christian college for young men." The Methodists of Mississippi pledged a like amount, and the name Millsaps was chosen for the new school—despite protests from the major. The college was located on the outskirts of the state capital, Jackson, where Major Millsaps owned a plantation. The college, separated from the city of some 6,000 residents by fields of cotton and corn, shared the space with Jackson College, a black school that occupied the eastern part of the present campus. When Jackson College (later Jackson State University) moved to its present location closer to downtown Jackson, Major Millsaps purchased that property along with 50 additional acres adjoining the campus. In September 1892 the new college for men opened with modest beginnings: two buildings, 149 students (two-thirds of whom were enrolled in a preparatory school because they were not yet qualified to do college level work), and five professors. Major Millsaps adjusted his plans for a males-only school when two women showed up with the first class. They were not turned away, and Mary Letitia Holloman became the first female graduate in 1902. By the time of his death in 1916, Major Millsaps had contributed over half a million dollars to the school.

The contributions of two other men, Bishop Charles Betts Galloway and Dr. William Belton Murrah, helped secure Major Millsaps's vision of a functional and demanding college experience. Bishop Galloway, who became the first chairman of the Millsaps Board of Trustees, governed the campaign to match Major Millsaps's gift. That end was achieved in 1894. Dr. Murrah was the first president of the college. From the outset these two men demanded an absolute classical curriculum that established a high standard of academic excellence. The purpose of the college, said Dr. Murrah, was to offer "the widest range of investigation and research and the fullest recognition of truth wherever found." Bishop Galloway discouraged denominational indoctrination and cultivated an atmosphere that emphasized hard work and personal freedom. In 1912 Millsaps became the first institution of higher learning in the state of Mississippi to be accredited by the Southern Association of Colleges and Schools. The generosity and insight of Maj. Reuben Millsaps, the weighty support of Bishop Galloway, the benevolent and sensitive attention of the Methodist Church, and the steadfastness of Dr. Murrah gave rise to the premier liberal arts college in Mississippi. The Millsaps Circle of Omicron Delta Kappa, a national leadership honor society, was founded in 1926, the 16th circle in the nation. In 1933, written and oral departmental comprehensive examinations were instituted. The Heritage Program, an interdisciplinary humanities program that integrated history, literature, religion, philosophy, and the fine arts into a single elective course of study, began in 1968. In 1979 the Else School of Management was established to offer full-time students and part-time students from business, government, and other professions the opportunity to acquire a quality undergraduate business degree and an M.B.A.

Mississippi's first adult degree program was established in 1982 and became a national model. In 1989 Millsaps became the first Mississippi college or university to earn a Phi Beta Kappa academic honorary chapter. A Millsaps alumnus, Dr. Otis A. Singletary, president emeritus of the University of Kentucky and the national president of Phi Beta Kappa Society, performed the installation ceremony. The college is routinely cited in national publications as an admired and prestigious contributor of quality academic quests. Millsaps is one of 40 institutions featured in Loren Pope's *Colleges That Change Lives*.

A valuable contribution that Millsaps College has made to the community, state, region, nation, and world over time is leadership training. Throughout its history Millsaps has been dedicated to the idea that liberal arts education is education for leadership. During the emotional and strained times of the civil rights struggle of the 1950s and 1960s, Millsaps took a positive stand for racial tolerance and justice. The college came under hostile attack from extremist members in Jackson and other parts of Mississippi for its moderate position. In 1965 Millsaps became the first all-white institution of higher learning in Mississippi to integrate voluntarily. These actions prompted Pulitzer Prize-winning editor Hodding Carter Jr. of the *Greenville Delta Democrat-Times* to call Millsaps "perhaps the most courageous institution in the nation," adding that "it is a candle burning in the darkness." This pursuit of knowledge continues to be demonstrated through the achievements and honors of Millsaps professors and graduates. Faculty members have published analyses of the Great Depression, poetry, and the first revisionist state history textbook in the United States. The school's notable graduates include Gen. Louis H. Wilson, Congressional Medal winner and commandant of the U.S. Marine Corps; National Book Award winner Ellen Gilchrist; Emmy Award-winning CBS News correspondent Randall Pinkston; and David Herbert Donald, distinguished Harvard historian and Pulitzer Prize-winning Lincoln scholar.

The prescient and unflagging leadership of George M. Harmon, president from 1978 to 2000, brought tremendous growth and change to the school. The picturesque campus welcomed a new science building, new athletic facilities, new and updated dormitories, expanded library and business school, and renovated Student Union. With an enrollment of approximately 1,200 undergraduate students, Millsaps College continues to make significant contributions to community service and lifelong learning.

CHARLES GRAVES SALLIS
Brandon, Mississippi

Millsaps College, *Are You One?* (2009), *Millsaps Timeline* (2006), *Self-Study Report, 1980–1981* (1981).

Mississippi, University of

Located at Oxford in the north-central section of Mississippi, the University of Mississippi was chartered in 1844 and opened in 1848. As Mississippi's only state-supported institution of higher learning, the university offered both undergraduate liberal arts degrees and professional degrees. Early presidents included Augustus Baldwin Longstreet (1849–56) and Frederick A. P. Barnard (1856–1861), who initiated pioneering scientific research and teaching programs. Even after specialized colleges and universities were established in the state, the University of Mississippi continued to offer a comprehensive program, including graduate and undergraduate degrees. The university encompasses the main campus at Oxford, a school of medicine, which opened in 1903 in Oxford and moved to Jackson in 1955, and branch campuses at Tupelo and Southaven. In 1861 the entire student body enlisted in the Confederate army. The university suspended operation during the Civil War but reopened in the fall of 1865, becoming coeducational in 1882 and adding its first woman faculty member, Sarah Isom, in 1885, who was also the first female faculty member at a coeducational institution of higher education in the South.

The University of Mississippi experienced two significant crises during its history. In 1928 Gov. Theodore G. Bilbo urged the legislature to relocate the state university from Oxford to Jackson, the state capital. His plans called for a gigantic increase in the state appropriation (from $1 million to $25 million), a restructuring of the university's curriculum, and sweeping personnel changes. Bilbo's effort to enlarge and relocate the university was unsuccessful, and the university lost its accreditation for two years. Recent scholarship has concluded that Bilbo's motives were much less political and punitive than formerly believed. A second major crisis occurred in 1962 when James Howard Meredith became the first black student to enroll at the university. Gov. Ross Barnett led the state's white power structure in resisting Meredith's admission and delayed his enrollment for nearly 18 months by a series of legal maneuvers. When the courts at last ordered his admission, legal proceedings gave way to violence. Throughout the night of 31 September 1962 rioters surged

The Lyceum, the oldest building on the Oxford campus of the University of Mississippi, built in 1848 (James G. Thomas Jr., photographer, University of Mississippi, Oxford)

across the university campus in a vain effort to prevent his enrollment. James Meredith did enroll and graduated from the university in August 1963.

The University of Mississippi is known universally as "Ole Miss," a name that became associated with the university in 1896 when students began publishing an annual, which was styled *The Ole Miss*. Within less than a decade alumni, students, and the media routinely referred to the university as Ole Miss, although it has never been formally or officially adopted. The university's traditional curriculum and degree programs are supplemented by several institutes and centers that offer Ole Miss students unique opportunities to enrich their collegiate experience and to broaden their intellectual horizons. Among them are the African American studies program; the Center for the Study of Southern Culture, which includes the Southern Foodways Alliance and the Blues Archive; the Sarah Isom Center for Women and Gender Studies; the William Winter Institute for Racial Reconciliation; the Trent Lott Leadership Institute; the Sally McDonnell Barksdale Honors College, one of America's premier honors colleges; and the Overby Center for Southern Journalism and Politics, funded by the Freedom Forum and named for Charles L. Overby, a former editor of the student newspaper.

In the early years of the 21st century Ole Miss is a beacon in the global village. At the Croft Institute for International Studies students from around the world are enrolled in East Asian, Europe, or Latin American studies and accelerated language programs in Chinese, Japanese, French, German, Spanish, Italian, Portuguese, and Russian.

Under the leadership of Robert C. Khayat, who served as chancellor of the university from 1995 to 2009, Ole Miss became a nationally recognized institution of higher learning with students from all 50 states and 65 foreign nations. Ole Miss is no longer a small, southern regional institution mired in the past, but a modern, multipurpose university renowned for developing leaders in a wide variety of fields. In addition to his commitment to making the University of Mississippi a great American public university, Khayat was also determined to preserve the grace and beauty of the Ole Miss campus. The classic oaks, the green swards, and majestic buildings that adorn the campus have been revered by generations of students and alumni. One of the most recent adornments to the campus is the Gertrude Ford Center for the Performing Arts, where the first presidential debate between senators John McCain and Barack Obama was held on 26 September 2008.

In July 2009 Dr. Dan Jones, former vice chancellor of the University Medical Center, assumed the office of chancellor. Total enrollment on the Oxford campus, the medical center in Jackson, and the branch campuses in the fall of 2009 was 18,344 students.

DAVID SANSING
University of Mississippi

Allen Cabaniss, *The University of Mississippi: Its First Hundred Years* (1971); David G. Sansing, *The University of Mississippi: A Sesquicentennial History* (1999); Gerald W. Walton, *The University of Mississippi: A Pictorial History* (2008).

Mississippi Freedom Schools

During the summer of 1964 the Council of Federated Organizations (COFO), a loose alliance of representatives from the major civil rights organizations, sponsored more than 40 "freedom schools" in the state of Mississippi. Staffed primarily by 200 white volunteers recruited on northern college campuses and reaching over 2,000 black children and adults, from preschoolers to the elderly, the schools formed one component of the "Mississippi Summer Project," an effort to promote black political mobilization through education and community organizing.

Coordinated by historian Staughton Lynd, the freedom schools combined academic instruction with activities calculated to promote psychological liberation and political awareness among local blacks. Enrollment ranged from a low of 10 to a high of several hundred students. Under the leadership of a black couple from Detroit, the freedom schools in Hattiesburg—the "Mecca of the Freedom School World"—registered over 600 students on the first day. In most schools academic instruction in subjects such as African American history, American government, French, and typing took place in the morning, followed by an afternoon break to escape the stifling heat. Activities resumed in the late afternoon and often extended into evening sessions that included political meetings attended by adults. The teaching methods were student-centered with desks arranged in a circle to avoid making the teacher an authority figure whose views must not be challenged.

The curriculum reflected the Student Nonviolent Coordinating Committee's (SNCC) emphasis on self-discovery and democratic participation, as well as the pedagogical ideas of John Dewey. Taking the daily lives of students as a starting point, teachers asked open-ended questions that would encourage students to name and value their own experiences. Adopting techniques common to progressive pedagogy, including practices previously employed at the Highlander Folk School and in training sessions for civil rights activists, freedom school classes typically featured singing, role-playing, dramatic compositions, and performance. Up to a point the teaching might be described as "nondirective," with students frequently being asked, "How do you feel about that?" However, the curriculum itself was highly purposeful in its psychological objectives and political aims. As one writer observed, the schools' object was not "to cram a prescribed amount of factual material into young minds" but rather to provide those present with a "first look into new worlds" that would "someday if not immediately" lead them to engagement with books and the world of ideas. Linking the classroom to the community meant challenging the existing educational system, encouraging school boycotts, and most immediately, mobilizing local support for the Mississippi Freedom Democratic Party—the primary reason for the 1964 summer project.

Operating in a climate of white hostility and constant danger of arrest or violent attack, freedom school teachers, who were unmoved by charges of indoctrination, saw no inconsistency in linking education to political action. Their work was rooted in an underlying optimism about the possibility of using education to foster interracial brotherhood and a corresponding belief that social change was best achieved through the mechanisms of electoral politics. As Len Holt would observe in 1965, the arrival of the freedom school teachers was "the rainbow sign that the Mississippi Summer Project would at least begin, and that the deaths [of civil rights workers] couldn't stop it."

As an independent undertaking the freedom schools ended with the departure of northern volunteers in the autumn of 1964. The spirit of idealism and pedagogical innovation associated with the freedom schools lived on, however, most notably in the activities of the short-lived and politically controversial Head Start Centers of the Child Development Group of Mississippi, which opened in the Mississippi Delta in 1965.

The historical significance of the freedom schools lies partly in their contribution to the political work of SNCC, partly in their adaptation of free-form progressive pedagogy to the repressive racial environment of the Deep South, and partly in the example they provided for the psychological empowerment of severely impoverished black children and their families. In that last respect the freedom schools may be said to cast the longest historical shadow. Writing in the autumn of 1964, historian Howard Zinn described the freedom schools as "an experiment that cannot be assessed in the usual terms of 'success' and 'failure.'" Operating without attendance records, grades, or examinations, and staffed by teachers chosen for their intelligence, enthusiasm, and social conscience without concern for conventional certification requirements, the schools led Zinn to call for a "forthright [national] declaration that the educational process cherishes equality, justice, compassion, and world brotherhood." Viewed in this light the Mississippi freedom schools stand out in retrospect as the most explicitly political manifestation of an educational debate that extends from the writings of A. S. Neil and John Holt in the 1960s to the "No Child Left Behind" legislation of the Bush presidency.

CLARENCE L. MOHR
University of South Alabama

John Dittmer, *Local People: The Struggle for Civil Rights in Mississippi* (1994); Kathy Emery, Sylvia Braselmann, and Linda Reid Gold, eds., www.educationanddemocracy.org/ED_FSC.html; Len Holt, *The Summer That Didn't End: The Story of the Mississippi Civil Rights Project of 1964* (1965; 1992); Elizabeth Sutherland Martinez, ed., *Letters from Mississippi* (2002); Doug McAdam, *Freedom Summer* (1988); Daniel Perlstein, *History of Education Quarterly* (Autumn 1990); Howard Zinn, *The Nation* (23 November 1964).

Mississippi State University

Established on paper in 1878 under the land-grant federal program designed to aid colleges devoted to agriculture and the mechanical arts, the Agricultural and Mechanical College of the State of Mississippi opened its doors in 1880. Established on acreage adjacent to the town of Starkville in northeast-central Mississippi, the new institution immediately took on a unique character.

The first president was Civil War general Stephen D. Lee, who still owns the record for the most years served (1880–99). His background led him to establish a military tradition that played a key role in the college's formative years, though eventually it faded, replaced by ROTC chapters. The first few years, male students who came from rural backgrounds dominated the student body, though some females enrolled, anticipating the ever-growing proportion of women students, who now outnumber the men. Students from foreign countries first attended the university in 1920. Once the unfortunate barriers of segregation came down with the enrollment of Richard Holmes in 1965, African American students have been enrolling in the university in continually increasing numbers. Students from countries around the world have likewise discovered the university. A number of sororities, fraternities, and other student organizations increase student opportunities to get to know each other. The university's social tapestry has come a long way from the beginning.

Representing the family atmosphere is the Alumni Association, originating in 1885. From that beginning and throughout its history, the association has served, and been supported by, its graduates, who number, as of the university's 125th anniversary in 2003, a grand total of more than 100,000. The Alumni Association remains one of the most active organizations on campus.

The college's reputation as the "People's College" originated from its embracing many students from low-income, rural, and small-town homes. The establishment of the Mississippi Agricultural and Forestry Experiment Station and the Mississippi Cooperative Extension gave the college an agricultural flavor that underscored the background of students' lives. Headquartered on the campus, the experiment station established regional stations to conduct agricultural research, and the extension service eventually had a presence in all of Mississippi's 82 counties to share information with farmers. Scientific farming became commonplace in the state thanks to the A&M college. Advances in the state's crops, dairy operations, and forestry have benefited from interaction with the university, and these beneficial relationships continue. Meanwhile the school has gone through two name changes, becoming Mississippi State College in 1932 and Mississippi State University in 1958. The university's agricultural research in such areas as food production and nutrition, forestry, and freshwater fish development has benefited Mississippi, the United States, and countries around the world.

The role of mechanical arts has had a similar history, growing from meager beginnings in education and research into a major power in the university's curriculum and carrying its technological advances into the world community. From research for U.S. military defense systems to innovations in the field of energy, the various engineering departments at the university and the work of talented students and superior faculty have attracted millions of dollars in grants. The Center for Advanced Vehicular Systems, for example, has gained national attention. In addition to the agriculture and engineering departments that have benefited Mississippi, the nation, and beyond, the university has established a College of Veterinary Medicine, a School of Architecture, and a College of Arts and Sciences, which today enjoys one of the largest enrollments of any of the university's colleges.

A notable achievement in recent years has been the expansion of the library, which did not occupy a separate building of its own until 1950. Library technology and major donations of historical collections have brought attention to the library from across the country. It contains many significant journalistic, civil rights, and political collections, which include the papers of Hodding Carter Jr., William "Bill" Minor, Senator John C. Stennis, Representatives G. V. "Sonny" Montgomery, David R. Bowen, Mike Espy, and Marsha Blackburn, as well as Mississippi state legislators, including important civil rights legislators. A major addition to these collections came in 2008 when the university and the library received the largest existing collection of papers of Civil War general and postwar president Ulysses S. Grant. The papers, comprised of some 15,000 linear feet of files, plus artifacts and hundreds of books, contain published and to-be-published items, plus thousands of unpublished items that will keep researchers busy for years.

The campus includes 160 structures, scattered across 4,200 acres. Campus enrollment that began with 354 students in 1880 has increased to a record 18,601 (2009), keeping MSU where it has been for several years—the largest university in the state of Mississippi, the people's university.

MICHAEL B. BALLARD
Mississippi State University

J. Wendell Bailey, *The M Book of Athletics: Mississippi A&M*, 2 vols. (1930); Michael B. Ballard, *Maroon and White: Mississippi State University, 1878–2003* (2008); John K. Bettersworth, *People's University: The Centennial History of Mississippi State* (1980); *Mississippi State University Catalogs* (1880–); *Reflector* (campus newspaper, 1898–).

National Humanities Center

In an essay on "Education and the Southern Potential" (1966) sociologist Rupert B. Vance observed, "Beyond the level of graduate training, a new pattern in American intellectual life has been the emergence of centers for advanced study, such as the Institute for Advanced Study at Princeton and the Center for Advanced Study in the Behavioral Sciences at Stanford. There is no comparable institution in the South and none in sight." In 1976, however, the American Academy of Arts and Sciences in Boston, after considering more than 15 potential sites across the United States, accepted the invitation of the Triangle Universities Center for Advanced Studies, Inc. (TUCASI), a consortium of Duke University, the University of North Carolina at Chapel Hill, and North Carolina State University, to locate the newly conceived National Humanities Center in the Research Triangle Park of North Carolina. TUCASI raised funds from North Carolina corporations and foundations for a 30,000-square-foot building, and it secured library support and partial administrative funding for the new center from the three universities. Among the North Carolinians who formed TUCASI and helped establish the National Humanities Center were John Caldwell, Archie K. Davis, William Friday, C. Hugh Holman, and Terry Sanford.

The center opened in 1978 and each academic year admits as fellows 40 scholars in the humanities to pursue individual research and to exchange ideas in daily conversation, lectures, interdisciplinary seminars, and conferences. A class of fellows includes young scholars (three to 10 years beyond the doctorate), scholars in mid-career, and distinguished senior scholars; fellows have private studies and are given fellowship stipends, library assistance, and manuscript typing. Most fellows are chosen in an open competition, for which the center receives applications from all parts of the United States and also from other nations. Scholars of southern history and culture who have been fellows of the center include Cleanth Brooks, Fitzhugh Brundage, Dan Carter, Richard Beale Davis, Laura Edwards, John Hope Franklin, Eugene Genovese, Glenda Gilmore, Dewey Grantham, Randall Jelks, Daniel Littlefield, Elizabeth Payne, John Shelton Reed, Anne Firor Scott, Stephanie Shaw, Tim Tyson, and Bertram Wyatt-Brown. The center also publishes a quarterly newsletter and from 1980 through 1996 produced *Soundings*, a weekly radio program on the humanities. The center also sponsors education programs intended to strengthen the teaching of the humanities in secondary and higher education. A 45-member national board of trustees composed of leaders from education, the professions, and public life oversees the center, and a director is in charge of its administration. Directors have been Charles Frankel (1977–79), William J. Bennett (1979–81), Charles Blitzer (1983–88), W. Robert Connor (1989–2002), and Geoffrey Harpham (2003–). Support for the center has come from private foundations, corporations, the National Endowment for the Humanities and other federal agencies, the Triangle Universities, the state of North Carolina, individual donors, and its own endowment fund. The center's stated purpose is "to encourage scholarship in the humanities and to enhance the influence of the humanities in the United States."

KENT MULLIKIN
National Humanities Center

http://nationalhumanitiescenter.org/

Newcomb, Josephine

(1816–1901) PHILANTHROPIST.
Josephine Louise Newcomb was the founder of H. Sophie Newcomb Memorial College, the first degree-granting college for women established within a previously all-male major university. Born in Baltimore, Md., 31 October 1816, she was the daughter of Alexander Le Monnier, a prominent Baltimore businessman. Orphaned in 1831, Josephine Louise moved to New Orleans to live with her only sister. While summering in Louisville, Ky., she met and married Warren Newcomb, a successful businessman who lived in New Orleans most of the summer because his wholesale business was located there.

In 1866 Warren Newcomb died, leaving to his wife and a daughter, Harriott Sophie, born to the couple in 1855, an estate valued at between $500,000 and $850,000. Under her own direction Josephine Newcomb increased her inheritance to over $4 million by her death in 1901. In 1870, at age 15, Harriott Sophie died of diphtheria. Devastated by the loss of her child, Newcomb began to search for a suitable memorial to her daughter. An Episcopalian, she donated generously to the support of her church. A native southerner, she gave to numerous causes to assist the recovery of the war-torn South. She contributed to the library of Washington and Lee University. She founded a school for sewing girls and supported a Confederate orphans' home, both in Charleston, as well as a school for deaf children in New York. In 1886, at the behest of Ida Richardson, a wealthy New Orleans woman, and Col. William Preston

Johnson, president of the recently established Tulane University of Louisiana, Newcomb agreed to found a college for women as a memorial to her daughter.

Although coeducational colleges and independent women's colleges existed, the H. Sophie Newcomb Memorial College was a unique experiment, the design of which influenced Barnard at Columbia, Radcliffe at Harvard, and the Women's College of Western Reserve. Part of, and yet separate from, Tulane University, the college had a separate administration and faculty, empowered to formulate its own academic policy. The college's stated aim, to offer a liberal arts education for women equal to that available for men, represented a departure in the history of female education in the South. In an age when higher education for women was viewed with indifference, Josephine Louise Newcomb initiated significant change in the patterns of women's education.

Tulane University dissolved Newcomb as a separate entity in 2006, in its reorganization in the aftermath of Hurricane Katrina. The heirs of Josephine Newcomb have mounted legal challenges to this plan, hoping to keep Newcomb a degree-granting college within the university.

SYLVIA R. FREY
Tulane University

Brandt V. B. Dixon, *A Brief History of H. Sophie Newcomb Memorial College, 1887–1919* (1928); John P. Dyer, *Tulane: The Biography of a University, 1834–1965* (1966).

New Orleans Public Schools

The division of New Orleans, in 1836, into three municipalities allowed leaders to develop a public school system without the rancor that had hindered other efforts. The Second Municipality, comprised of American immigrants imbued with the notion that democracy and an acquisitive political economy needed free public schools, started what would become the public school system in New Orleans. Joshua Baldwin led the effort and turned to some of that era's leading educators for assistance. Henry Barnard of Connecticut and Horace Mann of Massachusetts, for example, provided ideas on school design, curriculum, and personnel. The first school opened on 3 January 1842 with 26 students. Enrollment in the elementary and grammar schools increased each year, and school leaders opened a high school for boys in 1844 and one for girls in 1845. The early success in the Second Municipality influenced leaders in the First and Third Municipalities to start school programs.

The Civil War and Reconstruction periods brought additional changes to public education. Gen. Benjamin Butler used the Union occupation to unify the city's school districts and centralize control under a single superintendent. Unlike the top-down changes mandated by military leaders, change came to African American education from the bottom up, a pattern that persisted well into the 20th century. African Americans, like others throughout the South, often sought and gained literacy from Union soldiers, and their quest for education obtained greater structure and support under the control of the Freedmen's Bureau. Congressional Reconstruction brought additional changes, including the creation of a board of directors with control of all public education in one system. Reconstruction school leaders, and those that helped create the New South, believed that educational opportunity should mean something different for white females or for African Americans than for white males, and Reconstruction efforts to integrate the schools did not succeed.

In the ensuing decades school leaders responded to demands to expand educational access for white women and African Americans. At the same time, they worked to advance the overall quality of education. School leaders, for example, eventually embraced the high school movement of the early 20th century and built state-of-the-art high schools and adopted progressive curriculum standards for them. And two of the high schools were set aside for white females. African American students did not receive exemplary school facilities, but they, too, saw improved opportunities, including the opening of the first high school since Reconstruction. Other evidence of growth between 1900 and 1940 included additional evening schools, industrial schools, and extracurricular activities. On the eve of America's entrance into World War II, however, an extensive survey of the schools revealed that alongside pockets of excellence troubling problems existed, chief among them repeated student failures and high drop-out rates.

In the post–World War II years, school officials encountered the additional problem of increased demands by African Americans for educational equity within the racially segregated system and the challenge of implementing the *Brown v. Board of Education* decision. Changing residential patterns caused underutilization of school facilities in some areas and inadequate facilities in others, creating additional problems for school leaders like Superintendent Lionel Bourgeois, who attempted, in the 1940s, to close and consolidate some schools to reflect changing demographics and the judicial and political landscape as well. Often lurching from one crisis to another throughout the 1950s, school leaders were ill-prepared to successfully manage one of the public school system's biggest challenges: mandated school desegregation.

On 14 November 1960 four six-year old girls entered the formerly all-white McDonogh No. 19 and William Frantz schools. This second attempt to integrate New Orleans public schools did not end in failure as had the previous attempt during Reconstruction. Still, state and city leaders kept integration to a minimum through devices such as pupil placement exams and integrating one grade a year. These strategies proved less successful after 1965, thus quickening the pace of school integration and, eventually, the near complete withdrawal of white students. School officials then had to contend less with issues of race than with issues of class and urbanization.

In 2005 the devastation caused by Hurricane Katrina changed the educational landscape once again and, ironically, produced a fragmented school system similar to what had existed before the Civil War. How the various systems will fare in providing a quality education for all the children in New Orleans is not yet apparent. These new school leaders might draw inspiration from the knowledge that previous school officials encountered challenges as well, and at times solved them.

DONALD E. DEVORE
University of South Alabama

James D. Anderson, *The Education of Blacks in the South, 1860–1935* (1988); Liva Baker, *The Second Battle of New Orleans: The Hundred-Year Struggle to Integrate the Schools* (1996); Lawrence A. Cremin, *American Education: The Metropolitan Experience, 1876–1980* (1988); Donald E. DeVore and Joseph Logsdon, *Crescent City Schools: Public Education in New Orleans, 1841–1991* (1991).

North Carolina, University of

The University of North Carolina at Chapel Hill was authorized by the state constitution of 1776 and chartered by the General Assembly in 1789. The cornerstone of Old East Building, today the oldest state-university building in America, was laid on 12 October 1793. The first student arrived on 12 February 1795, and the first class was graduated in 1798. The university survived sectarian and political attacks, public apathy, and persistent underfunding. It began a slow emergence from obscurity as it strengthened its faculty and liberalized its curriculum. In time the natural sciences gained equal status with classical studies. And the constitutional reforms of 1835 and the success attained by many alumni in state and federal government helped to create a more favorable political climate for the university, accompanied by a greater emphasis on education for public service. Three 18th-century and five 19th-century buildings, still standing, met campus needs before 1861, when it was second only to Yale in the number of students enrolled. Although the university remained open through the Civil War, it was forced by general economic ruin and political bitterness to close from 1870 to 1875.

First to open a summer "normal school" for teachers (1877), the university introduced regular courses in education as early as 1885. Other guideposts to the future included the beginning of medical and pharmaceutical studies (1879), the first regular legislative appropriation (1881), the announcement of graduate studies leading to degrees (1876), organization of scientific laboratories and discoveries of major significance in industrial chemistry (1880–1900), administrative integration of the semi-independent School of Law (1894), and admission of the first women students (1897).

The period before World War I was marked by significant gains in academic standards and productive scholarship of the faculty, reorganization and orderly expansion of library services, and increased emphasis on the applied and social sciences. During the 1920s the state successfully met the needs of the university through enlargement of its physical plant. The university press was incorporated in 1922, the Institute for

Research in Social Science was organized in 1924, and the Southern Historical Collection was established in 1930. From 1930 to 1949 the university was led by Frank P. Graham, a former history professor (1915–30) who gained national recognition as an educator, statesman, and social activist. Expansion was halted by the Depression and by World War II but since 1947 has continued apace. A Division of Health Affairs was created that year and has resulted in greatly expanded schools of medicine, pharmacy, and public health, while new schools of dentistry and nursing and the North Carolina Memorial Hospital were established. A planetarium and astronomical observatory, a museum of art, a new library building, enlarged chemistry laboratories, and an indoor sports arena were added in the middle and latter portions of the 20th century. The university celebrated its bicentennial in 1993 with a yearlong observance highlighted by President Bill Clinton's University Day address. In 2000, North Carolina voters passed the multibillion-dollar Higher Education Bond Referendum, resulting in almost 50 building projects totaling over $500 million on the university's campus. It became the first major public university to announce plans guaranteeing low-income students a debt-free education in 2003, with the establishment of the "Carolina Covenant" program. As of fall 2009 its full-time enrollment was 28,916 students.

WILLIAM S. POWELL
JASON E. TOMBERLIN
University of North Carolina at Chapel Hill

R. D. W. Connor, ed., *Documentary History of UNC, 1776–1799*, 2 vols. (1953); William S. Powell, *First State University: A Pictorial History of the University of North Carolina* (1972); Phillips Russell, *These Old Stone Walls* (1972); William D. Snider, *Light on the Hill: A History of the University of North Carolina at Chapel Hill*; University of North Carolina at Chapel Hill, *The First Century of the First State University*, http://docsouth.unc.edu/unc; Louis Round Wilson, *University of North Carolina, 1900–1930* (1957).

Odum, Howard W.

(1884–1954) SOCIOLOGIST.

Howard Washington Odum (born in Georgia in 1884, died in North Carolina in 1954) was the South's best-known social scientist in the first half of the 20th century. In more than 20 books and 200 articles he assessed the level of the region's economic and cultural achievements, explored the forces that inhibited progress, and exhorted his fellow southerners to use their material, intellectual, and spiritual resources to rebuild their region. Odum's work was well known beyond academic circles, and he became an important symbol of the movement to use science and scientific open-mindedness as tools to unlock the region's potential and inspire a new sectional self-confidence.

Odum was educated during the height of the Progressive Era. He received his bachelor's degree in 1904 from Emory University, a master's degree in classics from the University of Mississippi in 1906, and Ph.D. degrees from Clark University (psychology) in 1909 and Columbia University (sociology) in 1910. As a young man he absorbed the spirit of the great

Progressive-Era teachers and orators who believed that science could reveal the secrets of social phenomena and pave the way for major leaps forward in the human condition. Odum brought this spirit to the University of Georgia, where he was on the faculty in the School of Education from 1913 to 1919. During this period he campaigned actively to improve rural education in Georgia and began a lifelong effort to encourage diversification of southern agriculture by developing the dairy industry (and later received national awards as a breeder of Jersey cows). In 1919 Odum became the dean of Emory College, but his vision of Emory as an instrument of social services clashed with the philosophy of the school's conservative chancellor. When the University of North Carolina offered Odum a post as chair of the sociology department and dean of the School of Public Welfare, he moved to Chapel Hill, where he remained for the duration of a remarkably productive career.

At Chapel Hill Odum concentrated on using the resources of social science to study the South's problems and to suggest solutions. Toward these ends he founded the *Journal of Social Forces* and the Institute for Research in Social Science. Between 1924 and 1954 Odum persuaded northern philanthropists to support studies of regional economic conditions, labor relations, race problems, welfare programs, and penal reforms. The most notable of the many products of this work was a massive statistical portrait of the South that Odum published in 1936 under the title *Southern Regions of the United States.* This book was used extensively by contemporary journalists and political leaders in campaigns for regional self-improvement.

Over the course of his career Odum also made major contributions to preserving the cultural history of southern blacks. He published collections of black folksongs in 1911 (in the *Journal of American Folklore*) and in 1925 and 1926 (in book form, with Guy B. Johnson), and between 1928 and 1931 he wrote a trilogy of books based on the life of a wandering black laborer.

Odum also participated directly in many social service programs. He helped lead three penal-reform movements in North Carolina, served as assistant director of President Hoover's Commission on Recent Social Trends, was a director of the North Carolina Welfare Commission, and helped found the Southern Regional Council. During the last two decades of his life Odum worked to develop a theory of regionalism that would encourage holistic analysis of all aspects of the South's condition and to devise means to ease the transition to a racially integrated society.

WAYNE D. BRAZIL
Hastings College of the Law

Paul Challen, *A Sociological Analysis of Southern Regionalism: The Contributions of Howard W. Odum* (1993); Katherine Jocher, Guy B. Johnson, George L. Simpson, and Rupert B. Vance, eds., *Folk, Region, and Society: Selected Papers of Howard W. Odum* (1964); Howard W. Odum, *An American Epoch* (1930), *American Regionalism* (1938), *Cold Blue Moon* (1931), *Rainbow Round My Shoulder* (1928), *Southern Regions of the United States* (1936), *The Way of the South* (1947), *Wings on My Feet* (1929); Lynn Moss Sanders, *Howard W. Odum's Folklore Odyssey: Transformation to Tolerance through African American Folk Studies* (2003).

One-room Schools

From colonial beginnings until early in the 20th century, one-room schools played an important role in southern education. These tiny schools that dotted the hills and valleys were, collectively, a salvation to a region recovering from the Civil War and, later, the Great Depression. In the 19th century, these early schools were located within walking distance of a few families who could pay the teacher. By the early 20th century, little had changed except that the teacher was paid by county and state governments. In 1900 there were more than 7,000 one-room schools in Georgia. Kentucky had 7,067 one-room schools in operation in the 1918–19 school year, and 4,551 one-room schools dotted the "hills and hollers" of West Virginia during the 1930–31 school year.

Between the end of the Civil War and 1930, rural southerners often cleared less than $100 per year for their backbreaking farmwork. To them, education was a luxury they could not afford. Though disinterested in many national economic issues, they bitterly opposed local property taxation to support education. Consequently many barns and most county jails were in better repair and more comfortable then the dusty, wasp-infested little schools where thousands of barefoot children studied without benefit of maps, globes, or other educational aids. A "trustee" administered the one-room in his district. A large percentage of these trustees were illiterate and were subordinate to thousands of state officials who also could not read or write. The trustee system was highly politicized, often corrupt, and simply did not exist as part of a more comprehensive educational program.

What these schools lacked in modern conveniences, they overcame with students motivated enough to endure hardships in order to learn and teachers willing to work under difficult circumstances to achieve progress. These forgotten heroes and heroines did not, according to one former teacher, "give poverty a chance to impede their love of learning." One-room school teachers received little recognition and few tangible rewards. Before World War II, many teachers received a Standard Normal Certification for a two-year, terminal-degree college program. Others became certified teachers by taking a qualifying examination that was developed annually by the state's Department of Education and administered by the county superintendent. The one-room school teacher was also nurse, counselor, janitor, playground director, and lunchroom supervisor. In spite of the hard work and long hours, the pay was very low. Some became teachers because economic and social conditions blocked other professional opportunities. "I don't think I chose to be a teacher," one former teacher reflected. "Economic conditions really made me become a teacher. The Great

Depression was four years old—there was no money anyplace. I had wanted to be a lawyer or an interpreter in the diplomatic corps."

To maintain appropriate school conduct, some teachers had a lengthy catalog of rules, which specified a punishment for each infraction. A teacher could maintain credibility as a disciplinarian if students knew they would be punished when they misbehaved; and parents were usually supportive of the teacher. Other teachers did not control their classes by punitive measures but induced their students to like them and to behave well to please the teacher.

The typical school day began with the Pledge of Allegiance and the Lord's Prayer. The routine of school life was occasionally interrupted by special social activities. Daytime events were student celebrations of holidays or scholastic competitions. Evening activities such as pie suppers were community socials that also provided operating funds for the school.

Transportation to and from school, by today's standards, ranked somewhere between inconvenient and impossible. Both students and teachers usually walked, and it was not uncommon for children to face a three-mile trek each way. Some teachers rode a horse or pony; others came in a horse-drawn buggy. By the 1930s some were driving cars to school. The automobile, however, did not greatly facilitate travel because of the poor roads and the isolation of the schools. There were no "snow days"; the teacher and students dressed warmly and walked through the snow. For the most part, transportation difficulties were accepted without complaint, and the hike to school often provided a time for unsupervised adventure and recreation for young people.

The school building was of wooden-frame construction. It typically had a front door that faced the road or path, three windows on each side of the building, and a painted blackboard across the back. Outside there was often a well, a coalhouse, and two outdoor toilets. Two long recitation benches faced the teacher's desk and blackboard. Because paper tablets were prohibitively expensive, students spent much of the day at the blackboard or using small slates at their desks. Rows of desks or benches, a "warm-morning" stove, and a water bucket completed the list of basic equipment. Teachers were often quite ingenious in equipping their classrooms. For example, a teacher who had no timepiece in her classroom cut notches in the doorstep on the east side of the building. When the sun hit the first notch, it was time to begin school. The second mark signaled recess, and the third indicated lunchtime; notches on a west window marked the afternoon hours. Another teacher cut up a calendar to help first graders learn to put the numbers in order. In many instances, the teachers spent much of their meager earnings on their school and students. "By the time I got through dressing those children and buying my materials, I never had anything left," remembered one former teacher. "I might as well have been staying at home. All I was getting was experience." Successful one-room teachers usually made good use of the skills and interests of older students. The older boys and girls often helped younger children with their lessons. Advanced students also conducted drills for lower-grade classes and supervised play activities. For many former one-room school students, the additional responsibility was a good learning experience.

By the mid-1900s, the one-room school was considered old-fashioned and ineffective by most educators, yet many were still operational. In the mid-1960s dozens of the War on Poverty's Appalachian Volunteers renovated eastern Kentucky's rural one-room schoolhouses. As late as the 1980s, a few one-room schools still operated in remote areas of the South.

Almost without exception, former one-room schoolteachers report happy memories of their teaching days and personal pride in their accomplishments. Although teaching eight different grades each day was hard, the teacher did not feel that the students learned less. Some of these former teachers even say that the old ways were preferable, claiming that one-room school education produced students with more creativity and greater self-reliance. Today, many one-room schools survive as museums on college campuses; others are maintained by local historical societies. They stand as monuments to thousands of "immortal teachers" and to millions of successful people who "learned their lessons and learned them right" in the one-room schools.

JAMES M. GIFFORD
Jesse Stuart Foundation

James D. Anderson: *The Education of Blacks in the South, 1860–1935* (1988); William A. Link, *A Hard Country and a Lonely Place: Schooling, Society, and Reform in Rural Virginia, 1870–1920* (1986).

Phillips, U. B.

(1877–1934) HISTORIAN.

Ulrich Bonnell Phillips has recently been described by historian Eugene D. Genovese as perhaps the greatest historian America ever produced. Author of six major works and 55 factual articles, Phillips almost single-handedly directed the social and economic history of the antebellum South away from pietistic antiquarianism to many of the major concerns of contemporary historians. An indefatigable discoverer and user of primary sources, especially plantation records, Phillips was undoubtedly the preeminent historian of the South in the first half of the 20th century. Still, his pervasive, if paternalistic, racism and his insistence that the plantation system was the social/economic system of the antebellum South caused his work to be virtually unread until his recent rediscovery.

Phillips was born 4 November 1877 in the small upland Georgia town of LaGrange. He received both his B.A. and M.A. from the University of Georgia and then went to Columbia, where he took his doctorate in 1902 under William Dunning. Phillips taught for short periods at both the University of Wisconsin and Tulane University and from 1911 to 1929 at the University of Michigan. On 21 January 1934, four years after leaving Michigan for Yale, Phillips died.

Phillips had four major ideas about the antebellum South: (1) its environment was an essential contributing factor to its development, and Frederick Jackson Turner's hypothesis of the frontier worked perfectly for the South of prewar years; (2) the region's political economy was a combination of geography, economics, politics, social structure, race, and ideology and dominated all aspects of southern life; (3) the key to antebellum political economy was the plantation, which was not a mere economic institution but an entire way of life; and, finally, (4) the plantation was primarily a method of social control of a "stupid," genetically inferior race and the necessary first step in what Phillips unabashedly regarded as the continuing, essential task of preserving the South as "a white man's country."

Phillips incorporated Turner's regionalism into his 1902 dissertation, "Georgia and States Rights," ostensibly a history of Georgia political thought. During the early 1900s he further developed the frontier thesis in numerous articles in major journals, the 13-volume *The South in the Building of the Nation*, and his introduction to the documentary collection *Plantation and Frontier*. Phillips's first attempt to view political economy as an interrelated system was his 1908 study of the development of the railroad industry, *A History of Transportation in the Eastern Cotton Belt to 1860*, which showed how the needs of the planter class created the type of railroads built in the South. Phillips then concentrated largely upon a systematic study of the plantation economy and produced two classic and highly influential works, *American Negro Slavery* (1918) and *Life and Labor in the Old South* (1929). In the late 1920s Phillips related his ideas of black social control to political history in such essays as "The Central Theme of Southern History" and was preparing a book on the subject at the time of his death.

MARK SMITH
University of Texas at Austin

Merton Dillon, *Ulrich Bonnell Phillips: Historian of the Old South* (1985); Richard Hofstadter, *Journal of Negro History* (April 1944); John Herbert Roper, *U. B. Phillips: A Southern Mind* (1984).

Piney Woods School

Dr. Laurence C. Jones founded the Piney Woods School in 1909 as a place to educate African American children during the height of segregation in Mississippi. Jones held the school's first classes in rural Rankin County about 21 miles south of Jackson. Today Piney Woods encompasses a 2,000-acre campus, including a 500-acre working farm.

Born in Missouri and schooled in Iowa, Jones moved to the South after developing a correspondence with Booker T. Washington about the industrial education provided at Tuskegee Institute. After teaching for a year in Jackson, Jones traveled to rural Rankin County, intent on founding an industrial school for African American children in the area. The early days of the school almost immediately became legend. As Jones recounted in his 1922 autobiography, he agreed to teach a "half-grown, barefoot boy to read." Jones held the first day of lessons on a

Story hour at the Piney Woods School in Mississippi, c. 1940s (Ann Rayburn Paper Americana Collection, University of Mississippi Library, Oxford)

log underneath a cedar tree, opening the day with the hymn, "Praise God from Whom All Blessings Flow." A symbolic re-creation of the cedar tree and log can be found on the school grounds today.

Over the next 20 years, Jones built the foundation of Piney Woods, beginning with the reappropriation of a rundown sheep shed on land donated by a local African American farmer known as Uncle Ed. Keeping with the principles of Washington's industrial education initiative at Tuskegee, the Piney Woods students learned trades as well as academics. The first building served as both a classroom and a dormitory for students, who came from all over Mississippi. One of only four historically black boarding schools in the United States, Piney Woods today continues the tradition of industrial education. In addition to the working farm, the campus has a printing shop, an automotive shop, and a daycare facility. Most students receive financial assistance, primarily in the form of a work/study program. Many of the school's day-to-day services depend on the labor of its students, including groundskeeping, cooking, assisting in the classroom, and maintenance.

Piney Woods serves as one of the best examples of the industrial school model and notions of middle-class uplift among African Americans in the South during segregation. Jones received the majority of his initial funding from northern philanthropists, particularly educators he met while in school in Iowa. Other notable contributors include the Maytag family, the Rosenwald and Jeanes Teachers' funds, Dale Carnegie, and the Kraft family. Like many industrial educators of his era, Jones courted northern white philanthropists by presenting Piney Woods as a way to create constructive and useful African American citizens for the New South.

Piney Woods served as a model for other educators and leaders throughout the world. Jones and his teachers traveled to countries in need of rural education programs such as India, Mexico, and China to teach local educators how to develop a school based on the Piney Woods model. In 1929 the school opened to blind students and served as the only educational opportunity for the blind African American community in Mississippi until the state opened a separate facility in 1950.

Although the school has no formal religious affiliation, Jones based the curriculum and philosophy of Piney Woods on strong Christian principles. The motto "head, heart, hands" embodies the tenets of academic, Christian, and industrial education that continue to guide the school today.

JENNIFER NARDONE
University of Mississippi

Beth Day, *The Little Professor of Piney Woods: The Story of Laurence Jones* (1955); Alferdteen Harrison, ed., *Piney Woods School: An Oral History* (1983); Laurence C. Jones, *Piney Woods and Its Story* (1922); Piney Woods School, *The Piney Woods Country Life School* (Pamphlet, 1988); Piney Woods School Web site, www.pineywoods.org.

Poteat, William Louis

(1856–1938) WAKE FOREST COLLEGE PRESIDENT AND INTELLECTUAL.

William Louis Poteat embodied Progressive Era leadership in the American South. He was a teacher of science, a college president, a Baptist liberal, an ardent Prohibitionist, a participant in myriad reform campaigns, and an advocate of freedom of thought and inquiry.

His parents, James and Julia Poteat, owned a large plantation and an enslaved labor force near Yanceyville in Caswell County, N.C. William, nicknamed "Bud Loulie" as a youngster and "Dr. Billy" later in life, initially enjoyed a privileged childhood, but the end of the Civil War led the family to become hotel keepers in Yanceyville, with tenants working the plantation. William left the turmoil of Reconstruction when he enrolled at the North Carolina Baptist State Convention's Wake Forest College in 1872. The institution was a natural fit, as his father had held positions of local and regional importance in the denomination.

William Poteat made Wake Forest College his life's work. He graduated in 1877, became a tutor of languages there a year later, and was named a science professor in 1880. He largely taught himself the scientific knowledge he needed, though summer stints at the University of Berlin and the Marine Biological Laboratory at Woods Hole, Mass., gave impetus to his relatively early adoption of laboratory work as a teaching tool. He dabbled in observation-based biology research with modest professional success, but he earned regional renown as a teacher of the subject.

By the close of the 1880s Poteat had reconciled his Baptist religious upbringing with his growing knowledge of evolutionary biology, largely by deciding that science and religion operated in the separate spheres of reason and faith. Though his published views on the topic caused mild controversy at the turn of the century, the trustees of Wake Forest chose him as president of the college in 1905, a position he held until June 1927.

Just as the study of biology influenced his religious views, so too did his reading of the so-called higher criticism, which historicized biblical writings. Poteat moved away from a literalist understanding of the Scriptures and toward emphasizing the duty of Christians to reform society. Although he did not fully adopt Social Gospel theology, Poteat did push fellow faithful in the South to mix their traditional evangelism with work for social improvement.

Even as he guided the development of Wake Forest College during his presidency, Poteat found time to take leading roles in the North Carolina Teachers' Assembly, the Southern Educational Association, the North Carolina Anti-Saloon League, the Southern Baptist Convention's Social Service Commission, the Southern Sociological Congress, the North Carolina Conference for Social Service, the North Carolina Society for Mental Hygiene, and the Commission on Interracial Cooperation.

Poteat's greatest intellectual legacy, however, is his willingness to defend the teaching of evolution during the 1920s. Facing intense criticism from supporters of conservative and fundamentalist Christianity, Poteat made a dramatic address at the December 1922 meeting of the Baptist State Convention. He forthrightly defended his religious faith and survived calls for his resignation as Wake Forest's president. Those calls continued through the mid-1920s, but Poteat nonetheless helped rally opposition to proposed state legislation that would have banned the teaching of evolution. In 1925 the University of North Carolina, led by Harry W. Chase, selected Poteat to deliver the McNair Lectures at the Chapel Hill campus. He put forth his trademark ideas about the compatibility of religion and science, again raising a statewide furor. The controversy continued when the young University of North Carolina Press published the three talks as *Can a Man Be a Christian To-day?*

Poteat delayed his retirement as president until he felt that freedom of intellectual inquiry was reasonably secure at Wake Forest College, and during his retirement he remained highly visible as a teacher, speaker, and Prohibitionist. In 1936 the Baptist State Convention chose him as its president, a fitting capstone to his long and varied career.

RANDAL L. HALL
Journal of Southern History
Rice University

George McLeod Bryan, "The Educational, Religious, and Social Thought of William Louis Poteat as Expressed in His Writings, Including Unpublished Notes and Addresses" (M.A. thesis, Wake Forest College, 1944); Randal L. Hall, *William Louis Poteat: A Leader of the Progressive-Era South* (2000); Suzanne Cameron Linder, *William Louis Poteat: Prophet of Progress* (1966).

Rainey, Homer

(1896–1985) UNIVERSITY PRESIDENT. Renowned higher-education leader, innovator, and administrator, Homer Price Rainey was born on 19 January

1896 in the town of Clarksville in northeast Texas. Rainey attended the private, Baptist-run Austin College in Sherman, Tex., where he majored in history, receiving his B.A. in 1919. After graduation, he went on to the University of Chicago, which at the time was in the vanguard of the education reform impulse then sweeping the country, especially in the North and Mideast regions. Rainey earned both his master's and doctoral degrees in education from the university, graduating with a Ph.D. in 1924. He was especially interested in institutional and curriculum finance, his dissertation topic, which he published in 1929. *Public School Finance* became one of the most respected books on the topic in the pre–World War II era.

After graduating from the University of Chicago, Rainey went on to teach education courses at the University of Oregon while simultaneously engaged in an extensive research project for the university concerning the state's funding of its public school system. In 1927, at the age of 30, he became president of Franklin College of Indiana—the youngest college president in the country at the time. Rainey remained at Franklin until 1931, when Bucknell University in Pennsylvania invited him to become that institution's president. Rainey accepted and remained at Bucknell until 1935 when Eleanor Roosevelt asked him to become the director of the American Youth Commission of the American Council on Education. This particular position proved especially pivotal in Rainey's career because it exposed him to New Deal liberalism, which he heartily embraced, particularly as the ethos applied to education reform.

Rainey gained national recognition during his tenure as director of the American Youth Commission, and while serving in that position he was asked by J. R. Parten, chairman of the University of Texas Board of Regents, to become UT's next president. Rainey accepted and took office in 1939. Despite significant accomplishments, from the moment he became UT's president, Rainey found himself in often bitter, acrimonious debate with the regents concerning the direction he wanted to take the university. Rainey and the regents were at ideological odds on a variety of issues ranging from tenure to faculty funding for research projects, to what should be taught in the classroom. After several years of such interference, Rainey had had enough, and in October 1944 he assembled his faculty and publicly spoke of the regents' constant harassment and opposition to his vision for the university. Unfortunately, the airing of his grievances ultimately cost Rainey his job; on 1 November 1944 the regents fired Rainey. His ousting made national headlines, creating one of the most protracted, bitter, and divisive controversies in the history of higher education in Texas, if not the nation. Despite ongoing student protests, overwhelming faculty support, and even letters from Eleanor Roosevelt and other New Dealers, the regents refused to reinstate Rainey. From the moment the news of Rainey's firing hit the national headlines, he became, for academics and progressives alike throughout the country, a symbol of both academic freedom and the survival of New Deal liberalism, especially in the South.

Indeed, so determined was Rainey to see liberalism prevail in Texas that he ran for governor in 1946 as a New Dealer and surprised many, especially the old guard, by forcing a primary run-off election. During that campaign, the conservatives, led by the former regents, accused Rainey of all manner of "radicalism," ranging from being a "Negro-lover" for allegedly advocating the integration of Texas public schools, most notably the University of Texas, to being in favor of a state income tax to supporting gay rights. Although Rainey was definitely a New Dealer and favored policies that would curtail the power of the state's plutocrats, he was not as progressive on the social issues he was accused of supporting. The more conservative Beauford Jester soundly defeated Rainey in the run-off. Nonetheless, Rainey's gubernatorial bid did have an impact; it marked the first time a candidate for a major state office put together a coalition of labor, minorities, and progressives.

In 1947 Rainey became president of Stephens College, an all-women's institution in Columbia, Mo. He left Stephens in the early 1950s, accepting a professorship in education at the University of Colorado where he retired from teaching in 1964. The university named him professor emeritus the following year. At student and faculty request, Rainey returned to UT in 1968 to give a speech not only about his career, but perhaps more important, about the state of higher education at that time in the United States, which had witnessed some of the most tumultuous times in the nation's history. Rainey's speech earned him a standing ovation and the accolades of both students and faculty. Rainey had returned to UT "the conquering hero" since 30 years earlier he had fought over many of the same issues that were currently affecting the university, its students, and faculty. The University of Texas somewhat atoned for its firing of Homer Price Rainey when in 1980 they renamed the school of music in his honor as well putting his bronze bust along the walkway to the main library alongside other UT notables.

JOHN MORETTA
Houston Community College

Alice Cox, "The Rainey Affair: A History of the Academic Freedom Controversy at the University of Texas, 1938–1946" (Ph.D. dissertation, University of Denver, 1970); Ronnie Dugger, *Our Invaded Universities: Form, Reform, and New Starts* (1974); George N. Green, *The Establishment in Texas Politics* (1979); Homer Rainey, *Public School Finance* (1929).

Randolph-Macon College

Randolph-Macon College began with the desire of the Virginia Conference of the Methodist Episcopal Church to have a clergy educated in the liberal arts and the desire of the leading citizens of Mecklenburg County to have a college. Fund-raising began in 1825, and a charter was acquired from the Virginia legislature on 3 February 1830, making Randolph-Macon the oldest chartered Methodist college in the country. The namesakes of the college, John Randolph and Nathaniel Macon, both well-known politicians, had no connection with the institution and were not Methodists. Instead, the choice of Randolph, a Virginian, and Macon, a North Carolinian, was designed to promote recruitment in both states and to make it clear the school was not strictly denominational. The college was erected west of Boydton, Va., near the North Carolina border, then at the center of the conference, and classes began in 1832.

At first the curriculum of Randolph-Macon followed the unique elective system of the University of Virginia, but the first formal president, Stephen Olin, persuaded the faculty in 1834 to adopt the rigid curriculum common to colleges at the time. In 1859 Randolph-Macon reverted to the elective system. The college achieved financial stability under President William A. Smith (1846–66). Smith taught a formal course defending slavery, and the college at one time owned two slaves. He and board of trustees chairman John Early, Methodist ministers both, were principals in the formation of the Methodist Episcopal Church, South.

The Civil War cut off the supply of students and forced the brief closing of the school. More damaging was the investment of much of the endowment in Confederate and southern municipal bonds. The war wrecked the regional transportation system and devastated the segment of the population that supported the school and sent sons to it. The board of trustees, pushed by the college president, Thomas Johnson, moved the college in 1868 to Ashland, Va., which had the virtue of being on a railroad line connecting the college with the Baltimore Conference of the Methodists, which included Maryland and northern Virginia.

The college remained small, with 100 to 200 students, but pioneered educational reforms in the teaching of English literature (1870) and physical education (1886). Under the leadership of the college president William Waugh Smith, the board of trustees established Randolph-Macon Woman's College (now Randolph College) in Lynchburg, Va., and three preparatory schools (at Bedford, Front Royal, and Danville, Va.), thus forming the Randolph-Macon system. The academies at Front Royal and at Bedford were boys' schools, while the Danville Institute was a school for females. W. W. Smith left the Randolph-Macon presidency to head the Woman's College, whose founding was primarily a response to his proposal to admit women to the college in Ashland. The system schools became increasingly autonomous until the dissolution of the system in the 1950s made the Randolph-Macon Woman's College and the Randolph-Macon Academy in Front Royal completely independent institutions, the Bedford and Danville schools having closed in the 1930s.

Modernizing the college in Ashland took more money than its rural, Methodist supporters could afford, and there was an appeal to northern financiers, especially Andrew Carnegie. When the Woman's College met the exacting standards of his pension fund (the first school in the South to do so), the money came with a stipulation that meant the board would cease to be entirely Methodist. This stipulation raised the question, voiced by alumnus James

Cannon, of whether the board or the Virginia Conference would own and control the system. After a protracted and debilitating quarrel, the Virginia courts supported the trustees, but the moral victory was with the church. Very little changed at the college until after World War II.

Many of the subsequent improvements at the college reflected the growing prosperity of Virginia. In the postwar presidency of J. Earl Moreland, the college expanded its student body from 300 in the 1930s to 900, with concomitant increases in buildings, curricula, and faculty. In 1964 the college decided to admit students regardless of race. Facing severe financial difficulties during the presidency of Luther W. White III, the college became coeducational in 1971, admitting its first 50 women residential students, although the college had admitted young women from the local community as day students since the 1890s and granted them the same degrees received by the male students. The college's curricular offerings, its student body, and its physical presence continued to expand in the 1980s and 1990s. The campus covers 110 acres with more than 60 buildings. The college celebrated the 175th anniversary of its founding in 2005, and inaugurated its 15th president, Robert Lindgren, in 2006. Modest enrollment growth over the next 10 to 20 years to potentially 1,500 students is envisioned, retaining small class sizes and close relationships between students and faculty.

The student body of 1,201 in the 2008–9 academic year was drawn primarily from Virginia (two-thirds of the enrollment), with the Mid-Atlantic states contributing most of the rest. The college resolutely emphasizes the liberal arts and sciences. Its graduates frequently move into the professions and business, with 65 percent enrolling in graduate or professional programs within five years of graduation.

JAMES EDWARD SCANLON
LAURIE PRESTON
Randolph-Macon College

Richard Irby, *History of Randolph-Macon College, Virginia* (1898); James Edward Scanlon, *Randolph-Macon College: A Southern History* (1983); Randolph-Macon College Archives, McGraw-Page Library; Randolph-Macon College, www.rmc.edu.

Reed, Sarah Towles

(1882–1978) EDUCATOR.

Sarah Towles Reed, a tireless advocate for academic freedom and economic justice, taught in the New Orleans public schools for nearly 50 years. Her political commitments to women, blacks, and labor made her a frequent target of authorities, who viewed the southern liberal as a subversive force.

Early in her career, Reed joined women teachers' fight for equal pay for equal work and in 1925 helped found a teachers' association to further their cause. By the time of the Great Depression, with teachers experiencing salary reductions and sporadic paychecks, Reed realized that teachers' interests could best be served by joining forces with other workers. In 1934 she took the courageous lead in persuading teachers to join the ranks of organized labor and form the Classroom Teachers' Federation (CTF), Local 353, of the American Federation of Teachers, AFT.

With the organization of the union, Reed and her colleagues entered a period of substantial progress for educational reform, including a strong tenure law for teachers and repeal of a rule prohibiting marriage for women teachers.

The New Deal and the beginnings of the civil rights movement in the 1930s propelled Reed into liberal racial activism. Although she did not support integration publicly, she did promote interracial cooperation among teachers, assisting black teachers in organizing their own union, campaigning for equal pay for all teachers regardless of race and calling for improvements in the chronically underfunded and ill-equipped segregated black schools of New Orleans.

The Cold War offered an opportunity for her detractors to rid themselves of the perennial troublemaker and discredit the union. In 1948 the Orleans Parish School Board charged Reed with "not stressing the American way of life as superior in every respect to Communism or other 'isms.'" Reed insisted on a public hearing. Confronted by overwhelming support for the teacher from her students and colleagues, the board had little choice but to exonerate her. Reed's victory may well have shielded other left-leaning teachers in New Orleans from similar charges.

After retiring from teaching in 1951, Reed continued to lobby the state legislature in support of bills providing retirement benefits and higher salaries for teachers. She died in 1978, at the age of 96. In 1988 the Orleans Parish School Board dedicated the Sarah Towles Reed High School in her honor.

LESLIE PARR
Loyola University New Orleans

Donald E. DeVore and Joseph Logsdon, *Crescent City Schools: Public Education in New Orleans, 1841–1991* (1991); Leslie Gale Parr, *A Will of Her Own: Sarah Towles Reed and the Pursuit of Democracy in Southern Public Education* (1998).

Rice University

Rice University, a private, independent, coeducational university located in Houston, Tex., opened its doors to students in 1912 as the William Marsh Rice Institute. It was chartered in 1891 by former Houston merchant William Marsh Rice with a $200,000 interest-bearing note payable to the institute upon his death. Rice was murdered in his New York City apartment on 23 September 1900, in a plot concocted by a lawyer who had written a fake will giving him most of Rice's money. After a spectacular trial and the settlement of the estate in 1904, approximately $3 million was available to the institute as a separate capital fund, added to the original endowment that had grown to almost $3.3 million. At the time the institute opened in 1912, the endowment stood at approximately $9 million, allowing all students to attend without paying tuition—a privilege not ended until 1965.

The board of trustees in Houston appointed mathematician and astronomer

Edgar Odell Lovett of Princeton University as president in 1907 with directions to plan the new institution. After worldwide travel, discussions, and faculty recruitment, Lovett oversaw the opening in September 1912 marked by an international convocation of scholars and an ambitious vision for the new university. The entering class of 77 students had an international faculty of 12 (Julian Huxley was the first professor of biology), one major academic building (with an elaborate plan for additional buildings by the Boston architectural firm of Cram, Goodhue, and Ferguson), and a large endowment. The honor code, a cherished Rice tradition, was adopted by the student body in 1916. By 1924 the entering freshman class was limited to approximately 450, and undergraduate enrollment has been carefully controlled ever since. In 2007 it stood at 2,690. The graduate enrollment has grown gradually to 2,144, with a full-time faculty now numbering 611 (and 146 part-time faculty). The endowment currently stands at $4.7 billion. The undergraduate student body is among the nation's most select, with average SAT scores over 1,400 and one of the highest percentages of National Merit Scholars. On-campus students live in one of 11 residential colleges, and there are no fraternities or sororities.

Under Lovett's direction the Rice Institute first developed major strength in the sciences and engineering, though distinguished instruction was offered from the beginning in the humanities and architecture. The curriculum broadened and the faculty increased greatly in size after World War II under the administration of physicist William V. Houston (1946–60), as the name change in 1960 to Rice University acknowledged. Moral, social, and economic imperatives drove the university—successfully, as it turned out—to seek legal authority in 1964 to break the founder's charter in two regards: to admit students without regard to race and to charge (a modest) tuition. Further expansion, especially in the humanities and social sciences, came in the 1960s and 1970s during the administrations of chemists Kenneth S. Pitzer (1961–68) and Norman Hackerman (1970–85). In 1961 the National Aeronautics and Space Administration located the Manned Space Flight Center (now Johnson Space Center) on land made available by Rice, and in 1962 the university established the nation's first department of space science. The *Journal of Southern History* has been published at Rice since 1959; *Studies in English Literature* was founded at Rice in 1961; and the *Papers of Jefferson Davis* project has been headquartered at Rice since 1963. The Shepherd School of Music and the Jesse H. Jones Graduate School of Management were added in 1973 and 1976, respectively.

In 1985 theologian George E. Rupp, dean of Harvard Divinity School, became Rice's fifth president. The 1990 Economic Summit of Industrialized Nations was held on the Rice campus, and the James A. Baker Institute for Public Policy was established in 1993. Malcolm Gillis, dean of the faculty of arts and sciences at Duke University, was appointed Rice's sixth president in 1993. He encouraged the further internationalization of the university and successfully completed a major fund-raising campaign. In 2004 David Leebron, dean of the Columbia University Law School, became Rice's seventh president. After a broad "conversation" with the Rice community, he announced a "Vision for the Second Century" that, among other goals, calls for a 30 percent increase in undergraduate enrollment and the launching of a $1 billion capital campaign. The university, in planning for its centennial in 2012, will acknowledge the continuing relevance of the founding president's vision and seek to articulate similarly ambitious goals for the future.

JOHN B. BOLES
Rice University

John B. Boles, *University Builder: Edgar Odell Lovett and the Founding of the Rice Institute* (2007), *A University So Conceived: A Brief History of Rice* (2006); Fredericka Meiners, *A History of Rice University: The Institute Years, 1907–1963* (1982); Sylvia Stallings Morris, ed., *William Marsh Rice and His Institute* (1972).

School of Organic Education

The School of Organic Education, in Fairhope, Ala., was founded in 1907. It is the oldest progressive school in the South and the second oldest in the nation. Marietta Louise Pierce Johnson, the school's founder and longtime director, moved to Fairhope in 1902. Born in St. Paul, Minn., on 8 October 1864, Johnson was an experienced teacher when she arrived with her husband and two sons. She had recently come under the influence of the writings of Nathan Oppenheim and John Dewey, both of whom had written extensively on the "new education," an approach to teaching and learning at odds with conventional beliefs about how children should be educated.

Fairhope attracted Johnson because it, too, was at odds with conventional beliefs. Designed in 1894 by members of the Populist Party in Iowa, it was led by Ernest B. Gaston, a young journalist and reformer. Its founding settlers came from several states (none southern) to a site they chose on the eastern shore of Alabama's Mobile Bay. They arrived in November 1894 with the conviction, as their constitution proclaimed, "that the economic conditions under which we now live and labor are unnatural and unjust, in violation of natural rights, at war with the nobler impulses of humanity, and opposed to its highest development."

The community they intended to establish was based on the theories of the political economist Henry George. His magnum opus, *Progress and Poverty* (1879), defined the "great enigma" of his time as the association of poverty with progress. To break the nexus between the two, George proposed to make land common property and to couple that reform with a modest form of municipal socialism in which "natural monopolies" would be communally owned and operated.

The Fairhopers, as the colonists called themselves, declared their purpose to be "to establish and conduct a model community or colony, free from all forms of private monopoly, and to secure to its members therein, equality of opportunity, the full reward of individual efforts, and the benefits of co-

Marietta Louise Pierce Johnson's School of Organic Education, Fairhope, Ala., 1913. The renowned educator John Dewey took this photo when he visited the school and subsequently included it in his book Schools of Tomorrow, *in which he devotes a chapter to Johnson's experimental school. (Photo courtesy Marietta Johnson Museum, Fairhope, Ala.)*

operation in matters of general concern." This "cooperative individualism," a term coined by Gaston, was to be achieved by communal ownership of the land, with farm, business, and home sites rented to lessees for an annual rental payment based on the value of the land. In return for the rental payments, the colony would pay the county and state taxes levied on its lessees. Before the era of income taxes this "single tax" on land values was an approximation of the Georgist program. The colony also adopted democratic practices advanced for the time, including female suffrage and office holding.

The Fairhopers thought of themselves as radicals—radicals in the sense that they would get to the root of the economic problems besetting their country. Johnson likewise thought of herself as a radical. She would get to the root of the educational system that she believed warped the growth of America's school children. Fairhope appealed to her because of the spirit of radical reform that infused its residents.

A strong supporter of the colony, Johnson nonetheless believed that the creation of a just and fulfilling society required more than the economic and political changes the colony existed to demonstrate. "No great economic reform," she said in a 1910 speech, "can be effected by people who have been trained during the growing up years to believe that success is in 'passing' at school and 'making money' in . . . life." It was in schools, she believed, that "false concepts" of justice were formed. Her school, unlike the conventional ones, would provide a daily experience free from "false concepts," an experience that nurtured a way of life consistent with democratic values.

From a tiny beginning of six students in a small cottage, the Organic School grew rapidly. By 1913, located on a 10-acre campus provided rent-free by the colony, its enrollment had swollen to 150, including two-thirds of the children living in Fairhope as well as children of several winter visitors from the north, attracted by both the school and the colony. By that time Johnson had won well-to-do friends and supporters in Greenwich, Conn. May Lanier, the most influential of them, tried unsuccessfully to persuade Johnson to move her school to Greenwich. She did succeed in establishing a Greenwich summer school, which Johnson conducted, training teachers and others in organic education. The Greenwich supporters also set up a foundation to raise money for the Fairhope school. It remained a generous contributor through the 1920s, vital to the school's continued existence.

Intrigued by the school's growing publicity, John Dewey decided to visit it in late 1913. His report on what he observed glowed with praise. In expanded form it was included in his book *Schools of Tomorrow* (1915), the most influential work on progressive education published by that time. The Fairhope school, he wrote, was a "decided success." It "demonstrated that it is possible for children to lead the same natural lives in school that they lead in good homes outside the school hours; to progress bodily, mentally, and morally in school without factitious pressure, rewards, examinations, grades, or promotions, while they acquire sufficient control of the conventional tools of learning and study of books—reading, writing, and figuring—to be able to use them independently." Natural, un-self-conscious growth, which Dewey believed was the main element, emerged from Johnson's commitment to structuring a curriculum addressed to what had meaning for children. In today's parlance, her school was "child-centered," not "results oriented."

Dewey concluded his report on the Fairhope school by stressing the revolutionary implications of organic education. Teaching the "whole individual," as both he and Marietta Johnson advocated, had the power to remake the social order. "The democracy which proclaims equality of opportunity as its ideal," he wrote, "requires an education in which learning and social application, ideas and practice, work and recognition of the meaning of what is done, are united from the beginning and for all." The Fairhope school showed "how the ideal of equality of opportunity for all is to be transmuted into reality."

Dewey's rave review was widely circulated by Johnson and her Greenwich supporters. It was a prominent factor in the growth of the school (its enrollment exceeded 200 during the 1920s); Johnson's reputation as a national figure in the progressive education movement; and the drawing power of Fairhope as a reform community attractive to northern progressives and intellectuals. "The Fairhope Idea in Education," as Johnson called the movement that sprang from her school, spread across the nation through her many lectures, her leadership role in the National Progressive Education Association, and in the nine satellite schools around the country she helped to create to demonstrate organic education.

By the 1920s the school had established its place as a major center of cultural and intellectual life in Fairhope. It had also fixed the curriculum that was to distinguish it. Children entered the school at age four for two years in kindergarten and stayed for another 12 years to graduation from the high school. It was open free of charge to all white children in Fairhope. (Both Johnson and E. B. Gaston knew segregation was contrary to their principles but, reckoning that the school and the colony, were they racially integrated, would be closed down by the surrounding white community, went along with the prevailing laws and mores.) Johnson wanted hers to be a private school, free from restrictions of which she did not approve. But she also wished it to be an example of what a public school might be, so she charged no tuition or other fees. A small number of tuition-paying boarding students was enrolled. The financial support necessary to survival came from the Greenwich foundation and other donors. The budget was always small and teachers' salaries low.

A typical school day included time in the wood shop, the arts and crafts studio, folk dancing, drama, and music. Johnson and her teachers saw that the youngest students went on nature walks, learned in other ways about their environment, were read to, and found innumerable creative outlets. No "home work" was required of younger students nor were they taught to read until they reached eight or nine years of age. As Johnson put it, the children under eight "have singing and dancing, a great deal of hand-work, stories, free play, and nature." Students were grouped by age; none failed and none skipped grades. There were no grades, rewards, or honors for "success," and no punishments for "failure." Both the teachers and the pupils, contrary to what some critics suspected, frequently testified to the fact that the Organic School was anything but a do-as-you-please school. All of the many activities took place in a consciously structured and regulated environment.

The academic curriculum for the older students was conventional. They studied history, literature, ancient and modern languages, mathematics, and science. The curriculum was distinguished not by what the students studied, but by the way they went about studying it. Freed from grades and the urgency of bringing students "up to standard," the teachers could more successfully nurture powers of analysis and expression. Competitiveness was diminished by encouraging group discussions and team projects and expecting students to share information. The pursuit of knowledge in this way more easily became its own reward.

The school reached the peak of its influence and impact in the 1920s. In the Depression years of the 1930s, however, it began a steady decline. Money had always been a problem but now the search for it became a quest for survival. At the end of the 1920s there were 215 members of the Fairhope Educational Foundation (the support group out of Greenwich) and northern tuition-paying students numbered as many as 79 in one year during the decade. Fund-raising campaigns launched by the foundation in the early 1930s met little success. Fewer and fewer students came from the North. Johnson's correspondence throughout the decade chronicles a growing sense of doom. In 1937 she wrote to a former Greenwich supporter: "We are now in the last ditch. Something surely must happen or it will be our last year." Unexpectedly, it was Marietta Johnson's last year. She died on 23 December 1938. The school would never be the same again.

The history of the school in the half century after Johnson's death, as told most authoritatively by Joseph W. Newman in *"Schools of Tomorrow," Schools of Today*, is a story of recurrent struggles for survival and loyalty to Johnson's concept of organic education; isolation from the larger progressive education movement; wildly fluctuating enrollments; frequent turnover of directors, principals, and teachers; conflicts between teachers and the governing board for control; an ongoing dispute over how or whether to preserve Marietta Johnson's core principles; and a bitter dispute between rival factions of Johnson supporters that, Newman believes, cost the school a "once-in-a-lifetime chance at financial security." At school opening in 1986 there were 25 students enrolled in a scaled-back offering of grades K–6.

Cut off from the national support that once sustained it, the Organic School also found itself without the complementary spirit of experimentation and reformism that had characterized the community in which it had taken root. The Single Tax Colony had lost its reformist vision and the ability to demonstrate the reform it had set out to exemplify. Fairhope was no longer animated by the radical spirit that brought it into being. Newman writes that the community "now rates in *Money* magazine as the nation's number two retirement community." Another historian describes Fairhope as a place where people went to escape social problems, not to solve them.

The spirit of Marietta Johnson, however, did not die. In 1989, as the historic campus became the site of a junior college, the school sought a new birth on a four-acre campus distant from the center of town. Free of most of the disputes that had plagued it, the newly named Marietta Johnson School of Organic Education today offers instruction in grades K–8. In addition, it has recently established a "learning center" for homeschooled high school children. The school honors Johnson as a guiding spirit, but, out of necessity, compromises some of her core beliefs and hopes. Grades are assigned, tuition is charged, and enrollment is small. No longer an example of what public schools might be, it nonetheless keeps alive assumptions and values as alternatives that might guide them.

Neither the school nor the colony defines the essence of Fairhope as they once did. Johnson's career and achievements, however, are kept alive by the Marietta Johnson Museum, prominently located on the original campus. The museum contains books, literature, artifacts, photographs, and videotaped interviews of former students and teachers—all in one of the original classrooms.

PAUL M. GASTON
University of Virginia

Paul E. Alyea and Blanche R. Alyea, *Fairhope, 1894–1954: The Story of a Single Tax Colony* (1956); John Dewey and Evelyn Dewey, *Schools of Tomorrow* (1915); Paul M. Gaston, *Coming of Age in Utopia: The Odyssey of an Idea* (2009), *Man and Mission: E. B. Gaston and the Origins of the Fairhope Single Tax Colony* (1993), *Women of Fair Hope* (1984); C. Hanford Henderson, *Education and the Larger Life* (1902); Marietta Johnson, *Thirty Years with an Idea* (1974), *Youth in a World of Men* (1929); Joseph W. Newman, in *"Schools of Tomorrow," Schools of Today: What Happened to Progressive Education*, ed. Susan F. Semel and Alan R. Sadovnik (1999); Nathan Oppenheim, *The Development of the Child* (1898); Mary Lois Timbes, *The Fair Hope of Heaven: A Hundred Years after Utopia* (2008).

Scopes Trial

The Scopes antievolution trial took place in the small town of Dayton, Tenn., from 10 July to 21 July 1925. The participation of William Jennings Bryan, the thrice-defeated Democratic presidential candidate, and Clarence Darrow, the celebrated criminal defense attorney, ensured that the trial would gain national attention, and the Scopes Trial remains the best-known clash between evolution's defenders and activists who seek to ban Charles Darwin's theory from the public schools.

Dayton became involved in the controversy almost by happenstance. The South had seen scattered skirmishes over teaching evolution ever since the publication of Darwin's *On the Origin of Species* in 1859, but these fights were confined to the college level. Public schools seldom taught the subject, and only a small percentage of youths stayed in school until the later years of secondary education, when evolution occasionally made its appearance. The issue became prominent only when northern fundamentalists, who proclaimed that evolution violated their belief in the Bible as the literal, inerrant word of God, turned their attention to the South. Under prodding from Bryan, who led the crusade, Kentucky lawmakers proposed the first statewide antievolution bill, but the legislature narrowly rejected it. However, in 1925 Tennessee passed the "Butler Act" making it a crime to teach evolution because it "denies the story of the Divine creation of man as taught in the Bible." Governor Austin Peay, who needed allies in his far-reaching program to modernize Tennessee's schools, signed the act into law.

The newly founded American Civil Liberties Union (ACLU) advertised for a teacher willing to create a test case for the law. Under prodding from Dayton "boosters" who saw an opportunity to publicize their small town, a young high school teacher named John Thomas Scopes agreed to be arrested for the misdemeanor of violating the Butler Law. The boosters' hopes were fulfilled when Bryan volunteered for the prosecution and Darrow joined the ACLU in Scopes's defense. The "trial of the century," as it quickly became known, attracted reporters from throughout the nation and was broadcast over the first radio network, which a Chicago station had set up expressly for the trial.

Although the trial was celebrated as a duel between science and religion, it raised numerous other issues. At a time when Tennessee's school system was rapidly expanding, the trial pressed the question of whether education should be controlled by majority rule, as through the legislature, or by educational experts, such as the scientists who testified at the trial. The sides also raised arguments over the separation of church and state, although the Supreme Court did not yet apply the First Amendment's Establishment Clause to the states. The best-known moment of the trial came on the seventh day, when Darrow cross-examined Bryan as a hostile expert witness and persuaded him to admit that the "days" of creation in Genesis might actually have lasted thousands of years—a common fundamentalist position for the time, but one that was damning for the purposes of the trial. Nevertheless, the jury found Scopes guilty. The defense planned to appeal the law up to the Supreme Court, but the Tennessee Supreme Court reversed the conviction on a technicality, thus ending the legal debate.

The South saw a flurry of antievolution activity in the next three years, including Arkansas's 1928 passage of the only antievolution measure ever put to popular referendum. By that time, the antievolution movement had reached its geographical limit and made little headway in the North. Even in the South, legislatures passed no further major antievolution legislation, but less formal local pressure, as well as teachers' own beliefs, nearly quashed the teaching of evolution until national science curricula began to be adopted in the 1960s. Tennessee repealed the Butler Law in 1967.

The Scopes Trial set no legal precedents. Although it was partly a consequence of educational progress in Tennessee, it firmly affixed the label of backwardness to southern education. Decades later, the play *Inherit the Wind* and the film derived from it were loosely based on the Scopes Trial, though their message was aimed more at the anticommunist hysteria of the 1950s than the fundamentalism of the 1920s. The South remains the region most sympathetic to antievolutionism.

JEFF MORAN
University of Kansas

Willard B. Gatewood, *Preachers, Pedagogues, and Politicians: The Evolution Controversy in North Carolina, 1920–1927* (1966); Edward J. Larson, *Summer for the Gods: The Scopes Trial and America's Continuing Debate over Science and Religion* (1997); George M. Marsden, *Fundamentalism and American Culture: The Shaping of Twentieth-Century Evangelicalism, 1870–1925* (1982); Jeffrey P. Moran, *The Scopes Trial: A Brief History with Documents* (2002).

Sheats, William N.

(1851–1922) EDUCATOR.

During his lifetime William N. Sheats became variously known as Florida's "Little Giant of Education," "Florida's Progressive Educator," and the "Father of Florida's Public School System." His fame grew during more than two decades as superintendent of public instruction, and his efforts set the foundations for a modern state system of public education.

Born 5 March 1851 on a small cotton farm in the red clay foothills of the Appalachians near Auburn, Gwinnett County, Ga., Sheats was proud of his roots and often referred to himself as a "Georgia cracker." His inspiration in life was his widowed mother, who though beaten down by sickness and poverty made every effort to get her children to school. Adopting her creed, Sheats worked his way through Emory College, eventually obtaining a master's degree, and while principal of a Georgia high school, he completed by correspondence an accounting course from Moore's Business College. Believing that Florida had a healthful climate, he accepted an offer to become vice principal of the East Florida Seminary at Gainesville in 1876.

A very popular teacher, Sheats was induced to run for superintendent of Alachua County schools. He developed his philosophy of administration during three terms as county school superintendent. Reading journals, consulting with educators, and touring school facilities convinced Sheats to emphasize centralization of authority and uniformity of procedure. He revoked all teaching licenses, forcing teachers to take his examination based on a series of textbooks. Facing reexamination every one, two, or three years, teachers flocked to Sheats's institutes on pedagogy. He led the county school board in adopting a rigorous code of conduct for teachers, uniformity of textbooks, and consolidation of schools. He believed so strongly in the separate-but-equal doctrine that he provided excellent teacher training for blacks and attempted to establish for them an industrial training school comparable to Booker T. Washington's Tuskegee Institute. After 12 years of his leadership the quality of Alachua County schools went from near the bottom among Florida's school systems to near the top.

Sheats gained statewide recognition at the 1885 constitutional convention. The only school man present, he dominated debates that shaped the education article, which was destined to remain in effect for 84 years. The document included provisions that mandated special tax districts be developed to fund high school education, that the state superintendent of public instruction be elected, that racial integration in the public schools be prohibited, and that the state organize teacher-training colleges, one for each race.

In 1892 Sheats became Florida's first elected state superintendent of public instruction. He soon showed the same passion for centralization and regimentation that had characterized his earlier work. He shocked teachers by revoking their licenses as a means to compel them to sit for his long and difficult examination. He proposed a uniform course of study, an effort at consolidating schools into larger units, and a state-aid formula for high schools. In black education he caused a national sensation by having the sheriff close a Congregationalist school and arrest the teachers for instructing blacks and whites in the same school.

Educators from around the nation read about "Mr. Sheats" in a National Education Association article on the ideal chief state school officer, but his opponents, referring to "Tsar Sheats," schemed for his election defeat. They succeeded in 1904 by portraying him as too liberal on the race question. He was turned out by the voters, even though during his administration 32,000 additional children registered in school, raising the proportion of registered children from 66 percent in 1892 to 71 percent in 1904, and expenditures per student had increased from $4.25 to $8.10.

Sheats made an election comeback in 1912, and during his last years he put a personal stamp on Florida's compulsory attendance law and administered one of the South's most effective uniform textbook laws. On 19 July 1922 he died in office.

ARTHUR O. WHITE
University of Florida

William N. Sheats, "Journal," William N. Sheats Papers, Southern Historical Collection, University of North Carolina at Chapel Hill; Arthur O. White, *One Hundred Years of State Leadership in Florida Public Education* (1979).

Snavely, Guy E.

(1881–1974) COLLEGE PRESIDENT. Born in Sharpsburg, Md., Guy Everett Snavely was tutored by a local minister after exhausting the education offered by local public schools. He graduated from the Johns Hopkins University in 1901 and began his career by teaching in local academies while studying for his Ph.D. in Romance languages, which he received from Hopkins in 1908. His first academic appointment was to Allegheny College in Meadville, Pa. During World War I he served as director of the American Red Cross for the Deep South. His success at raising funds led to his appointment as dean at Converse College in Spartanburg, S.C., charged with leading the college's capital campaign.

Two years later Snavely began his long association with Birmingham-Southern College (BSC), a struggling Methodist school set on a hill above Alabama's churning iron and steel furnaces. When he arrived in 1921, BSC's total enrollment was a scant 250, and the graduates took their photograph standing around a Model T Ford. When he left in 1937, the student body stood at over 900. Meanwhile, the faculty grew from 10 to 55, the campus from 60 to 125 acres, and the endowment from $100,000 to $1 million. Not content with just a few ramshackle frame buildings, the president persuaded wealthy Birmingham industrialists to erect substantial brick buildings befitting a proper liberal arts college. Snavely worked hard to turn BSC into Alabama's premier liberal arts college, a milestone that procuring the state's second Phi Beta Kappa chapter signified.

Snavely was successful at BSC because of a rare combination of experience, opportunity, and personal charisma. Consider his youth and early education. He came from a family of Republican farmers who believed in self-help and cooperation. His relationship with public education ended before high school, and a local minister began tutoring him in exchange for firewood and feed corn. Time and again, generous individuals would step in to help the hardworking young scholar, sometimes with personal loans. It is also significant that Snavely, who was a Methodist himself, found at BSC a strongly Methodist college (as was Allegheny) dedicated to the Social Gospel. Not a mile away, Methodists had already established settlement houses to minister to immigrant families. All of this fit into his Progressive values. In his inaugural address, with President Warren Harding beside him on the stage, Snavely urged a moral and religious education for the new urban world. "Education for Service," he called it, to be accomplished through selfless commitment and voluntary association. (He belonged to a seemingly endless number of clubs.) Snavely seemed to thrive on enlisting others in cooperative endeavors for the common good, as he had during his stint in the Red Cross. A successful college president, he once noted, "has to be a salesman *par excellence*." And that he was. A man with an unusual degree of personal success, he would eventually garner at least 18 honorary degrees, multiple appointments to various national committees and commissions, and even membership in the French Legion of Honor.

In 1937 Snavely left BSC to assume the executive directorship of the Association of American Colleges (AAC), a typical Progressive professional organization founded in 1915 to promote liberal education. Under his directorship its membership rose by the early 1950s to over 550 colleges and universities. But these numbers are deceiving, for education was expanding largely in response to an influx of federal dollars that Snavely opposed. When he took over, he was in his mid-50s and still a committed Progressive; more importantly, when he took over during the middle of the New Deal, the size and role of the federal government was being drastically reevaluated. Even after World War II and passage of the G.I. Bill, Snavely continued to oppose federal scholarships as "just another method of driving the nation into becoming a socialist state." He would advise penniless students, "Where there's a will, there's a way." Federal aid to colleges, he warned, would destroy their independence. But students, colleges, and universities were not about to turn off the spigots of federal largesse that were pouring dollars into education.

Snavely stepped down from the AAC directorship in 1954, returning briefly to Birmingham-Southern as its president. After serving as Lafayette College's interim president for a year, he finally retired in 1958. In one sense, Guy Snavely's Progressive vision, Education for Service, belonged to another age; and yet it remains the vision of Birmingham-Southern and other religiously affiliated liberal arts colleges like it.

G. WARD HUBBS
Birmingham-Southern College

Guy E. Snavely, *The Church and the Four-Year College: An Appraisal of Their Relation* (1955), *A Search for Excellence: Memoirs of a College Administrator* (1964).

South Alabama, University of

The University of South Alabama (USA) was established in May 1963 and has grown into one of the largest universi-

Mitchell Cancer Institute at the University of South Alabama in Mobile (Photo courtesy of University of South Alabama Department of Public Relations)

ties in the region. Over the past 45 years, the university has strengthened its community ties through historic preservation, medical research, and outreach programs.

In 1944 the University of Alabama began offering extension courses in downtown Mobile in a small facility on St. Louis Street near Bienville Square. From 1944 until 1960 the University of Alabama refused to offer advanced degrees or increase funding for the Mobile extension center. In 1960 Frederick Palmer Whiddon, a native of Newville, Ala., and a newly minted Emory University Ph.D. in philosophy, became the director of the Mobile Extension Center. Finding his improvement efforts rebuffed, Whiddon, with the support of prominent Mobile businessmen, began the process of removing the extension center from the control of the University of Alabama. In February 1961 these men convinced the Alabama legislature to create the Mobile County Foundation for Public Higher Education to encourage the development of a state-supported university in south Alabama.

After two years of negotiations with the University of Alabama and the Mobile delegation to the Alabama legislature, the University of South Alabama was chartered in May 1963 and Whiddon was named the university's first president. At 35 years old, he was the youngest college president in the country. USA was the first public university chartered in Alabama in almost 70 years. The new board of trustees acquired land in West Mobile and moved into its first new building in April 1964. The first class at USA had 928 students and 34 full-time faculty members, all of whom occupied a single building on the new campus that was originally designed for only 600 persons. Plans for expansion were being finalized even before the dedication of the facility in October 1964. Four years later, USA was accredited by the Southern Association of Colleges and Schools.

The first major expansion of the campus came in 1969, when the university acquired Brookley Field, a former U.S. Army base near downtown Mobile. Following the Brookley Campus expansion, President Whiddon and the board of trustees began working to establish a university medical school that would revive the tradition of the Medical College of Alabama, which served the area from 1859 to 1920. These plans won approval by the Alabama legislature on 9 August 1969. The prospect of another medical school in the state outraged University of Alabama officials, who had invested a great deal of money and effort in a large medical school in Birmingham (as part of the UAB campus). Despite these objections, Mobile residents welcomed the return of a medical college to the area. The Mobile city and county commissions allocated $4.5 million for the college and in November 1970 transferred ownership of the old Mobile General Hospital to the university, which turned the facility into a teaching hospital for nurses and physicians.

Over the next three decades the university grew rapidly, adding professional programs in engineering, education, business, computer science, and meteorology. Graduate work at the M.A. level became available in most disciplines, along with Ph.D. programs in instructional design, psychology, and the medically related biological sciences. A doctoral program in marine science was housed in the Dauphin Island Sea Lab, a nearby costal research facility, and a doctor of pharmacy curriculum on the USA campus was administered jointly with the Auburn University Harrison School of Pharmacy.

Throughout the 1980s and early 1990s, the university and its foundation prospered under Whiddon's direction. The foundation made extensive purchases of timber acreage, a move that generated some controversy at the time but later resulted in a critically important income stream after the Wall Street debacle of 2008. Conflict between Whiddon and the USA Board of Trustees escalated in 1998, leading to the president's resignation. He was succeeded by V. Gordon Moulton, a longtime administrator at USA.

Since its founding in 1963, USA has made a significant impact on the educational and economic climate in south Alabama. It has built an expansive, 1,200-acre campus in West Mobile that features state-of-the-art technology and is home to the Mitchell College of Business, named for the families of Mayer and Arlene Mitchell, the single-largest contributors to an Alabama university in state history. Among the Mitchell family's other gifts to USA was a $22 million contribution to the USA Mitchell Cancer Institute, a $125 million research and treatment facility that opened in 2008.

Like most urban schools, USA welcomed part-time and nontraditional students and rejected few applicants, resulting in graduation rates considerably lower than those on traditional residential campuses. Serious students rose to the challenge, however, and seized the opportunity for intellectual growth. As of December 2007, the university had awarded 60,000 degrees.

The USA medical system treats 250,000 patients each year at its hospitals and clinics. The university continues to be a major economic benefit to the Mobile area, employing almost 6,000 residents and having an estimated $2 billion impact on the local economy. Eighty-five percent of Mobile's K–12 teachers receive training and degrees from USA, and one out of every three physicians in south Alabama has been trained at a USA hospital. These improvements ensure that the University of South Alabama will remain a force in Alabama higher education for decades to come.

SCOTTY E. KIRKLAND
University of South Alabama

James F. Caldwell, *Magic? No! Miracle? Yes!: The Founding and Early Development of the University of South Alabama* (1998); Tennant S McWilliams, *New Lights in the Valley: The Emergence of UAB* (2007).

South Carolina, University of

The institution that would become the University of South Carolina was first chartered by Federalist and Jeffersonian legislative leaders of the state as the South Carolina College in 1801, part of an effort to unite South Carolinians in the turbulent wake of the American Revolution. Opened in 1805 near the state capitol in Columbia (intentionally distant from Charleston interests), the new college was regarded by South Carolina's leaders as a way to bring together the sons of the elite from the up-country and the low-country to promote, as they said, "the good order and harmony" of the state.

In the antebellum era, the Palmetto State government generously supported the South Carolina College with regular appropriations, and the institution boasted a cosmopolitan faculty, including such noted scholars as Europeans Francis Lieber and Thomas Cooper. Offering a staunchly traditional classical curriculum, the South Carolina College became one of most influential institutions in the South, earning a reputation as the training ground for South Carolina's powerful antebellum white elite, who later led the state out of the Union.

The institution closed during the Civil War, and for the next century it struggled to regain the leading role in the region it had held during the antebellum era. State leaders revived the institution in 1866 with ambitious plans for a diverse university, but soon the political controversies of Reconstruction buffeted the newly established University of South Carolina. In 1868 state Republicans appointed black members to the board of trustees, and in 1873 Republicans insisted that black students be admitted. White faculty resigned and the state's white elite abandoned the institution they had revered. The University of South Carolina became the only southern state university to enroll and grant degrees to black students during Reconstruction. Black and white students lived and attended classes side-by-side, a concept that was anathema to the old white elite.

Following the turmoil of "Redemption" in the Palmetto State, South Carolina's white conservative leaders closed the institution to purge it of so-called radical influences. They reopened it in 1880 as a whites-only Morrill land-grant institution, but thereafter it became enmeshed in the class-based political upheaval of the last two decades of 19th-century South Carolina and was reorganized several times as a college, then a university, and back again.

The height of uncertainty came in the early 1890s when Gov. Benjamin R. Tillman harshly attacked the institution, arguing that the state should support an agricultural college, not a comprehensive liberal arts university. Jeering that the university was "the seedbed of the aristocracy" and promising to close it forever, the Tillmanites never followed through on their threats, but their attacks crippled the institution. Nonetheless, the school's leaders admitted the first women in 1895 and gradually broadened the curriculum. Enrollment rose, and the state rechartered the college as a university in 1906. Since that time, the institution has served the state as the University of South Carolina.

The University of South Carolina struggled to compete with other state colleges, but a small, poor state like South Carolina simply could not afford to support a total of six separate colleges and maintain a high standard of scholarship at any of them. At a time when the leading universities in other states were laying their foundations for the future, the University of South Carolina was one of the weakest state institutions in the South and not even a leader within the Palmetto State. The 1920s saw a brief revival with expanded programs, but the Great Depression delivered a cruel setback. State appropriations plummeted, programs were curtailed, and faculty salaries were paid in scrip. However, New Deal spending brought a building boom and stabilized the university by the late 1930s.

The outbreak of World War II set into motion forces that would completely remake the institution during the next three decades. During the war, the campus hosted U.S. Navy training programs. In the postwar period, boosted by the G.I. Bill, enrollment boomed. In the 1950s, led by charismatic President Donald Russell, the university began to attract prestigious faculty and expand academic offerings. Increased funding in the 1960s and the arrival of the baby boom generation transformed the campus, with enrollment growing from around 5,000 in the early 1950s to nearly 25,000 by the early 1970s. In these years the University of South Carolina became a full-service "multiversity."

Change was constant. In 1963 Henrie D. Monteith, James Soloman, and Robert Anderson became the first African American students at the university since Reconstruction as a result of a court order prompted by Monteith's application. The campus expanded dramatically beyond the "Horseshoe" of the original campus into the surrounding

Columbia neighborhoods. New colleges such as the University of South Carolina Medical School offered new opportunities.

The 1980s and 1990s saw a drive for increased national recognition, which did not come without a cost. A scandal that brought down high-flying president James B. Holderman was a setback that showed the risks of a strategy for advancement based on star faculty hires rather than the more mundane tasks of institution building. A long-term decline in relative state support combined with intense competition in higher education meant that private fund-raising became ever more important. Major gifts such as the total of $70 million committed by financier Darla Moore for the university's school of business helped "raise the bar" in the Palmetto State.

In the 21st century, the University of South Carolina has continued its expansion toward the Congaree River, and the development of a public-private research campus called "Innovista" has been a major focus. The university has emphasized the development of research centers for nanoscience and hydrogen-based energy with the expectation that the university will therefore remain competitive into the next century.

HARRY LESESNE
Charleston, South Carolina

Michael John Dennis, "Educating the 'Advancing' South: State Universities and Progressivism in the New South, 1887–1915" (Ph.D. dissertation, Queen's University at Kingston, 1996); Walter B. Edgar, *South Carolina in the Modern Age* (1992); Edwin L. Green, *A History of the University of South Carolina* (1916); Daniel Walker Hollis, *The University of South Carolina, vol. 1: The South Carolina College* (1951); Maximilian LaBorde, *History of the South Carolina College, from Its Incorporation, Dec. 19, 1801 to Dec. 19, 1865* (1874); John C. McKinney and Edgar T. Thompson, eds., *The South in Continuity and Change* (1965); Michael Sugrue, "South Carolina College: The Education of an Antebellum White Elite" (Ph.D. dissertation, Columbia University, 1993).

Southern Cultures

The Council of Editors of Learned Journals has called *Southern Cultures* "indispensable to a number of fields" and "a hallmark of what ambitious journals should be attempting in the 21st century." The flagship publication of the University of North Carolina's Center for the Study of the American South covers all aspects of the region's mainstream and marginalized cultures—including their history, art, literature, and sociology—through interviews, essays, articles, personal reminiscences, and surveys on contemporary trends. *Southern Cultures* has published numerous theme issues (which often include free CDs or DVDs) on such topics as southern biography, photography, sports, politics, tobacco, food, Hurricane Katrina, the civil rights movement, Native Americans, and the global South, as well as three editions entirely devoted to music.

Founding editors John Shelton Reed and Harry L. Watson began publishing the quarterly in 1993. In 1996, UNC Press redesigned *Southern Cultures* and entered into a long-term collaboration with the center to produce the journal.

Lisa Eveleigh signed onto the editorial staff in 1996, too, and her 12-year run as copyeditor and then consultant was marked by distinction. Reed still writes for the quarterly and remains active in an advisory role but resigned his formal title in 2005 for another renowned southern sociologist, UNC's Larry J. Griffin, to serve as editor alongside Watson, the director of the center and a longtime professor in UNC's Department of History. Dave Shaw (executive editor), Ayse Erginer (deputy editor), Michael Chitwood (poetry editor), and Josh Guthman (music editor) round out the masthead, and the peer-reviewed journal's editorial board reads like a *Who's Who* in southern studies.

In 60 issues across 15 volumes *Southern Cultures* has published an extensive array of award-winning scholars, authors, and icons. In addition to interviews with Walker Evans, Alex Haley, B. B. King, Pete Seeger, Alice Walker, Eudora Welty, and Robert Penn Warren, the quarterly has published writing from Doris Betts, David Cecelski, James C. Cobb, Peter Coclanis, Pat Conroy, Hal Crowther, Drew Gilpin Faust, William Ferris, Allan Gurganus, Sheldon Hackney, Trudier Harris, Fred Hobson, Doug Marlette, Melton McLaurin, Michael McFee, Robert Morgan, Michael O'Brien, Michael Parker, Tom Rankin, Shannon Ravenel, Louis D. Rubin, Anne Firor Scott, David Sedaris, Alan Shapiro, Bland Simpson, Lee Smith, Henry Taylor, Timothy Tyson, Charles Reagan Wilson, C. Vann Woodward, and many others, as well as the original letters of Zora Neale Hurston and William Faulkner.

The quarterly occupies a unique position among publications about the South by targeting both academic and educated lay audiences, and over the last decade *Southern Cultures* has expanded its circulation in large part due to its emphasis on reader-friendliness. According to the Council of Editors of Learned Journals, "The rich array of photographs and graphics, and the sincere and effective attempt at readerly appeal, go well beyond what is attempted by most journals. This dimension of *Southern Cultures* is truly impressive." Each printed issue now reaches 3,000 to 4,000 readers, up from only a few hundred in 1998, and tens of thousands of visits every year to its online editions through Project Muse. The publication's rapid growth prompted the 2008 release of UNC Press's *Southern Cultures: The Fifteenth Anniversary Reader*, an anthology of the quarterly's most requested material for classroom use.

AYSE ERGINER
DAVID SHAW
University of North Carolina at Chapel Hill

Southern Education Foundation

The Southern Education Foundation (SEF) was incorporated as a private foundation in 1937 with the merger of four institutions that had pursued educational work in the South after the Civil War. The Peabody Educational Fund (1867) had worked to increase the availability of qualified school teachers and to promote public education in general. The Slater Fund (1882), built on the $1 million gift of New England textile manufacturer John F. Slater, supported the South's black colleges and, beginning in 1911, public high schools for African Americans. The Jeanes Fund, created in 1907 when Philadelphia Quaker Anna T. Jeanes donated $1 million to promote educational progress in the South, worked to support rural schools for southern blacks, placing teachers in black schools in 500 counties in 15 states by 1941. And the Virginia Randolph Fund was established in 1931 to honor the African American woman who had been the first Jeanes Fund teacher.

The SEF built on these historic origins of philanthropic educational work in the South, establishing in 1938 its prime mission of improving the academic performance of black students. In its early days, the SEF increased the number of Jeanes teachers, encouraged the employment of blacks in state departments of education, introduced audiovisual materials into black schools, and started graduate training programs for administrators in African American schools. In the 1950s the SEF encouraged desegregation of the public schools and helped prepare the South for this educational transition. It also granted scholarships in that decade to increase the number of black Ph.D.s, and in 1960 it began efforts to aid Historically Black Colleges and Universities (HBCU) to meet new accreditation standards.

In 1959 the SEF launched one of its longstanding reform efforts—to establish state-supported public kindergartens in the South. In 1968 the SEF granted funds in 13 states for conferences to promote kindergartens and the training of early childhood education teachers. From the 1970s the SEF has supported HBCUs, addressed the effects of educational testing on minority students, encouraged discussion of inequitable opportunities and resources in public education, launched the Consortium on Teacher Supply and Quality, and enhanced technological capabilities of institutions of higher learning. Its "Beyond Racism" research project studied race, inequality, and the imperative for public investment in education in South Africa, Brazil, and the United States. Beginning in 1998, the SEF's "Miles to Go" reports have focused attention on the need to close continuing gaps in educational achievement by race and income in the South. In 1983 the SEF's status changed from a private to a public foundation.

CHARLES REAGAN WILSON
University of Mississippi

www.southerneducation.org

Southern Historical Association and Its Antecedents

The Southern Historical Association (SHA), established on 2 November 1934 by 20 historians from colleges and universities across the South, is the leading professional organization for historians of the South and historians in the South. The association sponsors publication of the *Journal of Southern History*; holds annual meetings that are well known for their collegiality, with programs that offer sessions in the fields of American, European, and Latin American history; and awards several yearly prizes that recognize excellence in the field of southern history. The association also maintains a number of affiliates, such as the European History Section and the Latin American and Caribbean Section. The SHA is governed by an executive council consisting of the president, the vice president (as president-elect), the secretary-treasurer, the editor of the *Journal*, past presidents (who serve for two years past the expiration of their presidential terms), and nine elected members (who serve three-year terms, staggered so that three new members are added each year). Other work of the association is conducted by committees appointed by the president or by the council. Since 1980, the business office of the association has been located at the University of Georgia.

Two intellectual movements converged in the founding of the SHA in 1934. The first was the professionalization of historical study in the United States, whereby the university, specialized training represented by the Ph.D., and the claims of "science" came to hold authority over the representation and interpretation of the past. The second was the intellectual resurgence of regional identity that fostered the Southern Renaissance. Together, these commitments meant that early proponents of the SHA wanted to wrest control over interpretation of the southern past from "amateurs" in the Lost Cause tradition (and their organizations, such as the Southern Historical Society) while creating academic legitimacy for specifically "southern" history. This was not an easy balance. An earlier organization, the Southern History Association, established in 1896, had similar ambitions and commitments (and also produced a journal, the *Publications of the Southern History Association*) but managed to sustain itself for scarcely more than a decade, foundering in 1907. Although among the SHA's charter members there were a few advocates of deemphasizing the South as the focus of study, the founders' decision to limit the SHA's journal to articles and reviews in southern history gave public face to the association's priorities.

Despite the Great Depression, which hit the South and its institutions particularly hard, the SHA grew quickly, surpassing 500 members in 1936 and approaching 1,000 by 1940. The annual meetings, held in various southern cities, became important networking opportunities for professors and graduate students and provided the kind of intellectual camaraderie that scholars and teachers in small colleges and departments often lacked. World War II, however, disrupted both the association's membership and its activities, threatening the organization's viability. Professors and students were called into military service and often let their memberships drop. Paper rationing delayed the publication of journals and drastically reduced the production of books (the *Journal* reviewed 91 books in 1942; in 1945 it reviewed 23). As a result of wartime travel restrictions, the annual meeting was cancelled in 1942, 1943, and 1945. Members were eager to return to normal functioning after the war: the 1946 annual meeting posted the second-largest registration to date.

Indeed, as flush times returned to the South and its institutions of higher education, the health of the association was restored.

The postwar years, however, also brought renewed consideration of what it meant to be a "southern" history organization, as social, cultural, and political forces combined to call into question the region's racial politics. For the SHA these debates culminated in the specific issue of the integration of the association. The association had never officially excluded African Americans from membership; in practice, however, black members were barred from full and equal participation in the association's activities. For example, the association deferred to local custom and the segregationist policies of hotels and convention sites, which rendered the annual meetings inaccessible to black historians. Starting in the late 1940s, however, African American historians and their white allies began working together to move the association into taking a proactive stance against Jim Crow. A black historian appeared on the program for the first time in 1949. Through the 1950s the association increasingly prioritized the physical accommodation of all members at the meetings, trying to balance the moral obligations of inclusion with practical considerations of organizing a large convention. It was a protracted, contested, and imperfect path toward integration, but one that ultimately kept the Southern Historical Association as a relevant and enduring organization in a vibrant and diverse field. Today the SHA has approximately 2,500 individual members and 1,200 institutional members.

BETHANY L. JOHNSON
Rice University

Fred A. Bailey, *Journal of Southern History* (November 2005); Bethany L. Johnson, "Regionalism, Race, and the Meaning of the Southern Past: Professional History in the American South, 1896–1961" (Ph.D. dissertation, Rice University, 2001); Walter B. Posey, *Journal of Southern History* (February 1977); Southern Historical Association Records #4030, Southern Historical Collection, University of North Carolina at Chapel Hill; George Brown Tindall, ed., *The Pursuit of Southern History: Presidential Addresses of the Southern Historical Association, 1935–1963* (1964).

Southern Methodist University

Southern Methodist University (SMU) was founded in 1911 and opened in 1915. During its first century, the private university in Dallas grew from a liberal arts college and theology school to become a nationally ranked comprehensive university. SMU offers a strong liberal arts foundation and more than 80 undergraduate majors, along with nationally competitive graduate and professional programs, through seven degree-granting schools. They are Dedman College of Humanities and Sciences, Cox School of Business, Meadows School of the Arts, Bobby B. Lyle School of Engineering, Annette Caldwell Simmons School of Education and Human Development, Dedman School of Law, and Perkins School of Theology. The university is nonsectarian in its teaching and committed to academic freedom and open inquiry.

SMU is diverse geographically, racially, economically, and religiously. The enrollment of nearly 11,000 includes students from all 50 states and the District of Columbia, as well as more than 900 international students from nearly 100 countries. Minority students number more than 20 percent. Nearly 80 percent of first-year students receive some form of financial aid. Of the students reporting a religious affiliation or preference, 24 percent are Catholic and 21 percent are Methodist. Also represented are other Protestant denominations and religions such as Judaism, Islam, and Hinduism.

SMU was founded by what is now the United Methodist Church, in partnership with Dallas civic leaders, and is shaped by the entrepreneurial spirit of the region. The first president, Robert S. Hyer, chose "*veritas liberabit vos*" ("the truth will make you free") as SMU's motto and selected Harvard red and Yale blue as the school's colors. He borrowed from the University of Virginia's Neo-Georgian architecture for the design theme that still unifies the SMU campus.

Two later presidents, both SMU alumni, guided the fledgling university toward becoming a mature institution of higher education. Umphrey Lee (1938–54), who steered SMU through World War II, increased the university's emphasis on faculty research and scholarship, along with teaching. Willis M. Tate (1954–72) affirmed the university as a "free marketplace of ideas" and effectively interpreted the concept of academic freedom to conservative Dallas leaders. SMU was ahead of many universities in its region in achieving a smooth integration of the campus, beginning with Perkins School of Theology in the early 1950s.

SMU has a long history in literary publication. The *Southwest Review*, which began publication on the campus in 1925, is the third-oldest continuously published literary quarterly in the United States. The SMU Press, established in 1937, publishes scholarly works and books for general readership.

SMU has experienced major advancements since R. Gerald Turner became president in 1995. In the past 10 years, the average SAT score of the first-year undergraduate class has risen 97 points, and applications for the incoming first-year class have more than doubled. External funding for research and sponsored projects has more than doubled, and the endowment has nearly tripled, surpassing the $1 billion mark in 2005. Since 1995 SMU has added six new doctoral programs, bringing to 25 the fields offering doctorates on campus. Education abroad opportunities for students have nearly doubled, with 30 programs currently offered in 16 countries.

SMU's main campus has grown from 60 buildings and 176 acres in 1995 to 76 buildings and 210 acres in 2008. One of the new buildings, in the engineering school, was among the first academic buildings in the country to achieve LEED Gold status for its environmentally sensitive design and construction. SMU-in-Taos, the university's campus in northern New Mexico, offers courses on the site of a historic fort and a 13th-century Indian pueblo.

Today, SMU's 10 libraries house the largest private collection of research materials in the Southwest. The internationally acclaimed Meadows Museum on campus houses one of the finest collections of Spanish art outside of Spain and presents outstanding special exhibitions and educational programming for youth and adults. As part of SMU's focus on leadership, the Tate Distinguished Lecture Series and Hart Global Leaders Forum bring national and world leaders to the campus and community for lectures and interaction with students.

SMU made history in February 2008 with the announcement that the university had been chosen as the site of the George W. Bush Presidential Center, consisting of a library, museum, and institute. As SMU nears the end of its first century, it looks to the past with pride and to the future with optimism.

PATRICIA ANN LASALLE
Southern Methodist University

Marshall Terry, *From High on the Hilltop: A Brief History of SMU* (2001); Mary Martha Hosford Thomas, *Southern Methodist University: Founding and Early Years* (1974).

Southern Regional Education Board

Governmental leaders of southern states formed the Southern Regional Education Board (SREB) in 1948 as a nonprofit, nonpartisan advocacy group to work with 16 states to improve public education from kindergarten to university. It was the nation's first interstate compact devoted to public education, working directly with governmental leaders, schools, and teachers to advance student achievement through improved teaching and learning environments. The SREB is governed by a board that includes the governor of each state in the collaborative and four gubernatorial appointees from each state, including at least one state legislator and one teacher. Annual appropriations from the states involved fund the SREB, along with support from philanthropic foundations and state and federal agencies.

The SREB brings critical educational issues to the attention of the public, government leaders, and educational authorities through research reports and makes recommendations for policy changes. It collects and studies data on education, trains teachers in best practices, makes resources for students and teachers accessible, gives legislators information for policy making, delivers resources for online and adult education, and generally facilitates interstate access to educational programs.

Recent programs illustrate the diversity of approaches the SREB uses to foster educational progress in the South. The SREB State Teacher Center (www.theteachercenter.org) offers services for teachers and educational administrators, including locating educational curricula; understanding state-mandated qualifications for "highly qualified" teacher status under the federal No Child Left Behind project; and locating employment. The Electronic Campus provides online materials for high school and college students, as well as teachers. The Academic Common Market allows a student in one state in the compact to register with in-state tuition in another state university if registering for a specialized program unavailable in the student's home state. The SREB State Doctoral Scholars program began in 1993 and has provided assistance to over 900 minority scholars at 83 institutions. The Adult Learning Campaign aims to increase the number of adults enrolled in institutions of higher learning in the South.

CHARLES REAGAN WILSON
University of Mississippi

www.sreb.org

Spring Hill College

The first institution of higher learning in Alabama, Spring Hill College was founded by Michael Portier, the Roman Catholic bishop of Mobile, in 1830. A native of France, Portier came to New Orleans in 1816 as a seminarian. He arrived in Mobile as the first bishop of the city in 1826 and soon began making plans to establish a college there. Portier opened classes for six seminarians at a private home in February 1830 and soon purchased more than 500 acres six miles from downtown Mobile, in an area known as Spring Hill, to establish a larger school. On 2 July 1830 with the completion of two new buildings and an enrollment of 40 students, Spring Hill College was officially dedicated.

Established initially as a diocesan institution, the school was the fifth Catholic college founded in the United States, and the first in the Deep South. In 1835 the state of Alabama granted the college the title of university with the right to confer degrees, and five years later Pope Gregory XVI granted the college the power to award degrees in theology and philosophy. However, in 1846, after struggling with declining enrollments and four different administrations, Bishop Portier sent Father John Bazin to Europe to offer to turn over direction of the college to a willing religious congregation. The Society of Jesus agreed to assume direction of the school, and in January of 1847 six French Jesuits arrived in Mobile. That year, Father Francis Gautrelet was named president of the college, beginning the school's affiliation with the society, which continues today, as one of the nation's 28 Jesuit institutions of higher learning.

Under Jesuit leadership the school began to prosper, and the school received notoriety as one of its graduates, Paul Morphy (graduated 1854), was hailed as the world chess champion. During the early years of the Civil War, Spring Hill saw its enrollment increase as many parents sent their sons there to avoid being drafted, but following the fall of New Orleans the school suffered as both students and provisions became scarce. All the members of the Spring Hill faculty and staff were enlisted in the 89th Alabama Regiment but were furloughed to teach, although a number of the school's Jesuits served as chaplains in the Confederate army. One, Father A. Usannaz, went to the prison camp at Andersonville, Ga., to minister to the Union prisoners there. During the occupation of Mobile following the war, Union troops encamped upon the campus grounds.

One of the most significant chapters in Spring Hill's history came during the civil rights movement of the mid-20th century. In contrast to the infamous confrontation at the schoolhouse door by Gov. George Wallace at the University of Alabama in 1963, Spring Hill admitted its first black students almost a decade earlier, without fanfare or resistance, becoming the first all-white institution of higher learning in the state to do so. The call to integrate Spring Hill had first come in 1948, when President W. Patrick Donnelly announced at commencement, "Let the college that was the first . . . to raise the torch of education also light and lead the way to full democracy in Alabama and the Southland. Civil Rights? Spring Hill College is for them, for ourselves and for every other citizen, regardless of creed and color." While he received opposition from the school's board of governors in moving forward with desegregation, Father Donnelly quietly admitted a number of African American nuns into the 1949 summer session.

In 1952 Spring Hill officially went coed, admitting 40 full-time female undergraduates. The following year Julia Ponquitte, a student at Loyola University of Chicago, transferred to Spring Hill, becoming the first African American in the school's regular undergraduate program, and in the fall of 1954 nine black students were admitted as freshmen. The integration of Spring Hill College was kept quiet by the administration to avoid any conflict; even the school newspaper, the *Springhillian*, avoided mentioning the presence of the black students on campus. When asked by the *Mobile Register* if African Americans had been admitted, the school's president, Father Andrew Smith, stated, "I presume there are some in the classes. . . . We have never asked if they were white or Negro. We are not making an issue out of it." The success of the peaceful integration of Spring Hill was later cited by Dr. Martin Luther King Jr. in his 1963 "Letter from a Birmingham Jail," where he commended Catholic leaders of the state for integrating the college.

THOMAS J. WARD JR.
Spring Hill College

Charles J. Boyle, *Gleanings from the Spring Hill College Archives* (2004), ed., *Twice Remembered: Moments in the History of Spring Hill College* (1993); Michael Kenny, S.J., *Catholic Culture in Alabama: Centenary Story of Spring Hill College, 1830–1930* (1931).

Swann v. Charlotte-Mecklenburg Board of Education

For nearly 30 years, starting in the fall of 1970, Charlotte, N.C., operated one of the most racially integrated school systems in the country. During that time, the city served as the national test case for busing, a journey that began the preceding year when a U.S. district judge ordered busing as a remedy to eradicate segregation.

For Charlotte, the experience went beyond a landmark battle in the federal courts. Even as the community awaited a final Supreme Court ruling, which came on 20 April 1971, local citizens were caught in a political struggle as intense as any they had ever known. In the beginning there was strong opposition to the busing order, delivered in the case of *Swann v. Charlotte-Mecklenburg*. More than 10,000 people signed an antibusing petition; bomb scares and racial fighting became a regular occurrence in the schools, and on at least one occasion white parents threw rocks at a bus full of children.

The turmoil lasted for nearly three years, but finally in 1973 the community experienced a slow change of mood. Already there were parents, teachers, and students working to make the best of the new situation. Parents by the thousands volunteered in the schools, and within two years of the Supreme Court's decision affirming the legality of busing, many of the city's leading citizens were calling actively for compliance. The choice, they argued, was to make busing work or see the public school system destroyed.

By the spring of 1973, an interracial coalition of parents was pursuing a fair and stable busing plan that would involve every segment of the community. U.S. District Judge James B. McMillan ordered the school board to cooperate with an ad hoc citizens' advisory group in designing a plan that could win broad support.

In 1974 the schools implemented a new assignment system based on the pairing of elementary schools. In general, for the first four grades, inner-city children, mostly African American, were bused to the suburbs; and in the fifth and sixth grades, whites were bused to inner-city schools that had been all-black. The plan thus assured that most children had a chance to go to school close to home for at least a part of their elementary schooling, and almost none escaped busing altogether.

In junior high and high school, most students were bused, but with efforts to limit the length of the rides. All in all, most citizens regarded the arrangement as fair, and a broad consensus developed in Charlotte that the benefits of desegregation outweighed the inconvenience of busing. "Charlotte-Mecklenburg's proudest achievement over the past 20 years," wrote the *Charlotte Observer*, the city's morning newspaper, "is not the city's impressive new skyline or its strong, growing economy. Its proudest achievement is its fully integrated school system."

As the *Observer* noted, not only were test scores rising in the schools, where parental involvement continued to be high, but in many other areas of its life Charlotte had entered a period of progress. In the 1980s, the city's young black mayor, Harvey Gantt, an articulate civil rights pioneer, had lured new business into the city. By the end of the decade, two of the nation's largest banks had established their national headquarters in Charlotte, and the city had secured its first major league sports franchise, the Charlotte Hornets of the National Basketball Association. Another would follow in the 1990s, the National Football League's Charlotte Panthers, as the greater Charlotte area continued to grow, its population soon topping a million.

For the schools, however, the growth was double-edged. Many of the new arrivals in Charlotte had little interest in the goal of integration. They often came from northern or midwestern cities where the school systems tended to be more homogenous, and they saw busing as an anachronism or worse. In 1999 a group of white parents returned to court and secured a ruling from a new federal judge that Charlotte schools were now unitary, or fully integrated. U.S. District Judge Robert Potter ruled that any consideration of race in pupil assignments, even as a strategy for desegregation, was unconstitutional.

In the wake of that ruling, Charlotte schools began to resegregate, with large concentrations of minority students—many of them from low-income families—in inner-city schools. Particularly at the high school level, some of Charlotte's schools began to struggle. At West Charlotte High School, where in 2004 only 3 percent of the students were white, 70 percent tested below grade level. That same year at Garinger High School, where the student population was similar, 75 percent of 10th graders failed the state reading exam.

One school board member who had supported integration recalled how Charlotte recently had been a beacon for the nation. Now, she said in 2004, "We are becoming typical."

FRYE GAILLARD
University of South Alabama

Frye Gaillard, *The Dream Long Deferred: The Landmark Struggle for Desegregation in Charlotte, North Carolina* (2006); Gary Orfield and Susan E. Eaton, *Dismantling Desegregation: The Quiet Reversal of* Brown v. Board of Education (1996); Bernard Schwartz, *Swann's Way: The School Busing Case and the U.S. Supreme Court* (1986); Stephen Samuel Smith, *Boom for Whom?: Education, Desegregation, and Development in Charlotte* (2005).

Talladega College

Talladega College is one of several historically black colleges and universities established by the American Missionary Association (AMA) after Emancipation. Established in 1867 at the urging of local blacks, including William Savery and Thomas Tarrant, the institution was chartered by the state of Alabama in 1869. Hundreds of students enrolled in the primary, intermediate, normal, college preparatory, and theology departments, with the school graduating its first normal class in 1876. In 1879 the AMA appointed Henry Swift De Forest as the school's first president. For 17 years De Forest helped the school to fulfill its promise of becoming a full-fledged university. The first college class entered in the fall of 1891 and graduated in 1895. For the next twenty years George W. Andrews (1896–1904), Benjamin M. Nyce (1904–7), and John M. P. Metcalf (1907–16) led Talladega College. During their tenure, the school struggled financially, moved slowly toward strengthening its college program, and provided the only opportunity for higher education for many Alabama blacks.

Frederick A. Sumner led Talladega College from 1916 to 1933. During Sumner's administration the school developed into a first-rate institution, with better students, a superior interracial faculty, and a modern physical plant. Sumner began a successful "Million Dollar Endowment Campaign" and helped Talladega College to achieve the highly coveted "A" rating from the Southern Association of Colleges and Secondary Schools. The college's sixth president, Buell G. Gallagher, (1933–43), guided the institution through the final years of the Great Depression and the first years of the Second World War. Only 29 when he arrived on campus, Gallagher "gave Talladegans a sense of confidence, movement, and energy." Under his leadership, the institution implemented a more modern general education program and introduced the College Council, which promoted democracy on campus by giving all segments of the college a voice and a sense of responsibility. Gallagher strengthened the faculty, completed the endowment begun by Sumner, built a new library, and enhanced the college's national prestige.

Talladega dean James T. Cater, an African American primarily responsible for Talladega's educational growth during Gallagher's tenure, served as acting president while the board of trustees searched for the college's seventh president. Cater led the institution from the summer of 1943 to 1945 when the board named Adam D. Beittel to the post. Beittel, more publicly than his white predecessors, vigorously attacked segregation and racism and quickly earned a reputation as an agitator and radical. The Ku Klux Klan made two visits to campus during his administration. Student enrollment increased during the Beittel years, as did faculty salaries and the school budget. The National Alumni Association also became more involved, giving much-needed support. Faculty factionalism as well as salary and tenure issues stirred up bitter campus discord, which ultimately led to the dismissal of Cater and Beittel in 1952.

Arthur Douglass Gray, a 1929 graduate of Talladega College, became the school's first black president in 1952 and successfully courted the approval of students, faculty, and alumni. The college experienced growth in almost every area during Gray's leadership. Enrollment rose steadily, and increasing numbers of graduates continued their education at the nation's premier graduate institutions, won national fellowships, and held top administrative positions. Gray solicited funds that allowed Talladega's faculty to pursue their doctoral degrees, and he modernized facilities. When whites beat a Talladega student on 2 January 1961 in Anniston, Ala., the college became an active participant in the civil rights movement, and President Gray devoted much of his time to preserving the institution and protecting the students. The board of trustees reluctantly accepted the popular president's resignation in December 1963.

Herman H. Long, another graduate of Talladega, succeeded Gray and served until his death in August 1976. Like Gallagher, Long brought a new energy to campus, but spent a good deal of his time attempting to justify the existence of Talladega College and similar black institutions at a time when formerly segregated colleges were open to all. Long continued the tradition of introducing new programs, expanding and modernizing campus facilities, and strengthening and enlarging the faculty.

Talladega was an academically strong institution with many of its graduates attending professional and graduate schools. When desegregation seriously affected recruiting and enrollment, the school partially shifted its focus from training elite students to providing opportunity to the largely unschooled African American population. Talladega College, the "Alpha Lyrae Vega of them all," continues to survive. With its 20th president, Billy C. Hawkins, at the helm, it serves approximately 350 students with a full-time faculty of 30. Ninety-eight percent of the students receive financial aid. The college boasts that it attracts the top 5 percent of students nationwide and that 80 percent of its students pursue advanced degrees.

MAXINE D. JONES
Florida State University

Maxine D. Jones, *Alabama Review* (October 1988); Maxine D. Jones and Joe M. Richardson, *Talladega College: The First Century* (1990); Joe M. Richardson, *Alabama Historical Quarterly* (Spring 1975), *Christian Reconstruction: The American Missionary Association and Southern Blacks, 1861–1890* (1986).

Tate, Allen

(1899–1979) WRITER AND CRITIC.
The most cosmopolitan of major modern southern writers, John Orley Allen Tate was a prime exemplar of his own theory that the highest artistic achievements come from a combination of native and foreign influences, and he helped make Vanderbilt University a main southern cultural force in the early 20th century. He was born on 10 November 1899, in Winchester, Ky., a town in the heart of the bluegrass country. Family loyalty first led him away from home, for he followed his elder brothers to Vanderbilt University in Nashville and there encountered the writers who were to determine the course of his life. John Crowe Ransom and Donald Davidson were his teachers, Robert Penn Warren was a younger fellow student, and all became colleagues in the *Fugitive* magazine, which began appearing in 1922 while Tate was still an undergraduate.

By 1930 Tate had produced the centerpiece of modern southern poetry, the "Ode to the Confederate Dead," using techniques of imagery and deliberate fragmentation learned from foreign poetry to portray the experience of a native southerner who felt cut off from the traditional society he wished to memorialize. His theme in this masterful poem, as in the equally masterful literary essays he wrote and in his only novel, *The Fathers* (1938), was the decline, not simply of southern tradition, but of the whole tradition of Western civilization, which he came to see as the result of the loss of religious faith. "Modern man suffering from unbelief," he wrote near the end of his illustrious career, was what all his writing was about.

Tate was by education and conviction a Renaissance man, a classical Christian humanist, but by force of circumstance he became a modernist, trapped unwillingly in what he called "the squirrel cage of modern sensibility," a "provincialism of time" (more constrictive than the old provincialism of place) where solipsism, or uniquely personal intuition, was the sole alternative to scientific determinism, or positivism, as the measure of truth and value. His theory was that traditional society, where people were bound into community by ties of family, locale, and religion, had been replaced by industrial society, in which the only ties were economic and political; the southern writer's vantage point, living in a place where the agrarian community was still alive, if rapidly vanishing, made him an eyewitness to the change from traditional to industrial society, which in other places was already an accomplished fact.

Tate's definition of the *fugitive* was "quite simply a Poet: the Wanderer, or even the Wandering Jew, the man who carries the secret wisdom about the world." He lived out this definition himself, as he went from Nashville to New York, where he became part of another group of writers, less regionally aligned, that included Hart Crane, Malcolm Cowley, and e. e. cummings, then to Paris on a Guggenheim fellowship, where he spent some time in the circle of Gertrude Stein, with Ernest Hemingway, F. Scott Fitzgerald, and Archibald MacLeish, then back to Southwestern College in Memphis, where he taught, to Princeton University, to the Library of Congress, as its first Consultant in Poetry, to the University of the South, where he edited the *Sewanee Review* for a few distinguished years, and finally to the University of Minnesota, where he became Regents Professor of English. His career had taken him far away from the South and earned him an international reputation and many honors, including the Bollingen Prize for Poetry and the presidency of the National Institute of Arts and Letters, but he had always remained a southerner as well as a fugitive. At the end of his life he returned to Tennessee, where he died, in Nashville, on 9 February 1979.

Southerner, American, and internationalist by turns, Tate retained his regional identity all his life, nowhere more convincingly than in his late poem, "The Swimmers," where he recalled his Kentucky boyhood in an elegant series of terza rima stanzas that are a triumphant blend of the local and the universal. He wrote and edited many notable books; much of his best work can be found in *Collected Poems, 1919–1976* (1977); *Essays of Four Decades* (1968); and *Memories and Opinions, 1926–1974* (1975).

WILLIAM PRATT
Miami University (Ohio)

Ferman Bishop, *Allen Tate* (1967); William Doreski, *The Years of Our Friendship: Robert Lowell and Allen Tate* (1990); John M. Dunaway, ed., *Exiles and Fugitives: The Letters of Jacques and Raissa Maritain, Allen Tate, and Caroline Gordon* (1992); George Hemphill, *Allen Tate* (1964); Mark G. Malvasi, *The Unregenerate South: The Agrarian Thought of John Crowe Ransom, Allen Tate, and Donald Davidson* (1997); Radcliffe Squires, ed., *Allen Tate and His Work: Critical Evaluations* (1972); Thomas A. Underwood, *Allen Tate: Orphan of the South* (2000); Thomas Daniel Young and John Hindle, eds., *The Republic of Letters in America: The Correspondence of John Peale Bishop and Allen Tate* (1981).

Tennessee, University of

The University of Tennessee enrolls more than 45,000 students on four campuses: the major campus at Knoxville, the Health Science Center in Memphis, and the predominantly undergraduate campuses at Chattanooga and Martin. The Knoxville campus is the state's flagship, research-intensive university, offering more than 300 undergraduate and graduate degree programs and serving more than 26,000 students. More than 300,000 alumni live throughout the state, nation, and world.

Established in 1794 as Blount College, a private, nonsectarian, coeducational school, it was rechartered by the Tennessee legislature in 1807 as East Tennessee College, a male-only institution, and endowed with a land grant of 50,000 acres. Often condemned by frontier politicians as a school for rich men's sons, it was a small, struggling institution with never more than 169 students in the antebellum period. During the Civil War, the faculty generally supported the Union, while the loyalties of the students were divided. The university buildings were badly damaged in the conflict. The Confederate army occupied the campus first; later it was used as a military hospital by northern troops.

In 1869 it was designated the land-grant university under the Morrill Act. For the next generation a debate ensued within the university over the significance of the land-grant designation. Most of the faculty and the president looked upon agricultural and mechanical arts as merely a branch of the university; the trustees generally supported its transformation into a predominantly agricultural and scientific institution. The victory of the agricultural and scientific forces was completed in 1887 with the election of President Charles W. Dabney. During his 17-year tenure, Dabney ended the military system on the campus, admitted women, and persuaded the state legislature to make its first appropriation to the university.

The first half of the 20th century witnessed the emergence of the modern university with professional schools of medicine, dentistry, nursing, social work, and architecture; the development of doctoral programs in a variety of fields; the physical expansion of the campus; and the growth of the student body. The university experienced phenomenal growth after World War II with veterans entering under the G.I. Bill, followed soon after by their sons and daughters. The first black students enrolled—under court order—in 1952.

In 1968 the university underwent an administrative reorganization that left the Knoxville campus as the "flagship" and headquarters of its new "system," now comprising the medical units at Memphis, a four-year college at Martin, the former private University of Chattanooga (added a year later), the Space Institute at Tullahoma, the College of Veterinary Medicine, the Agriculture Institute, and the Public Service Institute.

During the second half of the 20th century, the university experienced a period of steady growth and stable leadership. Andy Holt served as president from 1959 to 1970, followed by Ed Boling from 1970 to 1988. Former Tennessee governor Lamar Alexander succeeded Boling, serving three years before becoming the nation's Secretary of Education. Joseph E. Johnson, who served as an assistant to President Holt, was named UT president in 1991. The new century began with a few setbacks in leadership, but strides in academic, research, and outreach progress continued. John Petersen was named UT's 23rd president in 2004 and served until

2009. He quickly laid the foundation for a greater understanding of the university's value and impact on all citizens of the state.

A positive momentum continued throughout the university system as the Institute of Agriculture expanded its research programs, extension services, and testing facilities across the state. The ongoing relationship between the university and Oak Ridge National Laboratory (ORNL) was formally solidified in 2000 through a partnership between UT and Battelle Memorial Institute, making a significant step for the university's future in research and economic development. In 2008 the National Science Foundation (NSF) awarded a $65 million grant (the largest NSF grant in Tennessee history) to the university to build and operate a supercomputer through a partnership with ORNL.

While the university has acquired a national reputation in both men's and women's athletics, with several Southeastern Conference football championships and national women's basketball championships, the University of Tennessee has also produced some distinguished academicians and statesmen, including one Nobel laureate, six Rhodes scholars, five Pulitzer Prize winners, two National Book Award winners, nine U.S. senators, and one U.S. Supreme Court justice. These notables and any number of other successful if less prominent alumni bear witness to the university's fulfillment of its mission to the citizens of Tennessee.

CLINTON B. ALLISON
JENNIFER BENEDETTO BEALS
University of Tennessee

Clinton B. Allison, in *Three Schools of Education: Approaches to Institutional History*, ed. Agnes Bagley (1984); James Riley Montgomery, Stanley J. Folmsbee, and Lee Seifert Green, *To Foster Knowledge: A History of the University of Tennessee, 1794–1970* (1984); Aaron D. Purcell, *University of Tennessee* (2007); University of Tennessee, Office of Management Services, *A Graphic View of the University of Tennessee* (7th ed., 1985), Office of the University Historian, *Brief Historical Sketch of the University of Tennessee* (1995).

Texas, University of

For many years Texas lawmakers considered the establishment of a state university. Finally, the Constitutional Convention of 1875 decided that "the Legislature shall, as soon as practicable, establish, organize, and provide for the maintenance, support, and direction of a university of the first class, to be located by a vote of the people of this State, and styled, 'The University of Texas,' for the promotion of literature, and the arts and sciences, including an agricultural and mechanical department." On 28 March 1881 the legislature passed a bill establishing the university, and Gov. Oran M. Roberts signed the measure on 30 March. Later that year, Texans voted to locate the school in Austin. In November 1882 the cornerstone of the west wing of the original main building was laid in place on a 40-acre plot of land one mile north of the Capitol building, where classes were temporarily being held; and in September 1883 the first students (221 in number) began classes in the new building. Until 1895 the university was without a president, and the chairman

Tower, University of Texas at Austin, c. 1940s (Barker Texas History Center, University of Texas at Austin)

of the faculty served as the chief executive officer. The university's third president, William L. Prather (1899–1905), in addressing the students, adapted Robert E. Lee's words about the South and uttered the now-famous words, "The eyes of Texas are upon you." In 1903 the words were matched to the tune of "I've Been Working on the Railroad" and became the school song.

At the 1882 cornerstone ceremony, Ashbel Smith claimed prophetically, "Smite the earth, smite the rock with the rod of knowledge, and fountains of unstinted wealth will gush forth." In 1923 oil was discovered on UT's west Texas lands. The money generated goes into the Permanent University Fund, which supports the 15 institutions in the University of Texas system, established in 1876 by the Texas Constitution.

After World War II, the university's enrollment increased dramatically—from 4,001 just after World War I to 15,118 the year after World War II. In 1950 the university was integrated as a result of the Supreme Court's decision in *Sweatt v. Painter*. The university's official name changed to the University of Texas at Austin in 1967, and since then, it has maintained its status as one of three southwestern members of the Association of American Universities. A 2004 *Times* of London survey named it the 15th-best university in the world. UT's general library system, which consists of seven museums and 17 libraries, is the fifth largest academic library in the nation. The university's Ransom Center of Arts and Humanities began in 1957 as the Humanities Research Center and now houses the world's first photograph, rare first-edition books, letters, and original literary manuscripts. UT is also home to the Texas Natural Science Center, the Blanton Museum of Art, and the Lyndon B. Johnson Presidential Library and Museum. Academic divisions include schools of architecture, geosciences, information, law, nursing, public affairs, social work, fine arts, liberal arts, engineering, communication, business, and pharmacy. UT's graduate school was established in 1910 and has expanded to 100 fields of study with a student enrollment of over 12,000, and today UT awards the second largest number of doctoral degrees in the United States. The university's research programs include centers and institutes in geophysics, archaeology, electromechanics, biodiversity, energy and environmental resources, and nuclear energy, as well as computational engineering, robotics, and business and urban research.

Athletics are significant at UT; a 2002 issue of *Sports Illustrated* ranked UT first in Division I athletics overall. The university's athletic department offers men's baseball, basketball, cross-country, football, golf, swimming and diving, tennis, and track and field, and women's sports include basketball, cross-country, golf, rowing, soccer, softball, swimming and diving, tennis, track and field, and volleyball. The university has sent 137 athletes to the Olympic Games since 1936, winning a total of 116 medals, many in swimming and in track and field; recent medal winners include Aaron Peirsol, Ian Crocker, and Laura Wilkinson (2000, 2004, 2008). The Longhorns football team has won four national championships and is second in the nation in all-time NCAA victories.

In the fall of 2009 there were 51,032 students enrolled at UT, and the campus is still referred to as "the Forty Acres," although it occupies more than 350 acres and several off-site research campuses. Notable alumni of UT include Lady Bird Johnson, Walter Cronkite, Bill Moyers, and Lloyd Bentsen Jr.

NORMAN D. BROWN
University of Texas at Austin
MARY AMELIA TAYLOR
University of Mississippi

Margaret Berry, *UT Austin: Traditions and Nostalgia* (1975), *The University of Texas: A Pictorial Account of Its First Century* (1980); Ronnie Dugger, *The Invaded Universities: Form, Reform, and New Starts* (1974); Roger A. Griffin, *Southwestern Historical Quarterly* (October 1982); University of Texas at Austin Web site, www.utexas.edu (2010).

Texas A&M University

Texas Agricultural and Mechanical (A&M) University was the first public institution of higher education in Texas. The Texas legislature authorized the establishment of the institution under the terms of the Morrill Act in November 1866. The act organizing the Agricultural and Mechanical College of Texas was approved on 17 April 1871; it appropriated $75,000 for the erection of buildings and bound the state to defray all expenses of the college exceeding the annual interest from the endowment. Proceeds from the sale of 180,000 acres of land, located in Colorado and authorized under the Morrill Act, were invested in $174,000 of gold frontier defense bonds of Texas. Under the authority of the Texas Constitution of 1876, Texas A&M is a branch of the University of Texas, which was itself established in 1883, and participates in the Permanent University Fund of the State of Texas. A locating commission accepted the offer of 2,146 acres of land from Brazos County, and the college opened on 4 October 1876. With an initial enrollment of some 50 students in the fall term of 1876, the institution has grown to be one of the largest universities in the nation with 48,703 students registered in 2009. On 23 August 1963, the 58th Legislature of Texas changed the name of the Agricultural and Mechanical College to Texas A&M University.

The college began as an all-male agricultural and mechanical college with required military training and enrollment in the Corps of Cadets. As a Senior Military College, it remains one of three public universities with a full-time student Corps program. Participation in military training and membership in the Corps of Cadets became voluntary in 1965. Although fewer than 10 percent of the students are now in the Corps of Cadets, the school continues to furnish more reserve officers than any other institution in the United States and offers ROTC programs leading to commissions in all four branches of the service.

Women attended intermittently as special students over the years, but the institution officially admitted female students on a qualified basis after 1963 and adopted an open admissions policy in 1971. Women also joined the Corps of Cadets during this time and began to play a more prominent role in many aspects of university life, including athletics. Though women faculty and employees were present during the early days of the school, the coeducational movement spurred greater numbers in involvement at all levels. The first woman president of the university was Elsa Murano, who was appointed in 2008.

Texas A&M University offers

graduate study in most fields, with a doctorate in many. It supports a College of Veterinary Medicine, established in 1916, and a College of Medicine, authorized in 1971, which graduated its first class in 1981. The Texas A&M University system, whose present chancellor is Mike McKenney, provides administrative direction for Texas A&M University at Galveston, Prairie View A&M University, Tarleton State University, Texas Forest Service, Texas Agricultural Extension Service, Texas Agricultural Experiment Station, Texas Engineering Experiment Station, Texas Engineering Extension Service, Texas Transportation Institute, Texas Veterinary Medical Diagnostic Laboratory, and numerous other agencies and divisions. In 1971 Texas A&M University became one of the first four sea-grant designated institutions. In 2003 the university opened a campus in Qatar, with a graduate program commencing there in 2008.

The university offers leadership in many of the newer technological areas, including space, nuclear research, computers, oceanography, chemistry, and the traditional areas of agriculture, engineering, architecture, education, geosciences, business, and liberal arts. Texas A&M scientists are also on the forefront of new scientific discoveries and benchmarks, conducting experiments in areas as diverse as astronomy, cloning, and nuclear energy. The school has been recognized by the National Science Foundation as one of the top 20 research institutions in the country and consistently scores among the top universities in both national and international rankings. Its research libraries boast world-class collections and consist of over 4 million volumes. Texas A&M University aspires to preeminence in teaching, research, and public service.

HENRY C. DETHLOFF
CATHERINE COKER
Texas A&M University

Henry C. Dethloff, *A Centennial History of Texas A&M University, 1876–1976*, 2 vols. (1975), *The Pictorial History of Texas A&M University, 1876–1976* (1975); George Sessions Perry, *The Story of Texas A. and M.* (1951).

Texas Southern University

Texas Southern University (TSU), a state-supported institution of higher learning located in Houston, Tex., was established 3 March 1947. As evidenced by its original name, Texas State University for Negroes, it was established to serve the African American population. At that time, the 50th Texas legislature was intent on maintaining segregation in higher education and therefore stipulated that the university would offer courses and opportunities equal to those of the University of Texas, "including pharmacy, dentistry, arts and sciences, journalism, education, literature, law, medicine, and other professional courses." The idea of a "classical institution comparable to the University of Texas" had been on the minds of black Texans since the late 1870s. In the early 1880s Rev. John H. (Jack) Yates tried unsuccessfully to locate Bishop College in Houston. Failing that effort, he later established the Houston Baptist Academy. The academy was a college in name only, since the students were enrolled in primary, secondary, and industrial education classes. When the academy closed its doors in the early 1920s, advocates of black higher education then turned their attention to Wiley College to provide extension classes for teachers in 1925. The popular demand for such classes caused Houston school superintendent E. E. Oberholtzer to lend his support to the efforts of black educators. Consequently, the Houston School Board voted on 7 March 1927 to establish a junior college system in the city, thus giving rise to a colored junior college and a white junior college.

The Houston Colored Junior College kept its name from 1927 to 1934. Because blacks' demand for higher education continued to grow, as shown by the increase in enrollment from 70 to 700, in 1934 the Colored Junior College became a four-year institution, Houston College for Negroes. It lasted from 1934 to 1946 and held classes at the Jack Yates High School until it moved in 1946 to a 53-acre site in the Third Ward area of Houston.

Despite the efforts by the Houston College for Negroes to provide educational opportunities for blacks, African Americans still expressed concern over Texas's failure to keep its promise to provide them with a colored "classical branch university" that would be equivalent to the "white only" University of Texas. Four decades into the 20th century, this promise was still unfulfilled, and blacks began to express concern not only about a branch university, but also about graduate and professional training for people of color. A most significant step toward providing such training for black citizens of Texas was a lawsuit filed by a black mail carrier, Heman Marion Sweatt, in 1946 (*Sweatt v. Painter*) to desegregate the University of Texas Law School. In an attempt to keep Sweatt from going to court, the State of Texas made several offers to him. One of the offers was to establish a black university in Houston with a law school. On 3 March 1947 the Texas legislature passed Senate Bill No. 140, providing for the "establishment of a three million dollar Negro University including a law school to be located in Houston."

At the end of 10 months, on 2 July 1948, Raphael O'Hara Lanier, a recent minister to Liberia, took office as the first president of the university. Lanier's administration underwent considerable growing pains, marred by both internal and external difficulties ranging from the resolution of the *Sweatt* case to changing the name of the university to Texas Southern University on 1 June 1951.

Samuel M. Nabrit, dean of the graduate school at Atlanta University, was selected as the second president on 1 September 1955 and served for 10 years. He was succeeded by Joseph A. Pierce, dean of the TSU graduate school, who presided over the university in 1966–67. During the 1967–68 academic year, the administrative affairs of the university were handled by an interim executive committee: H. Hadley, A. L. Palmer, and Everett O. Bell. On 1 July 1968 Granville M. Sawyer, assistant to the president of Tennessee A&I State University (originally the Tennessee Agricultural and Industrial State Normal School for Negroes), assumed office as the fourth president of Texas Southern University. It was largely through his efforts that the 1973 legislature designated TSU as a "special purpose institution of higher learning for urban programming."

Upon Sawyer's resignation on 7 December 1978, Everett O. Bell became the interim president, serving from January 1979 to July 1980. He was succeeded by Leonard H. O. Spearman, who became the sixth president of the university in August 1980. When Spearman resigned in June 1986, Robert J. Terry, a former vice president for academic affairs, was named interim president (1986–87). Upon his death, a committee of three (Melvin Bergeron, William Moore, and Otis King) was entrusted with the duties of running the university for one year. In 1989, following a search, the Board of Regents selected William H. Harris as the seventh president. Upon Harris's resignation in 1993, JoAnn Horton became the first female president. She left office September 1995 and was followed by James M. Douglas, dean of the Thurgood Marshall School of Law. Douglas's presidency lasted from 1995 to 1999. He was then followed by Priscilla D. Slade, who presided over the university from 1999 to 2006. Currently, John M. Rudley sits at the helm of the university.

Born during the era of Jim Crow, Texas Southern was a party to the *Adam v. Adam* case that challenged segregation in higher education. As part of an agreement between the State of Texas and the federal Office of Civil Rights, a "Texas Plan" was devised in 1985 and again in 2001. The shortcomings of these plans notwithstanding, they led to the improvement in the physical facilities, new academic programs, and an increase in enrollment. As of 2008 the enrollment of Texas Southern University was approximately 9,000 with 481 full-time and part-time faculty members, 55 percent of whom hold terminal degrees. The university offers programs leading to 85 baccalaureates, 27 masters, one Ed.D., and four Ph.D.s in eight schools and colleges: the College of Liberal Arts and Behavioral Sciences, the College of Pharmacy and Health Sciences, the Thurgood Marshall School of Law, the College of Education, the School of Science and Technology, the Jesse H. Jones School of Business, the Tavis Smiley School of Communications, and the Graduate School. The university also operates a College of Continuing Education. Housed on a 145-acre campus just southeast of downtown Houston, as of 2008 the physical plant of the university was comprised of 46 buildings, including an FM radio station, a physical education complex with a 7,200-seat arena, a performance theater, several dormitories and apartment complexes, the Robert James Terry Library, which holds more than 457,000 books and bound periodicals and the Heartman Collection on African American Life and Culture, the Barbara Jordan Archives, and the Mickey Leland Archives.

MERLINE PITRE
Texas Southern University

Howard Beeth and Cary D. Wintz, eds., *Black Dixie: Afro-Texas History and Culture in Houston* (1992); Ira B. Bryant, *Texas Southern University: Its Antecedents, Political Origins, and Future* (1975); John S. Lash, Hortense W. Dixon, and Thomas F.

Freeman, *Texas Southern University: From Separation to Special Designation* (1975); Merline Pitre, *In Struggle against Jim Crow: Lulu B. White and the NAACP, 1900–1957* (1999).

Tulane University

Tulane University traces its origins to the Medical College of Louisiana founded by seven New Orleans doctors in 1834. For more than a dozen years the school flourished, and in 1847 it became one of four constituent faculties of the newly established, and nominally state-supported, University of Louisiana. In practice, however, the medical school remained largely autonomous, and development of the larger university was cut short by the school's extended closure during the Civil War and Reconstruction period. Upon reopening in 1878 the university's future remained economically precarious, leaving the way open for control to be shifted to a private body created to administer the large educational bequest of Paul Tulane, a former New Orleans merchant.

The Tulane University of Louisiana came into being between 1882 and 1884 when the Louisiana legislature turned over the assets and control of the old University of Louisiana to the recently established administrators of the Tulane Educational Fund. Several years later Josephine Louise Newcomb, a native of Baltimore but a resident of New Orleans, donated $100,000 to establish within Tulane University the H. Sophie Newcomb Memorial College—the first women's coordinate college in the United States. At her death Newcomb bequeathed to the college the residue of her estate, a sum in excess of $2 million. From the beginning male undergraduates enrolled in what would become the College of Arts and Sciences.

Between the 1890s and the beginning of World War II Tulane's curriculum expanded to encompass professional education in engineering, architecture, tropical medicine, social work, business, and other fields. (A law faculty had existed since antebellum times.) Prior to the 1950s, admissions standards were not especially rigorous and graduate training was confined almost exclusively to work at the M.A. level. Most students were local residents who lived off campus.

Tulane's transformation into a research university with aspirations for national recognition occurred during the presidency of Rufus Carrollton Harris (1937–60). Under Harris's leadership the university added 28 Ph.D. programs between 1944 and 1960 while increasing its sponsored research funding from just over $200,000 to more than $4 million during roughly the same period. Graduate enrollment nearly doubled over the course of the 1950s, and admissions standards became more demanding at all levels. In 1957–58 Tulane's claim to national stature received a coveted stamp of legitimacy when the school was elected to membership in the Association of American Universities. President Harris sought, with limited success, to decrease the emphasis on Division I football, but he was unable to persuade a conservative board of administrators to begin the process of racial desegregation. Inaction on the racial front excluded Tulane from

Gibson Hall, the first structure on the present Tulane University campus in New Orleans, constructed in 1894 (Photograph courtesy Tulane University)

the first round of a program of sizeable grants from the Ford Foundation aimed at creating "dispersed peaks of excellence" among American universities. Following protracted litigation the first black students enrolled at Tulane in 1963.

Graduate education and research, together with chronic medical school deficits and an ambitious program of dormitory construction (made necessary by the recruitment of out-of-state students), strained the school's finances. Despite major grants from a number of national philanthropies the school was forced to spend endowment capital throughout the 1950s and 1960s, while relying on tuition revenue for most of its operating budget. By the mid-1970s, as liquid endowment assets shrank to a low point of around $1 million, Tulane teetered on the brink of insolvency. Disaster was averted and for the next two decades the school struggled to support a diminished but still large graduate program with painfully limited resources. During the 1990s graduate school expenditures were slashed by over $1 million, leaving the university far behind peer institutions such as Duke, Vanderbilt, Emory, and Washington University in St. Louis.

Under President Scott Cowen (1998–) efforts to regain lost ground were sidetracked in 2005 by the forced closure of the university for an entire semester as a result of flooding from Hurricane Katrina. Faced with extensive and costly damage to the physical plant, loss of tuition revenue, and a burgeoning debt that soared to $100 million over a four-month span, President Cowen concluded that drastic measures were necessary to ensure the school's survival. The result was a sweeping plan of reorganization that cut the number of doctoral programs from 45 to 18, stripped the university of some 230 faculty (mostly in the College of Medicine), and abolished the graduate school, the College of Engineering, Paul Tulane College (previously the College of Arts and Sciences), and H. Sophie Newcomb College. In the aftermath of these changes Tulane's endowment has grown and undergraduate enrollments have steadily increased. Graduate education continues on a greatly reduced scale, and the school has become actively engaged with problems of the local community.

CLARENCE L. MOHR
University of South Alabama

John P. Dyer, *Tulane: The Biography of a University, 1834–1965* (1966); Clarence L. Mohr and Joseph E. Gordon, *Tulane: The Emergence of a Modern University, 1945–1980* (2001).

Tuskegee University

Tuskegee (tuh-SKEE-gee) University is located in the rural east Alabama town of Tuskegee (meaning "warrior" in the Muskogee [Creek] dialect), the seat of Macon County. The county was established on 18 December 1832, from land ceded by the Creek Indians. The school developed through the efforts of Lewis Adams, a former slave, and George W. Campbell, a former slave owner, who saw in the late 1870s a need for the education of African Americans in rural Macon County. The founding date of the university was 4 July 1881.

From a modest beginning in a one-room shanty located near the Butler Chapel AME Zion Church, Tuskegee University rose to national prominence under the leadership of its first president, Booker T. Washington (1881–1915). Washington was a highly skilled organizer and fund-raiser who counseled U.S. presidents and was a strong advocate of African American farmers and businesses. He worked tirelessly in developing methods to aid African Americans to succeed by establishing a variety of on-campus vocational classes, including carpentry, brick making, sewing, millinery, animal husbandry, and gardening. Students were also required to complete coursework toward general diplomas, which included mathematics, English, and history. Student enrollment was not limited to rural Macon County and the South, but was international in composition.

Washington's vision for Tuskegee University (originally called Tuskegee Normal and changed to Tuskegee Normal and Industrial Institute in 1893) involved recruiting the best and brightest available within the African American community, including scientist George Washington Carver as farm manager (1896), architect Robert R. Taylor as director of Mechanical Industries (1882), and sociologist and editor Monroe N. Work as founder of the Department of Records and Research (1908). Despite the enormous influence Washington had on the university's success, Tuskegee's prominence as an African American school of higher learning did not abate after Washington's tenure as president ended. In fact,

"Lifting the Veil," the Booker T. Washington Monument on the campus of Tuskegee University, Tuskegee, Ala. The inscription at its base reads, "He lifted the veil of ignorance from his people and pointed the way to progress through education and industry." (Tuskegee University Archives)

the university's history is intimately linked to the accomplishments of its presidents. During Robert R. Moton's tenure (1915–35), the university continued to grow in size and prestige. Moton actively sought better quality buildings and more modern equipment for teaching the trades, more comfortable housing for faculty and students, and enlarged and improved facilities for recreation, health, and academic studies. The highlight of his career at Tuskegee was the expansion and enrichment of the curricula. In 1927 Moton raised the university's academic program from high school level to full four-year college status with bachelor's degrees in agriculture, home economics, mechanical industries, and education. Furthermore, through his efforts, the university donated land for the Tuskegee Veterans Administration Hospital, the first and only one staffed by black professionals.

Tuskegee University's accomplishments continued with its third president, Frederick D. Patterson (1935–53), who founded the School of Veterinary Medicine (where nearly 75 percent of all black veterinarians in America are trained) in 1944, the year he also founded the United Negro College Fund (UNCF). The UNCF continues today as a critical source of annual income for a consortium of Historically Black Colleges and Universities (HBCUs), Tuskegee University among them.

During the 1940s, although the rest of the world was embroiled in war, the university (as of 1937 called Tuskegee Institute) continued to lead the way toward the betterment of African Americans nationwide. The Infantile Paralysis Center opened in 1941 as another unit of Tuskegee University's John A. Andrew Memorial Hospital. The center provided treatment facilities and services for African American patients (especially for treatment of polio) from the southeastern states as well as care for Alabama patients with other orthopedic conditions. Further accomplishments came with the university's participation in the Civilian Pilot Training Program (which began at Tuskegee in 1939) that eventually led to the formation of the 99th Fighter Squadron of Tuskegee Airmen in June of 1941.

The fourth president, Luther H. Foster (1953–81), led Tuskegee through the turbulent years of the civil rights movement, as well as overseeing the organization of the College of Arts and Sciences, the elimination of several vocational programs, and the development of engineering programs. Under Foster's leadership the university maintained an attitude of open dialogue, allowing a variety of controversial speakers such as Martin Luther King Jr., Malcolm X, Stokely Carmichael, Julian Bond, and Alex Haley to visit.

Furthermore, faculty and staff were not discouraged to be involved in the civil rights movement. Charles Gomillion, professor of sociology and dean of the College of Arts and Sciences, filed a lawsuit leading to the groundbreaking Supreme Court decision in *Gomillion v. Lightfoot* (1960), declaring that Tuskegee's black citizens had been illegally gerrymandered out of their right to vote. Tuskegee's student population was actively involved in organizations such as the Student Nonviolent Coordinating Committee.

In 1985, under the leadership of Tuskegee's fifth president, Benjamin F. Payton (1981–2010), Tuskegee Institute attained university status and began offering its first doctoral programs in integrative biosciences, materials science, and engineering. The General Daniel "Chappie" James Center for Aerospace Science and Health Education was constructed in 1987, which included the largest athletic arena in the Southern Intercollegiate Athletic Conference. By 2008 the Tuskegee University National Center for Bioethics in Research and Health Care and the Tuskegee Airmen National Historic Site were completed. During the final four years of Payton's guidance, the university added the Andrew F. Brimmer Hall for the College of Business and Information Science and rebuilt Margaret Murray Washington Hall.

Tuskegee University's enrollment currently averages over 3,000 students, representing most states and several foreign countries. The university is rooted in a history of successfully educating African American men and women to understand themselves against a background of a rich academic heritage and the promise of their individual and collective future.

DANA CHANDLER
Tuskegee University

Pete Daniel, *Journal of Southern History* (August 1970); Martia Graham Goodson, ed., *Chronicles of Faith: The Autobiography of Frederick D. Patterson* (1991); Louis R. Harlan, *Booker T. Washington: The Making of a Black Leader, 1856–1901* (1972); William Hardin Hughes and Frederick D. Patterson, *Robert Russa Moton of Hampton and Tuskegee* (1956); Robert J. Norrell, *Reaping the Whirlwind: The Civil Rights Movement in Tuskegee* (1985).

University of North Carolina School of the Arts

The nation's first public arts conservatory, the University of North Carolina School of the Arts (UNCSA) is a unique institute for training talented students for professional careers in the arts. Conceived under the progressive leadership of Gov. Terry Sanford, novelist John Ehle, and others, UNCSA was established as the North Carolina School of the Arts by the North Carolina General Assembly in 1963. The school's founding legislation directed the new school to serve not only the state of North Carolina but also the Southeast.

The school opened in 1965 after distinguished leaders in Winston-Salem raised nearly $1 million from citizens in a telephone campaign to win the school for the "City of the Arts." In 1972 the school became part of the prestigious University of North Carolina system. At UNCSA more than 1,100 students from middle school through graduate school train for careers in the arts in five arts schools: dance, design and production (including a visual arts program), drama, filmmaking, and music. With a full academic program, UNCSA is accredited and awards the high school diploma, the College Arts Diploma, the Professional Artist Certificate, and bachelor's and master's degrees.

Today, as in the 1960s, students are admitted by the strength of their audition or portfolio. To be chosen they must not only possess talent for their art, but also passion and dedication. They work in their art form from the day they arrive. Of the more than 1,100 students enrolled, half come from North Carolina, representing about two-thirds of the state's 100 counties; and the other half come from about 40 states and more than two dozen foreign countries. Students at UNCSA study with resident master teachers who have had successful careers in the arts—from the Kirov Ballet to the Los Angeles Philharmonic—and who remain active in their professions. They train, rehearse, and perform in some of the finest facilities available, commensurate with those in the profession. The school's primary performance venue is the 1,380-seat Roger L. Stevens Center for the Performing Arts, a former vaudevillian theatre and movie house located about a mile away from campus in downtown Winston-Salem. Since its renovation in 1983, the Stevens Center has played a significant role in the revitalization of downtown.

In addition to its educational mission, UNCSA was also founded to be a resource enhancing the cultural life of citizens. As such, the school offers some 300 public performances and screenings by students, faculty, and guest artists each year, both on and off campus. The school also reaches out into the state and region by taking dance, chamber music, opera, and other touring performances into the public schools, Brenner Children's Hospital, and retirement communities, to name a few. UNCSA also hosts statewide arts festivals and offers community-based music and dance programs.

In 2008 the North Carolina School of the Arts changed its name to the University of North Carolina School of the Arts to reinforce its long-standing ties to the UNC system and to let prospective students know that it is more than an arts magnet high school: It is a *university*.

Today, UNCSA is an arts school of international renown—primarily because of the reputation of its alumni, who have performed in or behind the scenes of Broadway shows, film, television, and regional theatre, and who are members of the world's finest symphony orchestras and opera and dance companies. They have won or been nominated for all of the major awards in the entertainment industry, including Tony, Oscar, Emmy, and Grammy.

Equal to its reputation, the school also has a chancellor of international renown: Tony-, Grammy-, Emmy-, and Olivier-winning conductor John Mauceri, founding director of the Hollywood Bowl Orchestra and former music director of four opera companies: Washington (National), Scottish (Glasgow), the Teatro Regio (Turin, Italy), and Pittsburgh. He has been chancellor since 2006.

MARLA CARPENTER
University of North Carolina School of the Arts

Leslie Banner, "A Passionate Preference: The Story of the North Carolina School of the Arts," North Carolina School of the Arts Foundation (1987).

University of the South

Ten Episcopal bishops and laymen from 10 southern states under the leadership of bishops James Otey of Tennessee and Leonidas Polk of Louisiana organized the University of the South from 1856 to 1860. Designed to be a regional, indeed, national university under the perpetual control of the Episcopal Church, the university would be dedicated to preparing young male undergraduates and seminarians to lead the South. Although no buildings were constructed or students enrolled before the Civil War, the university retained title to more than 7,000 acres on the Cumberland Plateau in southeastern Tennessee that had been given by the Sewanee Mining Company and others before the conflict.

After the war the second bishop of Tennessee, Charles Quintard, worked with others to revive the concept of the university and to preserve the title to the land. A fund-raising trip to England brought nearly $10,000, and the initial students matriculated in September 1868. A decade later the first stone buildings were erected. Thanks to generous bequests, including many from northern friends, by the late 1890s the university with its new neo-Gothic stone buildings had begun to resemble a smaller version of an Oxford University college. In the early 1890s the university started a law school and a medical school (with dentistry and nursing), both continuing until 1909 when all were closed. Also the *Sewanee Review* began publication in 1892, now the oldest continuously published literary journal in the United States.

In the next decades Sewanee, as the campus is popularly known, enjoyed economic prosperity, adding buildings, students, and a growing reputation. One asset initially helping the reputation was its football teams, champions of the South in 1899 and charter members of both the Southern and later Southeastern Conferences; it left the latter in 1940, never having won a game against other conference members.

From the start, Sewanee has produced a series of leaders for the Episcopal Church: priests, bishops, and presiding bishops. Considered one of the premier Episcopal seminaries in the world, the School of Theology usually has a student body of 100. The school pioneered the concept of theological education by extension in a program that now annually enrolls more than 7,000 students around the world. It also publishes the *Sewanee Theological Review* to wide acclaim.

From 1868 until 1981 the university operated a secondary school, first the Sewanee grammar school, then the Sewanee Military Academy, and finally the Sewanee Academy. In 1981 the Sewanee Academy merged with nearby St. Andrew's School to form St. Andrew's–Sewanee School.

The College of Arts and Sciences, formally organized in the 1890s, has achieved and sustained national acclaim as one of the nation's finest liberal arts colleges. Committed to a residential experience for its 1,400 students, the university retains a favorable student-faculty ratio, offers majors in 36 subjects, and promotes excellence in its language study-abroad programs. Women students were first admitted in 1969, matching similar steps at the same time by other liberal arts colleges in the South. With now more than 13,000 acres wholly controlled by the university, students have unique opportunities to major in the study of environmental and natural resources. Sewanee's long literary tradition, bolstered by a generous gift from playwright Tennessee Williams, offers students many chances to write, publish, and perform. Not surprisingly, the university has also sought to promote studies of the South, broadly defined in terms of religion, economics, politics, history, and literature.

These undergraduate educational experiences have produced 25 Rhodes scholars, ranking the university among the leaders of all American liberal arts colleges, while it has also produced 27 NCAA Scholar-Athletes. Many students also participate in the university's acclaimed outreach and community service projects, both locally and throughout the Western Hemisphere. Matching their efforts are those of the University Choir with its famous Lessons and Carols service just before Christmas and with its summer travel to sing in English cathedrals.

On the campus, visitors will see student leaders and faculty wearing academic gowns as they have done since 1871. Often students may represent the fourth or fifth generation of their families who have attended Sewanee, and these family connections remain an important part of the university's traditions. But so also does its capacity for inspiring devotion and loyalty, which for many centers on the All Saints' Chapel that dominates the central campus and provides the setting for the most important rites of passage for all students and faculty in the university community. Though isolated atop a 2,000-foot plateau, often shrouded in fog, and yet connected to the wider world through every aspect of modern technology, the University of the South remains what its founders intended: an Episcopal university that offers a broad and inclusive educational experience to all of those who come, whether to study or to teach. After 150 years, the university is poised for still greater years to come.

SAMUEL R. WILLIAMSON JR.
University of the South

Donald S. Armentrout, *The Quest for the Informed Priest: A History of the School of Theology of the University of the South* (1979); Arthur Ben Chitty, *Reconstruction at Sewanee* (1954); Samuel R. Williamson Jr., *Sewanee Sesquicentennial History: The Making of the University of the South* (2008); Samuel R. Williamson Jr. and Gerald L. Smith, eds., *Sewanee Perspectives on the History of the University of the South* (2009).

Vance, Rupert B.

(1899–1975) SOCIOLOGIST.

During his 40-year tenure as a scholar, author, and lecturer at the University of North Carolina at Chapel Hill (UNC), Rupert Bayless Vance sought to unravel the threads weaving the South's people and land into a tapestry of poverty, an effort that became a personal struggle both to understand his own ties to the South and to help break the vicious cycle of dependence and despair inherent in the South's cotton-based economy. With pioneer sociologist Howard W. Odum—founder of the Institute for Research in Social Science and of the Department of Sociology at UNC, the first sociology department created at a southern university—Vance developed the study of "regional sociology." His experience of living in the South shaped the forms of his scholarship and of his reform efforts.

Born at the turn of the 20th century

in Plummerville, Ark., Vance grew up in an area whose wounds from the Civil War had yet to be healed. His early life was filled with hardships. Contracting polio when he was three, Vance lost the use of both of his legs; through physical therapy at an orthopedic clinic in St. Louis, he eventually was able to walk with crutches and to enter elementary school when he was 10. In the depths of the 1920s agricultural depression Vance's father lost his farmland and went bankrupt. Vance later utilized the image of his father's failure to represent the general condition of the South. A love of reading, a bachelor's degree in English from Henderson Brown College in Arkadelphia, Ark., and contact with writers such as Edward Mims and the Agrarians at Vanderbilt University, where he received his master's degree in economics, fostered the clear, descriptive, and humanistic style of his essays. The close relationship that developed between Vance and Howard Odum when Vance joined UNC's fledgling sociology department in 1926 encouraged the young sociologist to pursue his desire for social and economic reforms in the South.

Vance's studies of southern life were interdisciplinary, covering the topics of southern politics, culture, history, demographics, the transformation of the South from a rural area into an urban one, societal conflict, and cotton tenancy. In *Human Factors in Cotton Culture: A Study in the Social Geography of the American South* (1929), *Human Geography of the South: A Study in Regional Resources and Human Adequacy* (1932), *All These People: The Nation's Human Resources in the South* (coauthored with Nadia Danilevsky, 1945), and other studies, Vance advanced the theory that the South's problems were manmade, that history—not geography—had arrested the South in a frontier stage of development. The social and economic patterns of the South had been shaped by the plantation. Locked into a rural economy based on the production of cotton while the North grew more urban and industrial, the South retained (until the mid-1940s) a colonial economy—an economy that necessitated the exploitation of natural resources and labor in order to afford goods manufactured in another region. Overpopulation, an unstable cotton market, Jim Crow laws, and parasitic diseases such as hookworm and malaria, Vance argued, had only worsened the South's problems.

As a scholar, government consultant, southerner, and president or founder of several important sociology societies (including the Southern Sociological Society, the Population Association of America, and the American Sociological Association), Vance lobbied for social reforms such as the 1938 Bankhead-Jones Farm Tenant Bill and constructive urban and industrial planning in the South. Decades after his death in Chapel Hill in 1975, Vance's search for reform and his southern cultural studies remain relevant.

ELIZABETH MCGEHEE
Salem College

Rupert B. Vance, in *Regionalism and the South*, ed. John Shelton Reed and Daniel J. Singal (1982).

Vanderbilt University

Vanderbilt University, a private university in Nashville, Tenn., was chartered in 1873 and opened in 1875. Its origins date back to frontier days when, in 1785, the Cumberland Academy was established. Remodeled as the University of Nashville, it was divided after the Civil War into a medical school that became a part of Vanderbilt in 1875 and an academic department that evolved into the George Peabody College for Teachers. Already in the 1890s, Vanderbilt had attempted to unite with Peabody; unification was achieved in 1979.

Vanderbilt University is named after "Commodore" Cornelius Vanderbilt, who donated $1 million, then the largest founding gift ever deeded to a university. Vanderbilt, from New York, was one of America's wealthiest men, but not known for any religious fervor. That he gave such a large sum of money to southern education under the auspices of the Methodist Church may be explained, as the founding myth has it, with cunning southern wit. The mastermind behind the scheme was Bishop Holland Nimmons McTyeire, who supposedly visited Thomas Jefferson's grave in the 1840s, where he was impressed with Jefferson's achievement as the father of the University of Virginia. After the Civil War, McTyeire successfully lobbied the Methodist Church for a central university, only lacking the necessary funds. When he fell ill, his wife Amelia Townsend sent him to recover at the home of her cousin, Frank Crawford Vanderbilt, the Commodore's second wife. The university came to be thanks to the wives behind the scenes.

Vanderbilt University aspired to educational greatness from the beginning. McTyeire, the first president of the Board of Trust, hired innovative scholar-scientists, including in 1886 a young German-trained professor of Latin, James Hampton Kirkland, who, in 1893, succeeded founding chancellor Landon C. Garland. Under Kirkland's administration, Vanderbilt briefly caught up with northeastern institutions in the number of graduate fellowships. But after the turn of the century a difficult period started. During the "War of the Bishops," Kirkland fought with the Methodist Church over control of the university. He argued that, as the Church did not provide sufficient funds, it should have only limited influence. The bitter fight ended with a 1914 court ruling that severed Vanderbilt's ties with the Methodists.

Kirkland's next major project was the medical school. Thanks to the medical reformer Abraham Flexner, who in the 1910s used to vacation next to the Kirklands in Canada, Kirkland established excellent relations with the General Education Board in New York and the Rockefeller and Carnegie foundations. The mission of these interrelated funding organizations was, among others, to support promising educational projects in the South. Kirkland's Vanderbilt seemed the right place to raise southern educational standards. By the mid-1920s the Vanderbilt Medical School reopened as a modern medical center. The Johns Hopkins Medical School had served as a model.

But it would not be justified to reduce

the early 20th-century Vanderbilt to its medical school. In the 1920s the Fugitives, a group of southern poets, added to Vanderbilt's fame. They evolved into the Southern Agrarians, 12 writers and historians who published their manifesto, *I'll Take My Stand*, in 1930. Ironically, Vanderbilt—always a little uneasy about being a *southern* university—thus contributed significantly to southern identity. Simultaneously, that is, during the 1940s, Vanderbilt had to face its *white* heritage in a segregated South.

In 1937 Kirkland was succeeded by Oliver Cromwell Carmichael, who served through World War II. In 1946 Harvie Branscomb took over. He was probably one of the university's most controversial leaders: while Branscomb pushed the institution toward gradual integration, he was also at the center of the infamous "Lawson Affair." James Lawson, one of the first African American students in the divinity school, in 1960 was expelled for organizing nonviolence workshops and thus for being central to the Nashville student movement, headquartered at the local historically black universities, that organized sit-ins to desegregate lunch counters. Lawson was almost immediately reinstalled thanks to the intervention of Harold Sterling Vanderbilt, the president of the Board of Trust, a great-grandson of the Commodore, and the only member of the Vanderbilt family to be actively involved in university affairs. Lawson nonetheless did not return until 1970. In 2006 he was given the title "distinguished professor," and the following year a chair of African American history was named in his honor.

Branscomb had previously been connected with Duke University's divinity school, which brought back memories of Vanderbilt's Methodist heritage. Branscomb, however, focused on striving for academic greatness; for example, in the late 1940s he established relations with Brazil, thus making Vanderbilt an institution particularly well-suited for the study of U.S. relations with South America. The tradition was continued in the early 21st century when the Center for the Americas was created, of which the Latin American Public Opinion Project was a part.

Chancellor Alexander Heard (1963–82) saw the university through the era of student protests, the Vietnam War, the integration of African Americans, and the admission of women; women had studied at Vanderbilt since its opening, though at first not officially. The Heard era illustrated that Vanderbilt attracts a different "type" of student, not generally inclined toward loud or violent protests. They find different ways of affecting society. During the Joe B. Wyatt (1982–2000) administration, Vanderbilt pioneered in establishing Alternative Spring Break, a social service movement that has since spread to campuses across the nation. This less noisy activism counterbalances Vanderbilt's rich fraternity and sorority life. During Wyatt's administration, Vanderbilt also became a national arboretum in 1988.

Under Chancellor Gordon Gee (2000–2007) Vanderbilt blossomed, instituting innovative and daring research centers where faculty and students could develop their scholarly/scientific creativity beyond restrictive disciplinary boundaries. In 2008 Nicholas Zeppos was named the eighth chancellor.

ANJA BECKER
Vanderbilt University

Paul K. Conkin, *Gone with the Ivy: A Biography of Vanderbilt University* (1985), *Peabody College: From a Frontier Academy to the Frontiers of Teaching and Learning* (2002), *The Southern Agrarians* (2001); Dale A. Johnson, ed., *Vanderbilt Divinity School: Education, Contest, Change* (2001); Melissa Kean, *Desegregating Private Higher Education in the South: Duke, Emory, Rice, Tulane, and Vanderbilt* (2008); Edwin Mims, *History of Vanderbilt University* (1946).

Virginia, University of

Conceived by Thomas Jefferson as early as 1800, the University of Virginia was formally established in 1819 and opened its doors to students in 1825. It was unique in its day for its elective system, offering freedom of choice for students, and for its fully secular orientation. Jefferson designed the curriculum and the architecture and selected the original library holdings. On the principle that the institution should be based on the "illimitable freedom of the human mind," the university opened with nine possible specializations. Its physical structure featured a rotunda at its center housing a library rather than a chapel. Ten pavilions, separated by student rooms, created an open "academical village" where faculty and students could interact and where classical architecture served as examples of European Enlightenment values. The university would be governed by a rector and a "board of visitors" and would be administered internally by a chairman of the faculty. The university's first rector was James Madison, and James Monroe served on the board of visitors. It has grown to be among the highest-ranked public universities in America.

Jefferson's vision of a university administered by its faculty survived throughout the 19th century but proved unsustainable by the early 20th century. By then the university had weathered the Civil War, one of the few southern institutions to remain open. A devastating fire in 1898, which destroyed the rotunda and its annex, required extensive rebuilding. Stanford White, the Gilded Age's most prominent architect, was retained for this project. White designed major new buildings that changed the original architectural vision at the turn of the 20th century. And the board of visitors moved to create the office of president, the first one of whom assumed his duties in 1904.

The University of Virginia has had only seven presidents through the course of its history. Edwin Anderson Alderman (1904–31), an innovator of southern progressive education, oversaw the tremendous growth of the student body from 500 to 2,450. He established much stronger connections with secondary institutions and created admissions standards. Under Alderman's direction, in 1920 women were admitted to graduate and professional programs, following a long-fought battle headed by Mary Munford. Alderman died of a stroke while traveling, and his able assistant John Newcomb assumed the interim duties of the president.

Both John Lloyd Newcomb (1933–

47) and Colgate W. Darden Jr. (1947–59) served the university ably. Newcomb, an engineer by training, oversaw major building projects and expanded curricular programs and departmental specializations through the Depression and World War II. Darden, a former member of Congress and Virginia governor, sought to control the elitism of the fraternity social system, to expand the university to become the "capstone" of public education throughout the state, to enhance the beauty of the grounds, and to enlarge the graduate business programs. The years of his presidency required him to act on desegregating the all-white institution, which he was prepared to do on a limited basis, admitting the first black graduate students, Gregory Swanson (Law) and Walter Ridley (Education). He was not supportive of desegregating K–12 education.

President Edgar F. Shannon Jr. transformed the university between 1959 and 1974. During his tenure, women were admitted to fully equal status as undergraduate students in the College of Arts and Sciences, and black student recruitment developed in earnest in the late 1960s. The size of the institution tripled (from 5,000 to 15,000 students), major government grants were obtained, and substantial disruption was averted by his skillful handling of Vietnam War protests. The distinguished Echols Scholars program was created in 1960, attracting honors students. Along with Edwin Alderman, his successor Edgar Shannon made the greatest strides in creating the modern university.

From 1974 to the present, three additional presidents have made their mark. Frank Hereford (provost from 1966 on), an eminent physicist who earned all his degrees at the University of Virginia, succeeded Shannon. Hereford believed his greatest achievement was the major capital campaign he initiated. He also ended the infamous Easter Week or "Easters" activities, begun in the 1890s as a weeklong celebration of athletics and dance, which had evolved into a disruptive, alcohol-abusing event. Robert O'Neil, lawyer and former president of the University of Wisconsin system, served as president from 1985 to 1990. As an outsider, he recognized the critical importance of making progress in the quality of experience for African Americans and women, and he instituted major taskforce committees to review the needs of both groups. He also focused considerable efforts on substance abuse by students. In 1990 he became the head of the Thomas Jefferson Center for the Protection of Free Expression and returned to teach at the law school. John Casteen (1990–), who like Hereford had received all his degrees from the university, had previously served as the director of admissions, the secretary of education for Virginia, and the president of the University of Connecticut. His focus has been on the necessary refinancing and restructuring of the university, as the state has withdrawn support. Fund-raising has been a major effort, and he has overseen the dramatic increase of the university's endowment over the years. His emphasis on student diversity and access led to the creation of AccessUVa, a fund of grants for low-income students.

In the past 20 years, a host of new programs and new buildings, including major new sports facilities, has been created. The University of Virginia has been consistently ranked one of the top two public universities in America ever since *U.S. News and World Report* began separate listings of public and private universities. Its students are highly competitive, and it boasts one of the highest graduation rates among public universities. The African American graduation rate is the highest among the "public ivies." The institution is well known for its systems of student governance and its single-sanction honor code—a tradition that was established in 1842. Total campus enrollment stands at over 20,000 students in 2009.

PHYLLIS LEFFLER
University of Virginia

Virginius Dabney, *Mr. Jefferson's University: A History* (1981); Susan Hitchcock, *University of Virginia: A Pictorial History* (2003); Christopher Lucas, *American Higher Education* (2006); Richard Guy Wilson, *The Academical Village: The Creation of an Architectural Masterpiece* (2009).

Virginia Military Institute

Established in 1839 in Lexington, Va., on the site of a state arsenal, the Virginia Military Institute (VMI) is the nation's oldest state-supported military college. Students in the Corps of Cadets, about 1,500 in number, choose their major from 15 departments that offer the bachelor of science or bachelor of arts degree. Among the departments with the most academic majors are civil engineering, mechanical engineering, biology, economics and business, international studies, psychology, and history. VMI is ranked at or near the top of public liberal arts colleges listed in the annual survey by *U.S. News and World Report*. About 60 percent of cadets are Virginia residents. African American cadets first enrolled in 1968, and female cadets were first admitted in 1997. All cadets must enroll in four years of ROTC courses (army, air force, navy, or marines), but contracting to pursue a commission in the military services is a choice that each cadet makes.

Francis H. Smith became VMI's first superintendent (college president) in 1839 and remained in that position for 50 years. He was a West Point graduate (1833) and then a math teacher when, at the age of 26, he came to VMI. During those early years, the academic emphasis was on science and teacher education for Virginia. Thomas Jonathan Jackson (later "Stonewall" Jackson) taught natural philosophy (physics) at VMI for 10 years prior to the start of the Civil War. During that war the Corps of Cadets was mobilized and fought in the battle of New Market in the Shenandoah Valley on 15 May 1864; 10 cadets were killed in action. Each year VMI commemorates that event with a dress parade during which the concepts of duty and service are cited. Each cadet who died as a result of the battle is recorded as "Died on the field of honor." The main entrance to the barracks, a National Historic Landmark, is named

Jackson Arch and contains one of Stonewall Jackson's quotes that is inculcated into every student: "You may be whatever you resolve to be."

VMI has long emphasized the citizen-soldier ideal, referring to those alumni (85 percent) who serve on active duty in the military for several years and later pursue a civilian career, compared to the 15 percent who make the military their career. In the latter category, VMI's most famous graduate was Gen. George C. Marshall, class of 1901, who was the U.S. Army's chief of staff during World War II. In 1953 he became the only military person ever awarded the Nobel Peace Prize in recognition of what he accomplished as President Truman's secretary of state in implementing the Marshall Plan for reconstructing postwar Europe. Other VMI graduates distinguished in their military careers include Gen. Lemuel Shepherd, commandant of the Marine Corps, Gen. J. H. B. Peay III, who commanded the 101st Airborne Division in Operations Desert Shield and Desert Storm, and Gen. John P. Jumper, who served as the Air Force chief of staff, 2001–5. In the civilian arena, VMI's John deButts was chairman of AT&T, and Bruce C. Gottwald was chairman of the Ethyl Corporation. Jonathan Daniels, class of 1961, was killed in 1965 in Hayneville, Ala., during the civil rights movement. In the words of Dr. Martin Luther King Jr., "One of the most heroic Christian deeds of which I have heard in my entire ministry was performed by Jonathan Daniels."

All cadets live in the VMI barracks and adhere to a fundamental cornerstone of the institute: the VMI honor system, which simply states that a cadet will not lie, cheat, or steal, nor tolerate those who do. Cadets attend small classes with a student-faculty ratio of about 16:1. A long tradition welcomes cadets each year from Taiwan and Thailand, and many VMI cadets participate in semesters abroad, some exchanging places with military college students from Germany, France, and England. Physical fitness is emphasized at VMI, which sponsors numerous NCAA Division I intercollegiate athletic teams. VMI was a member of the Southern Conference from 1924 to 2003 and currently belongs to the Big South Conference. Success in track and field and wrestling has a long history, and the basketball team has led the nation in points-per-game in the last three seasons, 2007–9.

Seven VMI alumni have been awarded the Congressional Medal, and 11 have been designated Rhodes scholars.

THOMAS W. DAVIS
Virginia Military Institute

Judith M. Arnold and Diane B. Jacob, *A Virginia Military Institute Album, 1839–1910: A Collection of Photographs and Manuscripts from the VMI Archives* (1982); Laura Fairchild Brodie, *Breaking Out: VMI and the Coming of Women* (2000); T. W. Davis, *A Crowd of Honorable Youths: Historical Essays on the First 150 Years of the Virginia Military Institute* (1988); Henry A. Wise, *Drawing Out the Man: The VMI Story* (1978); Jennings C. Wise, *The Military History of the Virginia Military Institute from 1839 to 1865* (1915, 2009).

Volker, Joseph F.

(1913–1989) UNIVERSITY PRESIDENT. The founding president of the University of Alabama at Birmingham (UAB), Joseph F. Volker, emerged out of a northeastern urban environment far different from Alabama but with political skills and social views well-suited for seeking change in that state. Born 9 March 1913, in Elizabeth, N.J., young Volker attended public schools in the Elizabeth area before heading to Rutgers University for two years of undergraduate study in biology and chemistry. He then enrolled in Indiana University, completing the D.D.S. degree in 1936. While in Bloomington he lived with an uncle active in American Federation of Labor (AFL) politics in exchange for his services as editorial assistant on an AFL newsletter. From Indiana, Volker took an internship in oral surgery and anesthesiology at Mountainside Hospital in Montclair, N.J. Here he met and married a nurse, Juanita ("Neet") Berry, with whom he ultimately had three children. Next, Volker headed to the School of Medicine and Dentistry of the University of Rochester, where he had a Carnegie fellowship to pursue the Ph.D. in biochemistry. With the rank of second lieutenant from Indiana's Army ROTC program, he almost had to postpone completion of his Rochester studies when the United States mobilized for World War II. At the request of the Carnegie Fellowship Committee, however, his doctoral pursuits—especially research on the new substance called fluoride—were classified "essential." With Selective Service deferment he completed the Ph.D. in 1941 and immediately accepted a position at Rochester as assistant professor and director of research in the Department of Biochemistry and Pharmacology. His four years at Rochester, an institution at the forefront of interdisciplinary science, were a seminal time of his life.

With the army desperately needing dentists, Volker kept the deferment in 1942 when he became professor of clinical dentistry at Tufts College Dental School in Boston. He stayed at Tufts for seven years, the last two serving as dean. He continued the interdisciplinary research agenda begun at Rochester, including the action of fluoride in limiting cavities, and published widely. But he also began to explore ideas outside of health science as an ecumenical Tufts faculty member and a civically engaged resident of Boston. Amid these influences, he left Catholicism, the religion of his youth, and became a Unitarian. This was accompanied by a compulsive study of Thomas Jefferson. Volker amassed a significant private collection of writings by and about Jefferson, and his efforts to understand the Virginian's approach to deity subsequently led him into Jefferson's perceptions that democracy could not work without effective public education and that all knowledge was interrelated.

As Volker's Tufts days closed, accordingly, he had become a cosmopolitan East Coast urbanite from a family of liberal activists who had two compelling ideas marinating within him. First, scholars—not just scientists but others as well—could find more truth if they thought at the juncture of many disciplines. Second, high-quality public education was crucial to social progress, especially among societies in desperate need of radical uplift. Over time these thoughts evolved into a strategy for building a university.

Although committed to Tufts through 1949, in 1948 Volker took the job as dean of the University of Alabama's nascent dental school in Birmingham and shuttled back and forth between Birmingham and Boston during 1949 as dean at two institutions simultaneously. At the end of his first year in Birmingham the start-up dental college functioned with significant use of part-time faculty from the surrounding private-practice community. Within three years full-time faculty outnumbered part-time faculty, with key leaders raided from the Tufts dental faculty. He garnered such accolades for fostering interdisciplinary research in the dental school (and for forming a joint basic sciences program with the medical college) that by 1955 his responsibilities expanded to being director of research and graduate studies at the UA Medical Center.

With his rare blend of intellectualism, idealism, and pragmatism, Volker rapidly ascended as the leader of UA's Birmingham operations. From 1962 to 1966 he served as Vice President for Health Affairs, reporting to the president in Tuscaloosa. From 1966 to 1968, he served as Vice President for Birmingham Affairs, which merged management of UA's Birmingham extension center (arts and sciences, teacher education, engineering, and business) with its medical center programs. During this time he became a confidant of U.S. Senator Lister Hill on what specific medical research should be fostered by the federal government. He also guided Birmingham's health-science faculty to the rapidly expanding research monies of the National Institutes for Health and the National Science Foundation. Likewise, after first being introduced to U.S. Senator John Sparkman by medical dean Kracke (who was Sparkman's college roommate), Volker cobbled together alliances between Sparkman and Gov. George Wallace and even Wallace's archenemy, the liberal Alabama congressman Carl Elliott, to acquire massive War on Poverty funds—such as grants from the Appalachian Regional Commission and Urban Renewal—for both the physical and programmatic development of the Birmingham campus. With crucial aid from prominent black and Jewish corporate leaders of Birmingham he also moved toward desegregating University Hospital for both patients and doctors, as well as campus life for faculty, students, and staff. Because of Wallace's tight grip on Alabama's higher education budget, however, Volker was unable to make some of his desegregation steps official and open until after passage of the Civil Rights Act of 1964.

By 1969, indeed, three UA campuses—Tuscaloosa, Huntsville, and Birmingham—comprised the new UA System, with Volker becoming president of the University of Alabama at Birmingham (UAB). Volker served as president of UAB from 1969 to 1976, and by the time he left the UAB helm the "start-up" campus comprised 190 urban acres, 1,023 faculty, 8,983 undergraduate students, and 3,059 graduate students. By 1976 UAB had a payroll of nearly $84 million and total grants and contracts of almost $42 million, the largest such figures in Alabama.

In 1976, Volker moved to Tuscaloosa as founding chancellor of the UA System, and he kept the chancellorship until 1982. On resignation he returned to the Birmingham campus as a distinguished professor and consultant to the medical center. He died 3 May 1989 in University Hospital and left his treasured Jefferson collection to UAB's Mervyn H. Sterne Library.

TENNANT S. MCWILLIAMS
University of Alabama at Birmingham

Virginia Fisher, *Building on a Vision: A Fifty-Year Retrospective of UAB's Academic Health Center* (1995); Tennant S. McWilliams, *New Lights in the Valley: The Emergence of UAB* (2007); Joseph F. Volker Collection, Archives of the University of Alabama at Birmingham.

Wake Forest University

The North Carolina Baptist State Convention, organized in 1830 by Baptist proponents of missionary activity, included among its goals the education of ministers. Accordingly the convention opened the Wake Forest Institute on 3 February 1834 on a former plantation approximately 16 miles north of the capital city, Raleigh. Only white males could enroll. The institution survived the early opposition of antimission Baptists, and in 1838 the trustees successfully asked the state legislature to recharter the institute as Wake Forest College. The new charter allowed Wake Forest to grant college degrees, and the school dropped its original requirement of manual labor by students.

Wake Forest had a tumultuous 19th century. Constant fund-raising among state Baptists by the Rev. Samuel Wait, Wake Forest's first president, and his successors had the college debt-free and on sound footing by 1860, and the faculty ceased offering precollege work that year. The Civil War then nearly destroyed the college, which closed from May 1862 until January 1866. The preparatory department reopened alongside the college-level instruction. The situation remained precarious, but funds raised among Baptists in the northeastern United States in the 1870s and early 1880s restored a sense of permanence to Wake Forest. Charles Elisha Taylor assumed the presidency from 1884 to 1905, and under his leadership the institution modernized by hiring the faculty's first Ph.D.s and starting a law school in 1894 and a medical school (offering two years of coursework) in 1902.

William Louis Poteat served as president from 1905 to 1927 and built on Taylor's success. The college grew significantly. In Poteat's first year in office 345 students enrolled, while more than 700 enrolled in his last, 1926–27. Resources remained tight, but Tarheel Baptists' donations, grants from the General Education Board, and funds secured in the early 1920s from tobacco magnate Benjamin N. Duke and New York Baptist Jabez A. Bostwick allowed the growth to continue. Poteat introduced electives into the curriculum but retained an emphasis on the liberal arts, including classical languages. A science professor who frankly taught evolution, he also vigorously defended the college's freedom of inquiry against Baptist attacks in the 1920s. Religion remained a significant part of student life, but undergraduate students' attention turned permanently from the long-revered Philomathesian and Euzelian literary societies to fraternities and intercollegiate athletics instead. Women were offered regular admission beginning in 1942 as well, further changing campus life.

Overcrowding (partly a result of the G.I. Bill) and limited resources plagued the college as higher education boomed after World War II. In 1941 Wake Forest moved its medical school to Winston-Salem, accepting the offer of the Bowman Gray Foundation to support a full four-year curriculum. In 1956 the entire college followed, moving more than a hundred miles to a new Georgian campus on the outskirts of Winston-Salem because the Z. Smith Reynolds Foundation offered long-term financial support. Guided by presidents Harold Wayland Tribble and James Ralph Scales and steady-handed administrators like alumnus Edwin Graves Wilson, the school made the transition and thrived in its new suburban setting. The college desegregated in 1962. Graduate instruction in the liberal arts expanded, and in 1969 a graduate business school enrolled its first students. A name change to Wake Forest University in 1967 reflected those broader ambitions.

The dramatic changes made many members of the Baptist State Convention uneasy about the school the convention had founded and supported, and in turn school leaders at times chafed under the Baptists' continuing role in university governance. President Thomas K. Hearn Jr. facilitated Wake Forest's becoming independent of the Baptist State Convention in the mid-1980s. The university continues to rhetorically honor its Baptist heritage, but its divinity school, launched in 1999, has no denominational ties.

Hearn served as president from 1983 until 2005, a period marked by growth of the faculty, the campus plant, the size and geographic diversity of the student body, and the university's national reputation. His successor, historian Nathan O. Hatch, oversaw a planning process that in 2008 announced a significant expansion of the student body to occur over the subsequent few years. The university reported an enrollment of 6,788 in 2007–8 (including 4,412 undergraduates) with a full-time undergraduate faculty of 393, an endowment of $1.27 billion in spring 2008, and an estimated total cost of attendance for 2008–9 of $49,820.

RANDAL L. HALL
Journal of Southern History
Rice University

Randal L. Hall, *William Louis Poteat: A Leader of the Progressive-Era South* (2000); George Washington Paschal, *History of Wake Forest College*, 3 vols. (1935–43); Bynum Shaw, *The History of Wake Forest College [vol. 4]: 1943–1967* (1988).

Washington, Booker T.

(1856–1915) EDUCATOR.

Booker Taliaferro Washington was the foremost black educator of the late 19th and early 20th centuries. He also had a major influence on southern race relations and was the dominant figure in black public affairs from 1895 until his death in 1915. Born a slave on a small farm in the Virginia backcountry, he moved with his family after Emancipation to work in the salt furnaces and coal mines of West Virginia. After a secondary education at Hampton Institute, he taught an upgraded school and experimented briefly with the study of law and the ministry, but a teaching position at Hampton decided his future career. In 1881 he founded Tuskegee Normal and Industrial Institute on the Hampton model in the Black Belt of Alabama.

Though Washington offered little that was innovative in industrial education, which both northern philanthropic foundations and southern leaders were already promoting, he became its chief black exemplar and spokesman. In his advocacy of Tuskegee Institute and its educational method, Washington revealed the political adroitness and accommodationist philosophy that were to characterize his career in the wider arena of race leadership. He convinced southern white employers and governors that Tuskegee offered an education that would keep blacks "down on the farm" and in the trades. To prospective northern donors and particularly the new, self-made millionaires such as Rockefeller and Carnegie he promised the inculcation of the Protestant work ethic. To blacks living within the limited horizons of the post-Reconstruction South, Washington held out industrial education as the means of escape from the web of sharecropping and debt and the achievement of attainable, petit-bourgeois goals of self-employment, landownership, and small business. Washington cultivated local white approval and secured a small state appropriation, but it was northern donations that made Tuskegee Institute by 1900 the best-supported black educational institution in the country.

The Atlanta Compromise Address, delivered before the Cotton States Exposition in 1895, enlarged Washington's influence into the arena of race relations and black leadership. Washington offered black acquiescence in disfranchisement and social segregation if whites would encourage black progress in economic and educational opportunity. Hailed as a sage by whites of both sections, Washington further consolidated his influence by his widely read autobiography *Up from Slavery* (1901), the founding of the National Negro Business League in 1900, his celebrated dinner at the White House in 1901, and control of patronage politics as chief black adviser to presidents Theodore Roosevelt and William Howard Taft.

Washington kept his white following by conservative policies and moderate utterances, but he faced growing black and white liberal opposition in the Niagara movement (1905–9) and the NAACP (1909–), groups demanding civil rights and encouraging protest in response to white aggressions such as lynching, disfranchisement, and segregation laws. Washington successfully fended off these critics, often by underhanded means. At the same time, however, he tried to translate his own personal success into black advancement through secret sponsorship of civil rights suits, serving on the boards of Fisk and Howard universities, and directing philanthropic aid to these and other black colleges. In his speaking tours and private persuasion he tried to equalize public educational opportunities and to reduce racial violence. These efforts were generally unsuccessful, and the year of Washington's death marked the beginning of the Great Migration from the rural South to the urban North. Washington's racial philosophy, pragmatically adjusted to the limiting conditions of his own era, did not survive the change.

LOUIS R. HARLAN
University of Maryland

W. Fitzhugh Brundage, ed., *Booker T. Washington and Black Progress: Up from Slavery 100 Years Later* (2003); Louis R. Harlan, *Booker T. Washington*, 2 vols. (1972, 1983), *Booker T. Washington in Perspective: Essays of Louis R. Harlan*; David H. Jackson Jr., *Booker T. Washington and the Struggle against White Supremacy: The Southern Educational Tours, 1908–1912* (2008); August Meyer, *Negro Thought in America, 1880–1915* (1963); Robert J. Norrell, *Up from History: The Life of Booker T. Washington* (2009); Raymond W. Smock, ed., *The Booker T. Washington Papers*, 12 vols. (1972–).

Washington and Lee University

Washington and Lee University traces its origins back to the mid-18th century when Scotch-Irish Presbyterian settlers in the valley of Virginia established a small classical academy. In 1776 another generation, fired by a zeal for independence and education, changed its name to Liberty Hall and began college-level studies based on John Witherspoon's Princeton curriculum. In 1782 the Commonwealth of Virginia chartered the school, which granted its first bachelors' degrees in 1785. In 1803 it moved to nearby Lexington. It was distinctive among southern colleges, having no official connection with either a church or state.

In 1796 the trustees convinced George Washington to endow the college with canal stock valued at $50,000. The saving legacy still pays a part of each student's costs. In honor of Washington's gift the school became Washington Academy and later Washington College. Until the Civil War it remained a typical, southern classical college training lawyers, doctors, and preachers for regional leadership, particularly in newly opened lands in the South and West.

By 1865 the Civil War had deprived the college of students, decimated its alumni association, and depleted its endowment. Union raiders had wrecked the campus. That year the trustees offered Gen. Robert E. Lee the presidency. He revitalized the place, raised needed funds, recruited able teachers, and attracted talented students. Under Lee's leadership, the honor system began to take its modern form.

In 1860 all but one of 95 students were Virginians. In 1869, a year before Lee's death, the student body numbered 400 strong from 20 states and one foreign country. Lee hoped to heal the nation's wounds by having boys from North and South studying together. As a pragmatist, he also strove to provide leaders in law, medicine, engineering, business, and journalism to rebuild a shattered South. Lee transformed the curriculum before his death in 1870. In 1871 the school, now Washington and Lee University, included a law school and pioneering collegiate courses in business instruction and journalism.

Washington and Lee struggled during the last two decades of the 19th century. During the 20th century, however, the school grew stronger with each generation. The school of law, enrolling some 400 students, became coeducational in 1972. The first women undergraduates enrolled in September 1985.

Two undergraduate divisions, the college and the School of Commerce, Economics, and Politics, comprise some 1,800 students from throughout the nation and abroad, who choose from nearly 500 courses, 68 percent of which enroll 20 students or fewer. Each year its freshmen, numbering about 460, are selected from more than 3,700 applicants. Washington and Lee is the only national liberal arts college that has accredited programs in law, commerce, and journalism.

Kenneth Patrick Ruscio, Washington and Lee's president since 2006, guides a southern institution with a national mission, stressing academic excellence and leadership development in an atmosphere of courtesy, friendliness, student self-government, and honor, long the hallmarks of Washington and Lee. This small, independent school combines the intimacy of a college with the broad offerings of a university.

TAYLOR SANDERS
Washington and Lee University

Ollinger Crenshaw, *General Lee's College: The Rise and Growth of Washington and Lee University* (1969); Charles Bracelen Flood, *Lee: The Last Years* (1981); William W. Pusey III, *The Interrupted Dream: The Educational Program at Washington College (Washington and Lee University), 1855–1880* (1976); Taylor Sanders, *W&L* (2000).

Weaver, Richard M.

(1910–1963) CONSERVATIVE CRITIC AND THEORIST.

Although still remembered for his work in the discipline of rhetoric, Richard Malcolm Weaver Jr. made a far greater impact as a conservative critic and theorist influential in the development of modern American conservatism. In particular, older conservatives have long credited Weaver's *Ideas Have Consequences* (1948), a biting attack on modern materialism, immoderation, and relativism, as an inspiration for a generation of tradition-minded critics of American cultural decadence. The conservative sociologist Robert Nisbet once labeled Weaver the "morning star" of the post–World War II conservative revival, although obscure in his lifetime. Weaver's attempt to fashion a workable conservative synthesis, which balanced tradition with individual autonomy, order with a limited state, remains an essential project of the conservative movement.

Born in Asheville, N.C., in 1910, Weaver lost his father to a stroke at the age of five. His mother, Carrye, raised him and three siblings while managing the millinery department of her brother's department store in Lexington, Ky. Growing up, Weaver spent summers with family relations in Weaverville, N.C. A lifelong bachelor, he remained devoted both to Weaverville and his mother, eventually purchasing a home in the small North Carolina town for her and various family members. As a student, Weaver was an expert debater and socialist activist, abandoning Marxism only at the end of the 1930s. He earned a bachelor's degree in English at the University of Kentucky in 1932 and a master's degree at Vanderbilt University in 1934. The poet and critic John Crowe Ransom became his mentor at Vanderbilt, and Weaver continued in the doctoral program for several years, eventually abandoning a thesis on the poet John Milton not long after Ransom left the university. At Vanderbilt, Weaver fell under the influence of the conservative antimodernism of Ransom and his Southern Agrarian colleagues. After various part-time teaching appointments, Weaver received his doctorate from Louisiana State University in 1942. He wrote a dissertation on the mind and culture of the Confederate South after the Civil War (published posthumously as *The Southern Tradition at Bay: A History of Postbellum Thought* in 1968). And he taught in the undergraduate college of the University of Chicago from 1944 until his untimely death from a heart attack in 1963.

Weaver's habit of mixing social, aesthetic, and historical theorizing in his cultural criticism was typical of his times. In analyzing the Humanist controversies of the 1920s while a student of Ransom, Weaver insisted that values, derived ultimately from the flux of experience, are most deeply illumined in great art. He rooted his analysis of the Confederate mind in the theory that civilization requires cultural veils or myths that contain the ontological truths and moral values that alone are capable of constraining human action. The South and its Lost Cause embodied such necessary civilizing values. In the 1940s, Weaver gravitated to the Right, expressing private disgust at America's intervention in World War II and, even more ardently, its use of the atomic bomb.

For Weaver the war revealed the loss of chivalry, an idea that became the kernel of *Ideas Have Consequences*. In the book, he reworked his cultural theory, now discussing the necessary "metaphysical dream" (rather than veils or myths) that must serve as the center of value in all healthy cultures. The South, which previously represented a concrete embodiment of Weaver's preferred cultural values, receded in prominence, both in *Ideas Have Consequences* and in Weaver's increasingly theoretical, even ideological, writings. By the 1950s, Weaver was a dedicated contributor to the burgeoning conservative movement, writing for the fledgling *National Review* and later helping to edit *Modern Age*, a conservative journal of ideas founded by Russell Kirk. Weaver gained the respect of influential conservatives close to the *National Review* circle, particularly Frank Meyer and Willmoore Kendall. In becoming a passionate advocate of order, Weaver would seem to favor the traditionalists, and yet symbols and myths, not the hard hand of government, remained the cultural mechanisms of fostering order, which gave comfort to libertarians. Near the end of his career, he advocated what he labeled "social bond" individualism, a concept neatly bridging the antagonistic camps in postwar conservatism. "Man is free in proportion as his surroundings have a determinate nature," Weaver wrote in 1953, "and he can plan his course with perfect reliance upon that determinateness." Weaver died at the peak of his powers, poised to take a one-year appointment at Vanderbilt University, which undoubtedly would have resulted in a permanent position.

PAUL V. MURPHY
Grand Valley State University

George M. Curtis III and James J. Thompson Jr., eds., *The Southern Essays of Richard M. Weaver* (1987); Paul V. Murphy, *The Rebuke of History: The Southern Agrarians and American Conservative Thought* (2001); George H. Nash, *The Conservative Intellectual Movement in America: Since 1945* (1976); Ted J. Smith III, *In Defense of Tradition: Collected Shorter Writings of Richard M. Weaver, 1929–1963* (2000), ed., *Steps toward Restoration: The Consequences of Richard Weaver's Ideas* (1998).

White, Goodrich Cook

(1889–1979) UNIVERSITY PRESIDENT.
Goodrich White was the 14th president of Emory University. Remarkably, except for six years immediately following his graduation from Emory, he spent his entire adult life there, rising through the ranks of administration. He served as its president from 1942 until 1957, leading the school through World War II and the difficult transitions that followed.

Born 13 November 1889, White spent his childhood in Griffin, a county seat town in middle Georgia. He grew up in town, working at a general store and excelling at school. His family life revolved around the Methodist church where his grandfather was the pastor. After graduating from Newnan High School, he entered Emory College (then still in Oxford, Ga.), earning his A.B. in 1908 at the age of 18. He worked briefly for the Methodist Publishing House in Nashville, and then earned a master's degree in psychology from Columbia in 1911. After three years teaching at Methodist colleges, he returned to Emory in 1914 as an associate professor of "mental and moral science." It was also in 1914 that the Methodist Church, smarting from its unpleasant separation from Vanderbilt, voted to establish a new university in the Southeast. Emory College would move to Atlanta and become the undergraduate core of that new university.

After serving in the psychological division of the Army Medical Corps in World War I, White returned to campus and was quickly promoted to full professorship. As affable as he was intelligent, he soon showed himself to be a talented and stalwart administrator. He became dean of the College of Arts and Sciences in 1923 and, after a leave of absence to earn his Ph.D. from the University of Chicago in 1927, he assumed additional responsibilities as dean of the graduate school in 1929. He held both these positions until 1938, when he was appointed vice president. He retained that post and continued as dean of the graduate school until he was chosen as Emory's president in 1942.

White's tenure was greatly complicated by war and its aftermath. His first years were consumed with ensuring Emory's survival during World War II, as civilian students all but vanished from campus and the institution's attention turned to the war effort. In the postwar era, White was reasonably successful at seizing the opportunities presented by the economic and demographic changes that swept the South and by continued federal investment in universities. He was also an important figure nationally in higher education circles, appointed by President Truman to the Commission on Higher Education in 1948. Using funds from the government as well as from private foundations, Emory embarked on a course of expansion and improvement in academic quality. White oversaw a spectacular building boom and significant growth in the number of faculty, students, and educational offerings. Emory approved its first Ph.D. program in 1946; by 1955 nine departments offered the doctorate and graduate programs were put in place in the professional schools. This steady but measured advance was typical of White, who carefully weighed every change and shied away from revolutionary innovations or potentially contentious issues. He largely avoided, for example, the growing debate over segregation throughout his presidency, and although he did successfully pursue outside funding, he did not do so with the vigor that characterized some other American universities. This caution contributed to a stable transition from college to true university, but although Emory was a far stronger intellectual institution when White retired in 1957, its relative lack of aggression left it falling behind its more ambitious regional peers such as Vanderbilt and Duke.

MELISSA KEAN
Rice University

Nancy Diamond, *History of Higher Education Annual* (1999); *Emory Alumnus* (April 1957); Thomas H. English, *Emory University, 1915–1965: A Semicentennial History* (1966).

Woodward, C. Vann

(1908–1999) HISTORIAN.

Born 13 November 1908 in Vanndale, Ark., to Hugh Allison and Bess Vann Woodward, Comer Vann Woodward was the most influential historian of the 20th-century South. Educated at Emory University (Ph.B. in philosophy, 1930), Columbia University (A.M., political science, 1933), and the University of North Carolina (Ph.D., 1937), Woodward did not come to the discipline of history by a straight line, but rather through a succession of student and teaching careers in the humanities, which course produced an undying interest in creative literature that kept him in the company of great writers, from Robert Penn Warren and Cleanth Brooks to John Updike. After briefly teaching English at Georgia Institute of Technology, he entered the study of history in 1934, was one of the attendees at the first meeting of the Southern Historical Association in that year, and subsequently taught at the University of Florida, Scripps College, the University of Virginia, Johns Hopkins University, and Yale University, where he became

Sterling Professor of History and kept an office until very late in the 20th century. Yale University has established a chair in history in honor of Woodward and his son, Peter Vincent, a student of political science who, like the historian's wife, Glenn Boyd Macleod, and a number of close friends, succumbed to cancer at an early age.

Woodward showed an unusual blend of activism and detachment, of aristocratic provenance and fascination with the masses, of great privilege conferred by family and friend and iconoclastic rebelliousness, of professional specialization and an eclectic training. Evoking irony in his writings, he also lived a life of considerable irony, demonstrating what David Minter has called "deep reciprocities" between experiences of his personal life and the history he wrote.

Growing up in Arkansas during a period of racial violence and of grinding regional poverty, Woodward was nurtured by a family of devout Methodists committed to moderate social reform. Forsaking their path, he left an Arkadelphia Methodist college for Emory University, studying philosophy there with LeRoy Loemker, who taught him German existentialism and demonstrated to him a life that successfully combined scholarly excellence with social activism. After brief seasons teaching literature at Georgia Institute of Technology and studying political science at Columbia University, Woodward entered the University of North Carolina, studying with Howard Kennedy Beale; there he developed a historical interpretation based on class analysis and economic determinism, writing a dissertation that became his first book and his only biography, a celebration of Georgia Populism entitled *Tom Watson: Agrarian Rebel* (1938). In subsequent years, during World War II, he began to integrate his understanding of creative literature with this economic history, producing his most enduring scholarship, *Origins of the New South, 1877–1913* (1951), and his most influential study, *The Strange Career of Jim Crow* (1955; subsequent revisions to 1974), which Rev. Martin Luther King Jr. called "the Bible of the civil rights movement." In his provocative biography and in his magisterial 1951 study of the region, he established certain themes of interpretation that set historians onto new paths of exploration—and considerable and continuing debate. In these works, and in all later works, he said there was a sharp discontinuity, or break, in southern history caused by the Civil War, with a new group of more bourgeois leaders replacing the old agrarian elite; he also insisted that certain aspects of race relations, especially the legal de jure segregation called Jim Crow, were essentially New South and neither products of Reconstruction nor of the Old South. In all these works, too, among many other things, he tried to use the tools of irony in his style of writing to belittle those with power and authority and to uplift those, especially black and white allies in the rural countryside, who sought radical economic redress of social injustice.

After distinguishing himself as a professor at Johns Hopkins University and as a visiting professor at Oxford University, he became Sterling Professor at Yale University in 1961. At both Johns Hopkins and Yale, he directed excellent graduate students, three of whom earned the Pulitzer Prize, one of whom became director of the National Endowment for the Humanities, and all of whom made their own impact on the study of southern history. At Yale he became an essayist and an editor, turning out the collections of poignant essays, *The Burden of Southern History* (1960) and *American Counterpoint: Slavery and Racism in the North-South Dialogue* (1971), while editing the Pulitzer Prize–winning *Mary Chesnut's Civil War* (1981). He continued to travel to conferences and to work with young scholars, and he continued to turn out essays both provoking and graceful, a number of which were collected usefully in an interesting set, *The Future of the Past* (1989).

His work received the Bancroft and Sydnor awards; and he served as president of the Southern Historical Association (which he worked mightily to integrate), the American Historical Association, and the Organization of American Historians. Inside the profession, his interpretation of history, a subtle melding of lyric determinants, has been criticized for underestimating the force of racism and understating the longevity of segregation; and many others have scored him for overvaluing the reformism inherent in agrarian movements at the turn of the 20th century. Although he paid attention to women in history in ways unprecedented by the scholars who went before him, it is likely a fair judgment that he failed to appreciate the variety of roles played by women in the South. Although his judgments in such controversies may finally be ruled incorrect in every instance by subsequent scholars, he, like Charles Beard, whom he so admired, will be long remembered as the starting point for the major debates in the discipline of history. Outside the profession, his essays, especially *The Strange Career of Jim Crow* and those in *The Burden of Southern History*, attracted and held the attention of nonspecialist readers and thinkers who appreciated his grace, wit, commitment to moral change, and his insistence that *southern intellectual* and *southern reformist* were not oxymorons.

JOHN HERBERT ROPER
Emory and Henry College

Journal of Southern History (November 2001); Glenn Weddington Rainey Papers, Emory University, Atlanta, Ga.; John Herbert Roper, *C. Vann Woodward, Southerner* (1987), ed., *C. Vann Woodward: A Southern Historian and His Critics* (1997); John H. Roper Papers, Southern Historical Collection (SHC), University of North Carolina at Chapel Hill (interviews: William G. Carleton, Georgia Watson Craven, Manning J. Dauer, John Hope Franklin, J. William Fulbright, LeRoy Loemker, Bola Martin, August Meier, Glenn Weddington Rainey, Bennett Harrison Wall, and C. Vann Woodward); C. Vann Woodward, *Thinking Back* (1985), ed., *Responses of the Presidents to Charges of Misconduct* (1974), taped interview with Charles Crowe, SHC; C. Vann Woodward Papers, Yale University.

INDEX OF CONTRIBUTORS

INDEX

Page numbers in boldface refer to articles.